D1131238

# Bombs Away!

# Bombs Away!

Dramatic First-hand Accounts of British and
Commonwealth Bomber Aircrew in WWII

Martin W. Bowman

Pen & Sword
**AVIATION**

First published in Great Britain in 2010 by
Pen & Sword Aviation
an imprint of
Pen & Sword Books Ltd
47 Church Street
Barnsley
South Yorkshire
S70 2AS

Copyright © Martin W. Bowman, 2010

ISBN 978 1 84884 187 1

The right of Martin W. Bowman to be identified as Author of
this Work has been asserted by him in accordance with
the Copyright, Designs and Patents Act 1988.

A CIP catalogue record for this book is available from the British Library

All rights reserved. No part of this book may be reproduced
or transmitted in any form or by any means, electronic or mechanical
including photocopying, recording or by any information storage and
retrieval system, without permission from the Publisher in writing.

Printed and bound in the UK by
CPI UK

Pen & Sword Books Ltd incorporates the Imprints of
Pen & Sword Aviation, Pen & Sword Maritime, Pen & Sword Military,
Wharncliffe Local History, Pen and Sword Select, Pen and Sword Military Classics,
Leo Cooper, Remember When, Seaforth Publishing and Frontline Publishing.

For a complete list of Pen & Sword titles please contact
PEN & SWORD BOOKS LIMITED
47 Church Street, Barnsley, South Yorkshire, S70 2AS, England
E-mail: enquiries@pen-and-sword.co.uk
Website: www.pen-and-sword.co.uk

# Contents

# Acknowledgements

I am most grateful to the following people, all of whom graciously contributed either stories or photos and sometimes both, for this book: Dr Theo Boiten; Noel Chaffey; Oliver Clutton-Brock, Editor, RAF Bomber Command Association; Rupert 'Tiny' Couling; the late Basil Craske; Tom Cushing; Edward A. Davidson DFM RAF Retd; Squadron Leader Bob Davies AFC; Neville S.C. Donmall; Dr Colin Dring; Wally Gaul; Peter Gibby; Dennis J. Gill; Alan Hague, Curator, Norfolk & Suffolk Aviation Museum; Bill Hough; Alfred Jenner; Mike Lewis; the late Squadron Leader Malcolm Scott DFC; Steve Snelling, *Eastern Daily Press*; Frank Tasker; Ken Westrope; Edwin Wheeler DFC; Captain Bill McCash; Tom Wingham DFC; Jenkin Williams MBA, 2nd TAF Medium Bombers Association.

# Introduction

Of all the stark, cold, statistics that emanate from WWII there is one set of figures which even today, outweighs all others when one talks about RAF Bomber Command. No matter what historians and commentators have to say about the ethics and the prosecution of the day and night bombing offensive, the inescapable fact is that no less than 55,500 aircrew in Bomber Command were killed in action or flying accidents, or died on the ground or while prisoners of war. Approximately 125,000 aircrew served in the frontline, OTU and OCUs of the Command and nearly 60 per cent of them became casualties. In addition, almost 9,900 more were shot down and made POWs to spend one, two or more years in squalid, desolate Oflags and Stalags in Axis held territory. Over 8,000 more were wounded aboard aircraft on operational sorties. Bomber Command flew almost 390,000 sorties, the greatest percentage of them by Avro Lancasters, Handley Page Halifaxes and Vickers Wellingtons. Theirs of course were the highest casualties.

To try to encapsulate every dramatic episode of RAF Bomber Command's long and distinguished history in one volume is therefore impossible but the unique selection that follows is wide-ranging and significantly, each experience is related by British and Commonwealth airmen themselves. Their enduring bravery and fortitude and sometimes their despondency and cynicism, shows through in these stirring, daring, often irreverent, humorous and sometimes sardonic but memorable stories. All reflect the ethos, camaraderie, fear and bravery of the largely ordinary men, most of whom were plucked from 'civvy street' and thrust into a frightening, bitter conflict which was made even more dangerous by the lethal advance of technology. Death would normally come from an anonymous assassin, either in the black of night, or from behind a cloud or out of the sun, or simply from the flak gunner on the ground. And, if all this was not enough, the often unmerciful weather was no respecter of mortality.

There was no escaping the all-embracing shock wave that rippled through the bomber squadrons after a heavy mauling over enemy territory. Nothing could be more poignant than the vacant places at tables in the depleted mess halls, the empty locker of the departed, or the dog pining by the barracks for its missing master. Each man had to deal with tragedy in his own inimitable way. Some hid their feelings better than others, only for the pain to resurface months or even years later. Some, who had survived the physical pressures and who completed their tours, then succumbed to the mental torture that had eaten away at their psyche during the incessant and interminable onslaught day after day, night after night. There was little respite. The valorous men of Bomber Command were, in turn, the Light Brigade, the stop gap, the riposte, the avengers, the undefeated. Always, they were expendable.

Martin W. Bowman, Norwich

# Chapter 1

# Battle of the Bight

During the evening of Wednesday, 23 August 1939 RAF units in Great Britain and abroad were secretly placed on a war footing and mobilization of the Auxiliary Air Force and 3,000 members of the Volunteer Reserve was begun. The British public, probably aware they were enjoying the last days of an August at peace for some time to come, went about their business knowing they too would soon be called into the Services. The fragile peace was quickly shattered during the early hours of 1 September. Poland was invaded by German armoured divisions supported by the Luftwaffe employing blitzkrieg ('lightning war') tactics developed from experience gained during the Spanish Civil War, 1936-39. In Britain full mobilization followed while units of Coastal Command began flying patrols over the North Sea. At bomber bases camouflage was liberally applied to buildings and aircraft alike and brown tape was stuck over every pane of glass in criss-cross patterns.

At the outbreak of war the overall strength of Bomber Command stood at 55 squadrons. On paper this sounds a respectable figure but by the end of September it had been pared down to 23 home-based first-line squadrons. These consisted of six squadrons of Bristol Blenheim IV light bombers of 2 Group and six squadrons of Vickers Wellington Is and IAs of 3 Group (with two in reserve) stationed in East Anglia. The rest of the force comprised five squadrons of Armstrong Whitworth Whitleys of 4 Group based in Yorkshire and six squadrons of Handley Page Hampdens of 5 Group in Lincolnshire. Vickers Wellingtons were first-line equipment for 9 Squadron at Honington, Suffolk; 37 Squadron at Feltwell, Norfolk; 99 and 149 Squadrons at Mildenhall and Newmarket, Suffolk respectively and 38 and 115 Squadrons at Marham, Norfolk while 214 and 215 (at Methwold) were similarly equipped in Reserve. On 1 June 1939 1 RNZAF Unit had begun forming at Marham to fly Wellingtons. A decision had been taken early in 1937 that the New Zealanders would have a complement of 30 Wellingtons, six of which would be ready to leave for the Antipodes in August 1939. When war clouds gathered the New Zealanders were put at the disposal of the RAF and the unit moved to RAF Harwell where it became 15 OTU. Under the RAF Bomber Command 'Scatter' plan, the majority of bomber squadrons were immediately dispersed to satellite bases. For instance, Wellingtons of 115 Squadron were sent to the satellite airfield at Barton Bendish. By 2 September all of 99 Squadron's Wellingtons had been moved to the famous Rowley Mile racecourse on Newmarket

Heath. The famous racecourse had been used as a landing ground for aircraft in World War I. HRH the Prince of Wales landed at the strip in 1935 before travelling by road to attend the Jubilee Review at Mildenhall. After the Munich Crisis in 1938, the Air Ministry took an interest in the area as a satellite for bombers at RAF Mildenhall. The Rowley Mile course, in about 300 acres north of the Beacon Course and Cambridge Hill, offered one of the largest grass landing and take-off runs – 2,500 yards – in an east-west direction. A Wellington IA filled with 1,500 lb of bombs and 720 gallons of fuel required a 1,080-yard run to become airborne, which left little margin for error. The Rowley Mile strip was the longest of its kind in Britain where a Wellington IA could operate carrying 2,000 lb of bombs. Although long and flat, crews had to remember to hurdle the 20 feet high Devil's Dyke running along one boundary. Accommodation for air and ground crews was in the racecourse administration buildings, the grandstand and requisitioned housing locally, until new huts could be built.

On the afternoon of 2 September 10 squadrons of Fairey Battles flew to France to take up their position as part of the Advanced Air Striking Force. It was a sombre Neville Chamberlain, the British Prime Minister, who announced his country's declaration of war over the air on the BBC the following morning, 3 September. His resigned tones had barely vanished into the ether when reconnaissance revealed German warships leaving Wilhelmshaven. At 1700 hours an order was sent to RAF Mildenhall for 12 Wellingtons of 99 Squadron to be made ready to attack them. No Wellingtons could be airborne until 1830 hours and then only three aircraft were operational. They took-off but bad weather and oncoming darkness forced them to abort. They returned to Suffolk after jettisoning their bomb loads in the North Sea. It was evident that the RAF was not fully prepared for an immediate strike at the enemy. The President of the United States, Franklin D. Roosevelt, had appealed to the belligerent nations to refrain from unrestricted aerial bombardment of civilians. The British heeded this request but the RAF was prevented from using a direct passage to the German industrial heartland because of the strict neutrality of both Holland and Belgium. France also requested that Bomber Command did not attack land targets in Germany for fear of reprisal raids on French cities, which her bombers could not deter nor her fighters protect.

The only way to carry the war to Germany then, was to make attacks on German capital ships. The task of bombing the German Fleet fell, therefore, to the Blenheim light bombers of 2 Group and Wellingtons of 3 Group in East Anglia, which were ideally placed to attack installations in the Heligoland Bight. However, British War Cabinet policy decreed that no civilian casualties were to be caused as a direct result of the bombing. RAF Bomber Command could strike at ships, at sea or underway, but vessels moored in harbours were not to be bombed for fear of injuring 'innocent' civilians. Plans were laid for the first RAF raid of the war to take place during the afternoon of 4 September. While 15 unescorted Blenheims took-off for a strike on the *Admiral von Scheer* at Wilhelmshaven, eight Wellingtons of 9 Squadron and six Wellingtons of 149 Squadron, also without escort, flew on over the North Sea towards Brunsbüttel. Their targets were the battle cruisers *Scharnhorst* and *Gneisenau*, which had earlier been spotted by a Blenheim reconnaissance aircraft from RAF Wyton. Squadron Leader Paul Harris was leading 149 Squadron this day. En route Harris ordered his gunners to test fire their

Brownings. He was startled to discover that not one gun was in working order. However, not wishing to miss the first action of the war, he decided to press on to the target. Unfortunately, bad weather added to the crews' problems and five of his squadron were forced to return early. Harris lost sight of the two remaining aircraft in thick cloud. As he flew over Tonning, his Wellington took a direct flak hit. Harris' bomb-aimer aimed his bombs at a bridge over the Eder and turned for home. Harris nursed the ailing aircraft the 300 miles back to England and landed at Mildenhall six and a quarter hours after taking-off.

Meanwhile, 9 Squadron had fared little better. Three Wellingtons, led by Flight Lieutenant Peter Grant, managed to reach the German battleships amid fierce anti-aircraft fire but although they succeeded in dropping their bombs, none struck the ships. A further three Wellingtons, which succeeded in penetrating the harbour, were attacked by Messerschmitt Bf 109s and two of the bombers were shot down. The day's losses reached seven when five Blenheims failed to return. Debriefing revealed that some aircraft had failed to find the warships. One crew mistook the River Elbe for the Kiel Canal and one even dropped two bombs on Esbjerg. Crews that had scored hits on the vessels had discovered to their dismay that the general-purpose bombs, fused for eleven seconds delay, had simply bounced off the armoured decks and fell into the sea without exploding. The only casualties suffered by the German Navy occurred when a stricken Blenheim crashed into the bows of the cruiser *Emden*. Despite the losses, 3 Group prepared for another shipping attack the following day, 5 September. Plans were quickly scrapped, however, when it was feared that the Luftwaffe was about to launch an all-out attack on bomber stations in East Anglia. The 'Blackout Scheme' was put into effect and squadrons were sent to safety further afield. 149 Squadron, for instance, flew their Wellingtons to Netheravon in Wiltshire and did not return to East Anglia until 15 September.

During a temporary respite from the shooting war, the Wellington crews of 9 and 149 Squadrons licked their wounds while others carried the war, albeit tentatively, to the enemy. On the night of 8 September, 99 Squadron flew its first operation when three Wellingtons were dispatched to drop propaganda leaflets over Hanover. One aircraft was forced to abort but the other two successfully completed the operation. The Wellington and Blenheim crews were rested while Hampden squadrons bore the brunt of bombing raids in East Anglia. Ground crews used the time to iron out the bugs and eliminate teething troubles inherent in the Wellington IA, which had been introduced almost overnight into squadron service.

A combination of bad weather and the lack of suitable targets as dictated by War Cabinet policy delayed squadrons from using their new Wellington IAs and during the next few weeks on several occasions aircraft took part in sweeps over the North Sea. Otherwise, they were mainly occupied in bombing and firing practice and formation exercises, some of them in cooperation with fighter squadrons. In 1939 the officially accepted theory was that fighters had such a small speed advantage over the 'modern' bomber that any attack must become a stern chase. It was also accepted that fighters attacking a section of bombers flying in 'Vic' would attack in 'Vic' formation. On 30 October three Wellington crews practised evasive flying with fighters of 66 Squadron near Honington. At 800 feet, just below the cloud base, the leading Wellington I, flown by Squadron Leader Lennox Lamb and a second Wellington flown by Flying Officer John Chandler, collided. The propellers of Lamb's Wellington tore through the rear fuselage of Chandler's aircraft below, completely severing the tail unit, which spun away like a falling leaf. Chandler's tail-less Wellington then reared up into a steep climb, turned over onto its back and struck the leader's Wellington again with its port wing. Both aircraft plunged earthwards. Chandler's Wellington crashed against a large tree and caught fire on impact while Lamb's machine dived nose first into a dyke and completely disintegrated. Both landed less than 50 feet apart in marshy ground near Sapiston Water Mill, only three-quarters of a mile from the Honington runway. All nine airmen from the two Wellingtons were killed in the tragedy. However, Sergeant Smith had cheated death. He had climbed aboard Lamb's aircraft and had taken his usual place in the rear turret but Flying Officer Torkington-Leech had come back and said that he would be rear-gunner for the exercise. Smith had decided that if he could not be rear-gunner he would not fly at all and promptly got out of the aircraft and returned to the crew room. The new Flight Commander was Squadron Leader Archibald Guthrie.

Tragedy continued to dog the Wellington units when, on the afternoon of 5 November, a Wellington I of 38 Squadron, flown by 30 year old Sergeant E.T. 'Slim' Summers AFM, an instructor, crashed while being ferried from Marham to the satellite airfield at Barton Bendish. Summers was one of the most experienced pilots in the squadron, having accumulated 1,102 flying hours, of which 167 hours were on Wellingtons. Slim was a very colourful and ebullient character and had earned his Air Force Medal earlier that year, on 2 January 1939. On 15 May he had saved the life of his rear-gunner during a low-level bombing exercise in a Wellington. The starboard engine had failed and Slim was unable to turn the aircraft against the port engine. A fire broke out between the tail and centre section and the aircraft was landed in a field near RAF Marham, on the port engine. A normal landing would have blown the flames into the area of the rear turret. After touchdown the bomber ran into a hedge and the undercarriage collapsed. The crew quickly vacated the aircraft, which was still burning but Slim, who was wearing an old style aircraft harness, became caught up in the side window. He extricated himself by releasing the harness and though the aircraft was burnt out, the crew escaped serious injury. Slim's fame spread and he was known locally, for when he was not on duty Summers lived at the Whitington 'Bell', near the Marham base, with his wife. On 8 August 1939 he was asked if he would fly a Wellington out of a field at Roudham Heath near Thetford after it had crash-landed with the undercarriage retracted during a night exercise. The daredevil Summers successfully got the Wellington off and flew it back to Marham. On the fateful day of 5 November he was not so lucky. On board Summers' Wellington were six ground crew – riggers and fitters who would maintain the aircraft when it arrived at Barton Bendish. Slim attempted a very dangerous manoeuvre near the ground (it is thought he was trying to fly wingtip low between two trees). It must be assumed that he did not allow for the keel action of a heavy aircraft in a steep turn; also he failed to judge the height of the trees. The aircraft crashed inverted at Boughton killing all seven on board.

Meanwhile, the Air Ministry planners were still of the opinion that close-knit formations of Wellingtons, with their healthy defensive armament, could survive everything the enemy could throw at them and penetrate heavily defended targets. Recent heavy losses in British merchant shipping, and pressure from Winston Churchill, the First Lord of the Admiralty, in particular, prompted the War Cabinet to order Bomber Command to mount, as soon as possible, '...a major operation with the object of destroying an enemy battle-cruiser or pocket battleship'. However, the directive added, '...no bombs are to be aimed at warships in dock or berthed alongside the quays'. The War Cabinet wanted no German civilian casualties.

During the late afternoon of 2 December 1939, 115 and 149 Squadrons at Marham and Mildenhall were alerted that a strike would be mounted against two German cruisers moored off Heligoland. Immediately, 24 Wellington IAs were bombed up with four 500lb SAP (Semi Armour Piercing) bombs and 620 gallons of fuel, ready for a strike early the following morning. Leading the attack would be 34 year old Wing Commander Richard Kellett AFC, a distinguished pre-war aviator, now Commanding Officer of 149 Squadron.[1]

On the morning of 3 December the weather had improved and, at 0900 hours, Kellett led his 12 Wellingtons off in four flights of three. He rendezvoused with three Wellingtons of 38 Squadron and nine of 115 Squadron from Marham and the force flew out over the North Sea towards Heligoland in four 'battle formations' of six Wimpys each.[2] At the head of the bomber force Kellett positioned his section well out in front. Following some distance behind and leading the remainder, was Squadron Leader Paul Harris. Off to his right and a little way behind and leading the remainder, flew the third section led by a young Canadian, Flight Lieutenant J. B. Stewart. The fourth section, led by Flight Lieutenant A. G. Duguid, flew directly behind Stewart. Two cruisers were spotted at anchor in the roads between the two tiny rock outcrops that are Heligoland in the German Bight. Kellett prepared to attack from up sun. As a result of the early losses, the bombing altitude had been raised to 7,000 feet (considered 'high level' bombing altitude at this time). Harris claimed hits on one of the warships and Stewart attacked a large merchantman anchored outside the harbour but a cloud obscured the targets and results were unconfirmed.

Although *Freya* radar had warned the German gunners of the impending raid, the thick cloud at their bombing altitude had fortunately hidden the Wellingtons from view. Four Messerschmitt Bf 109Ds of 1 *Gruppe Zerstorergecshwader* 26 at Jever led by Hauptmann Dickore climbed and intercepted the bombers after they had bombed but their aim was spoiled by cloudy conditions. Even so, the two pairs of Bf 109Ds damaged two of the Wellingtons in the attack. One pair attacked from above and the other pair from below. Leutnant Günther Specht, who damaged one of the Wellingtons, was shot down by return fire from Corporal Copley, 38 Squadron, rear-gunner in Sergeant Odoire's Wellington. One of the rounds from Specht's machine guns actually hit and lodged in the belt buckle of Copley's harness without injuring him. Specht ditched in the sea and he was later rescued. The German had been wounded in the face and later had to have his left eye removed.[3] Luckily for the Wellington crews, the three remaining Bf 109Ds were low on fuel and they broke off the engagement, while 16 Bf 109D/Es and eight of I./ZG26's new Bf 110Cs arrived too late to intercept the bombers.

Again the bombs were to fail miserably, although an enemy minesweeper was claimed sunk when one bomb went clean through the bottom of the vessel without exploding. It was, however, a trawler, formerly the *Johann Schulte*, which sank to the bottom. Back at the RAF bases hopes ran high now that the bombers had penetrated enemy air space, duelled with the Luftwaffe and escaped unscathed. These hopes were to be short-lived.

On 13 December, 10 days after the disastrous RAF raid on Heligoland, running silent and deep, the Royal Navy submarine HMS *Salmon* spotted the German cruisers *Nürnberg* and *Leipzig* in the cold waters of the North Sea. *Salmon* stalked its prey and fired a salvo of torpedoes, hitting the two cruisers. The submarine scurried away leaving the German ships to limp back to Wilhelmshaven. Coastal Command contacted Bomber Command to send bombers to finish them off. Flares were loaded into the Wellingtons for a night attack but this was later cancelled. By dawn the following day a force of Hampdens had taken-off to intercept the battle squadron but they returned to base without having spotted the enemy. An armed reconnaissance by 12 Wellingtons of 99 Squadron at Newmarket Heath was ordered. Each aircraft carried three 500 lb semi-armour piercing bombs and any large battlecruisers or cruisers seen were to be bombed if the weather allowed the aircraft to reach a height of 2,000 feet. Leading the formation were Squadron Leader Andrew 'Square' McKee, the New Zealander pilot[4] and Wing Commander J. F. Griffiths the CO. The formation, which consisted of four sections of three aircraft each, took-off from Newmarket at 1143 hours and set course for Great Yarmouth. There the visibility was down to two miles just below 10/10ths cloud and crews peered into the thick sea haze in a vain search for a horizon. The weather deteriorated even further and at 1305 hours, when the formation reached the Dutch coast, the Wellingtons were flying at 600 feet in fine rain.

Griffiths altered course in the direction of Heligoland in order to give the enemy flak ships the impression that Heligoland was the objective. The weather continued to worsen and the formation was now down to just 300 feet. At 1347 hours course was altered for the Schillig Roads near Wilhelmshaven. Visibility was down to half a mile and the Wellingtons were now flying at only 200 feet. Despite the weather conditions the aircraft maintained a good formation and they flew on towards Wangerooge Island. They were spotted by five stationary trawlers, one of which fired off a red signal flare. Shortly afterwards a submarine was sighted and also fired a red flare. The leader replied by firing two red signal cartridges in rapid succession on the off chance that this might be the recognition signal. The submarine immediately did a crash dive and the formation turned on a north-easterly course.

At 1425 hours the *Leipzig* and *Nürnberg* were sighted. Griffiths attempted to carry out an examination to assess any possible torpedo damage but the fast closing speeds made this impossible. He swung the formation around and was about to try again when eight cargo boats were sighted. Immediately, they opened fire on the Wellingtons. A minute later three destroyers steamed up directly under Griffiths' bomber and opened fire. The Wellingtons were only 200 feet off the water and a barrage of light anti-aircraft fire from the ships below buffeted crews. Five minutes after the destroyers had opened fire, the *Leipzig* and *Nürnberg* added their pom-poms and other anti-aircraft firepower to the battle. Sergeant R.H.J. Brace's Wellington was shot down in flames. Pilot Officer H.L. Lewis, whose Wellington was thought to have been struck by flak, turned and crashed into the following aircraft flown by Flight Sergeant W.H. Downey, causing both Wellingtons to crash in flames. Flight Sergeant J.E.K. Healy's Wellington was also thought to have been a victim of flak. Griffiths turned the formation away and shortly afterwards a formation of three single-engined fighters was sighted approaching the bombers from Wangerooge, which came up out of the mist. The fighters, which were Bf 109Es of II./JG77 that had taken off from Wangerooge together with four Bf 110s of 2/ZG26 from Jever, closed and the RAF gunners responded with rapid firing. Fighters approaching in line astern from sea level made their attacks. Corporal A. Bickerstaff, the rear-gunner in McKee's aircraft, fired at the attackers and saw a Wellington falling and believed it to be the Messerschmitt he had just shot down.[5] Flying Officer J.A.H. Cooper's Wellington was seen to break away and enter the clouds. It was last seen heading towards the German coast with its undercarriage down, apparently under control. Bf 110s badly damaged Flight Lieutenant E. J. Hetherington's Wellington and he was forced to jettison his bombs into the sea. He went into the clouds and was able to nurse his ailing Wellington back across the North Sea with petrol pouring from its tanks (the Wellington did not yet have self-sealing fuel tanks). Almost home, the machine crash-landed in a field near Newmarket racecourse. The aircraft was a write-off and Hetherington and two of his crew were killed. The injured were removed to Newmarket hospital. The loss of five Wellingtons was so disastrous that Air Vice-Marshal J. E. A. 'Jackie' Baldwin, AOC 3 Group was compelled to compare it with the Charge of the Light Brigade.

Despite the losses Bomber Command opined that the Wellingtons had survived repeated fighter attacks, and faith in the old adage that 'the bomber will always get through' seemed as unshakable as ever. Indeed, the debriefing report was to state later: 'After careful analysis of individual reports by all members of crews, it seems almost possible to assume that none of our aircraft were brought down by fire from the Messerschmitts.'

At Bomber Command the consensus was that in future, concealment was more important than defensive firepower. Henceforth bomber formations would fly at 10,000 feet and crews were urged to seek the safety of cloud cover whenever possible. In his report of the events of 14 December, the Senior Air Staff Officer at Bomber Command Headquarters, Air Commodore Norman Bottomley, wrote:

'It is now by no means certain that enemy fighters did in fact succeed in shooting down any of the Wellingtons...the failure of the enemy must be ascribed to good formation flying. The maintenance of tight, unshaken formations in the face of the most powerful enemy action is the test of bomber force fighting efficiency and morale. In our service it is the equivalent of the old "Thin Red Line" or the "Shoulder to Shoulder" of Cromwell's Ironsides...Had it not been for that good leadership, losses from enemy aircraft might have been heavy.'

In complete contrast to the British version of events, the Luftwaffe report stated: 'German pilots registered five kills, plus one probable but unconfirmed kill. One German fighter shot down.'

On the evening of 17 December, Wing Commander Kellett and Squadron Leader Paul Harris of 149 Squadron were summoned to Group Headquarters at Mildenhall, along with the squadron commanders and section leaders of 9 and 37 Squadrons for a briefing on another raid on Wilhelmshaven the following morning. Unfortunately, there would be little cloud cover, for the weather forecast for 18

December predicted clear conditions. Harris was informed that Peter Grant would be flying with him, together with three of 9 Squadron's aircraft. This was the first time they had ever flown together and as they strolled away from the briefing, Harris put his hand on Grant's shoulder and said, 'Stay close to me whatever happens'. At Honington crews knew 'something was up'. Sergeant Frank Petts, a pilot in 9 Squadron, recalls:

'On a number of previous occasions reconnaissance Blenheims had found German warships off the German coast in the Heligoland area and had been followed by a bomber striking force. In the short days of mid-December it was decided to dispense with the preliminary reconnaissance and to dispatch a bomber force in the morning to search for and attack German warships. It was established subsequently that security about the proposed operation on 18 December was extremely poor; certainly on the evening of 17 December it was widely known in Bury St Edmunds that 9 Squadron crews had been recalled because of an operation planned for early the next day. On reporting to the Flights at 0730 hours on 18 December we learned that 9 Squadron was to supply nine aircraft for a force of 24, with nine from 149 Squadron and six from 37 Squadron at Feltwell. There were to be four groups of six aircraft: three of 149 and three of 9 in front, six of 149 to starboard, six of 9 to port and six of 37 in the rear. Targets were to be any German warships in the area of Heligoland or the Schillig Roads. Bomb loads were four 500lb general purpose bombs per aircraft.'

9 Squadron was airborne from Honington at 0900 hours. At 1000 hours nine Wellingtons of 149 Squadron led by Wing Commander Kellett took-off from Newmarket Heath and rendezvoused over King's Lynn with the nine Wellingtons of 9 Squadron. The six Wellingtons of 37 Squadron took-off from Feltwell and flew straight across north Norfolk, falling in behind the rear elements of the formation while over the North Sea. Leading Aircraftman Harry A. Jones, rear-gunner in Sergeant Herbie Ruse's crew wrote: 'There was not a cloud in the sky, it was unreal. Wellingtons were scattered all over the sky.' The formation flew a dog-leg course over the North Sea, first flying northwards as far as possible from the concentration of enemy flak ships among the Friesian Islands and then they headed due east for the German island of Sylt. After fifteen minutes on this new heading Flight Lieutenant A. G. Duguid began to have trouble with one of his engines. As he lost speed and dropped back, he signalled by Aldis lamp to his two wingmen to close up on Kellett's Vic. Riddlesworth, his No. 3 obeyed but Kelly, his No. 2, apparently failed to pick up the Aldis signal. Kelly peeled away from the formation, followed his leader down and headed for home as well. At 1230 hours Kellett sighted Sylt about 50 miles ahead. The formation was still at 15,000 feet and there was not a cloud in the sky. It was an open invitation for enemy fighters. As the Wellingtons approached the German coast near Cuxhaven, Bf 109 and Bf 110 fighters of *Jagdgeschwader 1*, guided by radar plots of the incoming formation made by the experimental *Freya* early warning radar installation at Wangerooge and directed by ground control, were waiting. Petts recalls:

'We left Sylt to port and shortly afterwards turned left towards the Schillig Roads where we had been told at briefing there were likely to be warship targets. We saw none but continued on a south-westerly course and I wondered how far we were going in search of battleships and cruisers. My rear-gunner called, "There's a fighter attacking behind. They've got him!" Then to starboard I saw a Bf 109 with smoke pouring from it, change from level flight to a near vertical dive so abruptly that the pilot could hardly have been alive and conscious after the change of direction. At this stage I thought, rather prematurely, that encounters with German fighters were "easy". Repeated calls to my Section Leader to ask him to slow down brought no reply and in spite of opening up to full boost and increasing propeller revs to maximum, I still could not keep up. Over Wilhelmshaven we flew into intense Ack-Ack fire (joined by the anti-aircraft guns mounted on the battleships *Scharnhorst* and *Gneisenau*). In trying to work out whether evasive manoeuvres were any use against the black puffs bursting all around I was for a while less pre-occupied with the problem of staying in formation. Quite suddenly the black puffs stopped and there in front were the fighters (there must have been about forty of them). In spite of full throttle and full revs, I was lagging behind.'

Kellett led the formation through the flak-stained sky over Wilhelmshaven and each bomb-aimer prepared to drop his three bombs on the ships below. Suddenly, Kellett gave the order not to bomb. All the battleships and cruisers were berthed alongside quays and harbour walls. Kellett's orders were precise: he was not to risk German civilian casualties. Bomb doors were opened but no bombs fell. Moored in the middle of the harbour were four large ships that appeared to be merchantmen. Heavy anti-aircraft fire was coming from them. It was all the encouragement Paul Harris needed. They appeared to be fleet auxiliaries so he dropped his bomb load on them. Another Wellington in his section did the same but the results were obscured by cloud. Kellett's formation had become strung out and disjointed. 9 and 37 Squadrons had become detached and had fanned out in the face of heavy barrage. The Wellingtons were easy pickings and the RAF crews were caught cold as the cunning German fighter pilots made beam attacks from above. Previously, attacks had been made from the rear but now the German pilots tore into the bombers, safe in the knowledge that the ventral gun was powerless at this angle of attack. They knew too that the front and rear turrets could not traverse sufficiently to draw a bead on them. Petts dumped his bombs, hoping it would gain him a little extra speed:

'About this time Balch on the front guns got his first fighter. A Bf 109 away to port was turning in a wide sweep, possibly to attack the sections in front. I saw the tracer in Balch's first burst hit in the cockpit area and the canopy or part of it, fly off; the second burst also hit and the 109 immediately went into a catastrophic dive with white smoke pouring from it. At this period I decided that in spite of my full throttle and full revs I should never keep up. Pilot Officer Ginger Heathcote my second pilot pointed out the 37 Squadron six forming the rear of the formation and suggested that I drop back to them. It was as well that I did not. 37 Squadron were flying in their own formation of three pairs stepped up in line astern. As the attacks developed, one of the six[6] went to dump his bombs. To open the bomb doors he first selected master hydraulic cock 'on' not realizing that he had flaps selected down. The result was sudden lowering of full flap leading to a sudden gain of considerable extra height. Enemy fighters left this aircraft alone but shot down the other five of 37 Squadron.

One of these was N2936 flown by Sergeant Herbert Ruse, which was singled out North of Wangerooge by Oberstleutnant Karl Schumacher, *Geschwaderkommodore*,

*JGI*, who shot out both the Wellington's engines and raked the aircraft with machine-gun fire, killing Corporal F.J. Fred Taylor, the front gunner. LAC Harry Jones, the rear-gunner, wrote:

'You thought the flak was going to hit you straight between the eyes and then it veered off. We went through a huge barrage and you couldn't see anything except big puffs of black smoke. As we came through the barrage there were the Messerschmitts waiting for us. We hadn't got any guns at all. All our gadgets had packed in so we had no front gun, no rear gun or anything. We discovered afterwards that they got the wrong oil in our hydraulic system. During one of these attacks I was hit in the back and then through the ankle. I rang up the skipper and said, "I've been hit and it bloody well hurts." He told me to come to the front and get it dressed. I staggered to the front of the aircraft. The wireless operator [Sergeant T. W. 'Tom' Holley] saw my ankle and got a hypodermic syringe and bunged this stuff through my flying trousers into my leg, which killed some of the pain. He was hit and killed immediately. He went a funny sort of grey and purple and died. A Messerschmitt sat on our tail and shot right through the aeroplane, through the rear turret and through the front of the aircraft. I was sitting on the bed behind the wireless operator's area watching the blood coming out of my foot. The second pilot [Sergeant Tom May] had to stand with his legs astride the bullets going between his legs. Then a bullet hit him in the thigh. I heard the skipper say he had got to get down. We had caught fire. We were over an island [Spiekeroog] off the German coast and he found a bit of beach to land on. We were burning by now. I got to the hatch at the top and pulled myself up but I got stuck and I could feel the flames burning my rear end. They pulled me out and carried me to the sand dunes.'[7]

Petts continues:

'Having decided that I could not catch up with my Section Leader, I turned about 40° to starboard, put my nose hard down and with the dustbin turret still in the lowered position, screamed down to sea level. All the way down from 15,000ft and then for some time just above the water I kept full throttle and full revs except when I reduced power for short periods in an evasive manoeuvre as fighters lined up to attack. During the dive I was too pre-occupied with what was going on outside to pay much attention to my instruments. I did, however, notice my ASI[8] reaching the 1 o'clock position, second time round. It was not until we returned to the aircraft next morning that I looked to see what that meant in terms of indicated airspeed; it was 300 mph! This was about twice normal cruising IAS[9] and I could not help wondering how much faster I could have gone before something broke. I cannot remember just how many fighter attacks there were; the first came before I left cruising altitude; there were more on the way down with 110s passing us as they broke away and finally we were chased along the water by three 110s. Robertson on the rear guns kept me informed as each attack developed and there were commentaries from the other two gunners. We met each stern attack with a drill that we had agreed as a result of experience gained in fighter co-operation exercises. The usual sequence ran: "There's one coming in, he's coming in. Get ready...get ready...Back, back." Throttles slammed shut and pitch levers to full coarse. Bursts from our guns and enemy tracer passed the windows. "OK, he's gone." Open up again to full throttle and full revs. Mostly the tracer was on the starboard side and it was not until some weeks later when we started taking aircraft back to Brooklands to have armour plate fitted behind the port wing tanks that I realized that previously we had enjoyed this protection only on the starboard side. Altogether my gunners claimed three 110s and two 109s.

'There had already been calls from Kemp and Balch that they had been hit and Heathcote had gone back to Kemp. Whilst I started checking at my end he helped Kemp (who was losing a lot of blood from a thigh wound) out of the dustbin and onto the rest bunk. Kemp in full kit was a tight fit in the dustbin and this move must have called for quite an effort from both. Heathcote next let Balch out of the front turret and went aft again. Balch had been hit in the sole of one foot but he was not in urgent need of attention. Robertson reported that he had emptied his guns into the last 110 and Kemp had called that the centre guns were out of action. Heathcote reported that there appeared to be no major damage to the aircraft, although it was a bit draughty as there were plenty of holes. For my part I eased back to normal cruising throttle and propeller settings and checking round was shaken to find the starboard oil pressure gauge reading zero. The propellers on Wellington IAs did not feather so I had to be content with pulling the starboard engine right back as with that setting it would give less drag than if switched off and if it did not seize it might be of some use if I wanted it. I opened up the port engine to "climb power" and found that I was able to climb gently to 1,000ft or so. During this time I had turned onto a course of 270 degrees. When Heathcote came forward again he agreed that 270 degrees was as good as any because we did not know where we were and steering due west ought to hit England somewhere.'

For almost half an hour 44 Luftwaffe fighters had torn into the Wellingtons. 9 Squadron, which had dispatched nine Wellingtons, lost five aircraft shot down, including Squadron Leader Archibald Guthrie, one of the flight commanders. Sergeant R. Hewitt's crew with his rear-gunner, Leading Aircraftsman Walter Lilley dead, were shot up by Oberleutnant Gresens of 2/ZG76. The fuel tanks were holed but Hewitt managed to nurse the ailing Wellington to the coast of Lincolnshire, where he ditched. They were picked up by the Grimsby trawler *Erillas* 100 miles from the Wash. Fighter attacks had continued until the bombers were only 80 miles from home. Kellett remembered Paul Harris' suggestion after the 3 December raid and 'flew a little slower' to allow the stragglers to keep up. Off to his right Peter Grant obediently stuck rigidly to Harris' Wellington. The tightly knit formation of 10 aircraft of 149 Squadron fought their way through. '*B-Beer*' piloted by Flying Officer J.H.C. Spiers, was shot down during a beam attack by a Bf 110. There were no survivors. '*P-Peter*' piloted by Flying Officer M.F. Briden ditched near Cromer Knoll. All of Briden's crew perished before they could be rescued. Squadron Leader Harris circled the scene of the crash and attempted to drop a dinghy to the stricken crew but its attached rope snagged the tail of his Wellington and Harris was forced to land at the fighter airfield at Coltishall, near Norwich, which was still under construction. The one survivor from 37 Squadron, Flying Officer Lemon, crash-landed at RAF Feltwell where the Wellington was destroyed. 9 Squadron, which had lost five aircraft from the nine dispatched, suffered another loss when Sergeant Petts crash-landed on his return and the aircraft was written off, as he recalls:

'Towards the western side of the North Sea we encountered some broken cloud which, on first sighting, raised false hopes that we were reaching land. We were finally sure that we were seeing land when we made out the shape of a Butlin's holiday camp ahead and knew that we were approaching Clacton or Skegness. I had seen Skegness some months previously and when we reached the coast I was able to confirm that this was it. I turned south-west to skirt the Wash, as there was no point in crossing additional water on one engine. I first intended to carry on to Honington but in view of Kemp's condition and deteriorating weather ahead I decided instead to land at Sutton Bridge. Preliminary gentle checks of undercarriage and flaps, a slow approach and smooth landing and we stopped after a very short landing run – our damage included a burst starboard tyre. It was just 4 o'clock; we had been airborne for seven hours. My first concern was for an ambulance for our two wounded. Next, a call to Honington – but no transport was available until morning – a preliminary debriefing and then something to eat. Next morning we went back to the aircraft to survey the damage and to collect various loose articles that we had left inside. The damage was mostly down the starboard side of the fuselage and on the starboard wing the lost oil pressure had resulted from a holed oil tank. As a souvenir I took only a piece of wing fabric complete with a cannon shell hole. The operation of 18 December, carrying, in search of warships, bombs quite unsuitable for such targets, cost 12 Wellingtons, 11 complete crews and several wounded."[10]

The survivors returned from 10 days' special leave to discover that changes had been made. At Honington a new Flight Commander, Squadron Leader (later Air Commodore) L.E. Jarman joined 9 Squadron from Training Command. Shortly afterwards a new CO, Wing Commander McKee arrived from 99 Squadron. The RAF post-mortem into the disastrous raid on Wilhelmshaven had concluded that its Wellingtons and Hampdens could no longer cross German territory in daylight and expect to survive against Luftwaffe opposition. From thenceforth Blenheims, whose losses had been lower, were dispatched singly or in pairs, to overfly the German North Sea bases. However, a few daylight bomber sweeps were flown over the North Sea. On 2 January 1940 three Wellingtons of 149 Squadron were attacked by 12 Bf 110s. Two of the bombers were shot down and a third had a lucky escape. Meanwhile, RAF ground crews at the Wellington and Hampden bases installed armour plate and applied self-sealing covering to fuel tanks.

Notes

1. Kellett, the son of an Anglo-Irish Surgeon Rear-Admiral, joined the RAF rather than the Navy after being told that Cranwell cadets were given motorcycles to assist their training. In the late 1920s while serving in Iraq, he force-landed in the desert and was saved by a fellow pilot from capture by hostile tribesmen who were advancing on the rescuing aircraft as it took-off. In 1936 he had the unusual experience of being seconded to the Imperial Japanese Army to advise on engineering for the Japanese Air Force, his services being recognized by the Emperor with the Order of the Sacred Treasure of Japan. He returned home in 1937 and took command of 148 Bomber Squadron equipped with Wellesleys. On 5-7 November 1938, as leader of the RAF's Long Range Development Unit, he flew one of two Wellesleys to establish a new long-distance record-breaking non-stop flight of 7,158.95 miles in just over 48 hours from Ismailia, Egypt to Darwin, Australia. Kellett was awarded the DFC in 1940 and, in the autumn of 1942 in North Africa, he was shot down in a raid on Tobruk and taken prisoner, being sent to *Stalag Luft III* where he was SBO at the time of the celebrated Wooden Horse escape. He was awarded the CBE in

1943. Air Commodore Kellett CBE DFC AFC died aged 84 in January 1990.

2. The Vickers Armstrong Wellington was affectionately known as the Wimpy after the American Disney cartoon character J. Wellington Wimpy in 'Popeye'. The Wellington, the Handley Page Hampden, the Armstrong Whitworth Whitley and Bristol Blenheim – all twin engined bombers – were the mainstay of Bomber Command early in the war. The Wellington had been conceived by the brilliant British scientist, Dr Barnes Wallis using geodetic or lattice work structure. Like many of its genre, the Wellington was weakly armed. Following heavy Wellington and Blenheim losses in daylight, the elderly Whitley squadrons in 4 Group were immediately employed in night leaflet dropping operations and made no apprearance in daylight at all. The serious losses inflicted on 29 September, when a complete formation of five 144 Squadron Hampdens was destroyed over the German Bight between Heligoland and Wangerooge Island by Bf 109s of I./ZG26, soon convinced the Air Staff that a profound change of its daylight policy was necessary.

3. Later, in May 1943, after a long convalescence and post in fighter training schools, Specht became Gruppenkommandeur, II./JGII. He scored 32 confirmed victories, including 15 four-motor bombers and was awarded the *Ritterkreuz* (Knight's Cross) before being reported MIA on 1 January 1945 during the disastrous Bodenplatte operation.

4. Later Air Marshal, Sir and C.-in-C. Transport Command.

5. Hauptmann Restemayer, pilot of a Bf 110 was wounded and his aircraft badly damaged. Feldwebel Friedrich Braukmeier, one of the Bf 109 pilots, was shot down and killed.

6. Flying Officer 'Cheese' Lemon. Squadron Leader P. C. Lemon DSO DFC was shot down on 25/26 July 1942 flying a 12 Squadron Wellington.

7. Ruse crash-landed in shallow water on a mud flat off Spiekeroog. He, May and Jones were captured. Oberleutnant Johann Fuhrmann, Schumacher's *Rottenflieger* (wingman) carried out three beam attacks on another Wellington without apparent result and, making a pass from dead astern, was shot down in the crossfire and ditched his Bf 109D in the sea but was drowned before he could be rescued. Flying Officer P.A. 'Pete' Wimberley was believed shot down by Leutnant Helmut Lent of I./ZG76 in a lone Bf 110. Wimberley crash-landed on Borkum, his Wellington bursting into flames. He survived but his crew perished. Flying Officer O.J.T. Lewis, Squadron Leader I.V. Hue-Williams and Flying Officer A.T. Thompson piloted the three other 37 Squadron Wellingtons shot down. Lewis was Lent's second victim. There was only one survivor, AC1 G.W. Geddes but he too died of his wounds later. 2./ZG76 led by the *Gruppenkommandeur*, Hauptmann Reinecke, claimed another Wellington, while Bf 109Es of 5./JG77 claimed three bombers.

8. Air Speed Indicator.

9. Indicated Air Speed.

10. In addition to the 12 Wellingtons lost and the two written off in crashes, three others were damaged in crash landings in England. Flying Officer W.J. Macrae of 9 Squadron force-landed at North Coates with a damaged starboard wing, rear fuselage and rudder and two men wounded. Wing Commander Kellett and Flying Officer Riddlesworth were the other two Wellingtons that crashed. Luftwaffe fighter claims for aircraft destroyed on the raid totalled 38, which later were pared down to 26 or 27. Among these, Oberleutnant Johannes Steinhoff's claim for two destroyed was reduced to one. Only two of I/ZG76's 16 claims were disallowed, one of which was 2./ZG76's Hauptmann Wolfgang Falck's second. Falck was hit by return fire during an attack on one of the Wellingtons but managed to force-land on Wangerooge. His wingman, Unteroffizier Fresia, was credited with two confirmed destroyed. Leutnant Uellenbeck's claims for two destroyed was upheld, as was Leutnant Helmut Lent's claims for two bombers shot down. Uellenbeck's Bf 110 was hit 33 times by return fire but although he and his gunner, Unteroffizier Dombrowski, were wounded, they landed safely back at Jever. Though RAF crews claimed 12 German single and twin-engined fighters had been shot down, just three Bf 109 fighters were lost and a handful damaged.

# Chapter 2

# Night Offensive

Early operations against German shipping had proved, at the cost of many valuable crews, that unescorted daylight bombing was out of the question. The losses seemed to have shaken the War Cabinet out of its chivalrous attitude towards the German civilian population but it would not be until March 1940 that the so called 'niceties' of war were dispensed with and Bomber Command was allowed to bomb land targets for the first time. The RAF night offensive had opened in February 1940 with '*Nickel*' raids with propaganda leaflets or 'Bumphlets' being dropped on Germany. They, at least, provided an opportunity for crews to gain some valuable experience of flying at night.

Unfortunately, the darkness was to prove no greater ally than daylight had been. On 2 March a Wellington of 149 Squadron, intending to drop leaflets over Bremen, crashed shortly after take-off when one engine developed trouble and the other cut out altogether. All the crew perished in the crash. The following night a Wellington 1A of 99 Squadron crashed at Barton Mills, killing all six crew, after being recalled from a '*Nickel*' sortie to Hamburg.

In March significant changes occurred at RAF Mildenhall. The headquarters of 3 (Bomber) Group moved from Mildenhall to Harraton House at Exning, near Newmarket. On 3 March the first Wellington ICs were issued to 149 Squadron, quickly followed by 99 Squadron. The Mark IC had re-designed hydraulics and a 24-volt electrical system, which permitted the use of the new directional radio compass. Crews, ever mindful of the beam attacks made by the Luftwaffe; soon installed hand-held machine guns in the long narrow side windows. Mark ICs were first used on 20 March during a sweep over the North Sea. Next day Wellington ICs of 149 Squadron made a night reconnaissance over Germany. Then, on 23 March, Wellingtons reconnoitred the River Elbe and the port of Hamburg. One crew, which lost its way, was shot down by anti-aircraft fire near Dunkirk. All the crew managed to abandon their aircraft and reach the safety of Allied lines. On 7 April Wellington crews were brought to a state of readiness when it was realized that German ships, sighted heading for Norway and Denmark the day before, were part of an invasion force. During the afternoon Blenheims attacked but their bombs missed and another attempt by two squadrons of Wellingtons was thwarted by bad visibility. On 12 April six Wellingtons of 149 Squadron took-off from Mildenhall and followed in trail behind six Wellingtons of 38 Squadron from Marham. They were ordered to head for the Norwegian coast near Stavanger and search for German warships. No warships had been sighted when the Wellingtons were intercepted by a group of Me 110s. The enemy pilots, again employing beam attacks to excellent advantage, shot down two bombers of 149 Squadron. Twelve Wellingtons of 9 and 115 Squadrons, which were ordered to make a bombing attack on two cruisers, the *Köln* and the *Königsberg* in Bergen harbour, fared little better. None of their bombs did any lasting damage.

The next bombing operations against German forces were made at night on the airfield at Aalborg in Denmark where the Luftwaffe had established a large supply base for their Norwegian campaign. On the night of 17/18 April 75 Squadron dispatched three Wellingtons to Stavanger for its maiden bombing operation.[1] On the Stavanger operation two aircraft managed to bomb the target. Then, on 25 April, six Wellingtons of 149 Squadron took-off late at night in another attempt to bomb Stavanger. It proved abortive. Thereafter, the Wellingtons were again employed on North Sea sweeps and night reconnaissance operations over the island of Sylt to prevent minelaying seaplanes from operating.

On 9 May a Wellington of 38 Squadron at RAF Marham was brought to readiness for a security patrol to Borkum in the German Friesian Islands. The front gunner, LAC G. Dick, recalls:

'The object was to maintain a standing patrol of three hours over the seaplane base to prevent their flare path lighting up and thus inhibit their mine-laying seaplanes from taking off. We carried a load of 250lb bombs in case a discernible target presented itself. We took-off at 2130 hours. Holland was still at peace and their lights, though restricted, were clearly visible, the Terschelling lightship in particular, obliging by giving a fixed navigational fix. After three hours monotonous circling and seeing next to nothing, I heard Flying Officer Burnell, our Canadian pilot, call for course home. The words always sounded like music to a gunner in an isolated turret with no positive tasks to take up his mind, other than endless turret manipulation and endless peering into blackness. I heard the navigator remark that the lightship had gone out and the pilot's reply, "Well give us a bloody course anyway". One only had to go west to hit Britain somewhere, or return on the reciprocal of the outward course – drift notwithstanding. After an hour's flying with the magic IFF box switched on for the past thirty minutes, I gave the welcome call, "Coast ahead!" Much discussion occurred as to where our landfall really was. I told them I thought north of the Humber, which was 150 miles north of our proper landfall at the Orfordness corridor. I was told to "Belt up". As a gunner, what did I know about it? (I had flown pre-war with 214 Squadron for two years up and down the east coast night and day and was reasonably familiar with it.) Probably pride would not let them admit that they were 150 miles off course, in an hour's flying. Eventually, a chance light showed up and we landed on a strange aerodrome, which turned out to be Leconfield. Overnight billets were arranged at 0400 hours for the visiting crew. However, others were on an early start. They switched on the radio at 0600 hours and gave us the "gen" that at around midnight Germany had invaded Holland, Belgium and France – hence the extinguished lightship. The odd thing was, we had returned with our bombs, as it wasn't the done thing to drop them indiscriminately. We returned to base later on the 10th to be greeted with "We thought you'd gone for a Burton". Good news was slow in circulating in those days.'

At Honington Wing Commander Andrew McKee, the New Zealander CO of 9 Squadron could tell his crews little more than they had gleaned from their wireless sets. Rupert 'Tiny' Cooling, second pilot in Sergeant Douglas' crew, one of two new crews who had arrived on the base barely three days before, recalls:

'The mess was quiet at lunchtime. Serious groups gathered round the radiogram, listening silently to the news. A lot was said but little was learned: things did not seem to be going well. The murmur of voices stilled as McKee walked briskly into the crew room, followed by his flight commanders. The target was the aerodrome at Waalhaven. It had been seized by German troops. Junkers Ju 52s were flying in men, munitions and supplies. Dutch troops were to attack at last light. The Wellingtons would crater the airfield, destroy the transports and soften up the defences. Each was to carry sixteen 250lb bombs, nose and tail fused for maximum fragmentation. Weather was forecast to be fine. Flak, said the intelligence officer, would be light stuff, mainly 20mm. The Germans had had no time to bring in heavy anti-aircraft weapons. Single-engined fighters were unlikely but there were reports of Bf 110 activity. He did not mention that five out of six Blenheims had been shot down by 110s earlier in the day and over the same target.'

In all, 36 Wellingtons would be dispatched by Bomber Command. At Honington, 9 Squadron began taking-off for Holland at 1730 hours. Sergeant Douglas piloted 'U for Uncle', a Wellington IA. Second Pilot 'Tiny' Cooling continues:

'Away to starboard, England was reduced to a dark shadow, separating sea from sky. With it strangely, went those last niggling doubts; those faint tremors of fear were swamped by a rising tide of excitement. "Wireless operator to front turret. Second pilot to the astrodome." Sergeant Douglas made his dispositions. We were 6,000ft above the polders. In the distance I saw that the flickering curtain of flak was hemmed with orange flame and rolling curls of dense black smoke. "Bomb doors open. Target in sight. Right a little, right." The last word was drawn out, then chopped as the nose came round to the required heading. Now the lights were directly ahead. "Left, left. Steady. Bombs gone." The Wellington jerked perceptively, as 4,000lb of metal and high explosive plunged from the gaping belly. There was a sharp "twack" like some large and floppy fly swat striking the upper surface of the starboard wing. A triangle of the camouflage covering leapt up to dance upon the upper surface of the starboard wing. Surprised at his own calm and composure, Cooling said, "Pilot, we've been hit. Starboard mainplane. There's a patch of fabric flapping just outboard of the engine."

'U-Uncle flew on past the Dutch coast. Out over the North Sea Sergeant Douglas handed over control to Tiny Cooling before going aft to see the damage for himself. It was dark when U for Uncle crossed the Suffolk coast. Electric blue flashes from Honington beckoned us to within sight of the flickering gooseneck flare path. With a gentle bump the wheels touched, the tail settled. Then the Wellington tugged determinedly to starboard. In the light of the downward recognition lamp the flattened starboard tyre was clearly visible. Still hot, the engine exhaust rings ticked and cracked above our heads in the cool night air as we examined the wing, the wheel and the undercarriage doors by the light of our torches. A ragged piece of torn fabric as big as a dinner plate dripped intermittently, exuding the sweet smell of high-octane petrol. One undercarriage door, perforated like the surface of a cheese grater, reflected a scatter of silver streaks on the matt black paint.'

The following night six Wellingtons of 149 Squadron again bombed Waalhaven. The German violation of Dutch and Belgian neutrality had opened up a path for British bombers to fly directly from England to the Ruhr where 60 per cent of Germany's industrial strength was concentrated. However, political infighting between the French and British commands delayed matters. The French, with their hands full trying to repel an enemy force from its borders, were alarmed at the repercussions of such an action and Bomber Command, with its 16 squadrons of Wellingtons, Whitleys and Hampdens, was prevented from carrying out the action.

For the time being RAF Bomber Command had to content itself with inland targets in Germany. On the night of 14/15 May, Wellingtons of 149 Squadron bombed Aachen and the following day the War Cabinet authorized Bomber Command to attack east of the Rhine. On the night of 15/16 May, Bomber Command began its strategic air offensive against Germany when 99 bombers, 39 of them Wellingtons, bombed oil and steel plants and railway centres in the Ruhr. Throughout May 1940 the Wellingtons attacked tactical targets with limited success. By early morning of 2 June the remaining troops of the BEF (British Expeditionary Force) had been evacuated from the shores around Dunkirk. Thousands of French troops had still to be evacuated and during the daylight hours of 3 June Wellingtons stood ready, bombed up, to attack German positions near Dunkirk. Tiny Cooling at Honington recalls:

'9 Squadron were to wait by the Wellingtons, prepared to take-off at 1530 hours. The target had yet to be decided. We lay on the grass by our allotted aircraft in the warm sunshine. A daylight operation was a daunting thought. Take-off was delayed by two hours; hopes rose. Take-off would be 2000 hours, the target Bergues, German positions on the southern edge of the Dunkirk perimeter. "For God's sake," said McKee with uncharacteristic emotion, "make sure you drop your bombs over enemy occupied territory. Our troops have enough to cope with without the added burden of someone's misdirected aim. And keep well away from the Channel. The Navy will fire at anything overhead. In present circumstances, who can blame them?"

Sergeant Douglas decided Tiny Cooling would carry out the take-off and approach to the target.

'It was still daylight when I took-off. As the coast appeared at Orfordness, I looked to port. A few hundred feet ahead was another Wellington, beyond it a third.'

The moment of pride to be in such company made Cooling recall Shakespeare's *Henry V* before another famous battle in France: 'We few, we happy few, we band of brothers', he thought. The navigator's voice sounded over the intercom. 'Set course one-seven-one from Orfordness. ETA target 42 minutes.'

'The starboard wing dipped; the other aircraft were lost to sight. The turreted nose travelled round the horizon until, within the cockpit, the compass grid wires were aligned with the north-seeking needle. Level out, on course, the light is draining and darkness, like sediment, deepens in the eastern hemisphere. The sun has set and yet, due south beyond the bulbous nose, there is another sunset, a golden glowing arc resting upon the distant skyline. It is puzzling for a moment until we realize the glow is above Dunkirk; the light is from fires blazing ninety miles away.

'Douglas took over the controls; it was the second pilot's job to drop the bombs, whilst the navigator kept track of our wanderings as we sought out "targets of opportunity". From the bomb-aimer's position the sight was awesome. Six thousand feet below, Dunkirk was a sea of flame glinting like a brightly spot lit plaque of beaten copper. We turned and flew south, avoiding the coast; skirting the column of smoke like a deep grey stake into the heart of the town. A flare ignited and drifted above a pale grey sea of smoke. We might have been flying over a lake of milky water. Spot a gun flash in that sea of featureless mist; line up its imagined position to track down the aiming wires of the bombsight and then let go a stick of three or four. Did we deceive ourselves? Scatter enough bombs about and chance will ensure that something is hit. It was time we were buying; fragments of time to load another boat; to allow another ship to sail. We left the burning beacon behind and headed home.'

Italy's decision, at midnight on 10 June, to declare war on Britain and France caused Bomber Command to re-direct its bombing strategy. Mussolini's intentions had already been anticipated and it was agreed that as soon as Italy joined the war her heavy industry in the north of the country would be bombed by Wellingtons and longer-range Whitleys. Accordingly, on 3 June, preparations were begun to transform Salon in the Marseilles area into a refuelling and operational base. At 1530 hours on 11 June Wellingtons of 99 Squadron flew in from England and landed at the forward base. Behind the scenes chaos reigned as first one order to bomb Italy was given, then countermanded by the French. Finally, an exasperated Group Captain R.M. Field, the CO of 'Haddock' force at Salon, ordered the Wellingtons off (a force of Whitleys, having refuelled in the Channel Islands, was already en route to Turin and Genoa). The Wellingtons were prevented from taking-off when, at the last moment, a procession of French lorries were driven directly into their path and left there. When the political shenanigans had been sorted out, more Wellingtons made the seven-hour flight from England to Salon.

On 15 June, two Wellingtons of 99 Squadron and six of 149 Squadron took-off from Salon for a raid on Genoa. Violent thunderstorms en route prevented all but one of the Wellington crews from finding their targets and seven bombers were forced to return to Salon with their bomb loads intact. On the night of 16/17 June nine Wellingtons made another attempt to bomb Italy but only five crews were able to find and attack the Caproni works at Milan. Crews returned to Salon to discover that the French had sued for an armistice and effectively, all future operations were brought to an end.

Meanwhile, on the night of 14/15 June, 214 Squadron at Stradishall flew its maiden Wellington operation when it was dispatched to the Black Forest. June was also a month when Wellington crews in Norfolk and Suffolk got their feet wet.

On the night of 20 June Wellingtons of 99 Squadron were engaged in operations over the Rhine Valley south of Karlsruhe. Acting Flight Lieutenant Percy Pickard's Wellington IC was hit over Münster and he was forced to ditch about 30 miles off Great Yarmouth. Pickard and his crew were picked up by a high-speed launch 13 hours later and landed at Gorleston.[2]

During July 1940 the Wellingtons of 3 Group carried out attacks on west and north-west Germany, with the occasional raid on targets in Denmark. During the mid-morning of 8 July New Zealand and Commonwealth crews stationed at Feltwell, home of 75 Squadron RNZAF, knew there was a 'flap' on when they were commanded to air test their Wellingtons. Sergeant Robert Shepherd, a 19 year old Wop/AG and front gunner in Flying Officer Joe Larney's crew, recalls:

'We went out to dispersal to carry out our checks. In my case, I checked the radio and the front turret guns and changed the accumulators. Later on in the war radio and R/T checks were limited because the Germans were listening out on all frequencies. It would indicate to them what preparations for a raid were in the offing. Having completed the DI we flew a forty-minute NFT (Night Flying Test) for checks on engine and flaps, etc. After lunch we went back to the squadron for lectures on aircraft recognition and radio and gunnery. At 1700 hours in the station HQ we were briefed that our target would be Mors in Denmark. Our station commander, Group Captain Modin, was respected by all ranks. He was posted to the Far East in 1941 and was unfortunately taken as a POW in Singapore. Wing Commander Buckley, our squadron CO and Flight Commander, Squadron Leader Cyrus Kay, both of whom were Kiwis, were great commanders, highly respected and loved for the way they led the squadron on operations.

'After briefing we went back to the mess to pass the time away until after take-off, which in our case was scheduled for 2145 hours. Security was fairly lax. After briefing was over one could leave the station and quite unintentionally divulge the "target for tonight". Later, from the time briefing commenced, the main gate was closed and nobody allowed out until aircraft were over the target. Up to take-off one felt tense. We went out to our kite, P9206/L ("for Larney") and Joe, our Kiwi skipper and Pilot Officer Harry Goodwin, the navigator, inspected the bomb bays and flaps. Then it was all aboard. Larney ran up the engines. All OK. We got the green light from the control tower and soon were airborne. After take-off we were more relaxed; our minds occupied with our jobs. I put the "J" switch over to intercom and radio to enable me to listen out on base frequency for any messages like "BBA" (return to base) or change of target. There was none. We crossed the coast and our IFF was switched off. I test fired my guns with a short burst and reported to Larney by intercom that all was OK. I remained in my turret right up to the bombing, assisting the navigator by getting him fixes. The target loomed and I saw flak and searchlights for the first time. I thought, "We won't get through that" but as we got nearer it seemed to disperse. We dropped six eighteen-hour delay bombs, together with incendiaries and 500lb bombs from about 10,000ft.

'Crossing the enemy coast I got on the radio and checked in with base. The skipper was limited as regards communication by R/T. The equipment then was the TR9 with a range of only fifteen miles. Pilot Officer "Hank" Hankins, our Second Dickie, took a brief spell at the controls. Nearing the base we were given permission to land. Joe turned and landed without incident. Malfunctions were reported to the ground crews. One cannot praise them highly enough. How could we operate without them? They were highly skilled in all trades. Our lives were indeed in their hands every time we took-off. We headed for debriefing, anxious to get it over so we could go to the mess for egg, bacon and milk before bed.'

Unrestricted warfare now threatened from both sides of the Channel. On the night of 23/24 August the Luftwaffe rained bombs on London, the first to fall on the capital since 1918. Bomber Command was quick to retaliate, for on the following night, 24/25 August, it dispatched 81 Wellingtons, Hampdens and Whitleys to Berlin as a reprisal. The flight involved a round trip of eight hours and 1,200 miles. Seven aircraft aborted and of the remaining force, 29 bombers claimed to have bombed Berlin and a further 27 over-flew the capital but were unable to pinpoint their targets because of thick cloud. Five aircraft were lost to enemy action, including three which ditched in the North Sea. Bombing results had been unimpressive but the RAF had scored a great victory for morale. Berlin was again bombed on the night of 30/31 August while in September Wellingtons of 3 Group made repeated night attacks on invasion barges massed in the Channel ports ready for Operation *Sealion*, the proposed German invasion of England. Other desperate measures were called for by Bomber Command. Unrestricted warfare manifested itself again on 4 September when the Intelligence Officers told crews they would be dispatched to the Black Forest, where the Germans were massing heavy armament. They were to carry a new incendiary device called 'Razzle'. This consisted of a wad of wet phosphorous placed between two pieces of celluloid, which ignited to produce an eight-inch flame when the phosphorous dried. Wellingtons of 149 Squadron had first tried an experiment on the night of 11/12 August, carrying 50 biscuit tins each filled with up to 500 examples but Churchill, fearing that such tactics could lead to German reprisal raids, had ordered the scheme to be postponed. Bob Shepherd of 75 (NZ) Squadron, recalls:

'I took the lids off the tins and there were wads swimming about in a solution. I opened the flare chute and one by one, tossed out the contents of three tin loads from about 10,000ft. We also dropped a full load of incendiaries and six 250-pounders. There was hardly any flak at all.'

The RAF bombing directive of 21 September gave support to priority attacks on oil refineries, aircraft factories, railways, canals and U-boat construction yards while electric power stations and gas works in Berlin should also be bombed. On the night of 23/24 September, Berlin was selected for a special retaliatory attack and was bombed by 119 Whitleys, Hampdens and Wellingtons. However, most of the objectives were missed and many bombs failed to explode. In September 1940 the Luftwaffe had been forced to abandon massed daylight bombing and the invasion fleet was dispersed. Bomber Command could again turn its attention to city targets. On the night of 16/17 November, 127 bombers, the largest number yet dispatched, raided Hamburg. By the end of 1940 Berlin would have been bombed on ten occasions. A trip to the German capital on 26 November proved to be Bob Shepherd's 30th and final op of his first tour:

'I flew with Pilot Officer Saxelby; Joe Larney (later Squadron Leader Larney) having completed his tour on 29 September on our trip to the oil refineries at Magdeburg. We got through and I left for a long rest before returning, in 1942, to fly a second tour, on 57 Squadron Lancasters at Scampton. Saxelby did not make it. He was shot down in 1942 and was made a POW.'

Bob Shepherd had certainly led a charmed life in 75 Squadron. He was one of the last of the original pre-war air gunners stationed at RAF Feltwell to survive a first tour. Others were not so lucky and many of his pre-war contemporaries, like

19 year old Bill Hitchmough, had been killed. Hitchmough was a gunner in Pilot Officer W.J. Finlayson's crew, which failed to return on the night of 23/24 October 1940 when Bomber Command had dispatched some 79 Wellingtons to many targets including Berlin and Emden. Next morning Shepherd was airborne with Pilot Officer 'Spanky' McFarlane with orders to mount a search off the Dutch coast. A dinghy was found but there was no trace of the crew.

These continual high losses of crews could only be made good by young men passing out of the OTUs, even if they were not fully trained or as familiar with their aircraft as they would have liked.

Notes
1. Three Wellingtons had been dispatched from Feltwell on 4 April but had been recalled.
2. Group Captain Percy Pickard DSO DFC and Wellington *F for Freddie* were later featured in a propaganda film, *Target for Tonight*. Pickard would lose his life on the legendary attack by Mosquitoes on Amiens prison on 18 February 1944.

# Chapter 3

# Bombers' Moon

In 1940 the RAF was so desperately short of aircrew that training courses for new intakes were notoriously short. At 15 OTU at Harwell the gunnery course, which should have been one month, was in fact two and a half weeks. Sergeant Alfred Jenner, a Wop/AG, did at least make one flight over enemy territory – a 'very scary' trip to Paris on a leaflet-dropping sortie before being posted in mid-November to 99 'Madras Presidency' Squadron in 3 Group at Newmarket Heath, as he recalls.

'Incendiary bombs were exploding in 99 Squadron's sleeping quarters when I arrived on a cold, foggy November evening. They were going off in the open fireplace of the room under the Rowley Mile grandstand on Newmarket racecourse, which served as NCO aircrew billets. Fortunately, the bombs were British incendiaries, or pieces of them, which bored airmen were throwing into the fire to enliven their lives after the previous night's raid on Gelsenkirchen. The talk was all of earlier raids, old comrades on other stations and those who had already "gone for a Burton" (been killed). I soon found out that every other aspect of life on an operational squadron was different from that at disciplined training establishments. You were not, for instance, expected to parade at 6 am, or to worry about kit inspections, nor even to be particular about dress, unless you were down in the town of Newmarket where Army Police could never understand the camaraderie of the air. You were expected to be meticulous in the performance of the job you had been trained to do and when in the air to obey commands without question. Discipline was vital we soon discovered, not the least because of the primitive conditions in which we had to live and fight. Newmarket was a racecourse, not a sophisticated permanent station like other squadrons enjoyed. The grandstand was always dirty and we could never keep our clothes clean. Our mess was just another room under the seating enclosure of the grandstand. Our ablutions were a makeshift building outside. We boiled our guns clean in the erstwhile harness room, which served as an armoury. Our aircraft were dispersed all over the racecourse, wherever there were trees to provide cover.

'Casualties were light for my first two months at Newmarket. Then it began, first with a loud bang while we were at lunch one day. We rushed outside and there at the racecourse winning post was the twisted remains of a Wellington. All inside were dead, including a young pilot who only the night before had been proudly displaying the small revolver given to him by his father "in case he ever needed it in an emergency". Worst of all was the loss of the so-called Broughton bomber, bought by the good citizens of the English town of that name. We knew every member in the crew of that machine and were therefore devastated when it crashed on take-off at the end of the runway and burst into flames. There were only two survivors, badly injured. The others burned to death as we watched helplessly. The rest of us then had to take-off over the still burning funeral pyre of our comrades. Crews were very keen and the ground crews knew their job. Although bomb loads were small and we did not always hit our targets, we firmly believed we were very good for morale. It did people good to see and hear us going out.

'I made my first operational trip on the night of 16/17 December 1940 when I flew as front gunner in Sergeant Fletcher's crew. We were to scatter-bomb Mannheim in a "town blitz" in retribution for the destruction of Coventry a month before. Operation *Abigail*, as it was code-named, would be in retaliation for the German bombing of Coventry and Southampton. In all, 134 bombers, including 61 Wellingtons, were dispatched; the first "area" bombing raid on a German industrial target. Aircraft were dispatched to the target singly. At this time we could not afford crew losses from collision or bombs falling on each other's aircraft so this was the only practical way. It was cold and lonely in the front turret but my Brownings never froze up on any of the operations I would fly. However, if one carried an apple, we were warned not to eat it; it would break your teeth! From a safety point of view, the front turret was preferable to the rear, which could be an exhausting trek to reach in our flight gear. The rear-gunner was protected by two slabs of armour plate which could be joined together to protect his chest. However, in the front turret I could only rely on armour plate behind the pilots to stop bullets hitting me from the rear. The primary function of an air gunner at this time was to be a heavy flak spotter for the captain. He told us to keep our eyes peeled and report enemy aircraft and flak gun flashes immediately. We dropped our bombs on Mannheim from about 12,000ft and although it was my first experience of flak, we came through all right. We landed back at Newmarket after being in the air for six hours and ten minutes. Unfortunately, incendiaries carried as markers by eight leading Wellingtons were dropped in the wrong place and the subsequent bombing had been widely spread.

'In the New Year I was on ops again. On 29 January 1941 we were told to bomb the *Tirpitz* at Wilhelmshaven. My pilot was Pilot Officer Coote, an ex-public school type who would stand no nonsense. All he wanted was to do a good job. He taught us that each man was reliant on the others. He was also a great "jinker" (taking avoiding action against flak and fighters). Coote stayed over the target for three-quarters of an hour with German guns popping off at us. Our observer, who was in something of a panic, shouted, "Why don't we drop the bloody bombs and get out?" Coote said in no uncertain terms, "I'm the skipper of this ship and you'll drop the bombs when I tell you!" In fact we never did see the ship and we brought our bombs home.

'On 11 February we brought our bombs home again. Our target was Bremen but there was 10/10ths cloud and we got hopelessly lost. We flew back and saw a strip of coastline but we were not sure whether it was France, Germany, Wales or England. We flew up and down. I suddenly spotted two towers and realized it was the entrance to Lowestoft harbour (the town where I was born and had spent my childhood). We flew back to Newmarket and landed through a gap in the cloud with the bombs still aboard. We had not noticed they hadn't been dropped! We lost a lot of aircraft that night.[1]

'On 14 March I flew with Sergeant Kitely, a Canadian, on a trip to Gelsenkirchen. No one could ever find Gelsenkirchen because of the industrial haze. Kitely decided to bomb and shoot up an airfield in Holland on the homeward trip. It was very exciting and we dropped our bombs. He dived the Wimpy down to 300ft and I fired about 1,000 rounds at chance lights and searchlights and the rear-gunner had a go as well. Ten days later, on 24 March, 99 Squadron were briefed to attack the *Von Hipper* in Brest Harbour. Brest was very clear. From about two miles away I could see two ships when the pilot ordered, "Bomb bay doors open". The bomb-aimer, surprised, said, "But we're too far away". We dropped them anyway. Our pilot, who was only one short of his tour, was determined to survive. It was the only case of "sugaring" I recall during my operations.'

Meanwhile, Eric Masters, a sergeant pilot who had recently arrived at Newmarket from OTU, waited impatiently to fly his first op with 99 Squadron. Squadron Leader Stanley Black, the CO, explained that Masters would captain a crew whose previous captain had been grounded. Black added that he would fly as an observer on the first two operations. In the first three weeks five operations were cancelled because of the weather. Masters recalls:

'I was becoming desperate to get the first op under my belt, to discover for myself whether I would make it – to find out just how scared one would be. Whilst I knew I had a super crew, I also knew they would be watching me very closely to see if I had any of the faults of their previous skipper. Finally, the day arrived and we set off to bomb Cologne. I was very nervous, not at the prospect of enemy action but having the CO along as my second pilot! It was in fact quite enjoyable and the ack-ack fire was nothing more than a nuisance. At times the Germans seemed keen on playing possum rather than give away the locality of a town by defending it too vigorously. One felt sorry for the crew of the other aircraft, coned in ten searchlights, weaving this way and that, trying to get away but we were glad they were taking the attention of the enemy. My landing back at Newmarket was my one "black". I dropped the Wimpy on the deck from about 25 feet instead of the normal five – ten feet and she bounced quite violently. I had to give her a quick burst on the throttles to keep her flying and let down again more gently. Squadron Leader Black suggested that it was because I had been used to concrete runways which reflected what little light there was and enabled one to judge "hold-off" more accurately. Grass was comparatively non-reflective and one had to judge height entirely by the flares. I was feeling rather miserable about it myself. However, no harm was done. I did my second trip a night later, with the CO coming along, to Cologne again.'

By mid-March 1941 99 Squadron had moved 10 miles distant to the newly completed station at Waterbeach, six miles north-east of Cambridge. On 30 March the Wellingtons began their campaign against the German battle cruisers *Scharnhorst* and *Gneisenau*, or '*Salmon* and Gluckstein' (a famous London store), as they were known, while the Halifaxes went after the cruiser *Prinz Eugen* at Brest. The campaign was to last for more than 10 months.

On the night of 31 March/1 April 4,000lb bombs were used operationally for the first time when modified Wellington IIs of 9 and 149 Squadrons dropped two on

Emden. Four aircraft were detailed for this operation, two acting as cover for the two Wellingtons carrying the bombs. 149 Squadron's *X-X-Ray*, piloted by Pilot Officer J. H. Franks, successfully completed its mission but the second squadron Wellington failed to get airborne and slid to a halt in a barley field near the runway. The 'Wizard of Oz' painted on the aircraft had failed to work its magic.

On the night of 9/10 April Alf Jenner flew his first operation from Waterbeach, with a new crew captained by Squadron Leader David C. Torrens, an ex-fighter pilot:

'Torrens was our new Flight Commander. As he was new to Bomber Command it was decided to give him the most experienced crew. I was by now something of a veteran with twelve ops and I became Torrens' front gunner. First Wop was Arthur J. Smith; a splendid wireless operator who had served in the pre-war RAF in Iraq. The second pilot was Eric H. Berry, who came from a well-off Yorkshire family and who had flown private aircraft before the war. His wartime training had been short; converting straight from a Tiger Moth to a Wellington. Although he had only flown two or three ops he was well thought of and was about to skipper his own crew. Our rear-gunner was Pilot Officer J.F. Palmer and our observer, Pilot Officer P. A. Goodwyn, was from Ipswich.

'At Waterbeach we played a guessing game. If there was a "breeze" that an op was on that night we would watch the petrol bowsers refuelling the Wimpys and note the number of gallons. If it was about 400 gallons that meant a trip to the Ruhr; if it was over 650, it must mean Berlin! Everyone was worried but did not show it. We had things to do to pass the rest of the afternoon. The wireless had to be checked and guns cleaned. At 5 o'clock on the afternoon of 9 April we entered the briefing room and sat down. At the end of the room was a large map, covered with a curtain. The Briefing Officer dramatically pulled the curtain aside and we were startled to see a red ribbon that seemed to go on forever! It meant a four and a half-hour trip to Berlin. The RAF hadn't been to the big city since the previous September. We all thought, "Jesus Christ! Why me?"

'After briefing finished we ate our flying supper in the mess. It was rather poor fare; usually corned beef and chips, bread pudding and tea. Everyone was in a high state of nervousness and excited hysteria, although no one showed any sign of despondency. We were quite well trained and highly motivated.'

This was Jenner's 13th op and although he was not superstitious, he felt prompted to write to his wife. At 1900 hours the crew truck nicknamed 'Tumbril', took the crew to *R for Robert* waiting at dispersal. Jenner recalls:

'It was really dark, cold and clear. A bombers' moon shone overhead. I climbed into the astrodome area of *R for Robert* and stowed my parachute. Our pilots wore theirs in flight. As we taxied out and lined up on the new tarmac runway I gripped the astrodome hatch clips, in case I needed to get out quickly, as I always did. We were away first. Torrens thundered down the runway (our bomb load was small because of the need for extra fuel). With flaps full on we climbed slowly into the sky above Waterbeach. I climbed into the front turret immediately; enemy fighters might already be about. Grinding away slowly we headed for Southwold, our point of departure. Nearing the coast of Holland I exclaimed, "Enemy coast ahead!" There were a few shots then all was quiet again. The captain talked quietly to us, telling us to keep our eyes peeled. Then the fun began. A succession of searchlights picked us up and passed us on from one to another until we could see the multitude of coloured flak bursts over Berlin. We had been told that there were 1,000 guns at Berlin. They couldn't all fire at us but it felt like it. Down below, Lake Wannsee shone in the moonlight. Buildings, or imagined buildings, appeared in the Berlin suburbs below. We could actually smell flak. The Germans were very good gunners. A shell knocked out one of the engines. Fortunately, it did not catch fire. Torrens feathered the prop. We dropped our bombs and droned away. Nearing Brunswick Torrens came on the intercom. "Sorry to tell you chaps but we will not make it back. You will each have to decide if you want to bale out or stay in the aircraft for a crash landing."

'I had previously decided that should such an occasion occur, then I would jump. I looked at the altimeter. It read 1,100ft (300ft less than recommended). The ruddy bulkhead at the front prevented me from turning the turret door handle. (To bale straight out of the turret would have taken me into the turning props.) To my relief, Eric Berry opened it from the other side. Flying Officer Goodwyn and I baled out. The remaining four crew, including Pilot Officer Palmer, the rear-gunner and Sergeant Albert Smith, the Wop/AG, stayed with the aircraft and crash-landed at Wolfenbuttel, near Hanover. They set fire to the aircraft before being captured and made POWs. Goodwyn and I joined them in Stalag Luft III.[2]

At Waterbeach, one day late in April, 99 Squadron crews were awaiting the call to briefing when they were surprised to hear Merlin engines, as if two Spitfires were landing together. Sergeant Eric Masters recalls:

'We all rushed to the windows to see a very unusual Wellington landing. It had Merlin engines instead of Pegasus radials. I was told to report to Wing Commander Black, who told me it would be my aircraft and that I had better have a chat with the ferry-pilot who had brought her in to learn of any different handling features. He told me it handled very well except for being extremely nose heavy due to the in-line Merlins moving the c-of-g forward. He said the trimming wheel was right back with very little more adjustment and he hated to think how she would handle with "the" bomb on board. He then told me this Mk.II Wellington was made to carry one 4,000lb bomb – the first of the blockbusters!

'Next day I took the new aircraft up for a test flight and found that the increased power from the Merlin engines was most noticeable, especially on take-off and climb. The usual bomb bay, with its opening and closing doors, was not big enough, so the doors had been dispensed with, leaving a large indentation along the bottom of the fuselage. It was not rigged for any other selection of bombs and had just the one release gear. This harming of the aerodynamics of the airframe made the aircraft somewhat "lumpy" to handle but the smoothness of the in-line engine power with the increase in airspeed outweighed every possible criticism.

'I still had my standard Wellington Mk IA assigned to me and in fact did five more missions in the aircraft before my first in the modified Wellington. It was on 5 May that I first took a 4,000lb bomb on ops, to Mannheim. By then the squadron had received another Mk II Wellington and there were twelve others distributed amongst squadrons in the Group. There were plenty of spectators, including myself, at the bombing up to see the massive bomb being winched into the bomb bay. It appeared to be a number of metal barrels welded together with a slightly pointed nose cap stuck on one end – merely, I thought to tell which was the forward end. It was quite a shock to see that quite a proportion of it was protruding and I wondered what effect this would have on the handling of the aircraft. I thought, too, that the bomb would not fall in the way a normal bomb would but would most likely tumble over and over. However, our flash photo later showed the bomb bursting; a real fluke.

'Following this we had a very busy period. We went to Brest on 7 May and to Hamburg (with the second 4,000lb bomb) on the night of 8/9 May 1941.³ On the 10th we went to Berlin (with another), then one to Mannheim on 12 May and another, to Cologne, on 17 May, before receiving my commission to Pilot Officer.'

There was no let up. On the night of 12/13 June 1941 405 (Vancouver) Squadron at Driffield, Yorks, made its operational debut when the Canadian squadron dispatched four Wellington IIs to Schwerte. On the night of 23/24 June 1941 44 Wellingtons and 18 Whitleys made a heavy raid on Cologne. One of the Wellingtons dispatched by 115 Squadron was flown by Pilot Officer Douglas Sharpe. His rear-gunner, Sergeant R.F. 'Chan' Chandler, who had been involved in a 3 PRU Wellington prang the previous month, recalls: 'After bombing Cologne things seemed to go wrong. There was a lot of chatter on the intercom between the pilot and the navigator. There was no doubt whatsoever that we were lost. The crew were repeatedly instructed to keep constant watch for any sign of land through the cloud.

'Shortly we saw the coastline. There were repeated comments about "fuel state". The aircraft was throttled back and a gradual descent was made. I was invited by Pilot Officer Sharpe to bale out over land. I declined, thinking it was best to stay with the aircraft and crew.'

Sharpe nursed the ailing bomber back to Suffolk, where almost out of fuel, he decided on a crash landing. Chandler recalls:

'It so happens that the area around Bredfield, Burgh and Pettistree is very flat and a suitable length of pastureland was selected. Sharpe made a gradual descent and approach. I jettisoned my turret doors and my back was to the starboard side as we dropped to a height of about fifty feet. I lowered my goggles and eased myself out on the edge of the turret. Looking out and down with the ground rushing past at an alarming rate of knots, I thought of rolling out of the turret. Looking along the fuselage I could see trees ahead and slid back into the turret. The next second there was the most tremendous crash and I lost consciousness.'

The Wellington had hit the trees and crashed into some council houses at Debach. Incredibly, a man with a child in his arms jumped to safety from the bedroom window of the smashed house. 'Chan' Chandler suffered serious leg, head and arm injuries but would recover. Fred Tingley, the second pilot, died later as a result of his injuries. He was the only fatality. Sharpe was unhurt but was killed on his next trip.

The night of 7 July was full of incidents. One crewmember was killed in a Wellington of 75 Squadron when it hit a tree during a night flying exercise while trying to land on one engine at Methwold. A Wellington of 115 Squadron crash-landed at Marham after being damaged in combat with a Ju 88C intruder of NJG2 and another squadron Wellington, piloted by Sergeant O.A. Mathews RNZAF, crashed in the North Sea with the loss of all the crew.

That night, Eric Masters of 99 Squadron, was flying the 30th and final operation of his tour, a sortie to Cologne. Masters was philosophical about it:

'Our losses were running at approximately 5 per cent so one believed one was living on luck after the 20th trip. One was just as likely to "buy it" on the first as on the thirtieth.' All went well until Masters' crew approached the Rhine.

'Pilot Officer Don Elliott, my Canadian navigator, came to stand beside me. There were two areas of AA activity ahead and I decided to head between them so that Elliott could pick out the river reflecting the moonlight from the south and from his map would be able to place us exactly. We discovered we were just south of Cologne. I wanted to get a really good run at the target and needed to get north of the city. There was no need for navigation now and having passed over the river I turned north and flew past Cologne on its eastern side watching the flak exploding, flares dropping, flash bombs illuminating huge areas and bombs bursting. I felt remote from it all. North of Cologne I turned over the river and headed south. Elliott was now in the prone bomb aiming position, just below and in front of me, getting a very clear view of the river and giving me course corrections to keep us in line with the target. The activity over the target had practically ceased and it became very peaceful. One of the gunners remarked, "Everyone else seems to have gone home, skipper". In these last minutes I had kept straight and level and at the same speed for much too long. The Germans must have wondered about this crazy lone raider. We were caught in the bluish-white beam of a master searchlight. Six more standard searchlights coned us. Now the whole fury of the Cologne defences concentrated on us. I increased speed, still heading for the target. The flak followed us expertly, throwing the aircraft about. Johnny Agrell, the second pilot, who was watching it all at the astrodome ready to deal with the flash-bomb, called out that we had been hit.

'I had felt a judder in the control column and then found it rigid in the fore and aft direction (elevator control). As I had been holding it in the dive I was now unable to bring the nose up.' In vain Masters tried to correct.

'The flak was still after us. I told Don to jettison the bombs (live) in a last hope to get the nose up but when this failed, I realized we were virtually out of control at 10,000ft and losing height rapidly. I had no alternative but to give the order, "Bale out!" I was thankful my chest parachute pack was in its storage position. At times I had been known to forget to take it on a trip and I had delegated Don Elliott to make sure it was always on the "tumbril". I was glad that on this occasion he had not let me down.' Eric Masters baled out and was captured. He spent the remainder of the war as a 'guest of the German government'.

The following night, 8 July, Wellingtons of 75 Squadron raided Münster. On the return flight at 13,000ft over Ijsselmeer, Squadron Leader R.P. Widdowson's aircraft was attacked by a Bf 110 night fighter. The rear-gunner was wounded in the foot but managed to drive off the enemy aircraft. Incendiary shells from the fighter started a fire near the starboard engine and, fed by a fractured fuel pipe, soon threatened to engulf the whole wing. Sergeant James Ward RNZAF, the second pilot, climbed out of the astrodome into a 100 mph slipstream in pitch darkness a mile above the North Sea. By kicking holes in the fabric covering of the geodetics he inched his way to the starboard engine and smothered the fire, which threatened to engulf the aircraft. Ward's actions earned him the Victoria Cross. (He was killed two months later, shot down in a Wellington over Hamburg.)

Other Wellingtons came home on a wing and a prayer. On the night of 14 July Sergeant Tony Gee of 149 Squadron brought *N-Nuts* home to Mildenhall after being coned in searchlights at 8,000ft over Bremen and fired on by accurate flak. Gee finally escaped but he was down to 2,000ft. His navigator/bomb-aimer, The Right Honourable Terence Mansfield, who was flying his 11th operation recalls:

'No one was wounded but as daylight came we found lots of it coming in everywhere. Our wireless was not working so we could not tell base that, although we were a long way behind schedule, we were still coming. By the time we got back to Mildenhall we were classed as overdue. Someone classified the damage to R1593 as not repairable and *N-Nuts* was taken away in pieces.'

In the half light of dawn on 15 July Sergeant J. C. Saich and the crew of a Wellington IC of 9 Squadron was returning to Honington with six 500lb bombs still in her bomb bay after a raid on Bremen. Three hours and forty minutes earlier, *T-Tommy* had been caught in the glare of searchlights over Bremen at 11,000ft, hit four times by flak and set on fire. Sergeant English, the rear-gunner and Sergeant Telling, the second pilot, were wounded by shell splinters. Flares, stored in the port wing, ignited and two large holes were blown in the starboard wing and rear fuselage. Much of the fabric covering the tail fin was burned away before the fires were finally extinguished. The bombs could not be jettisoned because of damage to the hydraulic and electrical systems. One main wheel refused to lower, the flaps were inoperative and the fuel gauges had read 'zero' for the last two hours of the flight. The area picked out for an emergency landing was a large field near Somerton, Norfolk. However, telegraph poles had been erected in all fields in the vicinity as an anti-invasion measure in 1940 and these could not easily be seen in the dim light. *T-Tommy* touched down, went into a swing and slammed into one of the wooden poles, finishing with its fuselage broken in two. Incredibly, all six crew emerged from the wreckage with little more than a few bruises.

Saich and Telling were each awarded the DFM for their exploits. Saich and five other crew, including Sergeant Trott, who had been aboard *T-Tommy*, were killed when their Wellington was shot down in flames by a German night fighter near Terwispel in Holland during the costly raid on Berlin on 7/8 September 1941. Sergeant Telling was killed six months later when his Wellington broke up during a training flight near Thetford, Norfolk.

Meanwhile, on 24 July 1941, Wellingtons, Hampdens and Fortresses made daylight attacks on the *Gneisenau* and *Prinz Eugen* at Brest while Halifaxes attacked the *Scharnhorst* at La Pallice. Sixteen bombers failed to return and two other aircraft were lost when they ditched on the way home.

On the night of 11/12 August the first service trial over enemy territory of the *Gee* navigational and identification device was carried out successfully by two Wellingtons of 115 Squadron during a raid on Mönchengladbach. On 28 August three of the squadron's Wellingtons were lost landing back at Marham after runway lighting had been damaged by enemy bombers.

In September 1941, the Wellingtons were flying further afield, as Terence Mansfield, of 149 Squadron, recalls:

'On 26 September, while en route to Genoa, we had been recalled over France due to forecast bad weather at base.' Three days later the Wellingtons went all the way. Mansfield continues: 'We had a lovely view of the Alps but Genoa was mostly covered by cloud so bombing was on estimated position using the coast. After leaving Genoa our wireless blew up and cloud developed solidly below 10,000ft so navigation was solely on astro fixes. Fortunately, we hit the Mildenhall Lorenz beam almost on ETA. Duggie Fox, my pilot, turned on to it and descended in the low cloud. Honington had been alerted and they fired a massive assortment of pyrotechnics as we approached and we crawled in under a cloud base of, at most, 200ft.'

On 30 September the Wellingtons carried a new weapon, as Terence Mansfield recalls:

'We carried a new 65lb incendiary for marking purposes. This horrid weapon was a very light case, rather like a large oblong tin, the contents of which were spontaneously combustible on contact with air. The resulting fire was very visible but it was a menace, as a leak brought fire.

'On 12 October we again carried 65lb incendiaries, to Nuremberg. We had orders to drop only on visual. It was totally dark and although we flew around the area for forty minutes, we could see no ground detail. Then bombing started but it was not Nuremberg. Anyhow, we went over to investigate at just over 4,000ft and I was confident that I could make out a small town. Since the fires were well established, we added to them and sent a signal back that we had bombed a secondary target. Further astro fixes on the return trip confirmed my calculated positions. On landing, we were told that we were the only crew not to find the target but our photograph proved that we were right and that almost the entire attack had been against the wrong place. We got our haloes back!

'On 7 November, my last [trip] with Duggie Fox and 149, we carried the 65lb incendiary again. All the outward route was appalling, with high cloud, very bad icing, turbulence and rattling hail. Using the occasional breaks in the tops, I managed to get a series of astro fixes, so that at least we thought we were almost on track. Total cloud cover at the target meant that we could not drop our bombs and we brought them all the way back. That we crossed the Suffolk coast almost on track and only five minutes late on ETA, proved the value of my sextant. We saw no signs of any defensive action and felt sure that the high losses, 21 of 170, were due solely to the weather.'

In the closing days of 1941, 149 Squadron at Mildenhall began exchanging its Wellington IIs for the Short Stirling. 3 Group, since it operated Bristol-engined bombers, had, in August 1941, been selected for re-equipment with the Short Stirling. On 24 December there was a taste of things to come when the Avro Lancaster entered service with 44 Squadron at Waddington. Meanwhile, in the summer of 1941 some units like 10 Squadron were still expected to soldier on with the obsolete Whitley until the end of the year when conversion to the Halifax finally took place.

Notes
1. Of a total force of 79 bombers, 22 including 11 Wellingtons, crash-landed in England.
2. On 9/10 April 80 aircraft – 36 Wellingtons, 24 Hampdens, 17 Whitleys and three Stirlings – went to Berlin. Six FTR.
3. Three hundred and sixty aircraft (plus another three on mining operations), the largest number of aircraft so far dispatched, were sent mainly to Hamburg and Bremen.

# Chapter 4

# Whitley Wanderings – Basil Craske

'The whole atmosphere of an operational squadron as opposed to a training unit was very apparent as soon as we arrived at Leeming, Yorkshire, in January 1941. It is rather difficult to describe but it was quite obvious that 10 Squadron was there to do a job and everything seemed geared to that end. A serious approach certainly but not without its humorous interludes. The Squadron motto was *Rem Acu Tangere* (Straight as an arrow to the target). Some artistic wag amended the plunging arrow to become two fingers raised amongst the flames, with the caption *Ram Acu Rectum* – all beautifully drawn in coloured chalks on the blackboard in the crew room. There were periods of boredom when waiting for the next assignment but the time of inactivity did not last for long. Quite apart from operational flights there were many test flights for the aircraft, experimental navigation exercises and even a crash course in astro-navigation and the use of a sextant, which was invaluable, bearing in mind that from take-off until landing no radio communication was allowed except in emergency. Consequently, all navigation was by dead reckoning, directional loop aerial and the stars, none of which were very accurate more often that not. Navigation in 1941 was very basic. At briefing there was a large wall map with a red tape extending from Leeming to the target. Aircraft were expected to leave the country more or less at the approved coastal feature but getting there and back was very much in the hands of the pilot and navigator. An example of suspect navigation could be seen on the very large map of Europe and the British Isles in the crew room, which had a suitable pin and flag indicating the targets bombed by *Shiny Ten*. In the very middle of England at Bassingbourn there was a pin where some crew had unloaded their bombs upon an inviting but dimly lit runway. There were many others on the other side of the water, one of which showed a successful raid on Turin in Italy.

Our first operation was to bomb the docks at Rotterdam. The captain of the aircraft was a flight lieutenant and I was second pilot. This flight lieutenant was a RAF 'Regular' whose basic *raison d'être* was as an armament officer. I am sure that he was a better armament officer than a pilot. All his night landings were straight down from 15 feet – 'Hang on, chaps, we've arrived'. The normal bombing run was carried out on a straight and level basis with the bomb-aimer, the second pilot in a Whitley, directing the pilot left or right as the case may be. The height was constant and this figure was set into the bombsight together with other factors such as speed, type of bombs and order of release. There was another method of dropping bombs, which was the glide approach; this would only be considered by an armament officer. The relative merits of one system over the other are that a straight and level run at a constant height and speed and direction gives the ack-ack gunners a significant time in which to plot the position of the aircraft and the flak becomes increasingly accurate. With the glide approach method the theory is that the throttled-back engines allow the aircraft to silently glide down towards the target, the glide factor having been set on the bombsight and hopefully the enemy on the ground will not notice your presence. All very well in theory but if the glide approach is commenced too far from the target, the aircraft arrives over the target at a dangerously low height.

It was a beautifully clear night with something approaching a full moon and the target docks were plainly visible. I lined them up at the top of the graticule – the fine optical lines of the bombsight – and waited for the target to centre, when I could press the tit to operate 'Mickey Mouse' (the bomb release mechanism). We glided lower and lower and the flak became thicker and thicker. It is OK if you can see the bursts, OK if you can hear the explosions but when the cockpit fills with cordite fumes it is time for some concern! The impatience of our pilot was becoming increasingly obvious but in the end I did manage to make a good drop, although we did get a bit plastered in the process.

The bombsight is situated in the 'greenhouse' at the nose of the aircraft and is surrounded by perspex. I was naturally in rather a hurry to return to the body of the cabin but having forgotten that I had plugged my oxygen tube into the bomb-aimer's position, my hasty retreat was rather like an internal bungy jump. However, all's well that ends well and we managed to find our way back to Leeming for our 15-foot drop, having learned quite a lot from our baptism of fire.

Our next target was the Kiel Canal itself and the same crew duly took-off on another moonlit night. On the face of it, operations to Kiel, Hamburg, Bremen and Emden were not so hazardous or taxing as those to inland targets, as the majority of the flight was across open sea, leaving Yorkshire by Flamborough Head and flying due east. Apart from the flak ships off the islands of Texel, Terschelling and Borkum, if you got too close to the coast and the very strong defences of Heligoland, there was not much to worry about until it was time to approach the target. To get to north German targets we would leave the coast at Flamborough Head and there take a drift sight to check and adjust if necessary for a change in predicted wind direction. The lighthouse at Terschelling was usually operative and on a good night taking a bearing from it could confirm your position. Otherwise, it was astro-navigation all the way, always assuming that the stars could be seen.

On this occasion the sea crossing went without incident and from a considerable distance the renowned defences of Kiel and the Canal could be seen blasting away. The closer we got to the heart of the matter the more agitated became a certain ex-armament officer. I had the night's target in my bombsight but I regret to say that I did not have the opportunity of declaring 'Bombs gone!' – they were jettisoned early and short of the target from within the cockpit. There were some rude words expressed by the rest of the crew and at de-briefing. As diplomatically as possible without 'dropping him in it', we made our feelings apparent. It was not long afterwards that the flight lieutenant departed 10 Squadron, presumably back to his 'arms'. An unfortunate episode but these things did happen, as we found out. Our next captain was Pilot Officer Willi Freund, a Czech by nationality. I cannot recall the target attacked and presumably all went according to plan. I do remember his 'Zees ees Rarbit Zee for Zebra calling Bandlor'. That was the last trip I made as a second pilot/bomb-aimer and thereafter I had my own crew and aircraft. I was still only 20 years of age.

Hamburg was a well-defended city but I remember one very clear night when we had made a particularly good bombing run and had seen our bombs burst on target producing the usual rectangular box pattern of explosions. Many other aircraft were hitting the target and so impressive was the sight that I circled Hamburg to enjoy the view! It was not often that I hung around waiting to be shot at.

I recall on one occasion with a full moon, not a cloud in the sky and at about 12,000ft, I spotted a Ju 88 heading towards us and from abeam but at about 2,000ft below. I hastily changed places with the second pilot, who was 'driving' at the time but I am pleased to report that the Jerry obviously had elsewhere to go. We did have regular practice in evasive action in conjunction with Spitfires from Catterick, which amounted to the rear-gunner telling the pilot when to pull up the nose and do a semi-stall turn, hopefully to get the fighter to overshoot. Quite effective, although the 'arse-end Charlie' usually ended up being sick. On the way home on these runs it could be a pleasant experience if the cloud top was around 8-10,000ft, to engage 'George' (the automatic pilot) and spend time taking sextant shots of Polaris, which gave a pattern of latitude progress and was a good check for me on the navigator's prowess. 'George' was not very efficient and gently undulated the aircraft in and out of the cloud top – a very pleasant memory. There was always the constant monitoring ear for any imperfection in the drone of the Merlin Vs but I never did have the least spot of bother from a purely mechanical aspect.

Targets to the south involved the warships *Scharnhorst* and *Gneisenau*, which were very much part of Bomber Command's itinerary in 1941. I came into the picture while they were at Brest and I recall two trips there, mainly because the German defences produced the best fireworks display in Europe. In order to protect the warships, which were extremely well camouflaged, the Jerries used to 'hose pipe' the tracer flak in order to maintain a curtain of fire over the whole target area. All very lovely to look at but invariably all aircraft suffered some damage. The bombing run at Brest was always exciting, to say the least. Despite, or perhaps because of, our efforts to cripple these ships, the *Scharnhorst* slipped out of Brest in July 1941 and re-positioned herself at La Pallice, near La Rochelle and a long way south from Brest. Nevertheless, it was decreed that we should let her know that we were still after her.

The distance to be covered necessitated the fitting of auxiliary fuel tanks to the inside of the fuselage, so moving from one part of the aircraft to another required a crawl on your belly for part of the distance. The unusual weight distribution did not do a lot for the trim of the aircraft. Coupled with the extra fuel plus the bomb load, the take-off was a bit dicey but with brakes on at the extreme end of the runway, with full boost and almost full throttle, I could get the tail off the ground almost before we started to run. As the other end of the runway approached a little bouncing technique got us safely airborne and on our way.

The route was compiled specifically for this raid and took us down the eastern side of England to leave these shores eventually at Southampton, where the defensive balloons were grounded. Across the Channel to the French mainland, we had to go straight for La Pallice as opposed to an over sea route because of the distance but our bombing run was, I recall, to be from the seaward side of where the *Scharnhorst* was known to be 'parked'. Apart from the odd spot of flak, the journey there was not too difficult and having arrived, the target area (but not the ship) could easily be pin-pointed from the pattern of the shoreline, which is unique with its promontory at this point. Flak over the target was fairly intense but nowhere near as severe as at Brest.

And so to the return trip – again back across France and in at Southampton with balloons still on the ground. The next point of reference was the Abingdon beacon and from there up the country to Leeming and home. Unfortunately, after leaving the Abingdon beacon the cloud cover was 10/10ths up to about 3,000ft but flying on a dead-reckoning course we stooged on... Dawn was just breaking as I made a reasonable landing and taxied behind the vehicle sent to lead me to dispersal, where an airman with the usual two torches saw me safely parked and shut down. A ground crew appeared and secured the aircraft and as we emerged the question had to be asked: 'Where are we?' The answer was 'Squires Gate', which meant that we had been flying around Blackpool Tower in the dark. In the mess they were amazed that we had been airborne for more than ten hours, as the Beaufighters they were flying had a maximum duration of just 1¼ hours. A good breakfast and a few hours shut-eye saw us off again and back home to Leeming. A subsequent check of the aircraft suggested that the compasses were not producing the correct readings. Perhaps they were being kind.

The Channel ports (theirs, not ours) were fairly frequent destinations at this time and usually a nice easy operation to complete. On one occasion the target area was found without difficulty, even to the extent of seeing rows of invasion barges awaiting our attention. I was flying Q-*Queenie* (my regular partner and the nicest and fastest aircraft of the squadron; being the oldest, she was not encumbered by the bulbous addition of an astrodome). The bombs were dropped to good effect and my intention was a heading back home to our ritualistic eggs and bacon breakfast in double quick time. It was a pleasant night and *Queenie* enjoyed the straightforward flight home above the clouds. Bandlor (Leeming) responded to our call dead on ETA. I was given a QBB (cloud base) of 400ft and in accordance with usual practice, I confirmed that I would descend towards Linton and hedgehop home. The Leeming to Linton track avoided the Yorkshire Moors to the east and the Pennines to the west. Down and down we went and at 400ft we had not broken cloud – nearer to 200ft, visibility was just about passable by wartime standards, remembering that it was all happening just after dawn. The River Swale or the main railway line could usually guide us near enough to base to see the runway but that night the visibility was such that I found no landmarks.

In no time at all the cloud base came down and the ground went up, leaving me to take some quick evasive action to avoid an oak tree. I didn't quite succeed and the underside of the port wing scraped across the upper branches. A loud exclamation from my wireless operator came through the intercom and, in wireless operator's expressive language, apart from wanting to know what the hell was going on, he informed me that he had lost his trailing aerial, around somebody's chimney he thought. He did add that he had forgotten to reel it in! I considered that enough was enough and quickly climbed into the clouds; while gaining height I instructed my Canadian second pilot to call up base, telling them what the cloud base was and requesting a QFX (diversion airstrip). Unfortunately my second dickie had left the TR9 on transmit and when he eventually did get through to Leeming their immediate response was, 'Would you please moderate your language as there are WAAFs listening out at Dishforth.' At least they knew what I thought of their 400ft cloud base! Eventually we got our QFX to Silloth on the Solway Firth. Being the first aircraft to return, I had the same problems with the ground crew at the beacon and did a lob down ahead of every other aircraft on duty that night; there was a full house at Silloth that morning. The underside of *Queenie*'s port wing, which was canvas-covered, was in shreds, so we had a pleasant day or two at Maryport while they patched it up before returning to base. Another narrow squeak.

On another occasion we were bound for St Nazaire with the intention of demolishing the U-boat pens, which were well concealed and embedded in massive concrete structures. The weather was far from ideal with bags of cumulus cloud producing thundery conditions, particularly over France. In such conditions it was common for the propellers to look like giant Catherine wheels, with the blade-tips having a visible electrical charge producing this effect. This in itself caused no problem but, having emerged from one cloud bank and entered another almost immediately, there was a terrific sudden and violent noise with an accompanying flash sufficient to temporarily blind me. I think we must have gone from a positive cloud to a negative cloud, or vice versa and we were the spark between. In any event, we were at about 12,000ft and both engines decided that they had had enough and cut out. The Sperry panel (ASI, altimeter, artificial horizon, etc) also decided to go on strike and the radios had blown, not to mention the compasses, which had been de-magnetized. My first instinct was to maintain a 'flying attitude' and accordingly, once I had some sort of vision back; I put the nose down and hoped for the best. The propellers were still rotating even without power from the engines and apart from varying the throttle settings and altering the propeller pitch, there was little I could do. Much to my relief, at about 8,000ft the Merlins began to show some signs of life and eventually resumed reasonable health. It was later explained to me that in all probability the electrical charge had caused the magnetos to fail but the continued turn of the engines by the free-spinning propellers had had the effect of making them workable again.

So there we were over France, virtually without instruments but with a glimpse of Polaris we could deduce that England was 'over there'. Fortunately the night was clear and over the Channel the bomb load was jettisoned manually. Having crossed the coast it was possible to establish our position by means of the flashing beacons and reference to the rice-paper 'flimsy' and I virtually beacon-hopped all the way back to Leeming. Without a functional TR9 we could not announce our arrival and not having gone the whole distance we were not expected. However, the usual three 'glim' lamps indicated the runway and without instruments on a pretty dark night I made a good landing and taxied round to my dispersal point to wake up the ground crew! I actually got a pat on the back from the CO for this exploit!

The last area of operations relates to Germany itself and the targets were many and varied. The nature of the operations was more hazardous for two basic

reasons: the defences were more efficient and concentrated, being in defence of the
'Fatherland' itself and the time spent over enemy territory was much longer. One of
the most significant features of the defence system was a mighty bank of
searchlights some 20 miles or so across, stretching from about Emden in the north
to almost the French-German border in the south. Not only were these searchlights
used in collaboration with flak batteries but night fighters also prowled in
abundance waiting for an intruder to be 'coned'. (In 1941 with a full bomb load it
took a long time to struggle up to 12,000 feet, which was about the Whitley's
ceiling and at that height the indicated airspeed was in the region of 120mph, so
the searchlight barrier was something to be taken seriously.) At 12,000 feet a single
searchlight could not pick out an aircraft but a concentration of light working in a
cone shape certainly lit up the cockpit. By extraordinary manoeuvres and a bit of
good fortune the 'cone' could usually be lost. But the safest method was to hang
around outside the searchlight band until two aircraft were separately 'coned',
then, nose down, nip smartly between them and through the danger area while the
Jerries were otherwise engaged.

As well as the searchlight problem there were many and changing areas of
concentrated flak batteries, which necessitated taking avoiding action at all times
when over enemy territory. If a constant course, speed and height were maintained
for only a short period of time these factors could be plotted and, even without the
help of computers, a shell could arrive in the same piece of airspace as occupied by
the aircraft. Thus the continuous procedure was 2 degrees left, 2 degrees right, 50
feet up and 25 feet down, adjust your speed and hope you've kept close to the
average course required for navigation purposes. Believe me, when you've been
doing this for two or three hours' non-stop, you end up with a sticky shirt.

I can recall targeting Frankfurt on one night, which meant five hours over enemy
territory with five hours' evasive action. This was not a particularly memorable
operation but reasonably successful and home to bacon and eggs for breakfast and
head down until lunchtime. The rub was that there was an early afternoon briefing
to do exactly the same thing again that night. I was not very enthusiastic but having
revisited Frankfurt and returned safely, my memory of these two raids on
consecutive nights is the shattering physical experience.

Towards the end of 1940 for the defence of Germany the *Nachtjagd* had been
formed as an elite night fighter force within the Luftwaffe. Prior to that time there
were very few night fighters, most being Me 109s and they did not have any
effective ground coordinated control. As time progressed Me 110s and the new Ju
88 fighters came into prominence. The greater development, however, related to the
German radar and its ability to pin-point an intruder and guide a night fighter to
it and this facility was used to great effect along the Kammhuber searchlight barrier
now stretching from Schleswig-Holstein in the north to Liege in Belgium in the
south. Against such odds it will be appreciated that the chance of finishing a tour
of 30 operations was somewhat remote. In the early part of June 1941 I had ten
days' leave and upon my return to Leeming there were very few faces that were
familiar. There was less than a handful of pilots who had any length of operational
experience. My beloved *Q-Queenie* had failed to return and with her my navigator
Bill Rice, with whom I was very friendly and with whom I had completed a fair
number of trips. He was an excellent navigator (he had his 2nd Mate's ticket in the

Merchant Navy before the war) and a number of his 'logs' of trips we had completed together had been used as training examples at 4 Group HQ.

Certainly in my time all targets in Germany were of military importance or were industrial centres and of course the Ruhr was high on the list of target priorities and a constant source of attention by Bomber Command. Cologne, Düsseldorf, Essen and Dortmund were visited frequently, with peripheral targets such as Hamm marshalling yards and Mannheim included for good measure. For much of the early part of August 1941 I was not called upon to take part in every operation flown by the squadron. Bearing in mind the imminent conversion to the Halifax as the squadron aircraft, my egocentric thoughts produced the idea that as one of the few remaining pilots with operational experience I was being saved for this event. I had taken part in 25 raids and had more than 250 hours of operational flying under my belt; a complete tour consisted of 30 trips.

A relatively easy trip to Cologne came my way on 16/17 August.[1] My crew consisted of Sergeant Harold P. Calvert, navigator, Sergeant King, Wop-AG and Sergeant Bruce Robertson, rear-gunner. We took-off in *G-George* at 2203 hours, having been fully briefed in the afternoon. The meteorological part of the briefing promised us cloud cover from the Dutch coast to the target. Accordingly, as was the practice, I sat down with Calvert to plot our route and discuss possible problems. In view of the promised cloud cover we agreed upon a track directly to the target, as opposed to going in by the back door. It was a relatively calm night and after a bit of a stooge across the North Sea we obtained a good fix and some flak around the Hook of Holland. It was fairly obvious by this time that the promised cloud cover was a figment of the Met man's imagination, as it was as clear as a bell. But our die was cast, our course plotted, so we continued as planned. The searchlights were obviously working overtime and it was not going to be easy to sneak through by playing the waiting game. However, this was our best bet and sure enough, the dancing beams of light merged into strong cones both to port and starboard, balancing an aircraft, in full glare, on the tip of the cone like a jet of water holding a ping-pong ball target on a fairground rifle range. Our chance had arrived and with all the power that *G-George* could muster, I went for the gap. Alas, not much progress had been made through the searchlight belt when the cockpit was filled with dazzling light. Normally, with a few hectic manoeuvres there was a fair chance of losing the lights but on this occasion the centre light had a bluish colour and had fastened on to *G-George* and no amount of twisting and turning could shift it and its accompanying beams. It was obviously a DHF development that was new to me. Being so occupied with trying to get out of the illumination, it was something of a surprise to hear and to see cannon tracer shells flying around the aircraft and, in particular, flashing up through the unoccupied front gun turret.

I had no doubt in my mind what to do next. I put the nose straight down and kept it that way. I can well remember the ASI registering 320mph. In the meantime Robbie in the rear turret was more than a little disturbed and was yelling all sorts of things into the intercom. He thought we had all 'had it' and certainly I was not able at that time to put his mind at rest. We had been at our usual 12,000 feet and at about 7,000 feet I tried to get back on an even keel, which was easier said than done. At that speed the port wing had dropped. The only way I could get sufficient

purchase on the 'stick', which in fact was a large wheel, was to put my feet against
the dashboard and heave like blazes with the wheel turned as far to the right as I
could get it. With some relief I got *George* out of the dive and regained straight and
level flight once again. I took stock of our situation, having firstly calmed Robbie
with the news that I was still alive and flying. The engines were sounding good and
while we were somewhat battered, there seemed no reason not to go to the target.

However, before I had managed to check all aspects and make a final decision,
a further attack from the starboard saw cannon shells whistling through the
starboard engine, through the cockpit and within inches of my feet and out the
other side. The starboard engine caught fire and although I managed to extinguish
it from within, the port engine sounded a bit sick, to say the least. Thus I was left
flying on less than one engine and in such circumstances it is necessary to trim the
aircraft as far as possible. This was achieved by adjusting the rudder tabs by means
of a wheel at the side of the pilot's seat. However, when I endeavoured to do this
all I found was a coil of wire that, having been shot through in the fuselage, had
sprung to the other end of its tension – next to me.

It was amazing to me that the pilot of the night fighter did not finish us off but
presumably he lost us in the darkness. I have often wondered whether the original
attacker had followed us down and then made another pass, or whether by
chance another night fighter had picked us up. It was obvious from the damage
reported by the crew that the first attack had been from below. Mercifully the
rear turret was missed but gaping holes had been blasted in the underside of the
fuselage even to the extent of losing the Elsan (I wonder who was the lucky
recipient beneath). Having observed the cannon shells coming up through the
front turret, I am led to the conclusion that the bombs, being positioned beneath
the cockpit, had acted as armour plating and had saved the three of us in the
cabin – a sobering thought.[2]

Having survived, if that is what you can call it, and being unable to maintain
height, the next problem was where to go. It would be impossible to back-track
through the searchlight belt with any hope of success, so I had little option but to
head in a northerly direction with a view to reaching Holland and possibly a
friendly face or two. As we were gradually losing height, even with full boost
applied to the damaged and only engine, the crew were busy jettisoning everything
removable they could lay their hands on. The bombs were the first to go, followed
by hatch covers, bombsight, ammunition and indeed anything that was detachable.
I was flying marginally above stalling speed and the ASI hovered around the 60-
mph mark. It was something of a difficult juggling act to feel the balance of the
aircraft and keep it flying, with one leg stretched to the limit to counteract with
rudder the one-engine factor.

I decided that both King and Robertson should depart as soon as possible as they
would stand a better chance of evading capture if they descended silently from
above and away from a crashed aircraft. King went out of the front hatch without
any problem. The rear hatch was in fact on top of the Whitley's square fuselage.
Bruce Robertson later told me that, having clipped his parachute on to his harness,
he emerged from the hatch on to the fuselage, stood up and had to literally run off
the rear and over his turret. There was insufficient strength in the slipstream to
whisk him away as we were flying at such a slow speed.

Cal and myself stooged on hoping to reach a friendly reception. After Cal had rescued my chute from beside the open hatch, he went back to writing his log. We were getting lower and lower and eventually I persuaded him that it was more important to get his backside through the hole in the floor than to complete his log. He too disappeared, leaving me to find my own way out. By this time I had clipped my parachute on to my harness and had engaged 'George' for good measure. It was then my intention to make a quick dash for it, which entailed getting out of my seat, descending a few stairs to the well, turning round and facing backwards with legs through the hole. However, I encountered a hiccup in the first part of the intended procedure. When I left and moved towards the open hatch, I found that my intercom cable, which was still plugged in, had somehow got around my chute, which meant that I had to retrace my steps to disentangle the cord. By this time I could see that the aircraft was dropping a wing quite severely and I had to disengage 'George', straighten things up, then make a sharp exit. I can clearly remember falling away from the aircraft and being on my back, seeing it fly over my head and quickly going to ground.

You will have gathered that my parachute opened and for a few moments I experienced complete peace. The contrast from total mayhem to almost complete silence – from non-stop action to passivity – is an experience that I am sure could never happen again. But as I have implied, this heavenly suspension lasted but a very short while, as in no time at all treetops were whistling past my feet. It had been less than 1,000 feet above ground when I had left *G-George* to go it alone. We had never had any instruction about parachute jumping. I found the best solution naturally; let the breeze take you and make sure you land facing backwards – no problem at all! *G-George* did not have such a soft landing and was well ablaze some 200 yards away. I must admit that when I landed my heart rate was off the clock but I did have time for a quiet 'thank you'.

My immediate problem was the disposal of my chute and harness and the two £1 notes I had with me, which I should not have carried. I had gathered my equipment together and had buried the cash when I heard the clanking of chains. My first thought was that I had landed in some sort of concentration camp but the inmates turned out to be tethered cattle, presumably belonging to the farmer who emerged from his house to investigate the burning aircraft. He was followed in line astern by his wife and two children.[3] As I was in direct line between the house and his intended investigation he quickly spotted me and turned tail back to the safety of the homestead. Still in line astern the children were calling 'Papa, Papa', which sounded to me reasonably civilized and having been seen in any event, I joined the line and called 'Papa', hoping that this might be the Dutch for 'How's your father?' I never found out as the door was slammed and bolted.

Simultaneously around the corner of the farmhouse came a German policeman with gun at the ready, who made it clear that I was his prisoner. I did not like to gamble that he could not properly fire his revolver and push his moped at the same time. I did, however, win one small argument with him when he endeavoured to make me pick up my chute and harness and carry it. This I refused to do. After all, I was aircrew! And he had to do it himself, draping the lot over his saddle and carrier. On this basis we proceeded through the village. It was surprising to me how many people were out and about at that time of the night. I did ascertain that the name of the village was Oeding, situated exactly on the border of Germany and Holland. For all the good it did me, I did take consolation in the fact that I had almost achieved my last target on this August night, that of reaching Holland.

I was eventually delivered to the German Army. Guards came and went during the next day but it was very much later that the Luftwaffe appeared in a large Mercedes and spirited me off to Münster, the Luftwaffe HQ. Sergeant Calvert, who had been picked up not far away, accompanied me. As the cell door slammed I was told, 'For you zee war if oofer'. But for me the war was just beginning – what followed was three years and ten months of captivity.

Later, after a mass escape from *Stalag IIIE* Kirchhain, during which Cal and I both got away, a member of the *Polizei* apprehended Cal and another escaper. He shot Cal when he attempted to replace his footwear. Apparently he could not cope with the two of them. Cal was somewhat older than the rest of us and was 34 when he died.

Notes
1. When 72 aircraft – 37 Wellingtons, 29 Whitleys and six Halifaxes attacked rail targets.
2. Oberleutnant Wolfgang Thimmig of 2./NJG1 was credited with shooting Craske's Whitley down at 0230 hours near Winterswijk 20 km NE of Bocholt. Thimmig's kill was one of the earliest *Dunkelnachtjagd* ('dark night fighting') victories, being achieved in complete darkness and under the guidance of ground radar. In all seven Whitleys and a Wellington failed to return from the raid on Cologne, the majority of these losses being due to night fighters of I./NJG1. Major Thimmig survived the war with 22 night and one day victory.
3. Fifty-three years later Craske visited the farm and met the children, Derk-Jan and Johann-Willem Hesselink.

# Chapter 5

# Deep Sea Hunters – Bruce Sanders

Between 3 September 1939 and 30 September 1942 Coastal Command submarine-hunters made the amazing number of 587 attacks on U-boats. How many of these enemy under-sea craft were sunk or so seriously damaged that they were unable to reach home may never be told, for the sub-chasers of Coastal Command frequently have no means of checking the results of their attacks. An attacked U-boat commander will crash-dive as the depth charges or bombs rain down and he may never rise again. Sometimes wreckage or a patch of spreading oil gives the tell-tale clue to the watchers in a hovering Coastal Command aircraft, but often the sea jealously denies the attackers any sign that they have been uneventful. The deep sea hunters of Coastal Command strike and hope for the best. For the crew of one Lockheed Hudson patrolling the wide Atlantic there was an adventure, which ended in the most amazing U-boat versus plane result of the war. They struck and hope blossomed into an amazing certainty. They actually captured the U-boat they attacked.

The story of this, the first time in history a land-based aircraft ever brought a U-boat's crew to surrender, was released by the Air Ministry in September 1941. [On 27 August 1941] the Hudson was one attached to 269 Squadron [at Kaldadarnes, Iceland]. It was piloted by [31 year old] Squadron Leader James H. Thompson, a Yorkshireman. With him as crew were Flying Officer W. John O. Coleman, second pilot and navigator, a young agricultural student from Oxford who was rear-gunner and a wireless operator from London.[1] The Hudson set out over the Atlantic in the early hours and ran into bad weather, with poor visibility and squally showers. Thompson put the aircraft in the custody of the automatic pilot, for the patrol threatened to become a dreary routine with no highspots to write down in the log. Suddenly a shout came from Coleman: 'There's one just in front of you!' The words electrified Thompson. He glanced to where the navigator pointed. Twelve hundred yards away on the Hudson's port bow was a U-boat.[2] Thompson did not have to consider what he would do; he dived. Over the submarine the Hudson levelled off under coaxing from Thompson's skilled hands. Coleman pressed the bomb release [unleashing a stick of four 250lb depth charges set to detonate at 50 feet] and as the Coastal Command plane flew over the U-boat the crew saw mountains of water spring up around it.[3] Thompson climbed steeply and swung round full circle, preparing for another attack. At that moment a cry came from the rear-gunner. The

U-boat had surfaced suddenly. Coleman got out his camera. This was something to record: 'Machine-gun them!' he called back. The wireless operator unwound the Hudson's belly-gun and, when Thompson turned down the aircraft's nose, tracer bullets projected in slashing streaks to the shiny steel decks of the under-sea marauder. Front guns, rear guns, belly-gun – the Hudson's crew gave the German submarine all the firepower they could muster. As Thompson prepared to pull the craft once more out of a low dive, the surprised RAF men saw the U-boat's conning-tower hatch thrown open. An assortment of German sailors, possibly a dozen of them, tumbled on to the deck. It looked as though they were going to man their gun and fight back, so the Hudson's own guns swivelled in an arc as Thompson flattened out and kept up a sharp fusillade. But the Germans did not man their gun. They started scrambling back to the conning-tower where they collided with others of the crew who were trying to get on deck. The result was something thing like panic. While the struggling mass of men in yellow life-saving jackets swayed and fought on the submarine's deck the Hudson circled four times, with guns fully trained.

Thompson afterwards remembered hearing Coleman muttering to himself: 'I lived all my life to see those baskets scrambling out of a conning tower!'

As the Hudson banked and came round for the fifth time, crew saw a sailor waving a white shirt. Amazed, they realized that the U-boat had surrendered to them – a land-based aircraft. They had a submarine on their hands and no way of getting it to port. Thompson decided to stay with it. For three and a half hours he flew round and round the wallowing shape of the U-boat, while the wireless operator sent out a long string of calls for aid. In the early afternoon aid came in the shape of another Coastal Command aircraft, this time, a Catalina flying boat [of 209 Squadron, flown by Flying Officer Edward Jewiss, who had sank *U-452* two days earlier]. The Hudson's crew, as soon as the Catalina was identified for what it was, signalled: 'Look after our – repeat OUR – submarine, which has flown the white flag.' 'OK' came back from the captain of the Catalina.[4]

The Hudson, fuel running low, dived once more over its prize and then sped for home.[5] Coastal Command had brought a U-boat to surrender but had not yet got it to port.[6] That was the next stage in the capture. A call was broadcast to all Coastal Command aircraft in the vicinity of the submarine and for the remainder of the day relays of aircraft turned up to take turns in guarding the prize. The Catalina remained at guarding station for eight hours. Just before darkness closed down, after the weather had become very much worse, a warship arrived and a fresh signal was flashed to the U-boat's commander. The Catalina was relieved from duty. It too went home. However, before dawn had fully broken another Catalina was out over the U-boat, despite the gale that was blowing. Time and again the U-boat was blown off course, but always the Catalina found it, although for one long 15 minutes its crew were unable to locate the submarine's light. But with daylight came more warships and a procession to port began. From the moment the first warship appeared on the scene Coastal Command covered the U-boat for the next 40 hours. It was hazardous and dangerous work, in weather that sailors described as filthy. But the relays of Catalinas remained on the job and the submarine at last reached harbour.[7] For their part in the amazing capture, Thompson and Coleman were awarded the DFC.[8]

In those days the Battle of the Atlantic was still comparatively young. It had not attained the intensity of thrust that was to climax in Doenitz's displacement of Raeder hunters but the deep sea record of individuals stood out as milestones along the path that was to lead to the great convoy battles of 1943. In October 1941 for example, the Air Ministry released the details of a representative month's work by the crew of a Bristol Beaufort flying with Coastal Command. During that month the pilot and navigator both celebrated their birthday. The former his twenty-first, the latter his twentieth. They had been at school at Wellington College together. The other two members of the crew were sergeants, one a Lancashire man, the other from Canterbury in Kent. This crew made 16 long flights over the Atlantic during the month, logging 80 hours actual flying time. They searched for submarines and they searched for ships. They also laid mines in enemy waters. Fighting enemy aircraft became incidental to their operational excursions. But they found only one submarine. They found it after dropping through some cloud. There lay the U-boat on the surface of the sea right beneath them. It crash-dived the instant the Beaufort was sighted. As its conning-tower disappeared beneath the waves the Beaufort's stick of delayed-action bombs crashed across the white ridge of water where the U-boat had floated. Whether that lonely stretch of sea became the U-boat's grave was never known. At the end of the month the Beaufort's young crew of submarine hunters went on a flight from which they did not return. Other crews took up where they left off. The continuous search for U-boats never slackened. When U-boats were not to be found and enemy shipping was, the ships were attacked. When, in place of U-boats, enemy aircraft were sighted, they promptly engaged. But the most relentless search by Coastal Command was for U-boats.

The determination to send as many to the ocean's bed as the Command could only grew more adamant with the passing months. The U-boat commanders began a fresh drive to Allied shipping in the Atlantic. Then Coastal Command diverted more and more of its long-range bombers and flying boats to cover the convoy skies and to provide an air umbrella for the merchantmen beating eastwards, hulls deep-laden with the products of democracy's Lease-Lend scheme.

A Liberator[9] – D for Donald – its broad nose decorated with a sprightly Donald Duck smashing a U-boat with a mallet certainly lived up to its emblem's promise. It set out one day early in 1942 to patrol the Bay of Biscay and, after a brush with a Heinkel 115 floatplane, which escaped destruction by darting into a heavy rain-cloud, came upon a large German ship, with a U-boat surfaced beside it. The first thing the enemy knew about the new arrival was the pattern of bombs falling around them. Then the pilot got the conning-tower in his gun-sights. He raked the hull and conning tower with cannon shells as the bombs exploded. When the white fountains of spray had subsided the U-boat was not to be seen, but over the sea near the ship, a wide patch of tell-tale oil spread. When the Liberator climbed the oil-stain was 200 feet wide and growing.

Again the Liberator's captain put down the nose of his aircraft and four more bombs hurtled over the ship, followed by a savage fusillade of cannon fire, which raked the decks. As the Coastal Command craft banked to come in attacking for the third time, another Heinkel was reported. The British pilot swung round and shots were exchanged with the German aircraft, which retreated. The Liberator recommenced its interrupted strafing of the ship. Back came the Heinkel, seeking to take the British aircraft unawares, but the Coastal Command crew were awake to danger from above and around. For the second time the Heinkel was beaten off, only to come back for a third and fourth attempt. On this last occasion its temerity cost it dear. It received a mortal jet of cannon shells as the desperate German pilot hurled his plane straight at the Liberator from a bare thousand yards. It looked as though his intention was to ram the British machine with his floats. But he covered only 700 of those thousand yards before he went down, one engine blazing. The Liberator pilot reported afterwards: 'We turned our attention to the ship again and made a last leisurely attack. We had no more bombs, so we raked it with everything we had. It was an uncanny business, for we never saw a soul on board from beginning to end. It was like attacking a ghost ship – but there must have been somebody there, for she steamed all over the place, trying to dodge our attack. Finally she made a half-moon of foam, with the U-boat oil patch in the middle.'

Unable to damage the ship any more, the Liberator turned back to England and arrived at base after completing a patrol that had lasted 15 hours. The crew got into their bunks precisely 24 hours after they had got up the day before.

Deep sea hunting is a time-consuming business. In June that year a Spanish radio report asserted that an Italian submarine [the *Luigi Torelli* commanded by Augusto Migliorini] had been beached near Santander. The foreign radio reports that continued to mention the beaching added that two Sunderland flying boats of Coastal Command, which had attacked the U-boat, had been forced down. The foreign radio reports erred. The Sunderlands were back at base. This is what happened. The Italian U-boat was damaged by an unspecified attacker[10] and was afterwards reported as sighted proceeding in a crippled condition towards the European coast. The news resulted in a hurried consultation between Admiralty officials and officers of Coastal Command. On a Sunday morning out sped Sunderlands [of 10 Squadron RAAF] to find the damaged undersea craft. Flying Officer Thomas A. Edgerton from Melbourne, the captain of a Royal Australian Air Force Sunderland, found the U-boat and after circling it realized that the Italian commander was unable to submerge. But the Italian crew were at their gun station on deck, ready to fight it out with the flying boat. They got their wish. The fight was on as the Sunderland approached from out of the sun. And the Italian gunners were on the mark. They sprayed the flying boat's hull with shell splinters. The Sunderland's gunners replied hotly, sweeping the U-boat's deck and, as the Coastal Command craft roared over the submarine, a stick of depth charges was dropped. There was a tremendous explosion at the submarine's stern and the sea rose in a towering wall of green water. When the curtain of water had dropped the Sunderland's crew saw the U-boat zigzagging wildly away, but at a much reduced speed.

Then a second Sunderland flying boat arrived to give aid. It was piloted by another Australian, Flight Lieutenant Edwin St. Clare Yeoman from Victoria. The Italian gun crew still showed signs of fight. They knew their engineers were working like demons to get the submersion gear functioning and any moment might mean the chance to escape, even in their damaged condition. So they sighted their gun and fired and that morning their shooting was good. They riddled the second Sunderland's tail. But they could not stop Yeoman's swooping dive. The flying boat roared over them and another exploding stick of depth charges fell right alongside them. The explosions lifted the Italian undersea craft's keel right out of the water. It fell back into a great swirling whirlpool of foam. It remained bobbing up and down the water, unable to proceed or submerge. The first Sunderland with fuel running short had already started for base. The second Sunderland circled the submarine and then had to wheel to fight off an Arado floatplane, which appeared, probably in answer to a frantic SOS from the submarine. The Sunderland's rear and mid-ship's gunners poured a steady fire into the Arado as it came near and suddenly it dropped and scurried away across the sea. By now the second Sunderland's fuel was getting low. It followed the first back to base. Together they had put that Italian U-boat out of the war for keeps.[11]

The Bay of Biscay became a happy hunting ground for the deep sea hunters of Coastal Command. As the weeks went by more and more of their attention was given to that seaway, 500 miles wide, which is the U-boat's route to the wider hunting fields of the Atlantic Ocean. One RAAF Sunderland, skippered by Flight Lieutenant F. C. Wood of Sydney who, in 1936, rowed number four for Oxford, caught a U-boat in the act of submerging. The flying boat's bombs blew the submarine to the surface and there it lay, damaged internally. Desperately the gun crew ran to their stations while the mechanics below tried to get their craft to submerge. The Sunderland skimmed low over the marauder, its bombs gone and began a grim duel with the gun crew. The Germans were lucky. An early burst from their gun caught the Sunderland in the fuselage, but luckily rendered no vital harm. For two hours Wood flew round and round the U-boat, which gradually got up more speed and then finally began to submerge as the commander took a desperate chance with his damaged hydraulics. The chance, as it proved, was too desperate. A wide streak of oil came to the surface, spread and then mysteriously stopped. Then, 100 yards from where the oil trail ended, a great gush of bubbling oil appeared and spread in a large stain over the water.

The Sunderland turned for home, to meet en route a four-engined Focke-Wulf Kurier and although the encounter was not decisive, it was the German aircraft that broke off the engagement, speeding for the French coast and rapidly gaining height. Wood's report on the brush gives a glimpse of life aboard the Coastal Command long-range flying boats. He says: 'We had been so busy with the submarine that we had forgotten to eat and one of the crew was just preparing a meal when the Kurier appeared. We took evasive action making a diving turn to port, which brought a strong protest from the cook. His flour basin was upset and fish heads – it was fish and chips for tea – were thrown about and slithering all over the galley floor. We were busy with the Focke-Wulf for about an hour and the cook apologized for the meal being a little cold when we finally got down to it. We carried out an improvised repair to the rear turret by putting surgical sticking plaster over a hole in an oil pipe. The only casualty in the crew was a slight scratch on one man's leg but the Sunderland had half a dozen holes big enough to put your head in, as well as something like a hundred little ones. As some of the damage was below the waterline we had to rush her up to the slipway when we landed in case she sank. The ground crew were on her like a lot of ants and had her safe on her beaching chassis almost before we stopped moving.'

The Coastal Command deep sea hunters had to set out prepared to take punishment. Some of them certainly received plenty, for they always engaged the enemy when there was a chance of scoring a victory. One Catalina tried to rescue survivors, only to be beaten by the high sea running at the time. The captain of this craft was Flight Lieutenant D.E. Hawkins DFC of Loughton, Essex. He had with him as second pilot, Pilot Officer J.C. Parry, from Rhyl and the navigator was Sergeant J.C. Greenhaugh, a Liverpool man.

'We first saw the U-boat when it was some distance away. It was going along pretty fast on the surface. Instead of submerging as we came up, it turned so as to bring both its heavy and light guns to bear, presenting me with a broadside target. It was obviously going to fight it out on the surface, hoping no doubt to wing us before we got it. The U-boat opened fire as we closed and I could see the flashes and smoke of its guns. My navigator at our front gun returned the fire as I took avoiding action. We attacked low across the beam of the U-boat. The bombs burst right across the stern and covered it in a cloud of spray. Then it dived and we thought it had got away but after about four minutes it surfaced sluggishly. The submarine's crew dashed from the conning tower on to the deck and manned the guns but we got in a burst that silenced their heavy gun. More of the crew came running up and a lot of them jumped overboard. Then we saw the U-boat was settling slowly by the stern and within a few minutes it disappeared stern first, leaving about 30 survivors in the water. I decided to try to land and pick up some prisoners. We dropped a smoke-float to mark the spot and made an approach to land up wind. But there was a heavy swell running and as we touched the water we were thrown into the air again and stalled. We hit the water a second time with a tremendous thump. The hull was split open underneath, the wireless set collapsed in a heap and the crew were thrown about and cut and bruised. Only the second pilot and I escaped injury because we were the only ones who could see the crash was coming and we instinctively braced ourselves for the shock. I pushed the throttles full open and we managed to remain in the air. It was obviously impossible to get down, so we had to leave the U-boat's crew in the sea and set course for base.'

Despite their damaged condition the Catalina made base safely, but only because the injured crew had worked hard to make her watertight against the moment of landing. That September the Air Ministry announced that Coastal Command had stepped up its U-boat attacks to the rate of an attack a day. Craft like *F for Freddie*, a Liberator, became relentless in the searching for and striking at U-boats. *F for Freddie* sank three U-boats within one calendar month. Another Liberator attacked two submarines within two hours. *H for Harry*, a Wellington, spotted a U-boat surfaced eight miles distant and began stalking it. Closer and closer crept the Wellington out of the sun, handled very clearly by a pilot who was determined to get the submarine if it was at all possible. He proved that it was. He had covered the entire eight miles and was roaring down over the U-boat before its crew awoke to their danger. Three men were still struggling at the conning tower hatch when the redskin of the skies charged overhead with machine guns chattering. They tumbled this way and that like broken dolls and the bombs broke across the under-pirate's slim back.

So intense became the anti U-boat campaign waged by the captains and crews of Coastal Command that the Air Ministry was able to announce: 'The enemy's increasing protection for his U-boats the Bay of Biscay testifies to the challenge of

Royal Air Force attacks in this area, where it is estimated that one in three U-boats crossing the Bay of Biscay is attacked.' The U-boat commanders had plenty to worry about as they set forth on their predatory missions. They were finding themselves with a war of their own on their hands, pitting their wits against an enemy who was monthly growing more determined in his onslaughts and stronger in numbers of aircraft.

One Wellington skipper, a Canadian, Sergeant A.S. Hakala from Sioux Lookout, Alberta, got a submarine on the first patrol he made with his crew. It was not beginner's luck in this case, for the U-boat's lookout spotted the plane and the aircraft did not arrive before the submarine crashed but the bombs went down to burst just ahead of the feather of foam betraying the sunken periscope. Hakala recalled:

'It was some explosion. The U-boat surfaced groggily until the conning tower and part of the hull were awash. The Wellington readily took this second opportunity, guns blazing away. To my surprise and joy flames and smoke poured from the conning tower. The bombs must have started it, but I hope the bullets helped.'

The U-boat was still on fire when a thick mist came down and the Coastal Command aircraft had to make for home. A Czech sergeant pilot, flying as a Coastal Command captain, equalled this feat and seriously damaged another U-boat on his first patrol.

What is said to be one of the most spectacular U-boat kills in the Bay of Biscay came as the result of the combined tactics of two Coastal Command aircraft. [On 17 July 1942] Flight Sergeant A. R. Hunt DFC of Oxford [flying Whitley *H-Harry* of 502 Squadron] attacked the submarine [*U-751* commanded by Gerhard Bigalk] and left it surfaced and helpless.[12] Flight Lieutenant Peter R. Casement DSO DFC, an Irishman from County Antrim [piloting Lancaster R5724/F of 61 Squadron, seconded from Bomber Command] came upon it drifting helplessly on the fringe of an oil patch larger than a football field. He too attacked, just before two o'clock in the afternoon. At two o'clock, according to his log, he bombed the submarine again. The U-boat was now so low in the water that at times it disappeared in the wash of the bombs. At a minute past two the submarine's crew jumped to the deck gun and fired at the aircraft. A minute later the aircraft replied. Two minutes afterwards the aircraft bombed again. After another six minutes the U-boat began to sink for the last time and the crew threw themselves overboard. Three minutes afterwards the sea was undisturbed save for the bobbing heads of the German crew.[13] A killed U-boat, in most cases, dies quickly. This one died in less than a quarter of an hour, fighting strenuously every minute. Doenitz had given his orders; there must be no cheap victories for the British deep sea hunters; U-boat captains, if they could not escape by crash-diving, must stand and fight it out. Coastal Command asked nothing better.[14]

In October 1942 a large convoy, Europe-bound, was successfully guarded from the attentions of a U-pack, which trailed the ships for four days. The Royal Navy, Coastal Command and the US Naval Air Arm cooperated in making things difficult for the submarine commanders. When the pack was reported, US Catalinas swept down from Iceland to provide an air umbrella for the convoy. The pack held off. The next day the danger area was reached. Coastal Command

Flying Fortresses, Liberators and Hudsons and a Catalina from a Norwegian squadron of Coastal Command joined the Americans. Two U-boats partly surfaced. American Catalinas pounced upon them like cats on unwary mice. The U-boats had to dive without being able to attack. Oil patches marked the scene of their diving. The same afternoon a submarine dived before a Liberator could reach it and afterwards the same aircraft forced another U-boat down before it could fire its torpedoes. In less than an hour this same Liberator attacked a third submarine with bombs and machine guns. Some miles away a Hudson stormed at a submarine with all guns firing. It then bombed the pirate and in a few seconds masses of oil and exploding air bubbles festooned the sea surface. Ten minutes later wreckage floated up. A Fortress spotted two U-boats, attacked one and caused the other to slink away into the ocean depths. When evening came the American Catalinas had another chance to hit at the underwater buccaneers. They attacked two. The next day the crisis was over. Only two U-boats were sighted. A Hudson got to one and attacked; the other chose discretion rather than valour. Another watchful 24 hours passed and then the giant convoy was in British waters, the danger past.

It was the same story when the North African landings were made. The Air Ministry stated:

'Night and day without respite, from the day the first convoy left port, an unending stream of flying boats and long-range land-based aircraft patrolled the Bay of Biscay neutralizing the Axis U-boat threat before it could develop. Probably not one of the aircraft was seen by the men on the troopships. The airmen were tackling the threat at its source – harrying and attacking the U-boats as they left the French Atlantic ports. And far to the west the ships sailed safely on. This great aircraft umbrella was laid by RAF Coastal Command, assisted by aircraft from Bomber Command and from the United States Army Air Corps. Sunderlands, Liberators, Halifaxes, Wellingtons, Whitleys and Hudsons all flew the Bay patrols and Coastal Command Beaufighters intervened against German long-range fighters which attempted to intercept the U-boat hunting aircraft. So complete was the secrecy surrounding the operation that not even commanders of the squadrons, providing the protection against the U-boats, knew what was afoot. All they knew was the greatest submarine hunt of the war was on.

'The men in Air Chief Marshal Sir Philip Joubert's command put on one of the finest shows of the war in the manner in which they successfully provided air cover for the invasion armada. Later they took toll among the U-boats stalking the seas off Gibraltar. The U-boat menace to the Allied invasion forces was completely nullified.'

In December one of Coastal Command's ace U-boat hunters came into the news. Squadron Leader T.M. Bulloch, a stockily-built Belfast man, joined the RAF in 1936. After establishing a brilliant record with Hudsons he transferred to Ferry Command and when the much-needed aircraft were coming across the Atlantic steadily he went back to Coastal Command to fly Liberators in the anti U-boat war.[15] 'The Bull,' as he was affectionately known to his crew, brought the first Flying Fortress to Britain and in doing so set up a Trans-Atlantic record for the crossing from Newfoundland to England. His searches and sweeps in operations against the U-boat commanders of the Third Reich had been made from bases in

Britain, Ireland, Gibraltar and Iceland. He came into the news when he made the following report:

'I saw the submarine just as we came out of cloud and made for it right away. We got it while it was still on the surface and our depth charges fell all round it. Naturally I couldn't see much after the attack, but the rear-gunner gave me a graphic description over the intercom and took some wonderful pictures. Bits and pieces from the U-boat flew all over the place and a cylindrical-shaped object was thrown into the water. We circled for a while but the submarine had disappeared by the time I had turned and I saw only a large swirl on the water and bubbles rising steadily to the surface. The cylindrical object floated for a while and then sank. Later we saw quite a large patch of oil on the surface.'

One of the ace pilots in [500] County of Kent Auxiliary Squadron, famed for its U-boat hunts, was Flying Officer M. A. 'Mike' Ensor DFC* a New Zealander. On [15 November 1942] off North Africa, he went so low in an attack on a German U-boat that his own aircraft was wrecked. His adventure has few equals even in the amazing annals of Coastal Command.

'When I dropped my depth charges I must have scored a direct hit on the sub, for it blew up just below the surface. The first I knew of the explosion was when the Hudson was shot up about 300 feet into the air like a rocket. Then, when I steadied it a bit, I found that the rudders and elevators had been blown off, the ailerons damaged and about six feet of each wing-tip bent upwards at almost right-angles to the rest of the wing. All the loose equipment had been thrown about and broken and what astonished me most after seeing the damage was that the Hudson could still fly. All the way back to Algiers – about forty miles – was a nightmare. The Hudson behaved in the most freakish manner. Sometimes the nose would dip steadily and I had to signal to the crew to run back to the tail to balance the aircraft. Then the tail would drop and back would run the crew to the nose. When we got over the bay and were congratulating ourselves that all was well, the port engine conked out and the Hudson became uncontrollable. We baled out as fast as we could and the Hudson dived into the water. I landed in the sea and was picked up by a sloop.'[16]

Just about a nightmare by any reckoning. But Doenitz had one U-boat less to send lurking along the convoy lanes.

Lynx-eyed Flight Sergeant V.W. Croft, of Bishop Auckland in Co. Durham had a similar experience, but one with a luckier ending. The Controller at his Coastal Command station in Iceland said to him one day, 'There's a damaged U-boat in this position'. He pointed to a spot on a chart. 'Go out and prang it.' Croft flew in his Hudson but was spotted by the German undersea raider, which managed to dive before the Hudson could get near enough to attack. Bitterly disappointed, Croft flew off. He recalled:

'Imagine our excitement when only a few miles farther on I sighted another German submarine. This one wasn't quite quick enough. It crash-dived but I was over him within two or three seconds and down went our bombs. Then the fun started. I flew very low and the bombs exploded close to the surface of water. Their blast threw our plane up into the air and behaved like an uncontrollable horse. However, I eventually managed to get it level and under control again. Our photographs were spoiled but so was the U-boat, I'm quite sure. That was a lucky break all right.'

Most of Coastal Command's lucky breaks were the results of a grim determination to engage the enemy and a split-second judgment in attack.

In January Bulloch was back in the news.[17] He and his men flew to protect a vitally important Atlantic convoy,[18] which was driving eastwards through bad weather and mountainous seas. In four days there were no less than 35 grimly fought air and sea battles staged by the convoy's escort. Bulloch got one submarine and probably a second and then gave the piloting of his aircraft over to 'George', the automatic pilot and started to eat a meal of steak and potatoes, which he had propped on his knees.

'I was going to enjoy that steak but another U-boat popped up. The plate with its steak and potatoes went spinning off my knee as I grabbed the controls and sounded the alarm and there was a clatter of plates back in the aircraft as the rest of the crew jumped to it. We dived on the sub and opened up on it with cannon and machine-gun fire. Our lunch was ruined, but that U-boat didn't get within torpedo range of the convoy. Instead of his lunch Bulloch got a bar to his DSO.[19]

One Liberator commander singed Admiral Doenitz's chin by boldly sailing over a French Atlantic harbour and bombing a U-boat as it was entering. Home was no longer safe for the U-boat crews. Not even a barrage of shore flak could keep the deep sea hunters away. If one had to choose the most celebrated deep sea hunting aircraft of Coastal Command the choice would have to go to a famous Catalina flying boat. Her captain once described her as a 'much-travelled little lady. But she has had several captains. At her home base she is down on the flight schedules as *L for Leather*. She is one of the most widely-travelled operational aircraft in the world and she had already earned an enviable reputation when she flew out over the Atlantic with Flight Lieutenant Douglas A. Briggs DFC at the controls and succeeded in locating the German battleship *Bismarck*.[20] She has made many flights over the Atlantic and has flown to Russia by the long route across the dangerous ice-floes of the Arctic Circle. She sank at least one German submarine in the Atlantic before flying to the other side of the world, for she was at work in the Orient shadowing and reporting on the Japanese fleet before the attack on Colombo. Hung from a nail over her navigator's desk is always a small bunch of white heather. In 1943 she had already been mention in reports for the way she attacked a Japanese submarine. "Like a much-travelled and rather battered old suitcase," wrote one RAF officer of her, "plastered with the labels of the famous hotels of many continents, *L for Leather* traverses the world's oceans.'

Flight Lieutenant D.A. Briggs DFC, an ace Coastal Command skipper, once got back to base after actually being forced down on the sea. The occasion was more than two years after he found *Bismarck*. He was commanding another Catalina, which was sent out on patrol far into the Atlantic to aid in escorting a convoy. At night, when only 800 feet up, the engines stopped suddenly and unaccountably. As the aircraft lost height the fitter set to work and when it was down to 500 feet, he got the engines restarted, only for them to cut out again a few seconds later. There was nothing for it but to go down on the sea, which was running very high at the time. Slipping into the first pilot's seat, Briggs got the wind direction from the navigator, turned on the landing lights, lowered the floats and by brilliant work at the controls succeeded in carrying out a very difficult stall landing on the choppy waves, while the wireless operator busied himself sending out a SOS. Distress signals were set off and one member of the crew scrambled out onto the rocking mainplane and flashed a SOS on an Aldis lamp. But in the night the convoy sailed by, not noticing. Briggs explained:

'We kept the air power unit running to enable us to use the wireless and to pump out the bilges, which were making water. The fumes from the air power unit, combined with the movements of the sea made most of the crew ill. Meanwhile the floats were being subjected to a severe buffeting from the waves and it looked as if we might have to abandon the aircraft. All precautions were taken in case that happened. The dinghies were inflated ready for launching and the rations were divided up. The wireless operator was maintaining contact with Coastal Command bases in Britain and Gibraltar and a report amplifying the SOS was sent. The air power unit could not be kept running continuously because of overheating, so arrangements were made to listen out every half-hour. Daylight came and with it the waves grew higher. By this time some of the crew were *hors de combat*. Despite their sickness, however, the greater part of the crew kept going, as there was a fair amount of work to be done. The air power unit had to be kept serviceable and one wireless operator had to be constantly on watch. During the morning the fitter, at intervals between being sick, sought to find the cause of the engine failure. The trouble was at last discovered and after a struggle to restart the air power unit the dinghies were brought in still inflated and the engines were started. The waves were even higher now and it appeared rough for a take-off. However, I taxied slowly into the wind while the engines were thoroughly run up and continued taxiing, awaiting a chance to take-off. The crew were warned for a take-off at any moment if a calm patch of sea should appear. By noon the sea was still increasing and as no sign of help was evident, I opened up to full throttle. The aircraft gathered speed. Three times we were flung off the sea by the waves before we finally remained airborne. We then set course for base, where we arrived safely.'

Well, that is how it is done with a seasick crew and Neptune, whipping his watery kingdom into a range of mobile mountains. One slight miscalculation, one tiny error in judgement and the Catalina would have been smashed to matchwood by those waves. Neptune must have rubbed his eyes that noontide. But the credit for fighting back to base against all conditions and overwhelming odds does not all go to Bomber Command and Coastal Command. Some of the smaller craft win their share of deserved glory when all hope of doing so might reasonably be considered to have vanished.[21]

Aircraft flying in the tradition of *L for Leather* saved a great Atlantic convoy [ON (Outbound North) 166] from disaster in February 1943. From bases in Iceland, Ireland and the Western Isles flew Sunderlands, Liberators, Flying Fortresses and Catalinas, in the worst possible Atlantic weather to protect ships with vitally needed war cargoes. Cargoes the U-packs were determined to send to the ocean's bottom. Cargoes the Royal Navy and Coastal Command were equally determined should reach the safety of British wharves and docks.

For five days [21–25 February] the U-boat pack dogged the convoy, at times as near as five miles from the great concourse of ships, at others more than 30 miles distant. The escort estimated that the pack was composed of at least 20 submarines.[22] Thousands of miles were flown by Coastal Command in less than four days. A single Liberator attacked three U-boats within four hours, depth-charging two of them and cannon-raking the third. Within 24 hours of the first German attack on a ship, three U-boats had been attacked and a fourth sighted. In one patrol period of eight hours Liberators and Fortresses made no less than five separate attacks and had three additional sightings. Two ace deep sea hunters, both squadron leaders, got kills. Squadron Leader Desmond Isted DFC, 22 years, whose home was in Reading, led a Liberator patrol that sighted two U-boats and attacked one [*U-623* on 21 February]. He flew six miles to reach his target and swept down so low that he was only 30 feet above the underwater craft when his bombs slipped from their racks.[23]

'The flight engineer, standing in the bomb-bay got the full effect of the blast from the explosion, which shook the plane. He actually heard the noise of explosion above the roar of our engines. It was certainly terrific and debris seemed to be falling on the water for several seconds afterwards. A large black object, probably the bottom of the U-boat, leaped out of the water and then slowly sank. The crew were convinced it was a kill, for when we left the spot there was an ever-increasing patch of oil and a two foot length of bright yellow timber was floating in the middle of it. The inside of a U-boat is painted yellow. Seagulls hovered, vulture-like, overhead.'[24]

The most spectacular air attack of the great defence put up by the convoy's escort was probably that made by Squadron Leader R.C. Patrick DFC, a Canadian from Ontario, who was leading a Fortress patrol. He too swept towards a U-boat sighted six miles away. The watchers in the Fortress saw five Germans standing in the conning-tower.

'They stood there and watched us just as though we were a friendly craft making a practice attack. Then down went our depth charges to straddle the U-boat just forward of the conning-tower. In the explosion that followed the U-boat was lifted out of the water and slewed round thirty degrees and when things had quietened down a little there was not a sign of the hatless men. All we saw was the sub, fully four feet higher out of the sea than before the explosions. There was a terrific up-rush of bubbles over a wide area and we saw that she had lost all forward way. Two or three minutes later, as my gunners raked her with cannon fire, she settled and sank.'

Such severe handling assured the Allied commanders that the menace of the U-boat was more than being just tackled. It was definitely being overcome. There was a second celebrated *L for Leather* in Coastal Command, a Flying Fortress [of 206 Squadron at Benbecula][25] and, like the Catalina of the same marking, it was regarded as a lucky aircraft in the job of deep sea hunting. One time [25 March 1943], with Flight Lieutenant William Roxburgh DFC of Glasgow as captain, this aircraft disposed of 'a peach of a target', as Roxburgh described the surfaced U-boat [*U-469* commanded by Emil Claussen] he sighted.

'We'd been stooging around for hours when, as we emerged from a cloud, someone shouted over the intercom, "Look-out". He was so excited he couldn't say another word. Less than two miles away was a U-boat, a peach of a target. I was too high and too close to make an orthodox attack and I knew if I circled down he'd crash-dive before I could get there, so, as seconds counted, I thought I might as well crack right in. I pushed everything forward and down we went, touching 270 mph! Everybody was momentarily airborne inside the aircraft, but the crew soon picked themselves up and made their way to action stations. The front upper gunner, Flight Sergeant Eley, opened fire at point-blank range and pumped over a hundred rounds into the side of the U-boat. We could see the bullets striking it. Then came "Bomb-doors open!" and down went the depth charges to straddle the sub. As I pulled out of the dive our target was submerging with a pronounced list to port and making very little way. Shortly after the explosions it popped up again, bows first, at a very steep angle and with a rolling motion. Results were apparent within seconds of the depth charges exploding. There was a terrific underwater explosion. Bits of wood, cylindrical objects, a piece of wood that looked like the top of a long table and a bundle that looked like clothes, jack-in-the-boxed to the surface, accompanied by a quantity of heavy oil which, when we left it, was over a thousand yards long.'[26]

Only 48 hours later, skippered this time by Flying Officer A.C.I. Samuel, of Sutton Coldfield, the same lucky Fortress found and attacked another U-boat. There were about 10 men in the conning-tower as Samuel swept down to barely 100 feet to deliver the cargo of depth charges. This U-boat sank under a spreading patch of oil 100 yards wide. 'Fizzing like a dose of Eno's' was the description supplied by one of the crew at base.

Hunting U-boats was a big-game sport for men with patience. One Wellington commander spent 1,300 hours on operational flying before he sighted and attacked his first undersea victim. There had been plenty of other work and adventure crowded into that long flying period, so the commander, a former student of the Scottish School of Physical Education in Glasgow, was not bored. But he may be forgiven if at times he seriously doubted whether he ever would see a submarine.

Early in June 1943 Mr Churchill announced in the House of Commons that Coastal Command were operating 'VLR craft – that is, Very Long Range aircraft. These were Liberators equipped with special long-range fuel-tanks. Their minimum range was 2,000 miles. Operating from the Atlantic's western shores, they cooperated with other Liberators from bases in Iceland and Ireland. The pioneer of these aircraft was Squadron Leader T.M. Bulloch DSO* DFC* ' who had operated mainly from Iceland and had made no less than 18 U-boat attacks.[27] On such flights 18 hours in the air is not an uncommon period of flying. The crews usually spent 24 hours on duty without a real break. All meals – breakfast, lunch, tea and dinner, as well as a supper snack – were eaten in the air on duty. Such crews flew prepared for anything. Only rigid disciplinarians, imbued with the spirit of working as a team, could hope to win through on such flights time and again, ready at moment to face up to the hazards of war and of the elements they were constantly challenging. Indeed, one Liberator 'VLR' captain had put it on record that 'Iron self-discipline is a primary requirement. Every man in the crew must be keyed up to maintain absolute efficiency over periods of eighteen hours or more, for the most; without the stimulant of fighting a U-boat.'

Small wonder such men came back through storms and tempest and despite the worst the enemy could do.

'Boy, this is it!' was the excited cry of Sergeant John Lloyd, a New Zealander and second pilot in a Liberator [Z-Zebra of 86 Squadron], when he spotted a German submarine [on 8 October 1943]. The captain of the aircraft, Flying Officer Cyril W. Burcher from Sydney looked to where the second pilot pointed and saw a 740-ton

U-boat [*U-643*] surfaced and making perhaps 10 knots. 'Three or four men were attempting to man the heavy guns fore and aft and another was trying to bring a smaller gun in the conning-tower to bear on us. We flew along the track of the U-boat to release our depth charges and passed over it at about 30 feet but none of us saw the guns fired, although they were trained on our aircraft. As we passed over the conning tower an officer jumped almost head first into the hatchway, followed by other members of the crew, who closed it after them. By the time we turned to make a second attack only 20 feet of the sub was above the water. The bombs fell just ahead of the swirl caused by the conning tower and soon after the explosion we were heartened see an ever-increasing patch of oil and a black object which looked like a body. The U-boat went down so quickly that at least one of the crew must have been left behind.'[28]

The truth was the U-boat commanders were getting jittery. They had orders to stay on the surface and fight it out, but the closeness with which Coastal Command pressed home their attacks shattered German nerves. Frequently only a half-hearted attempt to man the deck guns was made before the order to crash-dive shrilled on the U-boat's telephone. The sinkings went on apace and, on 30 May, the Air Ministry was able to announce the results of one intense period of 10 days' hunting – five U-boats destroyed.

Congratulations to Coastal Command on their successes against the U-boats in the month of May came from the Chief of the Air Staff Sir Charles Portal who wrote to the Air Officer Commanding-in-Chief, Coastal Command:

'I wish to express to you and all under your command my admiration and warmest thanks for your achievements in the anti-U-boat war during the month just ended. The brilliant success achieved in this vital field is the well-deserved result of tireless perseverance and devotion to duty and is, I am sure, a welcome reward for the air crews and others who have spared no effort during long months of arduous operations and training. Now that you have obtained this remarkable advantage over the U-boat, I know you will press it home with ever increasing vigour and determination, until, in conjunction with the Royal Navy, you have finally broken the enemy's morale.'

In June came the story of the triumphant crossing of another vast Atlantic convoy, in the defence of which the newly converted merchantman type of aircraft carrier was employed successfully in cooperation with aircraft of Coastal Command. In that great running fight the deep sea hunters were so much on top of the U-boats that 97 per cent of the great convoy reached British shores unscathed.

Signs were that the U-boat was slipping into a decline, as a commerce raider. The deep sea hunters of the RAF were beating them at their own game of sink on sight.

Notes
1. Frederick J. Drake and Douglas Strode.
2. *U-570* commanded by 32 year old Hans-Joachim Rahmlow, a recent recruit to the U-boat arm. On the morning of 27 August *U-570* was 72 hours out of Trondheim in Norway bound for Icelandic waters. *Hitler's U-Boat War: The Hunters, 1939-1942* by Clay Blair (Random House 1996).
3. Coleman saw two charges straddle the bow. The boat heaved violently and rolled almost completely over. Although new it had been rushed through work-up and was not seaworthy

in all respects while only four of the 43-man crew had previously made war patrols. When the boat had reached open seas, a large proportion of the crew had become desperately seasick. Thompson's attack panicked the men and a rumour spread that saltwater flooding aft had entered the battery, creating poisonous chlorine gas. Even so Rahmlow could have saved his boat but panic and indecision led to the boat's surrender. Blair, op. cit.

4. Hugh Eccles, pilot of another 269 Squadron Hudson had also homed onto Thompson's wireless call. He took photographs and served as a radio-relay station. Jewiss, having been airborne for about 16 hours, about 13 of them circling U-580, departed for Iceland.

5. Thompson crash landed at Kaldadarnes when the Hudson was caught by a violent gust of wind on landing and crashed nose first. The entire squadron had turned out to welcome the crew home. They were not seriously injured but the Hudson was written off. Blair, op. cit.

6. British Intelligence intercepted Rahmlow's plain-language radio call to Admiral Doenitz saying that he was unable to dive and was being attacked by enemy aircraft and a small armada of surface vessels was ordered to race to U-570. Blair, op. cit.

7. After Jewiss left, a holding presence was maintained by Catalina AH565 flown by Flight Lieutenant B. Lewin of 209 Squadron until the RN A/S trawler Northern Chief (Lieutenant Knight) arrived that evening. On the morning of 28 August the trawler Kingston Agathe and RN destroyers Durwell and Niagra arrived and the U-boat crew were taken off so that U-570 could be towed to safety.

8. The boat crew were taken prisoner and the officers were incarcerated in an officers' POW camp at Grizedale Hall, a country mansion in the Lake District. OL Bernhard Berndt, the IWO (1st Watch Officer) of U-570 was held accountable in a German POW 'court of honour' for the capture of the boat (Rahmlow was beyond their reach for 'trial'). Berndt (and Rahmlow in absentia) were found guilty of cowardice. When the Germans learned later that U-570 had been brought into Barrow-in-Furness, only 30 miles from Grizedale Hall, Berndt escaped in an attempt to scuttle the boat and regain his standing in the eyes of his fellow prisoners. He was shot dead by members of the Home Guard on 19 October while on the run. Rahmlow was later transferred to a camp for Luftwaffe officers. U-570 was re-commissioned in September 1941 as HM Submarine Graph and was used operationally until it was wrecked on Islay on 20 March 1944 when on passage to the Clyde from Chatham for extensive refitting. Blair, op. cit. and U-Boat Fact File 1935-1945 by Peter Sharpe (Midland 1998).

9. In September 1941, Liberator Is equipped with 'Stickleback' Air-to-Surface Vessel (ASV) radar aerials and a 20mm cannon pack under the fuselage, entered service with Coastal Command of the RAF. They were badly needed to help plug the Atlantic gap. Prior to their introduction, German U-boats could operate off West Africa or in the central Atlantic, the latter being beyond the range of other Coastal Command aircraft. Liberator Is first entered service with 120 Squadron at Nutts Corner, Belfast in September 1941. By January 1942 five Liberator Is had been converted into VLR aircraft whose range was 2,400 miles. The Sunderland had a range of only 1,300 miles. These were later supplemented by squadrons of Liberator IIIs, which were used for general maritime duties far out over the Atlantic. The Liberator V was equipped with additional fuel tanks in wing bays and centimetric Air-to-Surface Vessel (ASV) radar either in a retractable radome in the ventral position aft of the bomb-bays or in the 'Dumbo' or chin position.

10. On the night of 4 June, Squadron Leader Jeff H. Greswell and the crew of a Wellington of 172 Squadron, one of five Wimpys fitted with the Leigh Light (an airborne searchlight) picked up an ASV contact. His target was outbound from Bordeaux to the West Indies. Greswell homed on the Luigi Torelli by radar, then switched on the Leigh Light, which was designed to illuminate U-boats during the last mile of the approach when ASV metre-wavelength radar was blind. But owing to a faulty setting in his altimeter, his approach was too high and he saw no sign of the submarine. However, Migliorini, mistaking the

Wellington for a German aircraft, fired recognition flares, precisely pinpointing his boat. On a second approach with the Leigh Light, Greswell got the *Luigi Torelli* squarely in the brilliant beam and straddled the Italian boat with four shallow-set 300lb Torpex depth charges from an altitude of 50 feet. The blasts to his boat forced Migliorini to abort and he diverted to Aviles, Spain, where he ran aground. Blair, op. cit.

11. A total of 15 depth charges were dropped on the submarine by the two Sunderlands and they hounded the boat into Santander, Spain. A month later the *Luigi Torelli* escaped internment at Santander and limped into Bordeaux. Blair, op. cit.

12. Hunt dropped six 250lb Mark VII depth charges with Torpex warheads set for 25 feet. The close straddle literally lifted *U-751* out of the water. Then the Whitley mounted a second attack with ASW bombs and machine guns. *U-751* survived these attacks and, contrary to doctrine, Bigalk dived.

13. The Lancaster dropped ten close Mark VIII depth charges, then a string of ASW bombs. The bow of the U-boat rose vertically and she slid stern first beneath the sea. The crew spilled into the water, some of them shaking fists in defiance. No attempt was made to rescue the crew and all 48 hands died.

14. *U-751* was lost north west of Cape Ortegal with all 48 hands.

15. Squadron Leader Terence 'Hawkeyes' M. Bulloch DSO DFC an Ulsterman from Lisburn, County Antrim, became the most highly decorated pilot in RAF Coastal Command, credited with sinking more U-boats than any other pilot. In August 1941, when he had joined 120 Squadron at Reykjavik, Iceland, from 206 Squadron, Terry Bulloch DFC had already flown the LB-30A/B (early RAF version of the B-24 Liberator) since the spring of 1941, on the ferry service between Montreal and Britain. In the Bay of Biscay on 16 August 1942 in AM917 *F-Freddie* he seriously damaged *U-89*, a type VIIC submarine, which was homebound, commanded by Kapitänleutnant Dietrich Lohmann. Two days later Bulloch carried out attacks on *U-653*, another type VIIC Submarine, commanded by Kapitänleutnant Gerhard Fieler, near to Convoy SL (Sierra Leone) 118. Six depth-charges, cannon and machine-gun fire from the Liberator, and a passing shot with two anti-submarine bombs failed to deliver the *coup de grâce* but the boat was severely damaged and one crewman was killed in the attack. Fieler was ordered to give all the fuel he could spare to two other U-boats and then to abort. *U-653* limped into Brest on 31 August and was out of action for two months. On 12 October, while flying close escort to Convoy ONS 130 in AM929 *H-Harry*, one of Bulloch's crew, sighted a U-boat eight miles to starboard SSW of Iceland. Bulloch closed on the submarine, which was later identified as *U-597* and commanded by Eberhard Bopst, from out of the sun and lined up on its stern. He attacked along the length of the U-boat, dropping his depth charges at 25 feet spacing: one exploded next to the stern, two either side of the submarine's hull, and another next to its bow. With its pressure hull ruptured in several places, *U-597* sank with all 49 hands. Bulloch was awarded a bar to his DFC for this attack. On 5 November, while operating with Convoy SC 107, Bulloch and his crew sighted a U-boat, which dived before it could be attacked. They later found another U-boat, which Bulloch attacked with six depth charges from bow to stern. The U-boat disappeared, but a few minutes later, air bubbles came to the surface. At 1456 hours the crew found another U-boat, seen 25 miles from the convoy and this time Bulloch attacked with two depth-charges shortly after it submerged, but with no apparent success. On 1 December, Bulloch was awarded the DSO.

16. Ensor sank *U-259* 35 miles north of Algiers, which was lost with all 48 hands. He had shared in the damaging of *U-595* the day before when five Hudsons of 500 Squadron and two of 608 Squadron, north of Oran, attacked the boat. Due to the extent of the damage *U-595* was beached and blown up by its crew before all 45 hands were taken prisoner. In 1945 Wing Commander Ensor DSO DFC* was commanding 224 Squadron.

17. On 1 January 1943 he was awarded a bar to his DSO.

18. On 10 December 1942 Bulloch, in Liberator I AM921 was operating with Convoy

HX.217, which had left Canadian waters and was being trailed by 22 U-boats in mid-Atlantic. On arriving to lend his support, a U-boat was spotted travelling fast on the surface: it was attacked with depth charges and disappeared from view. An hour later, two U-boats were sighted 300 yards apart and Bulloch attacked one of them with his remaining depth charges. The other submarine submerged before he could attack it. With his depth charges expended, Bulloch continued his patrol while his gunner cooked lunch of steak and potatoes on the galley stove. He was credited with sinking *U-611*, commanded by Nikolaus von Jacobs, which sank south of Iceland with all 45 hands.

19. In Bulloch's own words: 'I was sitting in the cockpit with a plate on my knees, with "George", the auto-pilot, in charge. I was going to enjoy that steak, but then other U-boats popped up and the plate with its steak and potatoes went spinning off my knee as I grabbed the controls and sounded the alarm. There was a clatter of plates back in the aircraft as the rest of the crew also jumped to it, forgetting how hungry they were.' Bulloch dived on the U-boat and strafed it with cannon and machine-gun fire before it dived to safety. He made another attack 23 minutes after 'lunchtime' and then another 35 minutes later; another 54 minutes after that and a final attack after a further 24 minutes. On each occasion the U-boats were strafed with cannon fire and forced to dive to safety. In the space of five hours he made eight sightings and seven attacks. During all this, *U-254* was sunk and the convoy sailed happily on with the loss of only one vessel before reaching England. Escorts sank another U-boat and other aircraft accounted for a third submarine. Bulloch left 120 Squadron in December 1942. During his 18 months on the squadron he had sighted no less than 28 U-boats and had attacked 16 of them.

20. This is wrong on both counts. On 26 May 1941 after sightings had been lost for two days, Ensign Leonard 'Tuck' Smith from Higginsville, Missouri was actually piloting the Catalina of 205 Squadron, which was not *L-Leather* but *Z-Zebra*. Circling to confirm *Bismarck*'s identity, but unluckily breaking cloud only a quarter of a mile away, the Catalina was at once hit. It lost touch but another Catalina, of 240 Squadron, was soon there to regain contact. Blair, op. cit.

21. The only man to sink two U-boats in a single sortie was Flight Lieutenant Kenneth Owen 'Kayo' Moore, a Canadian pilot in 224 Squadron, on 8 June 1944. Moore and his crew had taken off in *G-George* at 2214 hours on 7 June and at 0211 hours on the 8th a radar contact was made dead ahead at 12 miles. At three miles a U-boat was sighted on the surface in the moonlight. It was actually *U-629*, a type VIIC boat, commanded by Oberleutnant Hans-Hellmuth Bugs on a war cruise from Brest bound for the Plymouth area. Moore did not need to switch on his Leigh Light and attacked from about 50 feet with six depth charges, which straddled the conning tower. *U-629* disappeared leaving wreckage and oil on the sea. It was lost with all 51 hands. Later, another U-boat was sighted, actually *U-373* commanded by Oberleutnant Detlef von Lehsten, which was on its 12th war cruise, from La Pallice, bound for the invasion front. Moore attacked with six depth charges and sank the vessel. (Moore had sunk both boats within 20 minutes). He took *G-George* in again and turned on his Leigh Light to pick out three dinghies on the surface of the sea and a few survivors swimming in the oil and wreckage. (*U-373* was lost with six hands, 47 survivors being rescued by French fishermen.) Moore received an immediate DSO, while DFCs were awarded to Warrant Officer Johnston McDowell, one of the navigators and Warrant Officer Peter Foster, the Wop/AG. Sergeant John Hamer the flight engineer received a DFM.

22. A running fight ensued over 1,100 miles with 21 U-boats, which sunk 14 ships of ON 166. *U-Boat Fact File 1935-1945* by Peter Sharpe (Midland 1998).

23. A few days earlier, on 6 February flying *X for X-Ray* of 120 Squadron near Convoy SC 118 after its signals were traced with HF/DF, listed damaged *U-465*. This boat was damaged again on 10 April 1943 by a Catalina of 210 Squadron. A Sunderland of 461 Squadron RAAF finally sank the boat on 2 May 1943 west of St. Nazaire. Sharpe, op. cit.

24. *U-623*, which was commanded by Hermann Schröder sank 540 miles north of the

Azores and was lost with all 46 hands. Sharpe, op. cit.

25. Fortress III FK105.

26. Roxburgh, who was escorting Convoy RU.67 sank *U-469* 80 miles SSE of Iceland and was lost with all 46 hands. Emil Claussen's brother was lost as commander of *U-1226*. Sharpe, op. cit.

27. In July 1943 Bulloch joined 224 Squadron. On 8 July he and his crew, in BZ721 *R-Robert*, took-off on patrol at 0853 hours. While on patrol north-east of Cape Finisterre, Flight Lieutenant Colin V. T. Campbell an armament specialist, was looking at some Spanish fishing vessels through his binoculars when he spotted a U-boat right in among them. It was *U-514*, a type IXC/40 submarine, commanded by Kapitänleutnant Hans Jürgen Affermann, which was on its fourth war cruise, from Lorient, bound for South Africa. Bulloch went into the attack and at 800 feet loosed off two rockets and a second salvo at 600 feet and four more at 500 feet from 500 yards. As the Liberator flew over, the front, rear and port-beam guns raked the U-boat along its length. However, the rockets had found their mark and had hit the U-boat below the waterline: the submarine plunged steeply beneath the waves, reappeared with its tail in the air, and finally went down at 1320 hours with all 54 crew. In all, Bulloch was credited with sinking three U-boats and severely damaging two more. He finished the war flying C-87s, and later RY-3 aircraft, in RAF Transport Command.

28. *U-643* was successfully attacked by *Z-Zebra* of 86 Squadron and *T-Tommy* of 120 Squadron from Reykjavik, Iceland flown by Flying Officer Dennis Webber but was then scuttled by Kapitänleutnant Hans-Harald Speidel. *U-643* was lost with 30 hands; 21 men survived. Sharpe, op. cit.

# Chapter 6

# Ninety Minutes in May – Bruce Sanders

At six o'clock to the minute that lovely May evening the briefing-room was packed. Pilots, air-gunners, navigators, wireless operators and flight engineers squeezed into rows of old cinema seats, rescued months before from a blitzed London building. They stood in rows along the wall and they were crowded together at the rear of the room. They were cracking jokes and laughing and filling the room with din. They were happy. All day long they had known something was in the air. Throughout the heat of the late morning and the afternoon the ground crews had been working feverishly on the machines, testing, checking gauges and radio circuits, running in the ammunition, trundling out the bombs and setting fuses. There was every indication that a big show was on the slate. A door opened and the hubbub died. The station commander entered. He smiled as he held up a hand. For a moment he stood watching the concourse of eager young airmen, waiting for his words; words that would send them hurtling through hundreds of miles of space to attack an enemy that was beginning to feel the shock of retaliation.

'Some of you have probably guessed that we've something special on the menu tonight,' he said. 'We have. We're bombing the Hun with over a thousand aircraft.'

The announcement was received with cheers. Excitement ran like a fever among them, until checked once more by the commander's upraised hand:

'I've a message for you from Air Marshal Harris.' They waited and he read to them:

'The force of which you form a part to-night is at least twice the size and has more than four times the carrying capacity of the largest air force ever before concentrated on one objective. You have an opportunity, therefore, to strike a blow at the enemy, which will resound not only throughout Germany, but throughout the world. In your hands lie the means of destroying a major part of the resources by which the enemy's war effort is maintained. It depends upon each individual crew whether full concentration is achieved. Press home your attack to your precise objective with the utmost determination and resolution in the knowledge that, if you individually succeed, the most shattering and devastating blow will have been delivered against the very vitals of the enemy. Let him have it – right on the chin.'

The commander looked up as his voice added the exclamation mark. The men broke ranks. Those seated rose to their feet. Arms lifted like lances in salute. The cheers broke in one vast wave.

The briefing finished in an atmosphere of buoyant enthusiasm. The crews trooped out of the long room. To a man they felt inspired by the words of the Commander-in-Chief, Bomber Command. They knew they were flying that night to make history. And their target was…Cologne.[1]

The scene, the instructions, the meticulous preparation and enthusiasm, were repeated over and over again that evening at bomber stations throughout the length of Britain. Men spent their last hours before darkness came writing letters, drinking a friendly glass, listening to the radio, playing darts, relaxing, getting ready for the great moment of take-off. They sprawled in messes and canteens in inelegant attitudes, smoking and chaffing one another and reading, in their own peculiarly British fashion, priming themselves to face possible extinction in the skies. This was to be a real pranging job. They were to go in and smother the target. Flak, searchlights, night fighters, anything the Rhineland defence could put up would not stop them. The defences were to be swamped. The raid was to provide a new high-level in concentrated bombing. Nothing short of saturation would be success. That was the new concept of air attack – saturation. Much was to be written and broadcast about saturation in the future. Even saturation raids were, in turn, to give place eventually to yet another concept – the cascade raid. But that night of 30 May 1942, the idea was novel and the men who were to try it out discussed it with the dreaded appraisal of a swimmer assessing a new type of underwater stroke or a cricketer summing up a fresh arrangement of the field to suit a new-style bowler.

Discussion was still in progress when the sun dipped at the close of the day and lights sprang up along the flare paths. The big bombers taxied down the illuminated runways and took-off. Where normally one flare path was lit on a flying field, that night two were lighted. In a great host the RAF's armada took to the skies. In one gigantic throbbing stream they poured over town and village, flowing to the sea. They flew in the steely sheen of the midnight stars. Over the British coast and out across the darkness of the North Sea; south-east over the dykes and fields of the Netherlands; on over the banks of the Rhine towards the clustered pile of Cologne, ringed in red on the navigators' charts. Leading the way flew the surest navigators, pilots and bomb-aimers in Bomber Command, the Pathfinders, as they were dubbed, the veterans with many such night operations marked in their log-books. They had been given the task, literally, of lighting the others in. Their showers of incendiaries would start the night's work, lighting up the city in preparation for the main weight of the attack, which would follow with a thunderous deluge of high explosives. The Pathfinders ran into a cone of searchlights and the German gunners twisted their rangefinders and began pumping steel at the invaders while, in the Rhineland towns, the sharp, strident notes of the air-raid sirens wailed their dreary warning. On Rhineland airfields German night-fighter pilots ran to their machines, took-off and climbed towards the stars. The battle was on before Cologne was reached, but the flak of the ground gunners could not split up that devastating surge of aircraft and the night fighters were flung aside before they could get in really close. The Pathfinders roared over blacked-out Cologne, weaving between the searchlights. Like steam escaping from a suddenly opened valve, the hundreds of incendiaries hailed down over the heart of the target area. Flame blossomed and bloomed in the darkness, and then the Pathfinders were in and away, and the first of the explosive bombs were raining down into the illuminated centre of the industrial city.

With clockwork precision the bombers came in, roared over the target area with bomb doors gaping wide and released the loads of bombs subscribed for by savings groups all over the British Isles. Smashing down into the industrial centre of Cologne, the steady and continuous rain of bursting steel took grim reprisal for the havoc wrought by the Luftwaffe on the English towns and villages in the preceding months. For 90 throbbing minutes the RAF kept up the carefully planned attack. One by one the blue ribbons of the searchlights faded, the red parabolas of the ground defence's tracers faltered and failed. The great downward rush of bombs smothered the defences.

In the city buildings collapsed, shattered by the blast of the new bombs. Fires started by the incendiaries took hold and devoured warehouses and factories. Mounds of smoking brick and rubble replaced orderly thoroughfares. Great stores of valuable war material were reduced to smouldering ruins. The city's civil defence army went into action, trying desperately to stem the tide of chaos and destruction, but in vain. Firemen, dispirited and defeated, drove back from infernos that could not be quenched, to try their skill and efficiency elsewhere, with like result. That night Cologne was in the front line of the war that had engulfed the world; battle was enjoined in the German homeland and the shocked and appalled citizens paid for their political and military crimes in the currency of total war.

To the British crews, watching the many coloured fires, the dense rising columns of dark smoke, the sudden rosettes of white flame marking fresh explosions, the effect was exhilarating. They were pitting themselves and their aircraft against a ruthless enemy, an enemy who had long paraded his preparedness to meet such an assault and the overwhelming success of their onslaught was as wine and meat to a hungry man. They were stimulated by the visual evidence of their own striking power. Since the days of the Battle of Britain they had trained and experimented, endured and struggled against odds, always looking to the time when the blows they dealt would make the enemy reel; when the potential of their striking power would make them a vital factor in the Allied offensive.

That night Bomber Command, as an air-striking force, achieved the fullness of military maturity; it made the efforts of the Luftwaffe appear second-rate. Within 24 hours all Europe was to know a new truth. The bright star of the Luftwaffe was in the descendant. In the space of that 90 minutes the balance of bombing power in Western Europe changed. The scales, so long tipped in favour of the Axis, swung in favour of the Allies. And to the men who worked the miracle it was just a night's work. In one Lancaster that approached the target with a mixed bomb load the bomb-aimer, lying in the nose, jotted down his impressions of the kaleidoscopic scene. When later he got back to base he put those impressions on record. He recounts:

'It looked as though we would be on our target in a minute or two and we opened our bomb doors. We flew on. The glow was as far away as ever. We closed the bomb doors again. The glow was still there, like a huge cigarette end in the German blackout. Then we flew into the smoke. Through it the Rhine appeared a dim silver ribbon below us. The smoke was drifting in the wind. We came in over the fires. Down in my bomb-aimer's hatch I looked at the burning town below me.

I remembered what had been said at the briefing. "Don't drop your bombs," we were told, "on the buildings that are burning best. Go in and find another target for yourself." Well, at last I found one right in the most industrial part of the town. I let the bombs go. We had a heavy load of big high explosives and hundreds of incendiaries. The incendiaries going off were like sudden platinum-coloured flashes, which slowly turned to red. We saw their many flashes going from white to red and then our great bomb burst in the centre of them. As we crossed the town there were burning blocks to the right of us, while to the left the fires were immense. There was one after the other all the way. The flames were higher than I had seen before. Buildings were skeletons in the midst of fires; sometimes you could see what appeared to be the framework of white-hot joists.'

Another eyewitness, also a bomb-aimer, who was lying prone in a Halifax, made an interesting comparison:

'There were aircraft everywhere,' he stated afterwards. 'The sky over Cologne was as busy as Piccadilly Circus. I could identify every type of bomber in our force by the light of the moon and the fires.'

For the RAF's meteorological experts had chosen the night for the big show with great care. There was a round bombers' moon to light up the Rhineland city and enable the peering bomb-aimers to pinpoint their targets as the aircraft went down to make the bombing run.

At times drifting clouds obscured the moon, it is true, and later a black pall of smoke rising 15,000 feet spread like a thick blanket over the city's blazing wounds. But with the moon lighting their way or the smoke cloud concealing the scene below them, the RAF crews made their runs over the target according to schedule and during each of the 90 minutes for which they kept up the heavy bombardment, dropped more than 10 tons of bombs. Over 300 acres in the centre of the city were devastated by the avalanche of explosives and severe damage was inflicted on the western suburbs and the industrial districts along the east bank of the Rhine. More than 250 factories and industrial premises were either totally destroyed by fire and bomb blast or very seriously damaged. The entire communications system of the city was disrupted. Yet the accuracy of the bomb-aimers, in view of the scope and nature of the raid, was truly amazing. 'In an area of 17 acres between the Cathedral and the Hange Brucke,' the Air Ministry reported after reconnaissance had been made, '40 or 50 buildings are gutted or severely damaged. Buildings immediately adjacent to the south-eastern wall of the Cathedral are gutted. There is no photographic evidence of damage to the Cathedral, although the damage to the adjoining buildings suggests that some minor damage may have occurred. The Police Headquarters and between 200 and 300 houses have been destroyed in another area of 35 acres extending from the Law Courts and the Neumarkt westwards almost to the Hohenzollernring. An area of three and a half acres between St. Gereon's Church and the Hohenzollernring has been completely burned out.'

The Luftwaffe had not the same target sense when it attacked Coventry.

When the preliminary reconnaissance, referred to by the Air Ministry statement, was made many large fires were still blazing. The reconnaissance revealed that no part of the city had escaped the scourging attack. The heavily damaged areas were computed to cover 5,000 acres. Cologne had been well defended. Over the industrial section of the city the RAF invaders had to fly through the electric brilliance of 120 powerful searchlights. Flak from more than 500 light and heavy anti-aircraft guns filled the sky over the city with whirling fragments of steel. Night fighters, stabbing with fiery jets of tracers, tried to interfere with the onrush of aircraft; their squadrons were placed strategically to defend either Cologne or the Ruhr. But, as one Canadian navigator remarked afterwards, 'The defences were just rubbed out.' The ideal of saturation was splendidly achieved. Cologne, the second largest city in the Reich, with the third largest population in Germany, a vast inland harbour with no less than three separate port areas and vital railway communications, a great centre of engineering and chemical industries, producing vast quantities of armaments and essential products for the German war machine, including diesel engines, explosives, fertilizers and synthetic oil, was taught the meaning of the word Blitzkrieg. 'It was almost too gigantic to be real,' was the opinion of one Halifax pilot, who saw the blazing city from many miles away. 'But it was real enough when we got there. Below us in every part of the city buildings were ablaze. Here and there you could see their outlines, but mostly it was just one big stretch of fire. It was strange to see the flames reflected on our aircraft. It looked at times as though we were on fire ourselves, with a red glow dancing up and down the wings.' 'And,' added another pilot, 'we had the guns absolutely foxed.'

The crews arriving back in Britain with the first flush of dawn were full of enthusiasm for the night's work and its results. All made light of the opposition encountered. When the final figures were known, their optimism was amply justified. The great raid had been made at a total cost of considerably less than 5 per cent of the concentrated attacking force. In short, double the weight of bombs had been dropped on Germany that night than had ever been dropped in a single night on England. The percentage of RAF losses on the operation was only half that sustained by the Luftwaffe in its previous concentrated raid on London more than a year before, on 10 May 1941.[2] Actually the night's programme employed upwards of 1,200 operational aircraft, for the tacticians of the RAF staged a large-scale side-show to pin down vital defence systems on the fringes of Germany and in the occupied countries. The way into the European mainland was swept by Hurricanes and Beaufighters and Havocs of both Fighter and Army Cooperation Commands, which swooped upon enemy airfields throughout the Low Countries and Northern France.

Tactics and execution of the strategic plan were, alike, successful. The enemy were out-manoeuvred at every stage in the night's enterprise and the next day, speaking for the whole nation, the Prime Minister gave his congratulations to Sir Arthur Harris:

'I congratulate you and the whole of Bomber Command upon the remarkable feat of organization, which enabled you to dispatch over a thousand bombers to the Cologne area in a single night and without confusion to concentrate their action over the target into so short a time as one hour and a half. This proof of the growing power of the British bomber force is also the herald of what Germany will receive, city by city, from now on.'

The Air Marshal's reply to the Prime Minister was succinct, but it contained a promise:

'All ranks of Bomber Command are deeply appreciative of your message. They will pursue their task with undiminished resolution and with growing means at their disposal until the goal is achieved.'

The congratulations which came from Sir Arthur Barratt, the Chief of Army Cooperation Command were every bit as cordial:

'This command is fortunate to have taken part in a great historical event when, for the first time in history, more than a thousand aircraft have concentrated their attacks. Heartiest congratulations to the aircrews and maintenance personnel of the squadrons concerned, who by their efforts, in conjunction with other squadrons of other commands, did their part successfully in assisting towards the success of the operations.'

The pilots and crews of Army Cooperation Command set out to play their roles in the great bombing festival just as light heartedly and with as much zest as the crews of the heavy bombers. Nearly all the Army Cooperation pilots flying in night reconnaissance squadrons were Army officers who had been seconded at one time or another to the RAF for special flying duties. As one of them, an ace pilot in his own special field of operations, said the following morning, 'We were all delighted when we knew we were to take part in the historic raid. Our part was, of course, less spectacular than that played by the crews who bombed Cologne, but I am quite sure if we had not attacked the aerodromes the losses over Cologne would have been heavier.'

In short, the complete and intricate cooperation between different commands, achieved on the night of the Cologne raid, had set a successful standard for the future. Men slaved to ensure they would not miss taking part in the great adventure. The pilot of one Blenheim, for instance, was told that it was highly improbable that his aircraft would be ready to take-off in time. He went personally and supervised the work on his machine throughout the heat of the day and that plane was airworthy five hours before zero hour. It left with the others of its squadron.

Little personal touches were not absent from the gigantic task of preparation. In one Blenheim flew a gunner from Bath, who had carefully chalked the name of his native city on each bomb fitted into the machine's racks.

'Those two Bath bricks went off with a good crack right on the runway,' ran a passage in the subsequent report handed in at base, 'much to the Hun's surprise. He must have thought we were on his side, for only a minute before somebody on the aerodrome had given us the OK to land. The landing was not quite the sort they had expected.'

Flashes of humour illuminated hundreds of the reports made by the triumphant crews.

Actually, despite the feverish work of preparation for the raid that went on throughout Britain until well on in the afternoon of the very day, there was an even chance that the great air armada would not take to the sky. Not until quite late were the RAF's meteorological experts able to advise the Commander-in-Chief about the night's weather in detail. But early in the evening a flood of satisfactory reports came over the telephone and Air Marshal Harris spoke that one magic word, 'Tonight'.

Armourers and mechanics, it is said, worked as never before. The bomb loads handled and fitted into the yawning racks, worked out in pounds weight, ran into astronomical figures. There was feverish competition between squadrons and between stations to get the maximum number of aircraft ready. The men selected to stay behind were disappointed. But once the assault was launched, once the armada was winging towards the Rhine, another branch of the RAF's far-reaching and intricate network of organization clicked into operation with the precision of a cog fitting its neat groove. For their brilliant work of coordination on that night of nights for aircrews, the Signals Branch of Bomber Command received special congratulations from Sir Arthur Harris. His words were sent to every group and every station in the command. For days before the raid was made 'Signals,' one of the most hush-hush departments in the RAF, was working at top pressure, at the same time contriving to keep its important work secret and to allow the enemy to suspect nothing of what was afoot. Due to the smooth departmental work of 'Signals' there was no hitch at any stage of the proceedings. Orders and instructions went through, preparations were made and when at length the 1,000 bombers were in the air, driving south-east under the midnight moon, 'Signals' saw that each separate bomber was linked by radio with its home base.

Before dawn next day, when the first RAF reconnaissance aircraft was out taking photographic records of the results, 'Signals' was again working at top pressure, saving crippled aircraft that were fighting to get back to Britain across the North Sea. 'Signals' came to the rescue of many aircraft and aircrews in the early hours of 31 May.

A navigator whose instrument panel was smashed by flak wished to fix his position without giving notice to lurking enemy night fighters. 'Signals' helped him out. Another navigator was killed and the captain of the aircraft, seated at the controls, had the task of getting his aircraft and men back without navigational aids. He told the wireless operator to get a special series of homing bearings, which would allow him to bring the aircraft directly overhead at any of 100 airfields. The plane arrived over a field and there the pilot was able to speak directly by radio telephone to the aerodrome control officer, who guided the aircraft down to a safe dispersal.

Again 'Signals' had functioned successfully.

One airfield was unable to clear its runways in time for the homecoming bombers. The group captain decided to divert some to another airfield and he had to make arrangements with a minimum of delay, for some of the machines possibly had fuel tanks which were very low. 'Signals' provided the special channel of radio communication that enabled this to be done expeditiously.

Some of the planes could not make the British coast and safety. They had to come down over the North Sea. But the aircrews taking to their rubber dinghies were comforted by the knowledge that 'Signals' would be on the job, fixing and charting by radio deductions the position where their machine came down and that news of their plight would be flashed to an air-sea rescue squadron.

One Wellington coming back from Cologne had its radio set shot away. The captain flew blind back to Britain and then, taking up the 'Signals' service by radio telephone, began tracking his way back through the skies to his own base. He flew from one air station to another, talking to each when he got over the field and being given exact bearings and a list of weather prospects for his route to the next. In all he visited six airfields in that way after crossing the coast, and before he found himself flying on his dispersal circuit over his home field.

An Order of the Day to the Signals Branch stated: 'The safety of aircraft and of their crews is found to depend again and again upon the methodical efficiency, care, intelligence and devotion to duty of the Signals Service. Captains of aircraft should know that, when the safety of their aircraft is endangered by fog or by other conditions of bad visibility, they can rely absolutely on the Signals Service to bring the aircraft home safely. The tradition of the Signals Service is that the safety of aircraft overrides every other interest; the personnel of the Signals Service spare no effort to bring every aircraft safely back to base. The Signals Service aspires never to lose an aircraft.'

However, aircraft were inevitably lost that May night, despite the efforts of the gallant crews to save them. Men gave they lives in heroic sacrifice to keep their machines flying and ensure the safety of their comrades in flight. The price paid by those who did not return was the price of victory. Some landed over the enemy countryside and were led away to prison camps; others found graves in foreign cemeteries and among strangers

Tradition was made that night. For as long as the RAF holds the skies the name of Flying Officer Leslie Thomas Manser of 50 Squadron, will be remembered and cherished by men to whom he set a great example in selflessness and utter devotion to duty. Manser knowingly gave his life in a desperate attempt to save his Manchester aircraft and to bring his crew to safety. It was beyond his powers to achieve the first part of his resolve; he died to make the second part possible. He came from the village of Radlett, in Hertfordshire, not many miles from London and, on the night of the big show, he was captain and pilot of one of 50 Squadron's Manchester bombers. He flew with the armada to the outskirts of Cologne. When he was caught in a blinding trellis of searchlights he tried to take avoiding action, but the ack-ack gunners, getting his range, turned their undivided attention on his desperately weaving aircraft. He was down to 7,000 feet and the ground fire was accurate. As he continued his run up to the target the Manchester was hit. The machine shuddered, but under Manser's skilful hands kept on course and the bombing run was made, right up to the target. The bomb doors swung wide, the bomb-aimer took his pinpoint bearing and down crashed the load from the racks. At once Manser turned. He set course for home. He started the trip back over hundreds of hostile miles with the searchlights still spotlighting his aircraft with their blue incandescent flame and with the ground gunners determined to make him pay for his daring low run. The flak caught him in a veritable trap. He pushed down the nose of the Manchester and continued in a dive to 1,000 feet. This manoeuvre however, was of no use. The German defences still held him in range. Searchlights and guns followed his descent and before he reached the outer suburbs of the Rhineland city, the Manchester had been badly hit several times. At the rear of the aircraft the tail-gunner was stretched out, badly shot up and in the front the cabin was filled with acrid smoke. The Manchester's port engine, at the same time, was overheating badly and threatening to cut out altogether.

At that stage in the fight to save the aircraft, Manser could easily have saved his own life by baling out. But he was resolved, if it was within his powers of endurance and skill, to get his aircraft back to its hangar on the flying-field [Skellingthorpe] of 50 Squadron. He pulled back the stick and coaxed the shuddering plane up another thousand feet, then he levelled off and, as he did so, he saw the port engine burst into flames. Inspired by Manser's cool example, the crew fought the wind-whipped flames for 10 desperate minutes, while the plane drifted in the sky, a bright prey for ground gunners and night fighters alike. At the end of that 10 minutes the flames were extinguished. But, as Manser had feared, by this time the port engine was dead. Moreover, part of the wing had been burned away, with the result that it was difficult to keep the plane on an even keel, while the Manchester's air speed had dropped dangerously. A brilliant pilot, Manser then exerted himself as he had never done before. Every trick he knew he tried in a vain attempt to gain height, to lift that heavy-growing mass of charred bomber higher in the sky, but to no avail. The plane dropped and continued to drop as it spun along the miles north of Cologne. 'At this crucial moment Flying Officer Manser once more disdained the alternative of parachuting to safety with his crew.' So runs part of the official citation on his bravery. 'Instead, with grim determination, he set a new course for the nearest base, accepting for himself the prospect of almost certain death in a firm resolve to carry on to the end.' [3]

The picture is one to inspire all who read. 'Soon the aircraft became extremely difficult to handle and when a crash was inevitable, Flying Officer Manser ordered the crew to bale out. A sergeant handed him a parachute, but he waved it away, telling the non-commissioned officer to jump at once as he could only hold the aircraft steady for a few seconds more. While the crew were descending to safety they saw the aircraft, still carrying their "gallant captain", plunge to earth and burst into flames.' The citation concludes: 'In pressing home his attack in the face of strong opposition, in striving, against heavy odds, to bring back his aircraft and crew and finally, when in extreme peril, thinking only of the safety of his comrades, Flying Officer Manser displayed determination and valour of the highest order.' He was posthumously awarded the Victoria Cross by the King. Back at the base to which he did not return his station commander, Wing Commander R.J. Oxley DSO DFC, has this to say of his passing:

'When I told the squadron how Manser on his last sortie on Cologne showed his determination by attacking the target with one engine out of action and then gave up his life to save the lives of the rest of the crew, we all felt humbled by what he had done. We realized that he had set an example for the rest of us to live up to and that he had established a tradition for the squadron. He was one of the most competent captains we have ever had in 50 Squadron. Whatever task was set him, he did it willingly and without question. All who met him became his friends and everyone in the squadron felt his loss as a personal blow.'

The Chief of Bomber Command sent a personal letter by special messenger to the home in Radlett where Leslie Manser had played as a boy. 'No Victoria Cross,' he averred, 'was more deservingly won.'

There were many awards truly earned over the holocaust of Cologne. Flying Officer Cyril Anekstein, a Londoner, who had enlisted in the RAF as an AC2 in September 1939, won the DFC for continuing a run up to the target, although his machine had been badly damaged by flying splinters. He got his aircraft over the target, saw the bombs away and then turned back and nursed his crippled craft along hundreds of miles, most of it over hostile territory. He was flying back over Germany with another cargo of bombs a few nights later.

Sergeant Cyril Terry, another Londoner, a chauffeur in civil life, that night was front gunner in one of our heavy bombers. His sharp eyes, cool nerves and shooting skill accounted for two of the black-painted night fighters that swarmed in a vain attempt to break up the phalanx of bombers. Near the target he saw one of our bombers being attacked by a night fighter who had cleverly positioned himself for the attack. His tracers were pumping into the British aircraft. Terry passed back instructions to his captain, who promptly manoeuvred into a position from which Terry could stalk the stalker. The distances between the three planes closed and when he was satisfied about the range, Terry pressed the gun button. He was dead accurate in his sighting. The very first burst tore open the night fighter's engine and set it alight. The German plane went down in a dive and continued diving. Not long afterwards, Sergeant Terry stalked another night fighter who was moving in to attack a bomber. Again he beat the German airman in that ghostly game of follow my leader. For his work that night Terry got the DFM. Like his fellow Londoner, Anekstein, he was back over enemy territory a few nights afterwards, when he destroyed a Focke-Wulf 190. He sent it down in the sea, blazing like a torch, just off the Dutch coast.

Flight Sergeant Thomas Oswald McIlquhan, a Canadian rear-gunner, played a similar role to Terry from the opposite end of his bomber. He got one Focke-Wulf at 9,000 feet by waiting until the night fighter had drawn in close. A second Focke-Wulf 190 fell to his guns later. For his feat McIlquhan deservedly wore the ribbon of the DFM a few weeks later.

With the crews on the Cologne raid flew a number of senior officers who wanted to gain first-hand experience of raiding on such a scale. Air Vice-Marshal J.E.A. 'Jackie' Baldwin was one of that number. As Air Officer Commanding one of Bomber Command's most important groups he was very anxious to see for himself how preparations, for which he had been largely responsible, worked out in practice. He worked at his desk throughout the day, then donned a flying suit and climbed into a bomber.[4] Doubtless it was due, in the main, to the personal reports of such high-ranking officers that the great follow-up raids were made.[5]

On 31 May the weather turned bad for bombing The big machines remained grounded. But on the next night [1/2 June], a Monday, the Air Council catapulted its second thousand-bomber raid on the Reich. As before, the operation went sweepingly according to plan. This time the target was the familiar 'Happy Valley', as the pilots and aircrews of Bomber Command had long since nicknamed the Ruhr, this narrow strip of industrial property, less than twice the size of Berlin in area, whose numerous mines and factories were the mainsprings of the German war effort. Essen was the chief focal point of attack, with the assault spreading over the continuous string of industrial towns, which merge their municipal boundaries above the richest deposits of coal and iron in Europe. Not a target such as Cologne, one city on a river, with countryside spreading out on every side of it. The Ruhr is maze of jumbled targets, each a landmark for a roving bomber captain, a crisscrossed sprawling mass of canals, railways, factories with chimney stacks and great squat industrial buildings.

The military defences of the Ruhr were possibly the most concentrated anywhere on earth. Yet of the large bomber force which attacked the district on the night of 1 June 1942, the casualty percentage amounted to less than 3.5 per cent.[6] The success of Cologne was repeated in every way. The defences were overwhelmed, while Fighter Command cooperated by staging intruder attacks along the flank of the main force of bombers. The significance of the repeat performance aroused tremendous enthusiasm in official circles. Sir Archibald Sinclair, as Secretary of State for Air, sent the following warm message to Bomber Command's Chief:

'Congratulations to you and the groups and squadrons of Bomber Command, on the bold and brilliantly successful raids on Cologne and the Ruhr. This double blow at the centre of the enemy's war industry and transport is the climax of months of patient work and cunning contrivance. The enemy knows that the next climax will be more tremendous still. Your crews are splendid, your maintenance personnel have done magnificently and the workmen who built the British aircraft, of which your force was wholly composed, share your triumph. Good luck to you and your men.'

Sir Arthur Harris, shortly to be dubbed the Scourge of Germany, replied to the Minister:

'All ranks of Bomber Command are very grateful for your message. As you rightly say, the effort put out was the result of the work put into building up and perfecting the force in the past. In that uphill task many now outside the limelight had a major share. As for those who built our aircraft – from taxpayer to tinsmith – the size of the force and the remarkably light casualties stand witness that they indeed give of their best. Our equipment is the finest in the world. Our crews never question workmanship or quality. They take it for granted and are never disappointed.'

Congratulations, however, came from farther afield. The thousand-bomber raids had kindled eyes and imaginations east of the fighting line in Russia. Bomber Command's Chief received a cordial verbal pat on the back from his Soviet opposite number:

'In the name of the personnel of the Long-range Bomber Force of the Red Army,' wrote Lieutenant-General A. Golovanov, its commander, 'I beg you to accept congratulations on the outstandingly successful initiation of massed blows on Hitlerite Germany by the British Bomber Command under your personal direction. The precision and effectiveness of this immense operation and the valour and skill of the men who took part, are highly appreciated by our pilots, who beg me to send battle greetings to their British brothers-in-arms.'

Sir Arthur Harris replied with his characteristic economy of words:

'The greetings you send are all the more appreciated because they come from airmen whose deeds fill us with admiration of their courage and efficiency. We will not cease our efforts until Hitler's Germany cries, "Enough!"'

Before the end of that month the RAF launched its third thousand-bomber raid. Bremen, second largest port in the Reich, received the concentrated pounding. The actual bombing operation was crowded into an hour and fifteen minutes – a quarter of an hour less than the time taken on the first raid. This time there was a complete RAF hook-up, with all operational commands taking part, Bomber, Fighter, Army Cooperation and Coastal. It was a climax in organization, a peak in operational coordination, but when it was announced there were further congratulatory messages.[7] The RAF had shown that thousand-bomber raiding had become part of its normal route. A black mood settled on the inhabitants of Western Germany. A partial evacuation of industrial areas was begun, to be accelerated a year afterwards, when the cascade and thunderbolt raid became part of the round-the-clock bombing routine, in which the American Army Air Corps cooperated. Letters to soldiers' relatives at the front were filled with gloom, so that in Berlin the Propaganda Ministry had to devise new tactics to counter the bad effect of the latest RAF strategy upon public morale. Rommel had shown his fangs in North Africa, but the good news from far away could not dispel the effects of experiencing disaster at home.

In Russia in the early days of July a Red patrol ambushed a group of Germans and wiped them out. Seeking military information, the Soviet leader of the patrol searched the dead bodies of the Germans for papers. Later these papers were sorted by Red Intelligence officers. In one scrawled letter from home appeared the following, which had escaped the German military censor: 'Our last mail made an overwhelming impression. The words "Cologne" and "Essen" are on everybody's lips. Relatives write terrible things. Friedrich was told that life at home had come off the rails and people simply cannot recover after this dreadful disaster.' Perhaps those words, stained with the blood of a German soldier, killed somewhere in the fighting before Stalingrad, are a sufficiently fitting, terrible and awe-inspiring comment upon the thorough technique and delivery of the crews who flew in the thousand-bomber raids. After all, it is the one who drains the cup who knows the bitterness of the dregs.

Notes
1. Harris could only accomplish this by using untried crews from the Operational Training Units (OTUs), many of them flying Wellingtons and even Blenheims and Hudsons. Five hundred and ninety-nine were Wellingtons, including four of Flying Training Command and no fewer than 367 of the aircraft came from OTUs. The rest included 88 Stirlings, 131 Halifaxes and 73 Lancasters, the remainder being made up of Whitleys, Hampdens and Manchesters.
2. In all, 898 crews claimed to have hit their targets. They dropped 1,455 tons of bombs, two-thirds of them incendiaries. Post-bombing reconnaissance certainly showed that more than 600 acres of Cologne had been razed to the ground. The fires burned for days and 59,100 people had been made homeless. The German defences were locally swamped by the mass of bombers and the 43 RAF losses. (Another 116 aircraft were damaged, 12 so badly that they were written off). It is estimated that night fighters shot down 30. These were mainly achieved on the return journey when the bomber stream had been more dispersed than on the way in.
3. Oberleutnant Walter Barte of 4./NJG1 claimed a Manchester, a Wellington 30km N of Hasselt and a Wellington NNE of Maastricht. The Manchester was L7301 of 50 Squadron flown by Flying Officer Leslie Thomas Manser. It had been seriously damaged by flak on the approaches to Cologne and Barte finished it off for his 5th victory. Manser and his crew could have safely baled out after leaving the target area but Manser ordered the crew to bale out only when it was clear that there was no hope of reaching England. He went down with the aircraft and was killed. He was awarded a posthumous Victoria Cross on 20 October 1942. Barte survived the war with 19 night victories and four day kills in NJG1 and NJG3. Oberleutnant Heinrich Prinz zu Sayn-Wittgenstein of II./NJG2 claimed a Manchester and a Wellington. Oberleutnant Reinhold Knacke StI/NJG1, claimed a Halifax 3km ESE of Weert, a Wellington 10km E of Weert and a Wellington 3km SW of Middelbeerer. Stabsfeldwebel Gerhard Herzog of I./NJG1 claimed two Wellingtons as did Oberleutnant Helmut Woltersdorf of 7./NJG1. *Nachtjagd* claimed 30 heavies. *Battles With the Nachtjagd: The Night Air War Over Europe 1939-1945* by Theo Boiten and Martin W. Bowman. (Schiffer Publishing. 2006).

4. During the afternoon Wing Commander Paul Holder, CO of 218 Squadron at Marham, received a telephone call from the Station Commander, Group Captain 'Square' McKee that the AOC wanted to fly with 218 Squadron that night. When the thick-set New Zealander asked Holder who they should put him with, the tall, quiet South African replied: 'He'd better come with me.' See *The 1,000 Plan* by Ralph Barker (Pan Books Ltd. 1967).

5. Baldwin borrowed McKee's Mae West, parachute harness and flying kit and took his place beside Holder in the second seat. He wrote: 'The weather forecast made it uncertain almost up to the last moment whether we should start. We had not been flying very long before we met much low cloud and this depressed me. The front gunner got a pinpoint on an island off the Dutch coast but the weather was still somewhat thick and there was an alpine range of cloud to starboard. Suddenly, 30 or 40 miles from Cologne, I saw the ground and then the flak. It grew clearer and clearer until, near the city, visibility was perfect. First I saw a lake, gleaming in the moonlight, then I could see fires beginning to glow and then searchlights which wavered and flak coming up in a haphazard manner. The sky was full of aircraft all heading for Cologne. I made out Wellingtons, Hampdens, a Whitley and other Stirlings. We sheered off the city for a moment, while the captain decided what would be the best way into the target. It was then that I caught sight of the twin towers of Cologne cathedral, silhouetted against the light of three huge fires that looked as though they were streaming from open blast furnaces. We went in to bomb, having for company a Wellington to starboard and another Stirling to port. Coming out we circled the flak barrage and it was eight minutes after bombing that we set course for home. Looking back, the fires seemed like rising suns and this effect became more pronounced as we drew further away. Then, with the searchlights rising from the fires, it seemed that we were leaving behind us a huge representation of the Japanese banner. Within nine minutes of the coast, we circled to take a last look. The fires then resembled distant volcanoes.'

6. The force of 956 bombers was again achieved by using 347 OTU crews and aircraft. Of the 37 bombers lost on the Essen raid, 20 were claimed by night fighters.

7. On the night of 25/26 June the RAF mounted the third and final 1,000 bomber raid when 1,067 aircraft were dispatched to Bremen. The force again mainly comprised Wellingtons and Halifaxes and included 102 Wellingtons and Hudsons of Coastal Command. Although the raid was not as successful as the first 1,000 raid on Cologne on 30/31 May, large parts of Bremen, especially in the south and east districts were destroyed. The price Bomber Command paid for this raid was very high. No less than 48 aircraft were lost; the highest casualty rate in the war so far.

# Chapter 7

# Happy Valley Excursion – Bruce Sanders

From time to time considerable controversy waxes in the messes of Bomber Command as to who first dubbed the Ruhr 'Happy Valley'. It is one of those points, which will probably never be satisfactorily explained, any more than will the origin of the word 'gremlin'. Perhaps the name arose spontaneously and naturally, for it is a typically British sample of sardonic humour. 'To ride the Ruhr,' one Canadian pilot explained graphically, 'on a night when Jerry's on his toes, is to switchback round the edge of hell. They sure brighten up the party and sling their greetings around with a free hand!' Anyone who has been on a Bomber Command 'special' to the Ruhr knows what he means.

It was put another way by a squadron leader who wears the DFC colours on his tunic. He led a flight of Halifaxes to the Ruhr in the big raid on the night of 16 September 1942.[1] Describing his experiences, he said of the Ruhr defences: 'We were over the Ruhr for about 20 minutes to make a reconnaissance report and we could feel the explosion of shells just beneath us and sometimes hear them. The defences are so strong and their area so vast that each of our aircraft must have been over it for at least 15 minutes, especially if they had to search for their targets. That is a long time when guns and searchlights are trying to get you.

'If you are attacking a target on the outskirts of the Ruhr it is not so bad. It is rather like attacking Cologne, where there are about 500 guns. But if it is right in the heart of the Ruhr, whichever way you go in you've got to get to the centre of a gun-defended area five times as big as that round Cologne. So to fly even within three or four miles of your target you will have to pass hundreds of guns.'

Happy Valley!

And the guns and searchlights are not the only defences. In the Ruhr night fighters swarm like wasps round a particularly sour dustbin.

On that same September night one of the earliest arrivals to meet the Ruhr barrage was a Wellington, which climbed above a heavy layer of cloud lying over the target, to find the sky above clear and moonlit. Perfect for night fighters. The Wimpy had not stooged around long when six Hun goggle goblins, as the crews had come to know night fighters, were sighted flying in pairs and clearly outlined against the moon. The pilot was about to open his bomb doors when a warning cry came from the watchful rear-gunner, 'Fighter dead astern!'

The sergeant's own words, told in his report when he got back to base, best describe what followed. He was captain of the Wellington and came from Edinburgh.

'I heard the warning, but then the intercom became weak so I could not hear the rear-gunners directions – only the stutter of his Browning guns as he opened up at the German. Simultaneously the fighter's cannon shells began tearing into us. The noise was terrific, but the most sickening part of it was the smell of cordite. As I did a 90 degrees bank-turn to port I saw out of my left window that the German fighter was falling away in a spiral dive with flames coming from its cockpit and both wings. It was difficult to pull the Wellington out of the turn. A length of trailing edge was ripped from the starboard wing and the starboard ailerons had gone. I pulled her out on the elevators, opened the bomb doors and our bombs dropped within the inner defences of Essen. We then surveyed our damage, which included the destruction of the electrical circuit and the hydraulic system, so that the rear-gunner's turret would no longer rotate. Then we saw another fighter. I was unable to bank fully, so I semi-banked, pushed down the nose and kicked on the top rudder. This got us away from the fighter but at that moment I thought I had been hit in the right leg. I have an old wound caused by a ground accident and I think the muscles must suddenly have knotted with the force of the kick. On the way back I continually had to use my right knee on the control column to keep the aircraft steady; the muscles seemed to be still knotted and were painful.'

But that is not all. This mild-mannered Scot, who must have been the very soul of inspiration to his crew, ran into more difficulties on this particular excursion to the Ruhr.

'The wireless operator was in real trouble. Both his feet were peppered with cannon-shell splinters. But it was not until he thought we were comparatively clear of danger that he said to me, "I think I have been hit". Before we left the Continent we were finding it difficult to maintain height because much of the geodetics and most of the fabric had been torn off aft of the flare-chute. Weaving violently, we scurried as fast as we could for the Dutch coast. We ran slap over the flare path of a fighter aerodrome and side-slipped out of searchlights down to 2,000 feet. Over the sea our port engine stuttered and oil-pressure went from sixty to zero. The navigator pumped in a gallon of oil and the engine picked up again, but not for long. Forty miles out over the sea we saw two more Hun fighters and heard them talking. Karl said something to Heinrich and Heinrich said "*Ja*", and then they both came in at us. I gave my knee another spasm as we side slipped into cloud at 1,200 feet. The port engine packed up 12 miles from the English coast. Because I had no useful flaps or undercarriage – when I worked the levers they merely flopped about – I asked the crew if they would like to bale out. But they decided to stay in the kite with me while I made what turned out to be a very difficult landing turn.'

Happy Valley!

But that was the type of pilot making the Happy Valley excursion run, the type his crews stuck with even when there seemed to be every chance of piling up on the home runway in a mass of tangled wreckage. As it happens, that particular pilot had a reputation for getting out of tough spots. He had, on three separate occasions, brought his machine back from raids over Hamburg after having to fight his way home. He had bought a packet over Bremen on another memorable occasion and he remembered a raiding trip to Oldenburg chiefly because that was where his Wellington, as he put it, 'acquired a few perforations'.

In October a force of Wellingtons, making use of heavy cloud cover, actually had the temerity to tackle the Ruhr in daylight.[2] Over one large marshalling yard, a key point in the Ruhr communication system, the cloud base was found to be only 400 feet. Three of the force promptly went down to reconnoitre and attack. As the bombs straddled the wide yard, with its trailing tracks of gleaming metal, stones and debris from the explosions were flung high above the low-skimming aircraft. The attack was virtually a house top swoop in the heaviest defended corner of Germany over which, according to Reichsmarschall Goering, no enemy raider would fly. And the time was two-thirty in the afternoon. One of the Wellingtons was lifted bodily by the blast from its own bombs as they detonated. The rear-gunner was thrown heavily against the roof of his turret. The pilot recalled:.

'The light suddenly seemed to fail and for a second or two I thought I was passing out, but then I realized that it was dark because debris had blotted out the light around my turret. The bombs had burst right across the yard.'

In short, the plane had flown through the middle of its own explosions. One of the other Wellington pilots had to make three runs before he could pick up his target properly. He then calmly turned round and returned for the fourth time because out of the corner of his eye as he swept down he had noticed a goods train piled with the products of the district. He went down still lower so that his gunners could effectively shoot up the train.

Wimpy pilots were notorious daredevils. This bunch lived up to their reputation. A third Wellington in the force was engaged by a determined Messerschmitt 109F. The German was a stickler, or maybe he thought the twin-engined medium bomber was a piece of Hun cake. He plainly believed in playing his luck, too. He swept in to attack the Wellington no less than seven times. His shells tore off the rudder and a good part of the plane's fin and ploughed up the fabric on the starboard side of the tail-plane. But after making his seven attacks without scoring a fatal hit he sheered off. Number eight was not his lucky sign. The Wellington in due course staggered home with a cheerful crew.

About this time the weather over Germany deteriorated badly and Bomber Command switched its attentions farther afield, to the industrial cities of northern Italy, so for a spell the Happy Valley excursion ceased to run. But a few days before Christmas the weather improved and the heavies were sent to make sure the Yule log was burning in the western Ruhr. Crews back on the old run got a thrill when again they saw the Rhine gleaming in the frosty moonlight when they were still all of 20 miles distant. The customary haze lay in patches along the valleys, but they could pick out quite easily the course of the Ruhr itself and the docks of the Duisburg-Ruhrort district.

Down out of the winter night dropped showers of flares. The scene below was suddenly lit up like a stage. One Lancaster pilot observed far below him the vapour trails spread by other aircraft going low to make their bombing runs. It was a concentrated attack in the new style that had developed from the thousand-bomber experiments. The defences, for once, seemed to be caught on one foot. Huge explosions were seen and large fires spread and grew more angry in colour.

But as they turned for home the heavy bombers ran into a circus of night fighters, mostly Fw 190s and Ju 88s. The weather favoured interception work. The pilots of the heavies had to jink furiously to shake off the angry swarm. One Lancaster had half a dozen running engagements, five with different Junkers and one with a Focke-Wulf. The pilot shook them all. One Halifax turned the tables and started after a twin-engined Me 110 and succeeded in damaging it before the German pilot turned tail.

Some of the later machines encountered night fighters as they flew in. One of these, a Stirling, was challenged by a Ju 88, as it approached Duisburg. The bomber actually was a clear target, for it was silhouetted against the glow of flares and searchlights. But the rear-gunner was alive to the swooping danger and got in the first burst. He saw the pieces ripped off the Junkers as his bullets found the enemy. But the German gunners had their sights trained. They flushed the Stirling fore and aft with cannon and machine-gun fire. The starboard tail-plane elevator and fin were holed and made useless and hits just behind the inner port engine set the dinghy storage blazing, while a starboard fuel-tank was drilled and petrol flooded the fuselage.

It only required one tracer to touch off that swilling petrol for the aircraft to become a solid sheet of raging fire.

Luckily that tracer was never fired.

But the German gunners, pressing home the advantage they had made, wrought more damage on the invader. A cannon-shell smashed through the window of the rear-turret and exploded on impact and, for a while, the gunner was blinded, with the freezing night air wrapping him like a shroud. The second pilot took a splinter in the knee, but he did not report the wound, although the captain of the Stirling, Squadron Leader G. M. Allcock, a New Zealander from Auckland, noticed the casualty as he noticed everything else that happened in those dire few minutes.

The flight engineer was folded up in his seat, suffering agonies. His face had been badly scorched by a shell, which had burst inside the aircraft. The wireless operator was likewise finding life somewhat trying just then. His radio set had been badly knocked about by another shell and he was trying to fix it with a hand bound in a blood-soaked rag. He kept tinkering with the set the whole way home. That was his job and he got on with it.

But retribution came with dramatic swiftness.

The mid-upper gunner had been biding his time and, as the Junkers lifted a trifle, he pressed his gun button. His bullets cut across the enemy plane like the teeth of a giant buzz saw. The Junkers turned slowly over and went down. Then the pilot set about finding the target, made his bombing run and the load of eggs were delivered precisely where ordered. All the frills and frolics of the old-time Happy Valley days again!

The Stirling turned back, with the fire in the dinghy storage still burning happily. The captain had a terrible responsibility to face up to then. If he continued the run and got over the sea and was then forced down into the bitterness of the wintry waves, the crew would have no chance to save themselves without a dinghy. Reluctantly he gave the order to prepare to bale out. Then began a tense period of waiting. The bomber flew on, maintaining height and the fire in the dinghy storage continued to burn, but did not spread. The miles sped away. They reached Holland

and the Dutch coast without further adventure and ahead stretched the white-flecked sea. Allcock still did not give the order to leave the aircraft and a few minutes later the charred and battered Stirling was heading across the North Sea. They crossed the English coast with the fire still crackling and reached their own base, only for the captain to discover, as he made his landing circuit, that his undercarriage was jammed. He made a risky belly landing well clear of the runway, so that it would not be blocked for the other planes of the squadron when they came in.

The following afternoon, on 21 December, Mr Jordan, High Commissioner for New Zealand and Air Commodore A. de T. Nevill, Officer Commanding New Zealand Air Headquarters in the United Kingdom, paid a visit to the bomber station where Allcock had landed, to meet the New Zealand members of the Stirling squadron. There they heard Allcock's saga at first hand.

The New Year opened with special greetings carried to the Ruhr in the form of 4,000lb 'cookies'. The Ruhr replied in kind with fresh batteries of anti-aircraft guns that had been rushed to strengthen the already very strong defences. 'Happy Valley was as spiteful as ever,' was the verdict of one veteran pilot who made the run. On 10 January the Air Ministry announced: 'For the fifth time in seven days aircraft of Bomber Command raided the Ruhr last night, dropping many 4,000lb bombs and causing large fires.' The principal weight of the attack was delivered on Essen, home of the Krupps combine of industries, which was said to employ 175,000 workers out of the town's total population of 700,000. The raiders plastered the town but it was only a faint promise of what was in store in the not distant future. Towards the end of February round-the-clock bombing was inaugurated and the crews of Bomber Command, for their part of the schedule, began carrying a new 8,000lb 'cookie'. This was the new era of cascade bombing and thunderbolt attacks.

It was not long before the Ruhr received another visit. Essen was the local town selected and the night of 5/6 March 1943 was the occasion.[3] The cascade that night included no less than 150 4,000-pounders and the entire weight of the raid was concentrated into a volcanic 40 minutes. For most of the way out the route was cloudy, but 15 miles from the target the weather cleared, although pilots reported that the Ruhr's best camouflage, its natural valley mists, were still seeping in from the river. The first big bombs wailed down and then erupted with violence and flame and the picnic was well underway. The defences opened up, employing somewhat new tactics.

A Halifax pilot reported: 'While I was over the target bombers were being caught and held in the searchlights and were twisting and diving to escape from the beams. Flak was being fired up the cones of the searchlights and bursting near the bombers. I saw three of our aircraft coned like this and hit.'

A Wellington pilot when he got back described how, despite his best efforts, the 'Ruhr searchlights held him in their beams for five minutes. We were hit time and again and when we landed our Wellington looked like the top of a pepper-pot. The extraordinary thing is that none of my crew got a scratch.'

Some airmen, like some seamen, live charmed lives; which must be an awfully discouraging thought for the German ack-ack gunners. The Poles who flew with the RAF that night were among the charmed ones. They were greeted when they returned to their station by General Sikorski himself, who stayed up and had coffee with them and listened to their enthusiastic narrative of the raid, which all agreed was one of the most effective in which any of them had taken part. They had scrapped with night fighters and one rear-gunner described in detail to the Commander-in-Chief of the Polish Forces how he had finished off an intrepid Me 110, which had tried interception tactics a short distance off the coast of Holland. The Messerschmitt had sneaked up from beneath the RAF machine and was only 30 yards off when the Polish tail-end Charlie opened up with his lethal stutter. His first burst reached the Me's vitals and the twin-engined fighter went spiralling headlong towards the cold sea with a trail of smoke pouring from it. The Polish crew looked back a few seconds later and saw it burning fiercely on the water.

The raid was a great military success.[4] A week afterwards the Air Ministry was able to announce, as the result of reconnaissance made, that no less than 450 acres of Essen were devastated. Of the Krupps plant alone, 53 separate large workshops were affected by the bombing. Thirteen of the main buildings in the works were completely demolished or seriously damaged. Nearly 1,000 tons of high explosive dropped by the RAF had caused the havoc. 'Essen,' said the special Air Ministry announcement on 12 March, 'is now the second most blitzed town in Germany. Only in Cologne is there a greater area of devastation.'

That very night [12/13 March] Bomber Command went back to help lessen the distinction.[5] This time the willing aircrews, carrying more than 1,000 tons of high explosives, found that the Germans had still further increased the Ruhr defences. 'Happy Valley was brighter and merrier than ever,' one pilot proclaimed. 'They seemed determined that we shouldn't get through,' another said. 'As we approached the town I saw three huge cones with at least 50 searchlights in each.'

The captain of a Stirling reported: 'When we arrived the whole of the target was lit up by fires. Suddenly there was a huge explosion below us; a great sheet of flame shot up to about 1,000 feet. Despite the thick cloud of smoke rising from the target we could see the glow of the flames when we crossed the Dutch coast on our way home.'

That cloud of smoke, it was estimated, reached a height of 15,000 feet – three miles!

The Germans, growing wily, had started a number of dummy fires outside the town, in the hope of distracting the bomb-aimers from the real targets they sought. But the veterans of Bomber Command were not to be fooled. Some of them went down to 500 feet before making sure of where their large bombs were being placed. One Stirling, diving still lower, went strafing searchlights on its own.

Here is what the pilot said: 'When we arrived over the target, explosions were going on almost continuously. By comparison, the tiny pinpoint flashes of the ack-ack guns seemed almost absurdly small. Against the background of one of the fires I could see a tall chimney stack. Immediately after we had bombed, the searchlights caught us and then the shells hit us fair and square. They burst inside the fuselage, just beneath the mid-upper turret. We were all blown out of our seats, but none of us was hurt. Then tracer came up all round us. We were still in the searchlight and I put the nose down and only flattened out when we were 200 feet above ground. We got clear and nothing more happened until we got to the Dutch coast. Then we were again coned by searchlights and again peppered by flak. I told the front gunner to shoot at the searchlights. I made straight for them and he put two of them out. The rear-gunner disposed of a third. The fourth searchlight came on, but it turned away from us as we went for it. We were almost suffocated by fumes from our own guns and from the shell that burst inside the fuselage.'[6]

There was, apparently, still entertainment to be had on the Happy Valley excursion route if one felt inclined to take time off for it. The next day reconnaissance aircraft flying over Essen found that large fires were still burning in the centre of the great Krupps works at three o'clock in the afternoon. The German fire fighters and civil defence organization had been unable to cope with the immediate effects of the thunderbolt attack. The results achieved by Bomber Command's tenacious onslaught on the greatest single armament works in the world brought official recognition from the Secretary of State for Air. Sir Archibald Sinclair sent the following appreciative message to Sir Arthur Harris: 'Your cunningly planned and brilliantly executed attack on Krupps has destroyed no small part of Germany's biggest war factory. Congratulations to you and all under your command on this achievement in the teeth of Germany's strongest defences.'

Some crews paid a heavy price to carry out their bombing orders. A few days afterwards the story of a Wellington belonging to the Canadian squadron that took part was told for the first time. An ack-ack shell burst beneath the aircraft when it was still some miles from the target and the navigator was killed instantly. His body collapsed on top of the bomb-aimer, who was sprawling in the nose adjusting the mechanism of the bomb sight. Glycol poured over both men, dead and living, running from a punctured tank and thick, choking fumes filled the forward part of the aircraft. At that moment the oxygen supply started to fail. The bomb-aimer continued to lie where he was, with the dead navigator on top of him, the fumes filling his head and the lack of oxygen making breathing very difficult. He continued to lie there and pass back the necessary directions to the Wellington's captain, so that the bombing run could be made and the bombs released. When the bombs were away the oxygen seemed to give out completely and the remainder of the crew were on the point of losing consciousness. The captain who, incidentally, was the commander of the Canadian Wellington squadron, next found that the aileron control had been damaged and the aircraft went staggering about the sky as he experimented with the controls. He put the machine down to 10,000 feet in order to get some air for their stifled lungs. When breathing was more normal the wireless operator reported that he had been hit. He sounded almost apologetic, for flak was still bursting all round them. The gunners had followed them down.

The captain turned to inspect the wireless operator's wound and received a shock. The man's right foot had been blown off as he was standing in the astrodome. 'But without a word of complaint he went back to his damaged radio set and tried to get it working,' the captain later reported. 'The bomb-aimer attended to him. Then, until we reached England, he remained at his set, trying to repair it and even managed to help me with the navigation. He put up a marvellous show.'

It was next found that the intercom wires linking the captain with his rear-gunner had been severed. The rear-gunner was brought amidships to the smashed astrodome to continue looking out for enemy night fighters from there, as it proved, just in time, for a Ju 88 pulled alongside and turned to attack.

The gunner, standing in the astrodome, passed back directions to the captain, which enabled him to take violent and effective evasive action. The Wellington was in no shape to start a shot swapping contest with the night fighter. But the Junkers hung on and swung in to the attack several times and, on each occasion, the joint partnership of gunner, observer and captain pilot produced a fresh manoeuvre, which got the Wellington twisting out of the Junkers' gun sights. At last the night fighter disappeared.

The long flight home continued and eventually, a flying sieve, with gaping holes ripped in the fuselage, the main spar and the bomb doors, with no chance of communication with base by radio, the Wellington circled its own flying field in the south of England and the captain effected a safe landing. The stoical wireless operator was rushed at once to hospital and the body of the navigator was taken from the machine. The damage was carefully inspected and it was found that a jagged piece of shell had passed through the front window of the cockpit, missing the captain by just a few inches. 'It was certainly a bad trip,' the captain agreed, 'but the crew put up a grand show.'

Nothing need be added to those words, except perhaps observation that such men are unstoppable. Seemingly, the Germans reached that conclusion for, when a fortnight later another strong force went to the Ruhr, the crews noticed that the ground defences had once more changed their tactics. One pilot's comment afterwards was, 'As we came over the Ruhr the searchlights seemed to have given up trying to pick up our aircraft and were just signalling to the fighters.'

Not that the changed tactics produced any different result. The Happy Valley visitors did their job and turned back for home, flying strongly and offering fight to any skirmishing night fighters. The Junkers squadrons posted as night guardians of the Ruhr had learned through months of bitter experience to be very cagey in their approach to the men of Bomber Command.

Krupps received another bomb-blasting visit from the RAF on 3 April, when 900 tons of explosives unloaded from the British bombers' racks. The concentration of the attack reached a new peak. At one stage it is estimated that 4,000-pounders were being dropped on the target at a rate of six a minute. April 1943, as it proved, was a month of wailing and much gnashing of teeth for the citizens of the Ruhr. Throughout the month Bomber Command stepped up its attacks, flying through good weather and foul, attacking the smaller towns and the larger industrial areas, such as Duisburg, which received two gruelling raids, one on the night of the 26/27th, when more than 30 tons of bombs a minute for a space of three-quarters of an hour rained down on the important inland port, the largest in Europe, which handled about 75 per cent of all the cargoes passing along the Rhine. On the last night of the month, Essen had a return visit from the bombers when the total of bombs dropped on the town was brought up to the amazing figure of 10,000 tons. At that time this was the heaviest weight of bombs dropped on any town in the world and considerably more than the total tonnage dropped on London during the Blitz. World observers were vastly impressed by the performance of steadily increased bombing made by the men in Sir Arthur Harris's command. The *New York Times* found it appropriate to comment in a leader: 'Germany is apparently reaching the point where she cannot cope, materially or physically, with the effects of bombing. Her enemies did not wait to pummel her cities until the population was strained by years of war and the armies were scraping the bottom of the barrel for men and material. They waited because they were unable to hit sooner. But if Allied strategy had been dictated not by necessity, but by a plan to reserve its full striking power until German force was spent, the results would be very much like what they are now.'

But the heaviest blows were still to come, incredible, as it seems, viewing the Ruhr onslaught with the perspective of twelve months from the time of the thousand-bomber raid.

The terrifying spectacle of Bomber Command going from strength to strength evoked admiration from Marshal Stalin himself who, in a message to Mr Churchill said: 'Every blow delivered by your air force to the vital German centres evokes a most lively echo in the hearts of many millions throughout the length and breadth of our country.' The Prime Minister passed on the message to Sir Arthur Harris who, in turn, circulated it to all his squadrons.

Those squadrons girded themselves for a fresh heavily-charged bombing offensive down the skyways of the now much blasted and shattered Happy Valley. Early in May it started and then, on the 12th, Duisburg-Ruhrort received a gift of more than 1,500 tons of high explosives and incendiaries, more than was dropped on Cologne in the thousand-bomber raid.

Whereas the Cologne raid had taken 90 minutes, concentration at Duisburg-Ruhrort was so controlled that delivery was made in half that time. Zero hour was fixed for two o'clock. The first flares and bombs went down dead on time. The last aircraft was winging home 45 minutes later. Flight Lieutenant D. F. Puddephatt of Brighton, gave a graphic description of the raid as viewed from his Halifax:[7]

'We arrived at the beginning and watched the bursts of high-explosive bombs making a continuous pattern. It was a grand night for the job. There was very little cloud and the moonlight showed up the country. Even without the flares which were dropped, we could easily have identified the target. The Rhine was very clear; we followed it part of the way, till I saw the finger-shaped docks of the port at Duisburg-Ruhrort. When the attack started searchlights were trying to work in cones and there was one cone with about 30 beams in it. But very soon they split up as more and more bombers came in. It looked as if they just couldn't manage to concentrate on any one aircraft. There seemed to be a thundering regiment of bombers behind and around us. We could see dozens of them and away in the distance I saw fighters attacking one of them and tracer bullets streaking across the sky. As we turned away the place was filled with fires. When we were over the Zuider Zee on the way home, about 150 miles from Duisburg, the rear-gunner could still see them blazing. I shall never forget all those coloured lights – the explosions, flares and fires. And there were "scarecrows" which Jerry seemed to be sending up to frighten us. They burst with a red explosion and then red and green stars poured out. It often burst near a bomber and did no harm.'[8]

Fireworks in Happy Valley!

Sergeant R. van Eupen from Wellington, New Zealand, a Stirling pilot, recorded his impression of the end of the raid. He was one of the last to arrive.

'There was one very large area of fire and we bombed this. But all round it there were other areas where the flames had got well hold. The only thing I could see in detail in this sea of fire was a large tower – perhaps a gasometer – standing out amongst the smoke and silhouetted against the flames.'

The following night it was the old Happy Valley route again for Bomber Command, this time to Bochum, a smaller town than Dortmund, but highly industrialized and an important transport centre for the entire Ruhr. Bochum lies at the eastern side of the central Ruhr. On this attack and others made elsewhere during the night, Bomber Command broke the record it had set up only 24 hours before for the biggest tonnage of bombs carried in a single night.

But then those were days when records were made only to be broken.

Wing Commander D.C. Smith, who took his Halifax on the raid, was surprised at the number of searchlights he encountered. He was a veteran on the Happy Valley run, but he had never previously seen so many as on that night.

'They were everywhere, in some places unbroken walls of them. We were in the early part of the raid and it was obvious by the way the searchlights waved about at Cologne, Duisburg and Düsseldorf that they had no idea where the attack was going to develop. It was as light as day and the whole Ruhr valley seemed to be lit up by the moon and the searchlights. When we flew through them they almost blinded us. Near Bochum itself there must have been about 15 large cones, with between 30 and 40 beams in each. The lights would wave about until they found somebody. Then all the beams in the area would fasten on to that aircraft and shells would be pumped up the cone. We could see bombers held like that a long way ahead.'

Change of tactics again. For that night there were not many encounters with night fighters. The Luftwaffe was probably licking its own wounds.

A few days later Happy Valley was flooded – literally – by the RAF. After the baptism by fire a deluge. The RAF had a nice sense of the fitness of things.

The brilliant low-level attacks on the Möhne and Sorpe dams and on the Eder River dam, were the logical culmination of a progressive policy of offensive raiding. The Möhne and Sorpe rivers are tributaries of the Ruhr and the two dams controlled about 70 per cent of the water catchment area of the entire Ruhr basin. They were built to ensure that the supply of water in the Ruhr would not fail in a dry season. If the great dams were breached and the reservoirs emptied, the resulting floods would be truly disastrous; 134,000,000 tons of water would pour from the Möhne reservoir alone. Taken together, the effects of both flood and water shortage for industry would be paralyzing.

These facts were in the minds of the men who planned the daring raid. The man they chose to lead the raid was sailing in Pembrokeshire two days before war was declared. A friend swam out to him with a telegram. The wire was an order to return at once to his unit. Forty-eight hours later, on the day Neville Chamberlain announced to the country that a state of war existed, this man was flying a Hampden loaded with bombs to the Kiel Canal. Over the canal there was so much cloud that the target could not be seen. The bombs were brought back, to be used on another foray. The man who brought them back was named Gibson.[9] He was twenty-one.

Preparation for the attack began with an intense training course, which was started on 1 April. Week after week the crews of the Lancasters chosen as the assault force practised approaching their targets and unloading their deadly mines until they could place them with chequerboard accuracy. The practice runs were made at a bomber station in a remote part of the country. Early in the morning of

17 May the assault was launched. Gibson, who throughout had been personally in charge of the operations, led the attack on the Möhne dam. He swept down and unloaded his mine and then deliberately turned and flew up and down to draw the heavy fire of the ground defenders, who were shooting with light anti-aircraft guns emplaced on the dam and projecting from defence slots cut in its walls. The gunners of his Lancaster replied hotly to the enemy fire and one or two of the German gunners wavered. The barrage weakened. In all Gibson was flying around over the reservoirs for an hour and a half and his luck was in that morning. When he got England the only damage his aircraft had sustained in the deliberate manoeuvre to draw the enemy fire away from the following machines was three small punctures in the tail. Flight Lieutenant H. B. Martin,[10] who arrived some time after Gibson and dropped his mine was better able to observe the actual breaching.

'I was able to watch the whole process. The Wing Commander's load was placed just right and a spout of water went up 300 feet into the air. A second Lancaster attacked with equal accuracy and there was still no sign of a breach. Then I went in and we caused a huge explosion up against the dam. It was not until another load had been dropped that the dam at last broke. I saw it very clearly in the moonlight. I should say that the breach was about 50 yards wide.' The crews assaulting the Eder dam breached it in two places. One hole appeared about 30 feet below the top of the dam wall, the other on the eastern side of the dam. A torrent of water poured into the valley beneath.

Air Chief Marshal Sir Arthur Harris and the air officer commanding the bomber group to which the Lancasters belonged, were waiting to hear Gibson's report on his return. 'We had high hopes,' the leader of the expedition told them, 'but the immediate results of breaching the dams were far beyond our expectations.' In the message he sent to the Lancaster crews, congratulating them on their brilliant work, the Chief of Bomber Command coined a new phrase, the Battle of the Ruhr. He said: 'Please convey to all concerned my warmest congratulations on the brilliantly successful execution of last night's operations. To the aircrews, I would say that their keenness and thoroughness in training and their skill and determination in pressing home their attacks will forever be an inspiration to the Royal Air Force. In this memorable operation they have won a major victory in the Battle of the Ruhr, the effects of which will last until the Boche is swept away in a flood of final disaster.' Congratulations came from the War Cabinet. They were addressed to Sir Arthur Harris by the Secretary of State Air, who wrote: 'The War Cabinet have instructed me to convey to you and to all who shared in the preparation and execution of Sunday night's operations – particularly to Wing Commander Gibson and his squadron – their congratulations on the success achieved. This attack, pressed home in the face of strong resistance, is a testimony to the tactical resource and energy of those who planned it, to the gallantry and determination of the aircrews and to the excellence of British design and workmanship. The War Cabinet has noted with satisfaction the damage done to German war power.'

Every bomber crew flying to the old bombing ground of Happy Valley knew henceforth that it was engaging in one of the major air battles of the war. The Ruhr was now a delineated battlefield. In such fashion had the mighty air offensive of the RAF grown in the course of a single year. On 23 May the biggest bomb load ever dropped anywhere in a single night – more than 2,000 tons – fell on luckless

Dortmund. The entire Ruhr shuddered when its most easterly town was subjected to this fearful pounding. It was another night of records, for that night the total weight of bombs delivered on Germany by Bomber Command in the course of the war rose to 100, 000 tons. Concentration broke another record. The great weight was dropped in the space of a single hour, between one and two in the morning. Planes all but jockeyed one another for position on the bombing run. For instance, Sergeant Ray Foster, rear-gunner in a Lancaster, was startled to see the starboard wing of another Lancaster flash by in front of his own tail-plane. The tip of the bomber's wing passed between the trailing edge of another bomber's main-plane and the leading edge of its tail-plane. 'I could have shaken hands with the bomb-aimer in the other Lancaster,' said Foster.

Flight Lieutenant H. C. Lee, of Felixstowe, piloting another Lancaster, made his attack late in the raid, but before then had circled round the target for nearly an hour, awaiting his turn. He was startled just as much as Sergeant Foster. 'As I made my attack,' he said later, 'a Stirling came streaking out only 50 feet above us and we were bumped by its slipstream. By this time it was difficult to believe that it was a real town below; the place was so covered with fires and smoke.' The next morning came more congratulations and another promise from the Commander-in-Chief, addressed to all the crews in Bomber Command.

'In 1939 Goering promised that not a single enemy bomb would reach the Ruhr,' Sir Arthur reminded them. 'Congratulations on having delivered the first 100,000 tons on Germany to refute him. The next 1,000,000, if he waits for them, will be even bigger and better bombs, delivered more accurately and in a much shorter time.'

The prospect was one of happier days ahead for Happy Valley.

Notes
1. On the night of 16/17 September 1942, 369 aircraft including aircraft from the training groups attacked Essen. Thirty-nine aircraft – 21 Wellingtons, nine Lancasters, five Stirlings, three Halifaxes and one Whitley, were lost – 10.6 per cent of the force. Many towns were hit, in particular, Bochum with 50 fires and Wuppertal, Herne and Cochem, a small town on the Moselle, 90 miles south of Essen.
2. A Bomber Command directive was now issued whereby crews stood down from night flying would be employed on daylight intruder sorties to keep the German sirens wailing and disrupt industry by driving the workers into air raid shelters. The RAF crews' only protection was cloud cover and it was essential that there was sufficient cloud to hide in. A Wellington was no match for a German fighter and all aircraft captains had strict orders to return to base if the cloud cover broke up. On 22 October 22 Wellingtons were on cloud-cover raids to Essen, the Ruhr and the Dortmund-Ems Canal at Lingen. Thirteen aircraft bombed estimated positions through cloud. One of the Wellingtons came down low and machine-gunned a train near Lingen, setting some of the carriages alight. No aircraft were lost.
3. On the night of 5/6 March, 442 aircraft, 157 of them Lancasters and *Oboe*-equipped Mosquitoes, began what has gone into history as the starting point of the Battle of the Ruhr. Fourteen aircraft – four Lancasters, four Wellingtons, three Halifaxes and three Stirlings – were shot down and 38 other bombers returned with damage.
4. For most of the way out the route was cloudy but 15 miles from the target the weather cleared, although pilots reported valley mists were still seeping in from the river. The eight *Oboe* Mosquitoes marked the centre of the city perfectly with red TIs and the Pathfinder

'backers up' arrived in good order and dropped their green TIs blind on the target. Only if there were no reds visible were the Main Force to bomb the 'greens'. These were followed by the first 'cookies', which wailed down and then erupted with violence and flame and the raid was well under way. The valley mists and industrial haze did not affect the outcome of the raid, which was bombed in three waves with the Lancasters bombing last, the entire weight of the raid being concentrated into a volcanic 45 minutes. Fifty-six aircraft turned back early because of technical problems and other causes.

5. Four hundred and fifty-seven aircraft – 158 Wellingtons, 156 Lancasters, 91 Halifaxes, 42 Stirlings and 10 Mosquitoes – were dispatched to Essen.

6. Twenty-three aircraft – eight Lancasters, seven Halifaxes, six Wellingtons and two Stirlings were lost.

7. Puddephatt and his crew of 77 Squadron were KIA on the night of 13/14 May 1943 on the raid on Bochum when Hauptmann Herbert Lütje of III./NJG1 shot down their Halifax.

8. 'Scarecrow' shells were said to be anti-morale shells, fired in the path of a bomber stream to dishearten the crews. They represented aircraft being blown up. As they burst nearby, they showered flaming oil and petrol, together with the Pathfinder flares and colour signals carried by RAF aircraft. In fact all the symptoms of an exploding aircraft. Briefings referred to the probability of 'scarecrows'. Having been briefed crews would report that 'scarecrows' were active tonight. They saw them often and said how realistic they were. Crews wondered how the Germans could portray an exploding aircraft so accurately. At the end of the war, when German anti-aircraft personnel were interrogated, it was discovered that they had no such thing in their armoury. The 'scarecrows' were real RAF aircraft blowing up.

9. Born on 12 August 1918 at Simla, the son of an official in the Imperial Indian Forest Service, Gibson was educated at St George's School, Folkestone and St Edward's School, Oxford, before being commissioned into the RAF in 1936. His first posting was to 83 Squadron as a bomber pilot. He was awarded the DFC in July 1940. In September 1940 Flight Lieutenant Gibson was posted to instruct at an OTU before transferring to 29 Squadron flying Beaufighter night fighters. In 99 operational sorties Gibson shot and claimed three enemy aircraft destroyed and was promoted to squadron leader with a bar to his DFC on completion of his second tour in 1941. After a short spell of instructing he had taken command of 106 Squadron.

10. Harold Brownlow Morgan Martin, born at Edgecliff, New South Wales on 27 February 1918, was probably the RAF's greatest exponent of low-level bombing. In Australia he had been pronounced unfit to fly because of asthma but he worked his passage to England, where he joined the RAF in 1940. Martin was commissioned in 1941 and he then served with 455 Squadron RAAF. He was transferred to 50 Squadron, with whom he flew a further 23 operations before being taken off operational flying and awarded the DFC.

# Chapter 8

# Boston Tea-Party Escorted –
# Bruce Sanders

On 9 March 1942 a brief announcement was made in the British Press which was probably missed by most readers. 'Yesterday's daylight bombing raids over France were carried out by American-built Douglas Bostons, which are now coming into service with Bomber Command.[1] It will be remembered that aircraft of this type have for some time been doing excellent work with Fighter Command, where they are known as Havocs.'[2]

The Havocs of Fighter Command were famous as night intruders, the planes that flew across after dark to lie in wait over enemy aerodromes for returning bombers. They and the Hurricane night intruders, as flown by the famous pair of intruder pilots, Flight Lieutenant Karel Kuttelwascher[3] and one-armed Squadron Leader J.A.F. MacLachlan, had won deserved fame.[4] The Bostons, escorted by Spitfires of Fighter Command during daylight hours, were to provide another logical development of the increased offensive in the air that began after the winter of 1941–42. Month by month the RAF was growing stronger. Week by week the bomb load it was carrying to the enemy was increasing in weight. Day by day its scope widened, its operations produced more gratifying results and the enemy was retreating farther south from the Channel skies.

Now a tactical fusion of commands was attained. What might be called the Battle of the English Channel was to be won finally when Bomber Command and Fighter Command joined forces and fought together in a common strategic plan.

Fighter Command's Spitfires were to provide escorts for the Boston medium bombers. They would tackle any Messerschmitts or Focke-Wulfs that attempted to intercept the bombers. The bombers would be left free to drop their bomb loads as ordered, on factories and power plants, on airfields and military buildings, on locomotive sheds and marshalling yards. Other forces of fighters would go strafing on diversionary sweeps, to use up the enemy fighter force and ensure a greater freedom for the bomber force. It was a well balanced plan of attack, full of punch, and it promised the RAF's young pilots the chance to go in and mix it with an enemy who had been showing considerable reluctance to come up and fight. The RAF wanted nothing better than to smite the Luftwaffe, to bring the German airmen within the view of their gun sights. The boot was on the other foot now. In the autumn of 1940 during the Battle of Britain, the RAF was on the defensive. It was on trial for its very life. The position had changed full circle. The Luftwaffe was on the defensive. Perhaps on trial for its life.

The outcome was bound to be interesting and exciting. So the Bostons made rendezvous with the Spitfires and, linking forces, roared over the Channel to attack the coastal ports and make life generally intolerable for the German garrisons. They had a few wrinkles to learn, as was only to be expected. But they learned fast. The wrinkles were memorized and smiles appeared. Mistakes were quickly rectified and rapidly a sound system of cooperative tactics was evolved. At first, for instance, the German fighters coming up to engage, got through to tangle with the Bostons.[5] Later on they never had the chance, for the Spitfires extended their cover into a veritable envelope.

One such day when the German fighters got through to the Bostons was 25 April. That day the Bostons, escorted, made several attacks in both the morning and the afternoon. They swept down over Cherbourg, then over Le Havre and another force dived on Dunkirk. Focke-Wulfs came up to greet the self-invited guests and these new speedy German fighters showed how they could manoeuvre in the fury of a dog-fight. There were not many of these intrepid Luftwaffe pilots but those who came up had an advantage. They attacked from the sun. This was the strategy employed by a couple of Focke-Wulf pilots over Dunkirk. Streaking out of the bright sunlight, they weaved through the fighter guard and began diving on the Bostons. They closed to within 100 yards before peeling off to starboard. Nowhere was the opposition of any real strength. It was chiefly of nuisance value. At Cherbourg the Bostons got right down over their target and the fighter pilots saw the bombs exploding on the submarine stores and straddling the docks.[6] The heaviest of the three raids was on Le Havre, the French naval base. There the Bostons did a good job of work. When they got back, after parting with the fighters, one young pilot enthusiastically reported to an intelligence officer that they had gone through quantities of German fighters and clouds of flak. He vividly described how a terrible burst of fire broke 'just where we had been a moment earlier'. His squadron leader happened to be an old stager and renowned for his reticence. His bombs got right home on their target but he claimed nothing for them because a small cloud at 3,000 feet had momentarily obscured his view. Most of his answers comprised one word. The intelligence officer tried hard to get a more comprehensive picture of the attack.

'Anything else of interest?' he inquired, looking up.

The squadron leader fingered his chin, frowning.

'What sort of thing – flak, for instance?'

'What about flak?' asked the intelligence officer, seizing on the suggestion.

'Well, the flak was there.'

'Thank you. This is more like a grilling than an interrogation,' he smiled at the squadron leader. 'Was there much flak?'

'Yes.'

'Fighters?'

'Oh, yes, there were fighters.'

'How do you know they were enemy fighters?'

The squadron leader rubbed his chin again and thought for a moment. 'They had

The port of Brünsbuttel, target for the Wellingtons on 4 September 1939. (*RAF Honington*)

Sergeant Frank Petts, a Wellington pilot on 9 Squadron. (*Petts*)

Group Captain Percy C. Pickard DSO DFC (left) a brave and revered leader, who as a Flight Lieutenant he and Wellington F-Freddie had appeared in the British wartime film, Target for Tonight. Pickard and his navigator Flight Lieutenant J.A. 'Peter' Broadley DSO DFC DFM (right) flying F-Freddie, a 487 Squadron Mosquito, were killed on the Amiens prison raid (Operation Jericho) on 18 February 1944.

A WAAF plotter. A total of 91 WAAFs died while on duty during World War II. (*via Andy Bird*)

Sergeant Alfred Jenner in the front turret of his 99 Squadron Wellington at Newmarket Heath in 1940. (*Alfred Jenner*)

(Below) Sergeant Basil Sidney Craske, a Whitley V pilot on 10 Squadron, 4 Group at Leeming Bar in North Yorkshire, who was flying Z6805, on his 27th op, to Cologne on the night of 16/17 August 1941, when he was shot down by Oberleutnant Wolfgang Thimmig of 2./NJG1 near Winterswijk 20 km NE of Bocholt. (*Basil Craske*)

Whitley I K7188 of 10 Squadron, which introduced this bomber type into RAF service in 4 Group at Dishforth, Yorkshire in March 1937 where it replaced the Heyford biplane bomber. (K7188 had been delivered to the squadron in 1937 and it was SOC on 10 October 1940). Whitleys were finally retired from Bomber Command in spring 1942. (*AW*)

Squadron Leader Terence 'Hawkeyes' M. Bulloch DSO DFC an Ulsterman from Lisburn, County Antrim, who was credited with sinking three U-boats and severely damaging two more. He became the most highly decorated pilot in RAF Coastal Command, credited with sinking more U-boats than any other pilot.

A 311 (Czech) Squadron Wellington crew.

Fortress II FL459/J of 206 Squadron with underwing and nose ASV (Air to Surface Vessel) radar antennae at Terceira, Azores in late 1943. Altogether, Coastal Command Fortresses sank twelve U-boats in World War Two.

Flight Lieutenant Kenneth Owen 'Kayo' Moore, a Canadian pilot in 224 Squadron, the only man to sink two U-boats in a single sortie, on 8 June 1944.

Liberator GR.IIIs of 120 Squadron at Aldergrove near Belfast. (*IWM*)

Flying Officer M. A. 'Mike' Ensor DFC* a New Zealander on 500 County of Kent Auxiliary Squadron who on 15 November 1942 sank U-259 35 miles north of Algiers, which was lost with all 48 hands.

Flight Lieutenant William Roxburgh DFC who piloted Fortress FK195/L of 206 Squadron on 25 March 1943 when he sank U-489 with depth charges during his patrol. (*IWM*)

Wellington XIIs of 221 Squadron, Coastal Command. (*RAF Museum*)

U-426 sinking by the stern on 8 January 1944 after a depth charge attack by Sunderland U-Uncle of 10 Squadron RAAF flown by Flying Officer J. P. Roberts. (*IWM*)

Catalina gunner manning the twin VGO .303 inch machine guns in the right blister in April 1941. (*IWM*)

Consolidated Catalina JX637. (*Boeing*)

Short Sunderland flight deck showing the pilot at the controls while the second pilot uses an electrical apparatus for signalling. Radio was not used as information might be picked up by enemy submarines. During a coastal defence patrol the flying-boat covered an average of 1,700 miles. (*IWM*)

Short Sunderland IIIA powered by Bristol Pegasus XVIII engines, which flew for the first time (W3999) on 15 December 1941. (*Shorts*)

A Lancaster crew pose for the camera in front of G-George.

Bombing up a Lancaster.
(*via Andy Bird*)

Rolls-Royce Vulture engined Avro Manchester BIA L7515 of 207 Squadron, RAF Waddington, November 1941. This aircraft was SOC on 6 November 1943. Initial batches of the Manchester were built with triple fins but with the IA the centre fin was deleted. Total production of the Manchester was 209, additional contracts for 300 Manchesters being cancelled. The Manchester's last Bomber Command operation was on the 1,000 bomber raid on Bremen on the night of 25/26 June 1942, when 20 were despatched, after which the type was withdrawn. (*BAe*)

Flight Lieutenant Dave J. Shannon DSO DFC RAAF, Flight Lieutenant Algernon Trevor-Roper DFC DFM, Gibson's rear gunner and Squadron Leader George Holden DSO DFC* MiD. Shannon was among those awarded the DSO for the Dam's raid. Holden, who as CO of a Halifax squadron had flown on raids over the Alps to Italy, took command of the Dam Busters' in July 1943. Squadron Leader George Holden was killed on the night of 15/16 September on the raid on the Dortmund-Ems Canal at Ladbergen. Trevor-Roper was KIA on the Nuremburg raid on 30/31 March 1944.

A Lancaster crew all smiles after bellying in at their home airfield. (*via Andy Bird*)

Halifax I crews having a cuppa from the YMCA tea wagon. (*IWM*)

Over Cologne on 28/29 June 1943 Halifax HR837 ND-F for Freddie of 158 Squadron had a bomb pass right through the fuselage without exploding. HR837 was repaired and served with 1656 HCU before it was SOC on 11 January 1945. (*IWM*)

Halifax II W7676 TL-P of 35 Squadron, which was lost with Sergeant D.A.V. John and his crew (all KIA) on the night of 28/29 August 1942 when it was hit by flak and crashed into the Westerschelde off Koewacht in Zeeland, Holland on the operation to Nuremberg. Of the 159 aircraft despatched, 23 including two Halifaxes and 14 Wellingtons were lost. Bombing was very accurate, crews having been ordered to bomb from as low as possible as Pathfinder aircraft marked the target with target indicators (adapted from 250lb bomb casings), for the first time. (*Flight*)

Stirling III EF464 ZO-P of 196 Squadron took off from Witchford, Cambridgeshire on 4 October 1943 but evasive action en route to Kassel caused the engines to over-rev and the port outer failed. Flight Sergeant G. H. Kogel, the pilot, turned back and made it across the North Sea but one mile from RAF Coltishall, a fighter station near Norwich, the port inner also failed and at 2143 hours the Stirling hit trees and crashed at Scottow, a small village near the airfield. Sergeant T. L. Dickie was killed and Sergeant C. D. Williams, who was severely injured, recovered and later flew on 514 Squadron. (*via Mick Jennings*)

During a 'Bullseye' on 6 November 1943, Stirling R9192 of 1657 HCU at Stradishall (an ex-75 and 15 Squadron aircraft) collided with Wellington III X3637 of 27 OTU in shadow of cu nim cloud at about 2000 hours. The Wellington, which took off from Lichfield at 1940 hours for an evening navigation detail, crashed at Raden Stick Farm, Little Walden, 2 miles north of Saffron Walden in Suffolk. The all-Australian crew including the pilot, Pilot Officer M. E. McKiggan RAAF were killed. R9192 was captained by Flying Officer D.W. Thomson RNZAF. Also on board were Flying Officer Vern L. Scantleton DFC RAAF, QMSII Colley and Flight Sergeant W. Mitson, army gunners for experience of AA. The Stirling, which returned to Stradishall and landed safely, was SOC on 12 June 1944. (*CONAM*)

Squadron Leader Smithers and his crew of Stirling W7455 OJ-B of 149 Squadron at Mildenhall on 15 January 1942. That night, 15/16 January, 96 aircraft set off to bomb Hamburg for the second night running. Three Wellingtons and one Hampden were lost and eight further aircraft crashed in England. This Stirling later passed to 1657 HCU and it was written off in September 1943 after being attacked by a Messerschmitt 410 intruder over Suffolk. (*Flight*)

Typhoon IB JP128 HF-L of 183 Squadron. (*Hawker Siddeley*)

Wing Commander Ian R. Gleed
DFC. (*IWM*)

a hostile appearance,' he explained. That reply became a classic, quoted on air stations all over the country as worthy of inclusion in the line-book of any mess.[7]

The regular afternoon offensives of the Bostons became 'tea parties' to their crews. Certainly as the fighter screen became of finer mesh and the chance of the most daring German airman slipping through, to get at the bombers, dwindled to a mere theoretical possibility, the description was not altogether unfitting. The Bostons, with their high-raised tails, making them look rather like miniature flying boats without floats, made their attacks with the regularity of a well-organized train service. The perfecting of the fighter-escorted bomber sweep allowed a wider range of operations. The Bostons began to penetrate deeper into occupied territory, sweeping over the coast and continuing to a target 60 or 70 miles inland. For the Germans, at any rate, this was a startling development. They saw plenty of trouble ahead and, as it proved, there was nothing wrong with their eyesight. They put up a show of resistance but it was beaten down by bombers and fighters alike. The days of air supremacy for the RAF were approaching and the pilots on those offensive sweeps over the Channel and into occupied territory felt the change coming and did all they could with gun and bomb, nerve and skill to hasten it, as on the day Spitfires escorted [18] Bostons to a 'tea party' at Lille [*Circus 141* on 27 April].

It was not a very formal affair, but a good time was had by all save the hosts. The Bostons were over France for 23 minutes, according to the log books when they returned. It was pointed out later that a similar offensive sweep carried out by German aircraft on Britain would have brought them to Guildford after, say, crossing the coast at Worthing and then, after bombing, sweeping across Surrey and Sussex and re-crossing the coast at Beachy Head.

In short, the Battle of Britain in reverse, except in the matter of results.

Over Lille the Focke-Wulfs came up and nosed through the flanking fighters. The Bostons were ready for them. A gunner in the leading Boston saw a German plane streak out of the sun a quarter of a mile away. He saw that the Fw 190 was hurtling to attack a bomber behind him and he turned the tables and played interceptor:

'He was coming in to attack the third Boston in formation. I got him in my sight and held my fire until he was 50 yards off. Then I fired and went on firing until he was only 10 yards from the Boston he was attacking. I could see bullets cutting into his fuselage all the time I was firing. Suddenly he turned completely over and dived straight down, with smoke coming from him. I watched him until he had fallen 4,000 feet below us. The Boston he had attacked got safely home.

'Another Fw 190 came up furiously from astern, cannon shells pouring from it in a continuous stream. The gunner of the attacked Boston sighted and returned the fire steadily. He saw his bullets spattering the Focke-Wulf's engine cowling. As I was firing I could hear the crackle of the enemy's bullets against our fuselage. One cannon shell exploded on our port propeller and knocked a chunk out of it. I don't think we were hit any more. Then there was a crimson burst above us, which warned the enemy fighters to keep off and warned us that flak was coming up. It was fairly accurate, but did not interfere with our bombing run.'

There was not much the German defences could do to interfere with the Bostons' bombing runs. The target at Lille was a chemical factory. When the bombers turned back for home, the German war effort was minus the output of that factory. While the bombers were going in over the target the Spitfire escort was finding plenty of work to be done on the fringes of the town. It comprised two wings, a British and a Polish. The British wing tangled with a score of enemy fighters and the skirmishing and manoeuvring kept up until the French coast was reached on the return journey. The Poles, with their accustomed dare-devilry, followed the bombers over the target through an intense flak barrage and more German fighters came up, until there were about 40 trying to break up the RAF formations of bombers and fighters. There was a sprawling mêlée of bullet spitting machines zooming and diving and banking and flattening out through thousands of feet of sky.

A Spitfire squadron commander destroyed a Focke-Wulf and then one of the Bostons [flown by Flying Officer W. A. Keech RCAF of 226 Squadron] got a bad hit [by flak]. Orders crackled over the intercom and eight Spitfires detached themselves from the milling formation to close-guard the damaged bomber. But the Boston was not able to keep aloft. It went down to make a forced landing after lagging behind the others and the eight fighters turned to battle their way home through fresh swarms of enemy machines sent to cut them off. Seven of the eight got back after avenging one of their number that was shot down.[8] They badly damaged two of the enemy and with concentrated fire literally sawed the tail off another, sending it down to earth in a vertical dive. The Germans had had a stomach full that day. When, in the late afternoon, more Spitfires returned over the Channel there was not a single enemy fighter to greet them. They had the skies to themselves. 'We cut ourselves a slice of cake with our tea to-day,' was how one of the Boston pilots felt about the show when he returned after the bombing.

Calais, Rouen and the docks at Cherbourg received regular attention from the Douglas Bostons. On many occasions during the spring these were escorted by the Middle Wallop Spitfire wing commanded by Wing Commander Ian R. Gleed DFC.[9] One of Fighter Command's ace commanders, he taught his men to stick close to the bombers and not to be lured away by the chance of attractive dog-fights. On one occasion [25 April] after the Bostons had plastered the Cherbourg docks, causing a great column of jet-black smoke to rise from the basin area, Gleed was quick to avenge a stricken bomber.

'It was impossible for us to see the full extent of the damage as it was just then that the fighter opposition got in among us. One of our bombers was shot down, but I got the man who did it and a Polish pilot of another squadron above us got another. After that most of the Germans kept away. We had very little opposition to meet with on the return journey.'[10]

When Fighter Command chaperoned the Bostons to attack the docks at Flushing [on 30 April] it staged its biggest single offensive of the war to that date – and brought every bomber back safely.[11] It was a brilliant piece of the new kind of combined work. Spitfires were under, above and all round the bombers for most of the journey, like an enormous suit of aerial chain mail. 'As the Bostons swung in to attack,' one of the Spitfire pilots was able to report, 'I saw the bombs go down. We watched the explosions and clouds of smoke, which followed and next saw another load go smack in the middle of some large buildings. Even larger explosions then occurred and the last I saw was direct hits on the pier, which must have been badly damaged.'

That day the Focke-Wulfs were aggressive. Thirty of them staged a fight at 20,000 feet but lost one of their number and had several others damaged. One Czech pilot officer who had previously had experience with the French Air Force in France was set upon by five Fw 190s after going to the rescue of a Czech sergeant. The sergeant [J. Hlouzak of 313 Squadron flying a Spitfire Vb] was being attacked vigorously by one German machine, which was covered by two others. It looked like a neat little trap of the old-style Richthofen kind. The pilot officer promptly attacked the leading Focke-Wulf and the German broke away. Five Fw 190s then milled round the sergeant. The pilot officer went through the entire German formation like a mean streak of vengeance. He beat off four, sending them wheeling all over the sky and he sent the fifth limping away. Then he saw why the sergeant had been the object of so much attention. He was having trouble with his engine. Whereupon the pilot officer flew after him and covered his retreat all the way back to England. 'He is a very brave pilot,' said the Czech squadron leader simply, speaking of the pilot officer later.

The Germans, in fact, never quite forgot how the RAF's famous 'Few' in the Battle of Britain successfully tore through the Luftwaffe's fighter screens and got at the bombers, clawing the Dorniers and Heinkels and Junkers out of the sky in fiery little shreds over the Kentish Weald. They fondly thought history would repeat itself over the brown-furrowed fields of enslaved France. They thought so when they rose in a cloud at midday on 28 April over St Omer.[12] Fifty of them, stepped up in layers, the better for diving to engage, desperately tried to get at the Bostons, hugged like a snug nut kernel within an enfolding sand bell of Spitfires. 'A horde of Huns' was how one pilot described the swarming mass of the enemy. Very soon fights were being decided in every corner of the cloudy sky. Swastika-crossed and target-ringed fighters fell out of the sky, guns blazing to the end, for that day it was bitter scrapping. The German nutcrackers squeezed with every ounce of firepower they could muster to break that Spitfire shell and get at the bomber heart of the British force. They were wasting their time. The bombs fell on the target and every Boston was brought back safely to Britain. A noisy tea party, but a party nonetheless.

The next day a gale raged over the Channel coasts. Spitfires took their [six] Bostons to Dunkirk to continue the offensive and although there was plenty of fire from the ground, not a single German fighter took-off to engage the invaders.

The Luftwaffe was learning to make one fight last a long time. It remained grounded the next day too [30 April], when a British force of Bostons and Spitfires went to Le Havre.[13] The flak was heavier than it had been but it provided the only opposition. On this occasion a Boston [flown by Pilot Officer Allen of 107 Squadron from Great Massingham] got safely home because a Spitfire pilot helped it to land. The bomber was the leader in the formation. It was going in for its bombing run when flak smashed the window and glass fragments struck the observer in the face. His head was jerked back from the bombsight, over which he had been crouching and for a moment he thought his eye had been cut out of his head. However, he got down to the bombsight again and observers in the following bombers saw the first plane's bomb load straddle the target. As the Boston flew on the air-gunner reported oil pouring from the port engine. The pilot banked steeply and as the machine approached the French coast again switched it off. But flying on only one engine he could no longer keep the leading place in the formation. He signalled number two to take over the lead and the formation, which had completed its bombing, flew on steadily past him and the damaged Boston limped along as best it could on the starboard engine. But the crippled plane was not alone. A full squadron Spitfires was giving it cover. 'We flew home on the one engine,' the pilot reported. 'My airspeed indicator was gone but a Spitfire helped to land. He signalled my speed to me as we went down and so on till we were safely on the ground.'

There's no pal like the friend who gets one home after a party. Occasionally other pieces of excitement intruded, as when two famous Fighter Command officers, Group Captain Barwell DFC and Wing Commander J. Rankin, DSO DFC*[14] took the Spitfire escort with [six] Bostons on another trip to Le Havre [power-station, on 4 May]. The Group Captain, a Warwickshire man, had made the headlines some months before. In the previous August he had crash-landed when his Spitfire cut out and broke his back. In hospital his back had been set in plaster of Paris but within a week he had gone back to his beloved Spitfires and, in September, was flying on local patrols, as he put it, 'to get his hand in again'. He flew, his back encased in plaster-of-Paris, for 17 weeks.[15] This is what one of the Spitfire pilots had to say when he returned from the Le Havre attack:

'The leader put us in such a position that we could watch the bombers and their immediate Spitfire escort and jump on any fighters that tried to attack them. On the way home, when our wing was several miles out to sea, we saw between 25 and 30 enemy aircraft below us and we were given the order to attack. We emerged from the fight with six enemy aircraft destroyed without loss to ourselves. Three were destroyed by [72] 'Basutoland' Squadron. These victories brought the squadron's bag to 101 enemy aircraft destroyed. You bet there will be a party of another kind to celebrate the squadron's passing the century mark. The Me 109 which Wing Commander Rankin destroyed gave out huge clouds of smoke and went down. Immediately afterwards he made another attack on a second Me 109. He went for this head-on but as he saw his shells the hitting the 109, he had to break away quickly to avoid a collision and he did not see what happened to the Hun. While the fight was going on, Group Captain Barwell found a Do 217, which chose the wrong moment to fly near Le Havre. The Group Captain gave it the whole of his cannon and machine-gun ammunition and it was followed down by a Basutoland pilot, who saw it crash.'

That new type German bomber, of the kind that was attacking the cities and towns of Britain at night, was something special for the day's menu. A couple of days later [on 6 May], announcing the day's sweeps, the Air Ministry chose these words: 'The impressive formations flew out to France together. And over the Channel the bombers divided and each with its escort made for its target – one to Calais and one to Boulogne. Not one of the Bostons was interfered with – their Spitfire escorts took good care of that. Indeed, all the bombers out, returned to their home bases in undisturbed formation.'[16] And the prime work of these bomber-fighter sorties was carried out effectively. The targets were pranged, as the leader of an Eagle Squadron reported the next day. 'I saw the bombs fall and they seemed to be concentrated well on the target. There was one terrific explosion and flame higher than I have ever seen broke out. As we were leaving the whole place was burning fiercely.'

That particular inferno was Zeebrugge.[17]

The routine continued with growing effectiveness and intensity throughout the summer months and the probing spearhead of the RAF's gathering offensive penetrated ever deeper and more destructively into the vital network of communications built up so painstakingly in the occupied countries. The Air Ministry announced the results of two months' steady and progressive striking at the enemy strung along the Channel coasts:

'Two million miles flown by Spitfires, the greater part over the English Channel or enemy-occupied France, tons of bombs dropped by escorted bombers on daylight targets, and 119 enemy aircraft destroyed.'

That was the tactical score for those two months. The résumé of the RAF's daylight activities throughout the period reviewed, contained this specific example of work by Bostons and their escorts:

'On one occasion a considerable force of Boston bombers attacked a target at Ostend. The Germans put up a strong fighter defence and there were many combats – so many, in fact, that our pilots were too busy protecting the bombers and attacking other fighters to see what happened to the majority of the enemy aircraft they engaged. One destroyed and two probables were the final claims; but cameras carried by our fighters later revealed that an additional 11 had been damaged. We lost one Spitfire… Hundreds of bombers were escorted during the two months to attacks on, amongst other targets, shipping in the ports of Ostend, Dunkirk, Boulogne and Le Havre. Considerable damage was done and at Le Havre direct hits were seen on a 7,000-ton merchantman. A number of direct hits were scored on shipyards at Le Trait; in addition, power-stations at Caen, Le Havre, Ostend and in the Lille area have been attacked and a number of direct hits scored. Marshalling yards at Hazebrouck and Abbeville have been bombed.'

The Luftwaffe in the occupied territories was stung into resisting and some of the best defence squadrons were ordered to fight back at the RAF's daylight storm troops. It made no difference to the result. The bomber sweeps went on. Attack squadrons of the Luftwaffe were brought back from the Russian front to stiffen the air resistance. The RAF asked nothing better than an adversary in its own class. Pilots of the calibre of Paddy Finucane[18] and Keith Truscott,[19] Hugo[20] and Gillam[21], thinned the Luftwaffe squadrons like a wheat field at harvest time. Indeed, that summer and early autumn of 1942 was a season of rich harvests for the day bombers and the fighters escorting them. One change brought about by the incessant day attacks was a greater employment by the German High Command of coastal shipping. With rail centres and marshalling yards repeatedly and consistently bombed, the overland routes became congested with frequent breakdowns. The solution appeared to be shipping. The RAF was ready for such a move. The Hudsons of Coastal Command attacked the ships while the Bostons of Bomber Command continued the good work along the coasts and inland, protected by the Spitfires of Fighter Command. The team work was brilliantly directed. German air aces of the fighting quality of Major Rudolph 'Rudi' Pflanz were ordered to go in and stop the RAF trip-hammer that was daily smashing down the German defences. Pflanz had 52 kills to his personal credit. Most of them, like Major Helmut Wick's impressive score of 56, were chalked up in Spain and Poland.[22] Pflanz took his squadron up to show the RAF how to fight when the

Spitfire-escorted Bostons arrived [on 12 July] over Abbeville; an old hunting-ground of the Channel sweepers.[23] As things turned out, Pflanz was no luckier than Wick, whose score he had seemed about to overhaul. Wick was shot down earlier by one of the most promising fighter pilots in the RAF, Flight Lieutenant John Dundas, off the Isle of Wight.[24] Pflanz never got back to base at Abbeville. He was sent spinning down in a death-dive somewhere over the Somme in a grim battle between 100 fighting planes. The Germans lost 11 that day, the RAF eight. The Bostons returned to England without loss, having done their bombing without interruption. By the end of the next month, August, American Flying Fortresses were joining in the Bostons' tea party. On the 29th the Air Ministry were able to open their bulletin in this way: 'Attacks on targets in occupied territory were made today by RAF Boston bombers and US Flying Fortresses escorted by Spitfires of the RAF and Dominions and Allied Air Forces. Target for the Bostons was the docks at Ostend. The Fortresses raided Wevelghem aerodrome near Courtrai, 40 miles south of Ostend. A number of combats resulted, in which two Fw 190s were destroyed and others damaged. All the bombers returned safely from these attacks. Despite very heavy flak the Bostons bombed accurately, bursts being seen by pilots of the fighter escort right on the docks and buildings.'[25]

There is a familiar ring to that announcement. It is the story that had been told daily for the past few months, with several additions. The story that was to be told regularly throughout the coming months, until in the following year the Ventura, the Mitchell and the Mosquito were to take on a considerable part of the daylight bombing previously handled by the Bostons. But even in the summer months of 1943 the Bostons were still making their attacks, escorted by a more heavily armed and faster Spitfire. But by that time the RAF had definite air superiority all along the Channel. On 15 January 1943 a Spitfire squadron leader who wore the ribbon of the DFC was able to take an interest in other things than flying when he flew as guard to the Bostons.[26]

'We kept well into the bombers all the way and, just as they were turning to come out, I saw several bombs explode right in the dock area at Cherbourg. There was a tremendous lot of flak but otherwise the show was rather uninteresting, because we saw no enemy fighters at all. However, it was very pleasant; nice, sunny and warm. I thought France looked lovely in sunlight.'

Pleasant trip – sunny and warm. In fact, all one could wish for any tea party.

Notes
1. At the beginning of 1942, 2 Group possessed just five bomber squadrons in Norfolk – two equipped with the de Havilland Mosquito B.Mk.IV and three with the Douglas Boston. On 5 January Wing Commander Alan Lynn DFC took over command of 107 Squadron at Great Massingham, while in Malta, Wing Commander Dunlevie RCAF and what was left of the squadron's Blenheims were waging war in the Mediterranean, where they would remain until the 12th. Training on the Blenheim continued until the first Boston III arrived at Massingham on 5 January. The new role for 107 Squadron (and 88 and 226, which also re-equipped with the Boston, at Attlebridge and Swanton Morley respectively) was to be high-level, pinpoint bombing with a dozen or more aircraft. For two months 107 and 226 Squadrons converted together, using the range at Brancaster on the Wash for firing practice. 226 Squadron was commanded by Wing Commander V. S. Butler DFC. They had been flying Blenheims at RAF Wattisham. Training in their new role took time and the Boston crews of

107 Squadron were not considered ready when Operation Fuller was mounted on 12 February. It was a vain attempt to prevent the 'Channel Dash' by the battle cruisers *Scharnhorst, Gneisenau* and *Prinz Eugen,* which were slipping through the English Channel from their French berths to Germany. Six of 226 Squadron's Bostons and four from 88 were involved. Only Flight Lieutenant Brian 'Digger' Wheeler and his crew in 226 Squadron found the German ships and they were beaten off by six of the escorting fighters. *The Reich Intruders* by Martin W. Bowman (Pen & Sword 2005).

2. The first Boston operation took place on Sunday 8 March with three raids on targets in France. In the early afternoon six Bostons of 226 Squadron at Swanton Morley, Norfolk led by Wing Commander V.S. Butler DFC and six from 88 Squadron at Attlebridge, Norfolk, took-off to make the first daylight-bombing raid of the war on Paris. The target, the Ford Motor Works at Matford near Poissy on the banks of the Seine. was turning out tanks and military vehicles for the Germans. Meanwhile, 107 Squadron provided six crews for a Circus operation to the Abbeville marshalling yards, escorted by the Kenley and Biggin Hill Wings in 11 Group. Fighters of 10 Group flew a diversionary operation and six more Bostons, three each from 88 and 107 Squadrons, attacked the Comines power station. The Matford works were at the extreme limit of the Bostons' range, so 88 and 226 Squadrons had to use Thorney Island on the south coast as a forward re-fuelling base. The Bostons had to fly at very low level to and from the target without fighter escort, which did not have the range to accompany them. All six 226 Squadron Bostons placed their bombs on the factory, though only two crews in 88 Squadron bombed the target but damage to the Matford Works was later estimated at 35–40 million French francs and it was out of commission for three months. The Boston flown by Wing Commander Butler hit trees and crashed, killing all the crew. This was the first operational loss of a Boston aircraft. Bowman, op. cit.

3. Flight Lieutenant Karel Miroslav Kuttelwascher joined the Czechoslovak Air Force in October 1934 at the age of 18 and clocked up 2,200 flying hours before the Germans occupied Czechoslovakia in 1939. Three months later, he made a dangerous and daring escape into Poland by hiding in a coal train. From there he was able to make his way to France where, flying Morane-Saulnier MS406 and Dewoitine D.520 fighter aircraft with the Armée de l'Air, he fought in the fierce but brief, Battle of France, claiming a number of German aircraft. When France fell, 'Kut' escaped to Britain via Algeria and Morocco and immediately joined the RAF. On 3 October 1940 'Kut' joined No.1 Squadron and became one of the 87 Czechoslovaks to fly with the RAF during the Battle of Britain. 'Kut' or 'Old Kuttel' as his fellow pilots affectionately called him served a full two years with 1 Squadron. During the early Circus operations in 1941 he shot down three Bf 109s and was credited with a 'probable. In July 1941 1 Squadron moved to Tangmere, three miles east of Chichester and it was from here that they commenced night intruder operations on 1 April 1942. The single seat Hurricane IIs were not equipped with AI radar equipment and the pilots flew long sorties of up to 3½ hours, with long range drop tanks fitted, often in poor conditions and completely alone. 'Kut' flew all his night intruder sorties in Hurricane IIc BE581 JX-E, which he christened *NIGHT REAPER*. In a brief three month period he cut down 15 enemy bombers over their own bases in France, including three Heinkel 111s in one night on 4/5 May and damaged a further five, and all this in only 15 night sorties. 'Kut' also shot up several E-boats and steam locomotives on nights when he had ammunition to spare on the way home. He was awarded the DFC and bar. Quite remarkably, the rest of the war was relatively uneventful for 'Kut'. While flying Mosquito night intruders he never even sighted another German aircraft. At the end of the war he returned briefly to Czechoslovakia but, in November 1946, on the day that the communists effectively took control of his homeland, he flew back to Britain to rejoin his English wife and family. He joined British European Airways flying Vickers Vikings as a first officer and, from 1951, as a captain. 'Kut' died of a heart attack on 16 August 1959. He was only 42.

4. James Archibald Findlay MacLachlan was born at Styal in Cheshire in 1919. He joined

the RAF on a short service commission in March 1939, and in November joined 88 Squadron on Battles, in France. He survived the operations of May 1940 and, after the withdrawal to England, transferred to Fighter Command in June. He received the DFC on 6 July for his activities in France as a bomber pilot, now serving with 73 Squadron until 20 August, when he went to 145 Squadron. He returned to 73 at the end of September, but, on 19 October, left the unit to join a reinforcement flight due to go to Malta. On 17 November he led six Hurricanes off HMS *Argus* to the island, at extreme range, two of his flight having to ditch when they ran out of fuel. Before seeing any action over Malta, he flew to Gibraltar in a Saro London flying boat where he undertook a number of patrols in a Swordfish. He returned to the island in a Sunderland on 5 January 1941 and thereafter, was very active over the island as a flight commander in 261 Squadron, claiming at least eight victories by early February when he was awarded a Bar to his DFC. On 16 February, however, he was shot down by a Bf 109E, baling out with his left arm shattered by a cannon shell, landing on the island after seven minutes in his parachute. By early March, following the amputation of his left forearm, he was sufficiently recovered to undertake some flights in a Magister. As soon as it could be arranged, he was evacuated back to the UK, where he attended the artificial limbs unit at Roehampton. Suitably fitted, he was posted to command 1 Squadron in November, undertaking a number of successful night intruder sorties with this unit, during which he claimed five victories, receiving a DSO at the end of May 1942. Two months later he was posted to OTU as an instructor, and then departed for the USA on a lecture tour. On return in June 1943 he joined the AFDU at Wittering. From here on 29 June, he undertook a low-level sortie over France in company with Flight Lieutenant Geoffrey Page DFC, both flying Mustangs. Between them they shot down six aircraft in 10 minutes south of Paris. On 18 July they commenced a second such sortie, covered by a flight of Typhoons, but as they reached the Dieppe area, smoke was seen pouring from MacLachlan's aircraft, although no enemy aircraft or ground fire was seen. He crash-landed at high speed in a small field, the aircraft shedding wings and tail before coming to a halt; no movement was seen. He had in fact been critically injured, and was removed to a German Field Hospital, where he died on 31 July. The previous day a second bar to his DFC had been announced. *Aces High: A Tribute to the Most Notable Fighter Pilots of the British and Commonwealth Forces in WWII* by Christopher Shores and Clive Williams (Grub Street London 1994).

5. Circus operations remained the order of the day and casualties were heavy. In April 107 Squadron alone lost seven aircraft from 78 sorties dispatched and 11 aircrew were killed. On 17 April, 88 and 107 Squadrons flew diversionary raids in support of Lancasters attacking Augsburg. Six Bostons from 88 Squadron bombed the Grand Quevilly power station near Rouen, while another six hit the shipyards nearby. Meanwhile, 107 Squadron attempted to bomb an artificial silk factory at Calais but their bombs were dropped on railway lines nearby and one of the Bostons was shot down into the sea by Bf 109s. Bowman, op. cit.

6. On 25 April all three Boston squadrons operated in concert with one another with two operations against French ports. 88 Squadron attacked Le Havre, while 107 bombed Morlaix airfield and harbour targets at Cherbourg and six Bostons of 226 bombed the dry docks at Dunkirk from 14,000 feet; buildings on the northern end of the Citadel Quay were hit. Two Bostons were lost. On the second raid of the day Fw 190s attacked 107 Squadron's Bostons and they also came under a heavy flak barrage. One of the Bostons, badly damaged, nevertheless managed to make it home minus part of its tail. Bowman, ibid.

7. Fourteen Spitfires were lost. *Fighter Command Losses Vol.2 1942–43* by Norman L. R. Franks. (Midland 1998)

8. Keech crash-landed at Raversijde (West Vlaaanderen) near Ostend. He and one other crew member survived to be taken prisoner. The third member of the crew was KIA. A second Boston, flown by Sergeant K. N. Carpenter of 107 Squadron, was shot down by Fw 190s. All the crew survived to be taken prisoners. Two Spitfires, including one flown by Sergeant Z. Kothera of 124 Squadron, were shot down. Oberleutnant J. Muncheberg of JG 26 flying

a Bf 109 claimed Kothera's Spitfire. Franks, op. cit.

9. He also commanded the Ibsley Wing. Flying Hurricanes May 1940–August 1941 Gleed destroyed 10 enemy aircraft, and three probably destroyed, before switching to Spitfire Vs and scoring a further three e/a destroyed and three probably destroyed. In May 1942 Gleed was awarded the DSO and in July was posted to Fighter Command, as Wing Commander Tactics. In December he was promoted to wing commander. In January 1943 Gleed was posted to the Middle East, where he was attached briefly to 145 Squadron for experience of operations in North Africa. He soon became Wing Leader, 224 Wing where he painted on the side of the fuselage below the cockpit of AB502 (which carried his initials IR-G) the same 'Figaro the Cat' cartoon that he had carried on his Hurricanes and Spitfires in the UK. On 16 April 1943 Wing Commander Ian Richard Gleed DSO DFC led a patrol over the Cap Bon area and a large formation of Axis transports was intercepted but escorting Bf 109s and Fw 190s shot down Gleed and his wingman. His Spitfire crashed on the Tunisian coast and Gleed was buried at Tazoghrane. His remains were later reburied in an Allied cemetery at Enfidaville. At the time of his death, Gleed's score stood at 13 and 3 shared destroyed, 4 and 3 shared/probably destroyed and 4 damaged. Shores and Williams, op. cit.

10. Gleed was credited with a Bf 109F damaged.

11. Twenty-four Bostons went to Le Havre and Flushing docks, Abbeville railway yards and Morlaix airfield. All targets were bombed without loss.

12. Circus 144. Six Bostons bombed St Omer railway yards accurately and without loss. Six Spitfires were lost.

13. Twenty-four Bostons to Le Havre and Flushing docks, Abbeville railway yards and Morlaix airfield. All targets were bombed without loss.

14. James 'Jamie' Rankin was born in Portobello, Edinburgh on 7 May 1913. He joined the RAF and was commissioned in 1935, becoming a flying officer in 1937, and was then attached to the Fleet Air Arm in 1939, but subsequently returned to the RAF as an instructor; he was a flight lieutenant at an OTU in June 1940. At the start of 1941 he was attached to 64 Squadron as a supernumerary squadron leader to gain some operational experience before being posted to command 92 Squadron in February. During the cross-Channel sweeps of 1941 his claims mounted rapidly, and he was awarded a DFC in June for nine victories and a Bar to this in August for 13. On 17 September he took over as Wing Commander Flying at Biggin Hill, receiving a DSO in October. His first tour ended on 17 December 1941 when he became Wing Commander (Training) at HQ, 11 Group, where he received a Belgian Croix de Guerre. In April 1942 he returned to Biggin Hill for a second tour as Wing Leader, which he completed in July with the award of a Bar to his DSO. In 1943 he was given command of 15 Fighter Wing in the new 2nd TAF, making one further claim while leading this unit. When the Wing was disbanded he commanded 125 Wing, leading this unit's Spitfires over Normandy during the invasion. He was promoted air commodore in 1945. Shores and Williams, op. cit.

15. Group Captain Philip Reginald Barwell DFC was born on 2 July 1907 at Knowle, Worcestershire. He joined the RAF in 1925. In June 1941 he took command of Biggin Hill. Sometimes he flew as No. 2 to 'Sailor' Malan on fighter sweeps. On 4 July 1941 Barwell shared a probable with Malan. A week later Barwell destroyed another enemy fighter. Early in 1942 Barwell's engine cut out on take-off and he crash-landed just beyond the runway and broke his back. Although he continued to fly he took no part in operations while in his plaster cast. On 1 July 1942 Barwell, in company with Squadron Leader R. W. 'Bobby' Oxspring, took-off from Biggin Hill an hour before sunset on a standing patrol between Dungeness and Biggin Hill. Control at Biggin Hill warned of unidentified aircraft in the area, which proved to be two Spitfires from Tangmere, flown by inexperienced pilots. Barwell, apparently oblivious to the warning, was attacked by one of the Spitfires and he was shot down into the sea. Although Oxspring saw him trying to open his hood, Barwell did not bale out. Despite intensive searches, no trace of him was found. Barwell's body was later washed

up on the French coast. *Men of the Battle of Britain* by Kenneth G. Wynn, (CCB Associates 1999).

16. Eighteen Bostons set out for Boulogne docks, Calais parachute factory and Caen power station. All targets were bombed without loss to the Bostons.

17. On 7 May, 12 Bostons went to the Ostend power station and the Zeebrugge coke ovens. Direct hits were scored at Zeebrugge, near misses at Ostend. No Bostons were lost.

18. Brendan Eamonn Fergus 'Paddy' Finucane was born in Dublin on 6 October 1920. Educated at O'Connell's Irish Christian Brothers School in Dublin he was a devout Roman Catholic, who reportedly took himself very seriously. Clearly he harboured no anti-British feelings, for after working briefly as a ledger clerk, he joined the RAF in May 1938. On completion of training, he was posted to 65 Squadron, seeing action with this unit during the summer of 1940 and spring of 1941. During this period he claimed five and one-shared victories, receiving a DFC on 13 May 1941. Meanwhile in mid-April he had been posted at a flight commander to 452 Squadron, which was just forming as the first RAAF fighter unit in the UK. He claimed this unit's first victory on 11 June, adding 17 and two shared by mid-October, receiving two Bars to his DFC during September and a DSO the following month. He then broke an ankle while jumping over a low wall in the blackout and was off operations until January 1942, when he was posted to command 602 Squadron. On 20 February his aircraft was hit by a Fw 190 and he was wounded in the leg, but again recovery was rapid, and he was back in action on 13 March. In another period of rapid claiming, he had added five and three shared to his total by the end of May. On 27 June he was appointed Wing Leader of the Hornchurch Wing, but on 15 July, while at the head of a formation exiting France at the end of a sweep, machine-gun fire from a gun position on the coast hit the radiator of his Spitfire. His wingman, Alan Aikman of 154 Squadron, dived down to strafe this, but as Finucane headed out over the Channel, his engine seized up due to coolant loss, and he attempted to ditch in the sea. The aircraft was seen to sink instantly on hitting the water, taking him down to his death. A telegram of sympathy was subsequently received from two of the Soviet Union's leading fighter pilots, Ivan Kholodar and Eugenyi Gorbatyuk. Shores and Williams, op. cit.

19. Keith William 'Bluey' Truscott, so nicknamed due to his red hair, was born in Prahan, Victoria, on 17 May 1916. After working as a clerk in South Yarra and playing Australian Rules football at senior level, he joined the RAAF in July 1940, undertaking most of his training in Canada. He reached the UK in March 1941, attending 57 OTU before being posted to the new 452 Squadron RAAF, as a pilot officer. In action during the cross-Channel sweeps of late summer and autumn 1941, he saw much action and made numerous claims, being credited with 11 destroyed and three probables by the end of the year, despite having been shot down into the Channel and rescued on 15 October. He was awarded a DFC, gazetted in March 1942. Meanwhile he had been promoted flight commander in October, while late in January 1942 he was given command of the unit, receiving a Bar to his DFC. On 17 March 1942 he left for Australia, now threatened by the Japanese. On arrival, after some leave, he converted to the Kittyhawk and was then posted to 76 RAAF Squadron as a supernumerary squadron leader, commanding a flight. The unit moved to New Guinea, where it was involved in much ground strafing, as the Japanese attempted a landing in Milne Bay. Subsequently it returned to Australia where, during the night of 20/21 January 1943, he intercepted three bombers over Darwin and shot one down. On 28 March he took-off to escort a returning Catalina flying boat, but while doing so, flew into the sea in his Kittyhawk and was killed instantly. Shores and Williams, op. cit.

20. Petrus Hendrik 'Piet' Hugo was born in Pampoenpoort, Cape Province, South Africa on 20 December 1917 and attended the Witwatersrand College of Aeronautical Engineering prior to travelling to the UK in 1938 to join the RAF on a short service commission in February 1939. On completion of training, he went to the Fighter Pool at St Athan and then 2 Ferry Pool at Filton, before joining 615 Squadron in France in December 1939. Known in

the RAF as 'Dutch', he was to claim one victory over France before the unit withdrew, but he was to add a number of successes during the Battle of Britain. On 16 August he was hit and slightly wounded in the legs by a Bf 110, whilst two days later he was shot down, crash-landing his Hurricane and being removed to hospital. A DFC was announced a few days later. He rejoined the unit in September, now out of the line, next seeing action during summer 1941 and becoming a flight commander in September. Operating over the Channel with cannon-armed Hurricane IIcs he took part in the sinking of over 20 ships and the destruction of three oil tankers, four distilleries and a railway locomotive. He was awarded a Bar to his DFC in November and during that month was posted to command 41 Squadron. In April 1942, when Wing Commander Michael Lister Robinson was killed on 10 April by Fw 190s of II/JG 26, he took over as Wing Leader at Tangmere. However during a fight with Fw 190s on 27 April 1942 Hugo was shot down, baling out into the Channel, wounded again. He was rescued and now received a DSO, gazetted on 29 May 1942. Posted to HQ, Fighter Command, on recovery, he resumed operations as Wing Leader at Hornchurch in July, following the loss of Paddy Finucane. However, his stay was brief, for he was posted to lead 322 Wing during the forthcoming invasion of French North-West Africa and here, during late 1942, he was to claim a further eight victories, two of them shared, and at least two probables. At the end of November he took command of 322 Wing, now as a group captain, holding the post until March 1943 and receiving a second Bar to his DFC during February. Posted to HQ, NW African Coastal Air Force, he returned to command 322 Wing in June 1943, leading it to Malta, Sicily, Italy and then out of the line to Syria for a time, subsequently returning to the active area, first in Corsica and then southern France. Finally the Wing moved back to Italy where it was disbanded in November 1944. He had continued to lead in the air wherever possible, adding several more successes to his long tally and undertaking much ground attack work. He then joined HQ, Mediterranean Allied Air Force, and was seconded to Marshal Tolbukin's 2nd Ukrainian Army in Romania and Austria. Returning to the UK towards the end of the war, he was posted to CFE. He remained in the RAF as a squadron leader, but with the acting rank of group captain, having added to his decorations a Croix de Guerre from France and a US DFC. Shores and Williams, op. cit.

21. Denys Edgar Gillam was born on 18 November 1915 in Teignmouth, Devon. He obtained his pilots' licence at the Public School Aviation Camp, Norfolk in September 1934, joining the RAF the following February. In March 1936 he was posted to 29 Squadron but a year later he was sent to the Meteorological Flight at Aldergrove in Northern Ireland. Here in June 1938 he received an AFC for flying food to Rathlin Island in a Westland Wapiti on two occasions when the island had been cut off from the mainland by gales. In September 1939 he was posted to 616 Squadron, the newest of the auxiliary units, to provide some 'stiffening' of experienced pilots. Whilst this unit suffered heavy casualties during the Battle of Britain, he emerged as its most successful pilot of the period. In his last action before the squadron was withdrawn (2 September) he had claimed one Bf 110 shot down when fire from another hit the engine of his Spitfire and set it alight, causing him to bale out. Four days later he was posted as a flight commander to 312 (Czech) Squadron and in November was awarded a DFC. In December he was posted to command 306 (Polish) Squadron, which he led until early March 1941 when he was posted to HQ 9 Group. He returned to operations in July 1941 at the head of 615 Squadron, undertaking attacks on coastal shipping with Hurricane IIcs. He received a Bar to his DFC in October but on 23 November was shot down by flak and baled out off Dunkirk, wounded in one arm and both legs; he was rescued by an ASR launch and, in December, was awarded a DSO. On recovery he was dispatched to the US on a lecture tour, on return from which in March 1942, he went to Duxford to form and lead the first wing of Typhoons. In October he attended the RAF Staff College, then going to HQ 12 Group, in February 1943. In August he returned to the US to attend the Command and General Staff School at Fort Leavenworth. At last in December 1943 he returned to operations as Wing Leader, 146 Wing in the new 2nd TAF, then commanding

Tangmere from January to March 1944, and 20 Sector, 2nd TAF in April 1944. In July he returned to 146 Wing to command as a group captain and in August was awarded a Bar to his DSO. On 24 October he led the Typhoons of his Wing against a building in Dordrecht where a conference of high-ranking German officers was underway, many officers of the 15th Army being killed. The award of a second Bar to his DSO in January 1945 brought a congratulatory note from his AOC, commenting that 'in World War I it would have been a VC'. In February 1945 he went to HQ 84 Group, as Group Captain Operations, where he remained until October, when he left the RAF. Shores and Williams, op. cit.

22. Helmut Wick's instructor during advanced training had been the great Werner Molders, who was also his StaffelKapitän in 1/JG53 from March 1939. Shortly after the beginning of the war he was transferred to l/JG2 and he scored his first victory on 22 November 1939. But only with the Blitzkreig did his score start to mount. He early showed a talent for multiple victories, with two French aircraft on 22 May 1940, two Swordfish torpedo bombers later that month (although these were unconfirmed for lack of a witness) and four Bloch 152s on 5 June and two more the next day. He ended the campaign behind Molders and Balthasar with a total of 14. He became Staffelkapitän of 3/JG2 Richthofen in July 1940; thereafter his rise was rapid. He reached 20 victories on 27 August, then on 7 September he was appointed Kommandeur of II/JG2. Wick was a remarkable natural marksman, with a gift for keeping track of events around him. If he had a fault, it was impetuosity, which often led him to tangle with the better-turning Spitfires and Hurricanes. He was promoted to Kommodore of JG2 on 19 October 1940. He claimed three victories on 5 November and five more the following day. On 28 November he finally passed Molders's score to become the – top-ranking 'Experte'. Later that same afternoon he led his Stab-schwarm out over the Channel on a Freijagd. A skirmish with Spitfires near the Isle of Wight saw his 56th victim go down, then Wick was bounced from astern by a Spitfire. His Bf 109 mortally hit, he baled out but was never found. His attacker, John Dundas of 609 Squadron, was almost immediately shot down by Wick's wingman Rudi Pflanz (eventual score 52).

23. Twelve Bostons bombed an airfield near Abbeville but results were not seen because of cloud. American crews in the 15th (Light) Bombardment Squadron flew in six of the Bostons, their last introductory flight with the Bostons of 2 Group. No aircraft were lost. The 15th (Light) Bomb Squadron had flown 13 sorties with 226 Squadron RAF, losing three crews.

24. John Charles Dundas was born in West Yorkshire, elder brother of Hugh 'Cocky' Dundas. Educated at Stowe and Christchurch, Oxford, he had graduated with First Class Honours in modern history, then spending a further year at the Sorbonne, Paris and at Heidelberg University. He then worked as a journalist on the *Yorkshire Post* and he joined 609 Squadron, Auxiliary Air Force, in 1938; he was mobilized with the unit in August 1939. He saw action over Dunkirk and during the Battle of Britain, being awarded a DFC on 9 October as the unit's top scoring pilot of 1940. On 28 November the Squadron engaged Bf 109Es off the Isle of Wight and he was heard to report, 'Whoopee, I've got one!' It transpired that he had shot down Major Helmut Wick, Kommodore of JG2 and at the time Luftwaffe top-scorer with 56 victories. Moments later, Dundas fell too, victim of Wick's wingman, Leutnant Rudi Pflanz, himself already a noted 'Experte'. Although Wick was seen to bale out, neither pilot survived. A Bar to Dundas' DFC was gazetted on 24 December.

25. Eighteen Bostons were dispatched – 12 to Ostend and six to Comines power station, both targets being bombed. One Boston and a Mosquito were lost on the day's operations.

26. Ten Bostons attacked a whaling factory ship at Cherbourg but scored no hits.

# Chapter 9

# The Flying Dutchmen – Bruce Sanders

On 1 May 1941 Sir Archibald Sinclair, the Secretary of State for Air, attended the Anglo-Batavian luncheon held in London. In the course of his speech he paid a tribute to a group of men who had, in the space of one brief year since the fall of their country, fought hard and well with their British comrades in the RAF – the flying Free Dutch:

'The Dutch airmen have been playing their part in the ceaseless watch and ward, which Coastal Command keeps round our coasts and shipping, work for which they were well fitted by their peace-time training among the Dutch islands and they have rendered great service carrying out those long, arduous sweeps over the sea which tax sorely a man's courage and endurance. They are here today in the ranks of those who are fighting the Battle of the Atlantic, a battle, which may well prove to be the most important of all. They are helping us to keep open the gateway to the West.'

The Flying Dutchmen did more than help to keep open the gateway to the west. They helped to push wide the door to the east when the RAF began its great air offensive. They flew with the bombers flying east, hitting back at the enemy that had spread like a great stain over the map of Europe. All over the world, Dutchmen living in freedom delved deep in their pockets to provide money for aircraft for these airmen of their race who had escaped to Britain, prepared to fight on like reincarnated Beggars of the Sea. The money poured into a fund and eventually purchased Lockheed Hudsons for the Royal Dutch Naval Air Service attached to Coastal Command. The Hudsons were presented to her countrymen by Queen Wilhelmina and very soon each had a grim decoration on its nose. An artist among the Dutch airmen had modernized the traditional figure of the stork carrying a baby suspended from a cloth in its beak. He kept the stork and the cloth but for the baby he substituted a bomb.

It was not long before these storks began unloading their cargoes. Nine days after Sir Archibald Sinclair spoke at the Anglo-Batavian luncheon on the night of 9/10 May 1941, they flew with Coastal Command Beauforts and Blenheims on a strafing expedition to the aerodromes at Kristiansand and Mandel in southern Norway. It was the first occasion on which the Dutchmen deliberately struck back offensively at the despoilers of their native land. Up to that time they had provided air escorts for shipping. Now a new life opened up for them. The attack was a gruelling one, made when the weather was not good and it was kept up throughout the hours of darkness. The Dutch roared in low over their targets, wheeling and banking as they came in from the sea and they dropped their bomb loads with good effect among the buildings and sheds round the airfields. They sprinkled wooden hutments with incendiaries and a stiffish wind whipped the flames into a crackling blaze. Into the fires they dropped HEs and bits of blazing debris were flung high into the air. The German gunners tried to get down to the work of destroying the intrepid invaders who had flown east across the North Sea but the Dutch were in their element. They gave the German defenders no chance to work up a concentrated fire. Again and again they whirled about the aerodromes, shooting up the pom-pom positions and making life for the machine gunners intolerable. When they got back they were bubbling over like schoolboys who had been on an outing. They were full of the thrill of paying back something for the many personal scores that remained to be settled. 'We have been waiting for a chance like this,' their squadron leader said gratefully. 'It was fine to be able to strike a real blow at the enemy.'

It was not long before the next blows followed. They were delivered on some of the Germans' most tender spots. Life for the Dutch began looking up. Frank Beresford was invited to join them and paint some pictures of life on their station, which would be kept as permanent records of their work with Coastal Command. Mr Beresford captured his subjects for sittings when he got them from spells of duty. He painted scenes and portraits. The latter included the commanding officer of the squadron (Lt. J. M. van Olm) who had been awarded the OBE, a famous Dutch airman with 19,000 flying hours in his log book and a flight lieutenant who already had the Dutch equivalent of the VC and the British DFC for performing a hazardous and secret enterprise of a very dangerous nature.[1] One of the most impressive pictures painted of the Free Dutch airmen was one Mr Beresford entitled *The Flag Flies Free*. It recorded the ceremony of breaking the Dutch national standard from the masthead in front of the squadron office on the anniversary of the German invasion of the Netherlands. Not that the Dutch needed reminders. They knew every minute of their flying time why they were in the air with bombs slung under their fuselage. They made it a point of honour rarely to waste those bombs. The Dutch took what to some might have been considered unnecessary risks, to ensure that their bombs fell truly. As on the night of 20 August Coastal Command had reported a German supply ship beating down the coast of southern Norway. One of the stork-nosed Dutch Hudsons, *De Vliegende Hollander* or The Flying Dutchman, sped to deal with the German merchantman. There was a great deal of low black cloud that night and picking out the ship was a tricky business. But she was located and the Dutch pilot made a preliminary run over the craft, so that his bomb-aimer could get an idea as to how the target showed up. This manoeuvre produced a stream of flak from the German machine gunners on board the merchantman. Undeterred by this, the Dutch pilot made another trial run over the target and more flak filled the air through which he flew. But at the end of that second run the bomb-aimer was ready for the job of hitting the target. He gave the word. The pilot swept over the ship for the third time. Up came the flak again. Down went the bombs. Those stork-delivered HEs straddled the ship, one crashing onto the deck dead amidships. Planking and pieces of deck furnishings were flung high into the air and a great dark column of smoke rose, was caught by the wind and smudged out the picture of the ship heaved to and listing in the sea. The Dutchmen returned home through the August night as full of joviality as though they had divided a bottle of schnapps.

After that the Dutchmen went ship hunting. It was a new sport, answering the call of their blood. Four centuries before, when the Duke of Alva was camped in their country, exiles like themselves had banded together to wreak vengeance on the foreign soldiery. The vengeance of the Beggars of the Sea, working from bases along the coasts of Britain, pouncing upon Alva's convoys, became a terrible red streak in history. These present day Beggars of the Sea struck in traditional fashion. They materialized out of the very clouds, struck their mortal blows and vanished as they came. The faith and will and courage that had been William the Silent's was all theirs. The luck that had been his they shared as another spiritual legacy.

The afternoon of 17 November 1941 was dark over the North Sea. Visibility was not good and the unbroken force of the wind had a biting snap to it. Through the murk, hunting for a possible victim, flew a Dutch sergeant pilot in a Lockheed Hudson. Away on his beam the occasional glimpses he caught of the distant coast of Norway, appeared unfriendly and hostile. It began to look as though he would have to return to base with his bombs unused, something that really lowered his spirits. Then, just as he was eyeing his petrol gauge thoughtfully he was attracted by a black mark against the low clouds, as though an artist had made a careless brushstroke on a grey canvas. He went down through the cloudbank. The black mark became a German supply ship escorted by a flak ship. The two vessels were steaming four miles off the Norwegian coast. Ahead the clouds broke. Down went the Hudson in a skimming dive, until it looked as though the pilot would not be able to flatten out in time. But he did, just above the tops of the curling waves. Amazingly he was unobserved by the German lookouts. He drove straight for the merchant ship, at the very last moment pulling back the stick and lifting his Hudson over the swaying masts. As he did so the bombs went down. Two of them landed squarely on the deck just fore of the bridge and as the Dutch sergeant raced away, wheeling to get out of range of the gunner of the flak ship, there were two large explosions from the stricken merchantman. A couple of flame-shot clouds of smoke rose from the vessel, merging into one broad column of fire-flecked blackness as the wind encouraged the blaze and the last glance the Hudson's crew had of the ship was her settling with a heavy list to port. Then, with the Dutch machine rapidly climbing out of range, the attack accomplished, the flak-ship belatedly opened fire – too late to be effective.

The surprise was 100 per cent. The bombing was probably the same, for an hour later another Hudson sped across the North Sea to make observations and when the crew got back they reported a 'constant red glow' from the position where the first Hudson's crew had last noticed the listing ship. Those were the days when the Germans were keen to get every ounce of supplies to the Russian front seaborne that could be stowed into the ships they had confiscated in the harbours of the countries they had overrun. The reason why so many of those heavily loaded freighters did not reach the Northern ports can be laid to the charge of the intrepid Dutchmen, who watched for the scurrying, furtive supply ships as eagerly as a cat lying in wait by a new-found mousehole.

The Germans increased the volume of flak, which greeted the appearance of the Hudsons of Coastal Command, but the modern Beggars of the Sea were not put off their aim by the threat of physical danger. They counted death a fair exchange for robbing the Germans of the means by which they waged war. They willingly died so that one day their beloved tulip fields would blossom and bloom in a free land. Six days after the brilliant attack on the escorted supply ship off the Norwegian coast, another attack on 23 November 1941 was made on a vessel deep-laden with vital supplies for the Russian front. The German ship was just off Lister when the captain of a Dutch Hudson sighted her. Not far off was a powerfully armed escort. A few hurried words in Dutch and the crew nodded their agreement to a hastily devised plan. The Hudson veered back towards the west, circling through a cloud formation and dropped into the very eye of a westering winter sun. Turning towards the supply ship, the Dutch pilot dived with the sun behind him. He went down from 1,300 feet to only 200. A stick of bombs swung clear of the diving Hudson just as the flak ship opened up a heavy fire. Even as the bombs were falling, the Dutch pilot cleverly checked his flight and turned, spraying the decks of the anti-aircraft vessel with his front guns.

The brave man died fighting. One of the last shells pumped up at the Hudson exploded just below the cockpit and a splinter killed the captain, Kwartiermeester C. A. E. van Otterloo. At the very moment he lurched forward over the controls there was a tremendous explosion in the merchant ship, somewhere just forward of the bridge and a thick black cloud of telltale smoke rose. It was his reply to the men who had slain him. The Hudson continued diving down and the observer, Officer vl. 2e kl. W. M. A. van Rossum, climbed over the dead captain's body to get at the controls. He was able to level off just before the plane's nose hit the dark sea. The Hudson trembled and for seconds seemed to hover, about to slip down into the water, but gradually it responded to the controls and climbed again. The remainder of the crew came forward and lifted the captain out of his seat. The observer dropped into his place his face set grimly. Only once before in his life had he flown a Lockheed Hudson. That had been in a training circuit on his home airfield. Now he set about the difficult task of getting the damaged machine back to Britain. It was a task that demanded all his powers of concentration and some measure of luck. The demand was supplied. That Hudson got back to base and those unnamed Dutchmen made their report and later followed their captain to his last resting place. Like the other pilots of Free Europe who were attacking the enemy in the van of the United Nations' air fleets, the gallant Dutch have to remain anonymous. Most of them had families somewhere in occupied territory and for them to be named would have brought German retribution upon the relatives they were fighting so desperately to free.

In the middle of December a sergeant-major of the Royal Netherlands Marine, a pilot with considerable flying experience, got another of those coast-hugging supply ships so badly needed by the German Northern armies. He too was flying a Hudson attached to Coastal Command and he was in that happy hunting ground of the flying Dutchmen, the seas off the Norwegian coast. He roared down to mast height and straddled the ship with delayed-action bombs. Three of them ploughed into the vessel's decks. He circled swiftly to observe the rest of the attack and saw the ship's crew in a wild scramble to lower the lifeboats.

'Some of them tried to lower the boats but most of them couldn't wait and jumped into the sea. I wondered what all the hurry was about, but found out in a few minutes. The ship blew up with a roar and a shower of debris and flames. I both felt and saw the explosion. It must have been a munitions ship and I don't wonder that the crew were in a hurry to get clear.'

Twenty-two year old Matr.2 (Seaman 2nd Class) Jaap Lub, a gunner in 320 (Dutch) Squadron in 1942, recalls:

'On 5 May 1942 I became a mid upper gunner in 320 (Dutch) Squadron on Lockheed Hudsons at Bircham Newton, Norfolk. The Hudson was terrible. It couldn't stick anything. No self-sealing tanks. It wasn't made for the anti-shipping strikes we flew, during the dusk and the dawn. Thank God we were never attacked by fighters: we would have stood no chance. Altogether, I flew 26 operations on Hudsons, all flown with an all-Dutch crew, mostly at night. (I later flew 75 more operations, on Mitchells, a much better aircraft.) My pilot was Ovl.2 (Officer Flyer 2nd Class) Tys de Groot, a bloody good pilot with whom I loved to fly. Observer was Ltz.3 Petri. I was a Matr.2 (Seaman 2nd Class) and our W/Op was Anthonie.

'Normally, we took-off at around 8 o'clock and returned after three hours. We usually flew at 4,000 feet over the North Sea, sometimes together with four or five others. Soon after taking-off you were on your "Jack Jones" (it was too dark to see one another). Losses were high because we flew at low level, belly on the water, straight at ships. Our targets were German convoys off Norway, France, Belgium and Holland. We'd take-off one after the other loaded with four 250lb bombs. We'd go for two lines of ships, left and right, straight and level. Usually, we approached from their stern. I never fired at ships. I used to save my ammo in case we were attacked by fighters. It wasn't necessary to rake a ship.

'On 27 November, my 14th shipping strike, we started out in Hudson "L" as dusk was falling. It was a beautiful evening. There was a calm sea and not a cloud in the sky. We went across the North Sea almost at sea level, and by the time we got to the other side it was practically dark. We were after a convoy off the Dutch coast. By the time we got to Ijmuiden, though, they were gone. We headed north for our secondary target at Den Helder, where my mother and father, a retired Dutch naval officer, lived. They did not know I was flying in the RAF. I had last seen them just before the German invasion of my country in May 1940, after which eight of us, all naval ratings, walked to Dunkirk and finally escaped to England from Boulogne. Some of us now flew under different names so that our families in Holland would not be persecuted. I hated the bloody Germans. I'd seen them bombing Rotterdam and in the *Freedom Paper* it told of how men were put up against a wall and shot and how many boys were sent to Germany. I thought: "Christ! I'm near mum and dad and they don't even know I'm flying!" (Later, in 1943, the Red Cross sent me a letter from them. You could answer them in no more than 25 words. I wanted to let my dad know I was now a sergeant. He being ex-Navy would know that if I said I was now a member of the "Golden Ball" he would know I was a sergeant. (Up to the rank of corporal, uniform flashes were yellow. Sergeant and above were orange). That would have made him proud. My letter survived the German sensor and he knew what I meant. He knew the quickest way to promotion was to fly, and so he knew I was flying.

'We flew up parallel with the Dutch coast. Up front, the W/Op, Anthonie, who came from the Dutch East Indies, was operating the ASV set, scanning the screen for ships. We found two lines of cargo ships 90 degrees north-west of Den Helder, steaming out to sea. Petri, the observer, looked out of the window and saw the ships. A long line of them, steaming slowly eastwards. He was so excited that he yelled out at the top of his voice:

"Ships on starboard! Ships on starboard!" He had hardly stopped shouting when they began firing at us. Our formation immediately broke up and we circled the convoy with our bomb doors open, ready to attack. The flak was getting heavy, about eight ships were firing heavy machine guns and pom-poms and an escorting destroyer was blazing away with a whole ack-ack battery. From every side Petri saw red, white and green tracer fly past, and as we dived for the attack the shells came uncomfortably close. I'd never seen so many golden balls coming up at us.

'De Groot singled out a heavily-laden ship of the convoy. We were going straight, then suddenly, nose down! De Groot opened fire with the two nose guns, giving it everything we'd got, as we dived. I was swearing because we had never done this type of attack before. We'd always gone in straight and level. He kept on shooting and shooting. I thought he would have to stop soon before the barrels melted. Petri stood in the astrodome and warned de Groot where all the heaviest flak was coming from and kept a look out for night fighters.

'As we passed over the ship de Groot released our bombs. As soon as the bombs were away, de Groot banked sharply. I don't know if we were hit. (I never ever checked to see if we were; it was always straight into debriefing and straight into the bar for me on return to England.) Up front it was a different story. Apparently, a few seconds later and after bombs away they felt a giant explosion. Petri suddenly heard a loud bang. The cabin filled with smoke and the wireless operator cried out: "I'm hit! I'm hit!" A cannon shell had exploded just behind his back.

'Petri went to his assistance, and as he turned around and looked backwards, saw that the ship we had bombed was on fire. Two of our bombs hit the ship. An explosion sent up a column of flames and smoke 100 feet high. As we set course for home, the other aircraft [the Flying Dutchmen and the Canadian Demon Squadron, also flying Hudsons], attacked and Petri saw bombs bursting and tracer crisscrossing like "fireworks". Our job was done. We didn't hang around. Petri managed to bandage up the W/Op's wounds. Bernet had several splinters in his back. Although he was in great pain he carried on throughout the return trip sending out messages as if nothing had happened. It was confirmed later that the vessel, a 2,500-ton cargo ship, was sunk. (Unconfirmed in postwar research.) Marvellous! Petri said the sight of all our aircraft, Canadian and Dutch, making a mess of that convoy was worth the many weary months of training and uneventful patrols, and we all felt we had done something in smashing the Nazis and to repay them for what they had done to Britain and Holland.'[2]

But not all the flying Dutchmen were in Hudsons. Some were flying Spitfires and it was these who first went back to Holland – to fight. One Dutch Spitfire ace earned a reputation as an individualist. He liked nothing better than to go scouting on his own. In early April he went on an offensive patrol and over the aerodrome at Flushing spotted a German dive-bomber flying at barely 100 feet off the ground. The Dutchman went into a steep dive, flattened out and attacked the surprised

German head-on, his machine guns blazing. He could only hold in the attacking position for one brief second before having to break aside. But in a matter of moments he had swung round and was attacking again. This time he came in on the beam and was able to keep his gun button depressed for a full three seconds.

The German's tail went up and it crashed as the other members of the Dutchman's squadron arrived and started giving the aerodrome buildings and hangars a real RAF workout. From the Netherlands East Indies came recruits for the ranks of the flying Dutchmen. They also came from Canada and the United States. Britain was their rallying ground, where their standard still flew freely. It was from Britain's friendly shores that they went back to Holland – with bombs for the invader who had lowered the flag of Orange. They went back in September 1942, flying Hudsons of the Royal Dutch Naval Squadron of Coastal Command and at night caught up with a convoy off Texel, which had been reported earlier. It was a dark night, with few stars, and the Hudsons began their attack by dropping flares, which lit up the scene like a theatrical stage. In the brilliance of the silver-burning flares they swooped to attack and found themselves diving through a barrage of heavy AA fire. Then from the Dutch coast came the shadows of night fighters, spitting hot streams of tracers. In a matter of seconds the falsely bright sky was crisscrossed with the whirling shapes of fighting planes. The bombs of the first Hudson went through the gaping bomb doors; pitching along the dark length of one of the convoy's ships. The observer in that Hudson watched closely, fascinated by the scene. He saw the bombs strike and noticed where the last of the stick struck on the after part of the vessel. Suddenly there was a zigzagging orange flash, which seemed to split the ship in two and then gushing clouds of heavy, oily black smoke. That was all the observer noticed. His Hudson was over the ship then and the next was going in for a strike at one of two ships keeping close stations. At the last moment the pilot of this Hudson pulled on the controls and the bombs slithered towards the larger of the vessels. The rear-gunner shouted excitedly in Dutch over the intercom. He had observed a direct hit on the after part of the bridge, right over the ship's heart. Then the third Hudson was weaving down through the flak, beneath the streaking fire from the night fighters and the pilot chose the ship as yet unscathed. Again the Dutch nerves were good. No throb of excitement robbed brain or muscle of its true function. The bombs crashed accurately on the target and, as in the case of the first ship, a great orange glow rushed upward as though to scorch the clouds. Then the flares died. The Hudsons raced for base, losing the night fighters in the covering darkness and behind them, dwindling like a fading will-o'-the-wisp, the glow of the burning ships hovered on the face of the sea.

There was plenty of cursing in Texel that night, but only in the camp of the invading army. To the proud free men of Orange, shackled to the economic and military chariots of the Germans, those fires were like a promise lightening the gloom of days that were lengthening into months and years.

The ship hunting went on. Out of the night came the vengeance-seeking Dutch, striking anywhere along the European coastline from Norway to the mouth of the English Channel. Over seas that had borne the warships of van Tromp and de Ruyter, they sought their enemies and struck repeatedly. In the messes of Coastal Command squadrons flying Hudsons it was said that the Dutchmen had the power of night vision. Winds rising to gale force did not stop them. Fair weather or foul they went out, always seeking; searching.

On 6 October their search was rewarded somewhere off the coast of France when, in the darkness, they spotted a large freighter cautiously creeping along under the cover of night, trying to make port before dawn broke. The pilot did not hesitate. He went down very low and released his bombs when he could still only barely make out the funnel and superstructure of the merchant ship. But at least one bomb hit the target plumb centre. 'We saw a great yellow flash and then a shower of red sparks.' With its usual thoroughness, the RAF sent a reconnaissance plane shortly after dawn to check up on the claim. Sure enough, at the spot indicated on the Hudson's chart, the reconnaissance crew found a broken ship beached on a sandy spit, in shallow water, the waves already beginning their grim work of pounding the wreck to pieces. Again the Dutch had written their defiance in deeds. The record of the Dutchmen became so impressive that the Air Ministry issued a special bulletin about their activities. That was on 3 December. After detailing the scope of the flying Dutchmen's aerial offensive, the bulletin stated:

'It was in May 1942 that the Dutchmen had their most successful month, putting out of action at least eleven enemy supply ships.[3] In every case the attacks were delivered from, or below, mast height, the pilots leap-frogging over the masts and releasing their bombs at the moment the aircraft swept up over the ships. It was a dangerous method of attack. A foot lower, a slight miscalculation by the pilot could end in disaster for the aircraft. But the Dutchmen cheerfully accepted the risks and continued to bomb from a low altitude to make sure of hitting the target with bombs. One Dutchman went so low that the explosion of the delayed-action bombs rocked his Hudson violently; another narrowly missed the cable of a balloon floating from a ship. But in both cases the ships were damaged. Enemy convoys suffered severely and, in the far north of Norway and on the Northern Russian front, German soldiers, sailors and airmen waited for food and equipment, which never arrived.

'Many of the Dutchmen now flying with the squadron escaped from Holland when their country was invaded; others have arrived from the East Indies. There have been many outstanding personalities among them. There was, for instance, the flight lieutenant – a superlative pilot – about whom a Royal Air Force squadron commander once said, "I'd give anything to have him in my squadron." There was the navigator who always typed his log in the aircraft while flak was still flying up at it; and there was the pilot who painted a stork flying to deliver a bomb on the fuselage of the Hudson. Some of these men have gone now. But always there are others to replace them. And the Dutchmen go on bombing Hitler's ships, helping to weave the pattern of victory that will release Holland from the grip of the invader.'

The Flying Dutchmen, as this testimonial attests, made their own tradition in the RAF. They have written large their own story in its bright-paged annals. For many of them their own personal story of struggle and endeavour began long before they reached a RAF recruiting office. There was, for instance, one pilot officer in the RAF, wearing the ribbon of the Dutch Cross of Merit, a fair-haired young man with a quick, ready smile and grave grey eyes that watched the war-tattered world through spectacles, who endured and suffered much to get to England and don air force blue. His eyesight would not allow him to become an operational flier, but he was an expert glider pilot. He had been referred to by the Air Ministry as Pilot Officer X. His story is representative of many of his countrymen's. It is a patchy story because much of it cannot be filled in today for military reasons, but he outlined it himself. He learned to speak English.

'I was with a companion in my bid to escape. Through the Dutch broadcasts from England we heard of people escaping from Holland, so we decided to try it. In December 1941 we made our effort and at that time my idea was to try to reach the Dutch East Indies, but when the Indies fell I had to revise my plans. In northern France we found the people fairly helpful, but in the Vichy territory in the south, it was rather different. People were suspicious and many seemed to have swallowed the German propaganda about Britain having let the French down.'

The two Dutchmen were, in effect, in a hostile country and it was not long before they found themselves under arrest. The Vichy authorities at Lons-le-Saunier clapped them into jail for a fortnight. From the jail they were removed to a concentration camp, where they had to work for the French Army. They were put into old French uniforms and, although they were not treated badly, they found conditions difficult at times. And food was scarce. They found that some of the French soldiers firmly believed that the British and the Germans would eventually exhaust themselves in the titanic struggle and then would come the French army's real chance to rise and establish order in Europe. The Dutchmen, having lived under the German heel and knowing the determination of the British never to give way, realized that these particular Frenchmen were living in a fool's paradise – or, perhaps, were living in a fool's world dreaming of a fool's paradise. For there was no aspect of life in Vichy France that could be described as paradise, even by the most blind of political fools.

'When we heard that we were to be sent back to prison we formed a plan to escape. It was not difficult to elude the guards, but the chief consideration was the provision of food for the long journey we contemplated on foot, as we did not wish to risk detection by asking help on the way. As the Dutch Indies had fallen, my companion and I decided to make for England. We set out from a place in southern France with a stock of biscuits and tackled the journey on foot, because we heard that those who travelled by motor or train were often detected. We navigated by pocket compass, keeping to the least-frequented roads. I was surprised at what we could do on only a few biscuits and a bottle of brandy each day. In all, my journey from Holland to England took eight months. When I escaped I intended to use my flying experience against the enemy and I liked life in the RAF.'

Eight months, from December 1941 to August 1942, scheming to get to freedom in order to fight and every step of a tortuous journey beset by danger. No mean feat. But that is the kind of road travelled by the flying Dutchmen before they found themselves armed and ready to hit back. Small wonder they struck so hard when the opportunity at last presented itself.

Twice within a week in January the Dutch in their Lockheed Hudsons struck at the German convoys off their own shores.[4] In bright moonlight, on the second occasion, they attacked a convoy steaming slowly past Terschelling, carrying supplies from France, Belgium and Holland to Germany. Flares and flak from an escort vessel guided them in their downward swoop. The second bomb of the first Hudson struck a medium-sized vessel amidships. A second Hudson flew straight 'up moon' – the target lined up in the first run and the last bomb of a stick struck the vessel somewhere aft of the funnel stack. The third Hudson made four runs over the targets selected, observing the effects of the other aircraft's bombing. When its own bombs dropped it was to score another direct hit behind a black squat funnel.

The Dutch bomb-aimers were deadly marksmen. The Dutch crews, too, had the knack of getting back safely even when their luck was not in. In March 1943 a story was entered in the log book of a Dutch sergeant-pilot, which needs no embellishing. The Hudson had been out bombing another convoy, this time off the Friesian islands. 'I was flying on a straight course home when I felt a terrific jar and the rudder jerked wildly. I didn't know what had happened at first but then the rear-gunner said we had just collided with another aircraft. He had not been able to identify it but it wasn't one of ours so we think it must have been a German. It was too dark and he got only the barest glimpse of the other aircraft, which he believed crashed into the sea. I straightened out the aircraft again and the gunner made a hasty inspection, reporting that both rudders had been badly damaged, but the elevators appeared intact. The radio operator reported that the radio loop aerial had been torn off. The aircraft must have passed right over us and struck us with his fuselage and propellers or engine nacelle.'[5]

Luck or intuition – call it what you will – the flying Dutchmen have it. Most successful air fighters have to a marked degree. It is their battle target, against which flak and cannon shells and machine-gun bullets cannot necessarily prevail. In dog fights or ack-ack barrage it frequently means invincibility.[6]

Notes
1. Lieutenant t.z. 2e kl. J. M. van Olm, CO of 320 Squadron, 1 June 1941-20 June 1942. Research by Theo Boiten.
2. 1. *The Royal Air Force At War: Memories and personal experiences, 1939 to the present day* by Martin W. Bowman (PSL 1997).
3. Postwar research only confirms the following two: 8.5.42 the *Burgundia*, Swedish MV of 1,668 tons damaged off Emden in 320 Squadron attack, and 29/30 May 1942 *Sperrbrecher* 150 of the 8th Spbr. Fl. of 750 tons bombed amidships by 320 Squadron Hudson, 10 km N. of Ameland and sank with loss of two of crew. Research by Theo Boiten.
4. One confirmed in postwar research: 18/19 January 1943 the *Algeria*, a 1,619 ton Swedish MV bombed at 23.50 hrs by Hudsons of 320 and 407 Squadrons N. of Vlieland. Taken in tow but broke in two and sank N. of Vlieland. Three of crew KIA. Research by Theo Boiten.
5. On average, 320 Squadron had 10 Hudsons available for operations between the late summer of 1941 and early 1943. During this period, 15 aircraft and crews of the Dutch Squadron were lost. Research by Theo Boiten.
6. In March 1943 320 Squadron was disbanded but shortly afterwards was reformed as a light bomber squadron in 2 Group, Bomber Command at Methwold, Norfolk.

# Chapter 10

# Over the Alps and Back – Bruce Sanders

In October 1940 RAF Bomber Command turned its attention to the Italian military cities and with such effect that, it was said at the time, 'the Italian people attributed almost supernatural powers to our bomb-aimers'. In October 1940 the last stand-up fights of the Battle of Britain were being fought and the night blitz on London had already run more than a month of its eight months' agony. The RAF was determined to show Mr Churchill that it was always prepared to switch over to the offensive at a given moment. Then winter came and a New Year with new resolutions, which apparently included more attention for the Italian home front. On the night of 11 January 1941 the bombers of the RAF went south over the snow-clad Alps and attacked the royal arsenal at Turin. It was a bitterly cold flight, so cold in the only long-distance bombers then in operation that, while crossing the Alps, one crew had their bomb release mechanism frozen solid. The pilot arrived over the arsenal only to find that the bombs were very undesirable frozen assets, for the flak curtain was thickest over the target area. He had to get rid of them somehow, as he depended on a lighter aircraft to make the long flight back to base. So he went on to the Fiat factory. Again the bombs would not go down. He flew on to another war factory and tried again. This third time the mechanism worked and the bombs went down. He saw them burst in the centre of the factory building and four fires were started by his incendiaries. Five minutes later while he was still stooging around, there followed a large explosion and a series of smaller ones. Most of our aircraft that night swept across the silver streak of the river Po, picking out the darkened streets and squares of the city, to pinpoint their target without much difficulty. As attacks went in those days, it was highly successful. The 'bomphleteers', who had brought supplies of a four-page pamphlet of Mr Churchill's recent address to the Italian people, sent them drifting over the city like a fall of snowflakes.

The next night Bomber Command left its customary visiting cards at Venice, or rather Porto Marghera, which is very near the city of the Doges on the mainland, and at Regensburg on the Danube, a port for Romanian oil distribution. They arrived over the Adriatic shortly before 0200 on a bright, frosty morning, with the starry sky clear and visibility good. The last of the attackers left an hour later, when the target area was well ablaze and a pall of fire-drenched smoke was rising to 500 feet. They also smashed the Duce's oil storage tanks and the fires of Porto

Marghera were plainly discernable when the bombers were climbing over the French Alps. Regensburg received its visit between 0230 and 0430. There conditions were not so good. Cloud formations concealed the target, but diving through the various rifts the pilots levelled off at about 1,000 feet and enabled bomb-aimers to sight accurately as the bombs were released. When the crews got back to Britain they were thrilled and excited. The long pull over the Alps in winter held no terrors for them, although icing conditions had been rather bad. The wing commander who led the attack on Porto Marghera gave a graphic picture of how he took his men in:

'There was fog over the foothills on the other side. It looked like a great sea of ice, with the high ground standing up like islands. The plains of Lombardy were also completely covered by fog. Then, as we neared the Adriatic coast, the fog disappeared and when we got to Venice, flying "up moon", it was like day. I had more or less made up my mind all along to go down low and the moment we got over the Alps I started losing height. Over Venice we circled round to draw their fire and see how much there was. They had quite a lot of light stuff. Some of it was getting pretty accurate towards the end. Having seen how much there was, I decided to go right down. We flew over Mestre, whistling among the chimneys. There was a sort of fort or citadel outside Mestre and two sentries standing on the ramparts had a crack at us. We could see them standing up with levelled rifles. I had given orders to the front and rear-gunners that they were to fire back on anybody who fired at us and they opened up on the sentries. A couple of years later Italian sentries were crowding civilian air-raid shelters when the RAF flew over. But one can learn much in two years.

'The time was now round about 0200 yet it was so light that one could see people in the street. I heaved the aircraft over a couple of factory chimney stacks; then we started to climb to do the bombing. We went up to 700 feet. We were carrying one of our heaviest bombs and when it burst it nearly blew us out of the air. The bomb landed either on or beside a large building with a lot of pipes all round it. There was a colossal belt of smoke and flame, which shot up almost level with the aircraft. The smoke died away but the flames persisted. Then there were a couple of great explosions. We went round again and dropped the other bomb in the middle of the flames, adding to it by half as much again. I knew of an aerodrome about 20 miles away at Padua so we went whistling along the railway tracks at about "nought" feet to find it. We passed three trains on the way. We were flying right alongside them. We flew over Padua itself, again doing tight turns round the chimneys and church spires and having dropped our leaflets there, flew on to Padua aerodrome, where the front and rear-gunners let fly, left, right and centre, at the hangars. We streaked across the aerodrome at 20 feet. We could see that there were no aircraft dispersed around the aerodrome, so we assumed that they were in the hangars. Immediately we came on to the scene the aerodrome defences opened up on us. Tracer was flying alongside almost parallel with us. I was behind the trees to get cover. I had wanted to have a crack at another aerodrome, but there was not much time and we'd got the Alps to cross again, so we left it at that and came away.'

Judged by any standards, it was a pretty effective night's work. One also that the Italians were to remember for eight months, for that was the interval before the next trans-Alpine flight. But the attack made on the night of 10/11 September 1941 marked a decided change in the weight of the offensive against the Italian mainland. That night four-engined Stirlings and Halifaxes joined the Wellingtons[1] in flying to bomb the royal arsenal and other targets in Turin. The interval of eight months had been well employed in the aircraft factories of Britain. The four-engined giants were coming out of the assembly shops and a new age of bombing was about to dawn in the Mediterranean skies. That night, for the first time, Bomber Command 'heavies' made the 1,200 mile journey out and back, crossing and re-crossing the Alps. Some of the crews taking part in the flight to Italy had only the previous night flown to Berlin. They were getting to know their way around Europe.

'It was as quiet as the grave,' was how one of the Stirling pilots described the passage over France. 'One of two searchlights poked into the clouds. We could see the splashes of light on the clouds below us, but they were ineffective and soon gave up. We started climbing well before we got to the Alps. As we made the crossing we were flying at one time at over 20,000 feet. We could see the snow on the tops of the higher mountains and, down in the valleys, the mountain villages. The moon was up and it was a really beautiful night. We could see very far; we picked out Mont Blanc high among the other peaks. We didn't stay at 20,000 feet for long because there was no need to go as high but I had never been over the Alps before and I wanted to make sure of getting well up. As soon as we had crossed the Alps we lost height again and came down to Turin. We were about the third bomber over and already there were three large blocks of fire in a row. We went on and the navigator found the railway station. We dropped one stick of bombs across it. We went round again and came back to drop a second stick. After we had bombed we climbed again and as we turned towards the Alps we saw the attack getting under way. There were lots of bombs being dropped.'

However, night fighters went up this time, but the Italian cat's-eyes men were singularly loath to engage the gun-bristling four-engined Stirlings. They were content to see the unwelcome callers off the premises, as it were, as the pilot goes on to explain:

'A few minutes after we had left Turin my rear-gunner told me that three fighters were coming up very fast astern in close formation. At first they were nearly 2,000 feet below us. I think they must have seen us against the moon. I told the rear-gunner to get rid of them because there would not be much room for evasive action over the mountains. He opened up on them at once and they split formation. One of them disappeared into cloud and the other two joined some friends of theirs who had come up. They made no attack and soon made off. One solitary gun in the foot of the hills on the Italian side of the Alps took a pop at us. It just fired once for luck. We crossed the Alps lower this time and later I left it to "George", the automatic pilot, to take us a good part of the way home. We came home very nicely.'

The entire business, in fact, seemed to come off very nicely. None of the crews suffered from the intense cold of the Alpine crossings and the majority of them appeared to be more impressed by the beauty of the snow-covered mountains in the moonlight than by any other feature of the night's work. It almost seems a pity Keats and Shelley did not live to become airmen and fly with Bomber Command.

They would have had a brand new angle on nature – especially on the Italian side of the Alpine range.

Poets, however, like other mortals, are not always lucky. They might have been briefed for the attack on Genoa, eighteen nights later, when the crews of the Stirlings and Wellingtons making up the force met cloud over the Alps and saw nothing of the peaks going out or coming back. That night the navigators did a particularly good job with their pencils and dividers. As one of the pilots reported:

'As we neared the Alps the clouds began to build up. We skirted a terrific electric storm going on over Mont Blanc. We could see great zigzag flashes of lightning. There were two layers of cloud over Genoa and a high bank of cloud had come up over the moon.' But the city where Columbus first saw the light of day soon had other illuminations.

'Our bomb-aimer decided to drop a few incendiaries. A cautious Scotsman, he would not put all his bombs down at once. The incendiaries went with a rush right into the factory and soon you could see the flames coming out of the roofs and the windows. The whole of one end of the factory – it was an enormous place – was lit up. We went round again and dropped our next stick. We gave them a bit of both this time, high explosives as well as incendiaries. This time we put a high explosive right on the doorstep of one of the factory buildings. We went round a third time and saw that the fires were still going strong. Then we dropped a stick of bombs along the docks. The fires in the factory were still burning when we left. We saw nothing of the Alps on the return journey. We crossed in pitch-black darkness and cloud. Until we got back to base we had only one glimpse of the ground.'

With the British bomb crews that night flew aircrews of the Czech and New Zealand bomber squadrons. The offensive was truly gathering weight. Again the Italians were given set things they could easily remember and once more an interval of eight months elapsed before the bombers returned. This time – the night of 12/13 April 1942 – the attack was made by a force of [eighteen] Whitleys, which flew to attack targets in that very vulnerable triangle formed by Turin, with Milan to the east and Genoa to the south. It was a dark night, clear but with no moon to light the bombers' path. Things had changed somewhat since the last journey over the Alps and the change began at the French coast, where plenty of flak and many searchlights tried to reach the high-flying force. But once through the barrage they continued steadily south-eastwards across France, climbed the Alps and then found a thick sprinkling of cloud in that triangle. They probed the cloud gaps like flying shuttles and found that the Italians had grown lax with inattention from the RAF. The blackout was broken by bright patches of unscreened lights. There was an amazed and hurried scramble to turn off switches when the first bomb exploded. The attack took the Italians completely by surprise and every one of the force of Whitleys returned to England. However, the raid was no more, really, than a tactical feeler and a psychological reminder to the civilian population they had no reason to feel neglected. The RAF in the matter of targets has no preference, save that dictated by our military strategy and policy.

As the Italians realized only too vividly half a year later, when, coordinating with the great North African offensive, the weight of Bomber Command was flung solidly against the war industries of Milan, Genoa, Turin and Venice. The famous vulnerable triangle then became very vulnerable indeed. On 22/23 October 1942 the first heavy and really concentrated attack was made, on the port of Genoa.[2] It was an attack comparable with what Bomber Command had been meting out to the industrial cities of the Reich and for the first time the Italians awoke to full realization of what participation in the Axis orgy of conquest entailed. The target area was saturated with 4,000 and 1,000lb bombs. The cascade of bursting metal and incendiaries overwhelmed the defences and all but left the port at the mercy of the heavy aircraft circling in the Italian skies.

An anti-aircraft officer [Major Mullock MC] who had flown as special observer with Bomber Command on its raids on Lübeck, Rostock and the Renault works went on the 1,500 mile round trip to Genoa. He watched the raid from the fall of the early bombs to the fading out of the resistance from the shore gunners and gave as his opinion when he returned, that the raid was the most concentrated made to that date. He saw only one stick of incendiaries miss the target area.

'As we came down the other side of the Alps the valleys were shrouded in mist and we were afraid that Genoa might be obscured. But over the plain the weather cleared again. From 30 miles away I could see the light of the flares dropping over Genoa. As we got nearer it looked as though the whole town was ablaze. There was a big oil fire, with flames spurting up into the air and clouds of black smoke on top of them – we circled round before making our bombing run and I counted 13 big fires and innumerable little ones. Clouds of smoke were coming up. When we first came in there had been AA fire and a good deal of tracer. As the attack developed, the guns almost entirely stopped firing. I could see tracers coming from the sea; the ships in the bay were evidently firing.'

It was the forty-sixth operational flight for one DFC flight lieutenant and when he got back to base he enthusiastically announced that it was by far his most successful. 'As we crossed the Channel on the way out we watched what was about the best sunset I have ever seen. We never saw land until we reached the Alps. The clouds above France were lit by the sunset glow. When the sun went down on our starboard side the full moon came up on our port and the clouds were still lit up. Up currents of air were driving the clouds away as we got to the Alps, mountaintops soared above the clouds in the moonlight. The mountains were glistening white and almost purple the shadows. We saw a wide glacier. As we passed the Alps the clouds were disappearing and the moon shone right down into the deep valleys. There was no mist or haze, we could see every river, lake and village.'

That part of his report reads more like an extract from a travel agency's booklet of tours. Perhaps the tourist booklet of the post-war era contained such reports and descriptions. An autumn night-flight over the Alps would seem to hold wonders to stir the jaded senses of the most inveterate globetrotter. But in his appreciation of the views on the way out, the flight lieutenant was not forgetful of the reason that took him to the Italian port.

'We were early on Genoa, so we circled the Mediterranean. I think that we and one other bomber were the first to drop flares. They went down at the same time and showed up the harbour, lots of buildings and streets. At first I thought they were the shimmering white haze above Genoa, but it was only the whiteness of the town, which has a great many white buildings. After the flares came our bombs. When I had seen them burst on the target we came down to just above the sea to watch the main attack. We never saw a bomb wasted. Oil storage tanks blew up a sudden red glow and gave off great volumes of smoke. We did a slow climb over the sea and as we did so, we saw eight fires glowing in the target area. They were all well concentrated and five of them were very large indeed. We saw a searchlight trying to find us, though it was in the midst a bunch of fires.'

That night the 600,000 Italians who lived and worked, played and went to daily war jobs in Genoa, knew that the Anglo-Saxon judgment was rapidly approaching. The next night they were back in their air-raid shelters, as were the citizens of Savona and Turin, for the RAF followed up the blitz on Genoa with a three-pronged attack.[3] The crews had to use oxygen all the way over the Alps but they suffered no hardship. Again it was a night when the mountain scenery was of breathtaking beauty and the navigators sent the aircraft low down. As one of them put it, 'we map-read our way over the foothills to the Gulf of Genoa'.

That night the *Regia Aeronautica* sent up night fighters to challenge the RAF bombers. Over the Lombardy plain shots were exchanged, but the Italian night fighter pilots had little heart for the work of close engaging the bombers. A squadron leader in a Halifax was surprised when a CR. 42 biplane suddenly swooped on him but the British gunners broke up two attempts to get in a vital burst on the part of the Italian pilot and then suddenly the biplane was falling away down the sky. A Stirling likewise met one of the biplanes and, after dealing with it effectively, encountered a Breda 88 and after that a Macchi 200. The aircraft was hit in the tailplane and fuselage and the rear turret's hydraulic apparatus was damaged. The gunner had to swivel himself round by hand, but he beat off the planes and saw his tracers biting into the Macchi. The next day, 24 October, Milan received a visit from British-based Lancasters – in daylight.[4] At 1704, the first Lancaster nosed down through the heavy clouds and unloaded. They came in rapidly, pinpointing their targets and wheeling round. Mixed in the general delivery of HEs and incendiaries was a goodly proportion of 4,000-pounders, which rocked the city's industrial heart with tremendous palpitations. Some of the large four-engined bombers went down to 50 feet to bomb their targets. Only when the bombers were well on their homeward run did darkness come down and afford them any protection. On the outward flight they had flown close together and very low, hedge-hopping in the manner in which the Augsburg and Le Creusot raids had been made possible. When the crews landed it was to hear news that brought ready grins to their faces. At the very moment they had touched down more bombs were scheduled to be dropped on the targets they had left. A large force of Stirlings, Halifaxes and Wellingtons were continuing the Milan blitz by night. The town from which Mussolini's march on Rome had been staged was being given a prolonged opportunity of revising its opinion regarding the regime it had helped to establish.

In early November, a fortnight after the first assault on Genoa, which had coincided with the Eighth Army's lunge in the desert, the heavies of Bomber Command returned.[5] It was a dark night and a large number of flares had to be dropped to light up the port. But the 'cookies' brought by the bombers began their work of pulverizing factories and key plants. Flak that night was heavier, especially from the dock area, but the results obtained were very satisfactory. So much so that Bomber Command went back the next night and gave Genoa its heaviest raid of the war. This time Lancasters joined the Halifaxes and Stirlings[6] in the night swoop over the Mediterranean. Weather conditions over the target were very favourable for bombing but all the way to the Alps the bomber crews had their work cut out. Rain and cloud brought visibility to only a few feet, while icing and sudden electrical storms gave the pilots some cause for anxiety.

'It was as if we were flying in the slipstream of another aircraft,' was the description given by a pilot later. One front gunner reported that, as his plane penetrated cloud, ice came crackling through the turret ventilators in handfuls, while up-currents threw the bombers about. Above the clouds when the pilots climbed, the night was bitterly cold and a thick hoar frost coated the windscreens. Over the Alps snow was falling steadily. Ice flew in large chunks from the whirling airscrews, rattling against the windscreen like hail. One of the RAF's Public Relations officers flew in a Stirling that night. He kept a very detailed log of the raid, noting times and his own personal reactions to the conditions of the flight. At 1930 hours he records:

'St. Elmo's fire round the propellers. Now again in the astrodome I can see the circles of flame round the propeller and the front-gunner reports blue darts on his gun-barrel and flames trickling around the metal of the turret. This lasted about ten minutes. We are climbing for the Alps and our flight engineer switches on oxygen. The smell and feel of the mask are strange at first and rather like an anaesthetist's apparatus.'

The PR officer was fresh to this kind of flight and his reactions and experiences are interesting to those who can follow the adventures of the bomber crews only through the media of the printed page. They are the experiences and reactions of the average man to one of the greatest flying sorties of war. However, at 2014 hours the RAF guest was becoming a little more accustomed to the journey and the cloud-top scenery. He jotted down:

'I am lying flat over the bottom blister. Though there is no moon, the Alps come into view – surfaces of a grade of purplish-white peppered with black. The captain suggests that if I come forward again I shall soon see Genoa. I take several deep breaths of oxygen and then plug out to struggle forward. Though the Stirling is a huge aircraft, it seems that nothing could be big enough for me, a novice, to move gracefully in. As I climb towards the nose my dangling intercom winds itself around everything, from the automatic pilot to the flight engineer's neck. Just visible in his macabre red light, the captain looks up, grins and shouts, "How are you feeling?"

"Fine," I say.

"Liar," says he. "Don't worry. It's always the same on your first trip." While talking, I have to stop half-way and plug in for oxygen and intercom. "If we are worried," says the captain, "think what those poor silly Eyeties must be feeling. Look over there. That's Genoa. No future being in Genoa on a night like this."

That particular Stirling was the leader of the raid. It was the first plane to approach the target and the searchlights wavered as they came on and the ack-ack fire was desultory and uncertain, though some red fireballs were thrown up with the light flak.

At 2105 hours the RAF officer put this down:

'Now it becomes frightening. There appears to be no way through the wall of searchlights and flak. The front-gunner goes down into the bomb-aimer's hatch and the captain starts violent jinking. From the astrodome I can see the glow of our exhausts and the great hump of the outer engines rising up and descending again against the vivid light of the flashes and the beams. As we wind our way along, the giant humps on either side continue to rise.

'Fifteen minutes later: "Bomb doors open!" comes through the intercom and then, "OK, bomb doors open." I lift my oxygen mask and bite into a small English Newton apple. For some reason it gives me great pleasure to munch an English apple over Genoa. As we get over the searchlights I am less scared. Down below, the gun flashes reveal the blocks of building. Searchlights wander across our propellers, edge and wing-tips, flick the tail and, fantastic as it seems, never catch it. But the flak comes nearer and the red fireballs closer as the captain levels out for the bombing run and calls to the bomb-aimer, "OK. Remember the precise target." We are steady for a mighty long 20 seconds before the bomb-aimer reports, "Bombs gone."

'The job then is to get home. At 0136 hours the next morning the RAF visiting officer sees the lights of the flare path spring up on the runway of the home base and that Stirling, which led the raid – *V for Victor* – gets the instruction from below, "You can land now".'

On 13/14 November [nine] Stirlings and [67] Lancasters once more went to Genoa, which was becoming daily more and more important as a supply base for the Axis armies in North Africa. In the six days that had passed since that last full day's raiding on the port, many more guns and searchlights had been rushed to defend the port against the RAF's return. Flak ships on the German model were stationed in the harbour. Among the individual targets attacked was the Ansaldo works, to the west of the port, which constructed naval armaments and marine engines. Night fighters were met going out and on the way back and over France one German machine was sent down in flames. The entire British bombing force, for the second time, returned without losing a bomber during a raid on Genoa. 'Another pair of white gloves,' was how Sir Arthur Harris smilingly described the exploit when he received reports of the night's work. A night passed and then to Genoa again flew Bomber Command, to bring off a third 'white gloves' raid. It was actually the sixth attack on the port since the opening of the Mediterranean offensive. The raid was crowded into one furious spell of 25 minutes and in that time hundreds of bombs, 1,000lb in weight or larger, were dropper over the target areas. The weather was again right for the intrepid bomber crews. There was a bright half-moon and visibility was good. Objects below were picked out with comparative ease and one Halifax observer, who had been told to look out for a statue of Mussolini in a new square, had little difficulty in pin-pointing it. The pilot of another Halifax was fascinated by a fire which he saw start at the end of a row of warehouses on a small peninsula extending into the inner harbour. The fire ran like liquid along the entire row. He also saw a stick of bombs straddle the western docks, where a large liner was berthed. On the way home Focke-Wulf and Junkers night fighters engaged the returning bombers, but the German planes got the worst of any encounter.

Some days later a message was received in England from a man who had stood on a hill above Genoa and viewed the stricken port. On six nights the RAF had gone to the port for the total loss of only 12 aircraft and the bombing had been concentrated into a period of no more than two and a half hours. In that short space Genoa had been completely knocked out as an effective Axis supply base.

'The burned and destroyed areas in Genoa are so large and many that it is useless to attempt to give details of the damage,' wrote the eyewitness. 'Seen from a height, one has the impression that half of the town has been destroyed and in the port almost everything seems to be destroyed, burned, or damaged. Among the few exceptions in the port area are the silos where the grain for Switzerland was stored. Lack of small craft in the port, as a result of a large number having been sunk or severely damaged, is causing difficulties to the port authorities.'

The RAF had, as usual, been thorough in its work. So thorough, indeed, that when a single high-flying reconnaissance plane flew over the Genoa area and the air-raid warning sounded there was a complete stoppage of work for two hours – although no bombs were dropped.

But Genoa was not to suffer devastation alone. Three nights after the third 'white gloves' raid – that is, on the night of 18/19 November 1942 – a cargo of 4,000-pounders was delivered on Turin [by 77 aircraft]. The raid went off with the customary precision and, at one stage, seven Halifaxes roared in over the target, flying almost wing tip to wing tip and bombed within a few seconds of one another. They crossed the target area with a broad ribbon of upward-leaping fires and tumultuous explosions.

The pilot of one of the Halifaxes said:

'It was even brighter than Genoa. All the streets and bridges across the river stood out clearly. There were thick clouds all the way across France and right up to the Alps, but on the Italian side the weather was perfectly clear. We stayed around the city for about half an hour and I saw fires increasing very rapidly. There was plenty of flak at the beginning of the attack, but it all died down towards the end. I did not see a single searchlight.'

When the RAF bombers left, smoke from the blitzed Fiat works and other industrial targets was drifting in a wide stream northwards across the town. On this raid was enacted the personal saga of Squadron Leader B. V. Robinson DSO DFC [of 35 Squadron] who fooled the Italians by sticking to his pilot's seat and tricked the Rome Radio into a false claim. Rome Radio announced triumphantly: 'The British Air Ministry communiqué today says that all the British aircraft which bombed Turin last night came back to their bases. The British have been misinformed because some of the members of the crews in the British planes which bombed Turin last night have been made prisoner after their planes were brought down.' As it happened, it was the Italians who were misinformed. They certainly had some prisoners to show, but all the aircraft got back to their Bomber Command stations. It was Squadron Leader B. V. Robinson who spoiled the Italians' claim. Robinson was captain of a Halifax, which unloaded flares and bombs over Turin. Shortly afterwards, however, fire began spurting from the bomb bay. An extremely powerful flare, one designed to light up practically an entire city, had got hitched and ignited. The fire swept across the Halifax in gusts, spread to the port wing and it was not long before the whole aircraft was filled with smoke and noxious fumes. There was an explosion, which staggered the aircraft and the bomb doors were quickly opened, but the blazing flare did not drop through. The fire continued to take stronger hold on the plane, which was now racing back towards the Alps, barely 1,000 feet above ground level. Robinson tried everything he knew to retain height, but slowly the aircraft sank. It looked as though nothing could prevent the

Halifax smashing into the granite sides of the Alpine peaks. There was only one thing to do and the captain did it. He ordered the crew to bale out. They did so. He saw the last man go down and was preparing to follow, when inexorably the fire went out. One moment flames were shooting up from the bomb bay, the next they were not. Robinson thought fast and took a chance. He stayed with his crewless aircraft. He got it over the white tipped peaks and continued the flight towards home knowing that he had no flight engineer if anything went wrong mechanically, no navigator to plot a course for him past the heavily defended areas of France and no gunners to fight off any night interceptor craft. He came down on an English airfield near the coast.[7]

Back to Turin went the bombers the next night. They found that German night fighters were posted far to the south inland from the French coast to attack a force of Bomber Command invaders should it return. One squadron, flying Lancasters that night for the first time, had a number of encounters with the desperate German pilots. Their wing commander's aircraft was attacked three times. First he had to fight it out with a Ju 88 on the French side of the Alps. By diving the wing commander got below the Junkers and the mid-upper gunner got in a burst that sent the German airman winging away. It was shortly afterwards that a twin-engined Me 110 rushed in with cannon blazing. The Lancaster replied, with fire too hot for the Messerschmitt pilot. He also disappeared. Later, on the way back, the Lancaster was approached by another Ju 88 but by rolling off into a patch of cloud an encounter was avoided. Wing Commander G. W. Holden DFC commanding a Halifax squadron that night, was over the city when the first flares sailed down. He had the task of remaining over the target area to make a special report. He stooged around while the fun was at its height for more than half an hour – 'fun', let it be understood, in the RAF's meaning of the word. At the end of half an hour a good many fires were blazing furiously and there was one enormous fire pouring from a large warehouse. A column of smoke rose to 8,000 feet and one hovering Lancaster, seeking its own special target, flew right through the black cloud.[8]

On the 28/29th of the same month 228 aircraft, 117 of them Lancasters were dispatched to Turin. That night, when a great many high explosives and 100,000 incendiaries were dropped on the city's targets, the RAF's new 8,000lb bombs were dropped on Italy for the first time. Wing Commander G.P. Gibson, who was to earn the VC months later for his brilliant attack on the Möhne dam with his Lancasters, was piloting a Lancaster over Turin that night.[9] He gave it as his opinion when he returned that Turin received a packet last night. The packet was made up of three wide areas blazing from end to end.

*H for Harry*, a veteran Stirling, was making its 66th operational attack when it glided down to attack a large factory in Turin from a height of 2,000 feet. The pilot had to spiral down over his target, which meant passing it about a dozen times. At 4,000 feet light ack-ack opened up on it. The Stirling's gunners answered back. The pilot recalled:

'We fought a kind of duel with them. We could see most of the details of the works. The long sheds looked to me just as if a small boy had carefully drawn his fingers along some sand. After bombing it looked as if the same boy had smashed his fist into the lot. Our stick of bombs dropped diagonally across the works. We were thrown up by the force of the blast and my rear-gunner reported that from his

Boston III of 107 Squadron in flight. (*via Nigel Buswell*)

Boston in flight over the sea. (*IWM*)

Hudson cockpit. (*IWM*)

A 206 Squadron Hudson crew about to start a patrol in T9303/V. (*Flight*)

Flight Sergeant Ken Brown RCAF is introduced to HM King George VI by Guy Gibson at Scampton on Thursday 27 May 1943.

The Möhne Dam the day after the raid on the Ruhr dams by Lancasters of 617 Squadron 16/17 May 1943. Nineteen Lancasters set out for the Ruhr dams but three were missing by the time that they arrived over the target. Wing Commander Guy Gibson went in and sent his mine successfully bouncing up to the concrete wall of the Möhne Dam, where it sank and exploded. The next two Lancasters missed - one of them being shot out of the sky but both the fourth and fifth hit and finally breached the dam. The Möhne reservoir contained almost 140 million tons of water and was the major source of supply for the industrial Ruhr 20 miles away. Three Lancasters went on to bomb the Eder, 60 miles from the Ruhr, which was also breached. The Eder was even larger than the Möhne, containing 210 million tons of water. Eight of the Lancasters and 56 of the 133 men who flew on the raid failed to return. (*René Millert via John Williams*)

Hudson I N7303 of 269 Squadron undergong servicing in 1940. (*IWM*)

Flight Sergeant Ken Brown RCAF and his crew of F for Freddie just prior to joining the Dambusters.

Wing Commander Guy Gibson VC DSO* DFC*.

Flight Lieutenant (later Squadron Leader) Harold 'Mick' Martin DSO* DFC*. By the end of the war Martin, who was awarded the DSO for his part in the Dams raid and who received a bar to his DSO and DFC, was the only Australian airman to have won five British awards in the conflict. He was granted a permanent commission in 1945 and commanded 2nd TAF and RAF Germany from 1967 to 1970, retiring from the RAF in 1974 as Air Marshal Sir Harold Martin KCB DSO* DFC** AFC. He died on 3 November 1988.

Flight Lieutenant Johnny Wynne, who brought Fortress III HB799/K back alone from Lützkendorf near Leipzig on the night of 14/15 March 1945, here seen in the cockpit of another Fortress, Take It Easy. (*CONAM*)

Sergeant 'Wally' Gaul. (*Gaul*)

Convoy under attack en route to Malta on the evening of 10 August. (*IWM*)

Seen from *Victorious* during Pedestal, the carrier *Indomitable* launches an Albacore aircraft. (*IWM*)

The American tanker *Ohio* enters Grand Harbour, Valletta. (*IWM*)

Wellington IC HEl15 N-Nuts of 40 Squadron which forced landed at El Adem (Tobruk) on 23 January 1943 with a stopped port engine, during a flight to Egypt after a three-month stint on Malta. On landing, the port fuel tanks, pipe lines, filters and carburetter had to be cleared of forty gallons of water which had got into the tanks on Malta! Left to right, Flight Sergeant R. G. Thackeray, Sergeant Art Harvey RCAF, Eric Kerbey, Bert Ward, 'Taffy' Ball and Bob Williams RAAF. (*R. G. Thackeray*)

Sergeant Cliff Mortimer's crew of 40 Squadron at ALG 104, Daba, Western Desert on 21 November 1942 with tented camp in background. Left to right, Sergeant Rowley Beatson RNZAF, front gunner; Sergeant Bert Horton RNZAF, WOp; Sergeant Gordon 'Reg' Thackeray, 2nd Pilot; Flight Sergeant Jeff Reddell RNZAF, navigator-bomb aimer; Sergeant Wally Hammond, rear gunner. (*R. G. Thackeray*)

'All back' is chalked up on a squadron blackboard on 16 June 1944 following the raids on 15/16 June by 227 aircraft on ammunition and fuel dumps in France. No aircraft were lost from the operation on Fouillard by 4 Group with 8 Group Pathfinder marking and the operation on the fuel dump at Châtellerault by 5 Group who destroyed 8 of the 35 fuel sites in the target area. (*via Andy Bird*)

Flying Officer S. T. 'Tom' Wingham DFC. (*Wingham*)

Hudson III V9158 OS-T, which was used to test the airborne lifeboat Mk.I designed by the celebrated yachtsman, Uffa Fox. (*MoD*)

Flight Sergeant Leslie Hyder of 149 Squadron, the second pilot of Stirling BF372 on the night of 28/29 November 1942 seen here recovering from wounds received on the raid. Hyder, Sergeant Cameron and Sergeant Gough were awarded the DFM for their actions on the operation. (*IWM*)

Acting Squadron Leader John Dering Nettleton of 44 'Rhodesia' Squadron, a South African, who led the daring daylight raid by Lancasters against the Maschinenfabrik Augsburg-Nürnberg Aktiengesellschaft (MAN) diesel engine factory at Augsburg on 17 April 1942. Nettleton survived and was awarded the Victoria Cross. Promoted wing commander and becoming CO of 44 Squadron, he FTR from a raid on Turin on 12/13 July 1943. (*IWM*)

American officers inspect the damage to Halifax II MZ559. (*Squadron Leader Bob Davies AFC*)

The crew of Halifax II MZ559 of 578 Squadron, 4 Group, taken at Riccall in 1944. Left to right: Flight Sergeant R.E. 'Bob' Burn RCAF, navigator; Sergeant R.G. 'Sam' Browne, rear gunner; Flying Officer B.D. 'Bob' Davies, pilot; Sergeant F.E. 'Wally' Scarth, flight engineer; Sergeant M.U. Hayward, top turret gunner; Flying Officer B.A. 'Ron' Corbett RCAF, bomb-aimer; Sergeant Tither, radio operator. (*Squadron Leader Bob Davies AFC*)

Warrant Officer Bert Noble MiD* (2nd from left, rear row) and his crew on 101 Squadron. (*via Bernard Noble*)

A Mitchell II of 180 Squadron taking off from Dunsfold in mid-1944. (*Paul McCue*)

Mitchells of 180 Squadron en route to their target. (*Smith-Carrington via Theo Boiten*)

Crews of 431 'Iroquois' and 434 'Bluenose' Squadrons RCAF are briefed at Croft for a raid on Essen. These two ex-Halifax units began operating the Lancaster Mk.X from 10 October and 7 December 1944 respectively. 431 'Iroquois' Squadron suffered the highest percentage losses in 6 Group.

The empty ruins of a bomb-shattered residential district in Hamburg, photographed from an AOP Auster communications aircraft on 3 May 1945, the day the city officially surrendered to the British. The last Bomber Command raid on Hamburg occurred on the night of 13/14 April with an attack by 87 Mosquitoes of the LNSF. By then there was little left to bomb. As he scribbled his notes in the aircraft, the photographer was moved to remark that 'almost the whole city is in ruins'. (*IWM*)

Warrant Officer Jack Laurens DFM and crew of Lancaster III DV267 of 101 Squadron at Ludford Magna. L-R: Laurens, who was a South African and had flown at least seven ops to Berlin; Sergeant W.F.D. 'Don' Bolt, mid-upper gunner; Flight Sergeant Les Burton, navigator, Sergeant A. E. 'Ted' Roystone, rear gunner; Sergeant R.N. 'Chris' Aitken, bomb aimer climbing aboard; Sergeant J.A. Davies, Special Operator, who is wearing body armour; Sergeant W.A.G. Kibble, flight engineer; and Sergeant C.H. 'Cass' Waight, WOp, who is also wearing body armour. This aircraft was one of many ABC-equipped Lancasters and carried an additional crewmember known as the Special Duties operator. On 19/20 February 1944 DV267 was lost on the raid on Leipzig and Laurens, Bolt and Waight, who suffered a broken neck, were killed. The five other members of the crew were taken prisoner.

Lancaster X Camart of 434 'Bluenose' Squadron RCAF.

Lancaster X Xotic Angel of 434 'Bluenose' Squadron RCAF which converted from the Halifax and began Lancaster operations from Croft in December 1944.

Lancaster B.I W4964 WS-J Johnnie Walker/Still Going Strong! of 9 Squadron at Bardney after returning from the raid on Stettin on 6 January 1944. 28-year old Flying Officer Flying Officer Albert Edward Manning, the pilot, was from Ipswich, the bomb aimer was from Winnipeg, the WOp was from Melbourne, the flight engineer was from Hornsey and two of the gunners were from Scotland and Chichester while Sergeant J. J. Zammit (centre, in the white flying suit) whose ninth op this was, came from New York. On 22/23 March 1944 Manning and five of his his crew including Zammit were killed on the operation to Frankfurt. Group Captain N.C. Pleasance who accompanied the crew on the raid was also killed. W4964 Still Going Strong! of 9 Squadron flew 106 ops between April 1943 and October 1944.

A shattered V-Victor back safely at Tortorella shows what a miraculous escape Wally Lewis, the mid-upper gunner had. Cliff Hurst, the wireless operator, got the worst of it. (*Ken Westrope*)

USAAF P-38 Lightnings buzz 614 Squadron Liberators at dispersal on Foggia Plain. (*Hunt*)

Three Wellingtons of 149 Squadron fly low over the hangars at RAF Mildenhall. (*IWM*)

Wellington crews back from a raid. (*IWM*)

turret he could see stretches of the roof being held up among showers of burning material.'

Huge fires raged in the locality of the royal arsenal, flames shot with bright reds and yellows and vivid greens. The way back was strewn with night fighters. One Lanc crew sighted as many as 23 over Northern France and had a running fight with eight, sending one Fw 190 down in flames.

In December the RAF went three times to Turin to round off the work of reducing the armament industry of the city to near impotency. On the 8th the fires raised by incendiaries and more 8,000-pounders were reflected on the white summits of the Alpine peaks. The *Duce* had made a solemn promise to the people of the raided northern plains that more ack-ack guns were coming from Germany. The crews of Bomber Command were on the qui vive for a hotter reception from newly positioned guns, but they had not arrived and there were only some half-dozen searchlights flickering wanly and dispiritedly across the inferno, which engulfed the target area. When Bomber Command returned the following night the inferno had not completely subsided. Fires were still sending up hungry tongues of flame and a pall of smoke still floated across the city. Again the fires, left when the bombers started for home, revealed the Alpine peaks silhouetted darkly against the roseate glow to the south after the aircraft had passed the range. On 11 December the Turin-bound bombers flew though a thick curtain of snow. One Lancaster bomb-aimer reported:

'Only a small part of the glass of my compartment was clear of ice and through it I searched for a gap in the clouds. Ice had formed all over the aircraft and snow fell as we approached the Alps. When I went into the front turret after bombing I found several inches of snow behind the gunner's seat.'

It was like flying through Arctic skies, but Bomber Command's crews made the runs and bombed to schedule and returned home ready to go again and again as many times as ordered. That was how the air offensive south of the Alps was maintained because the bomber crews were ready to endure and strive against the weather as well as against the enemy. It was why Rommel did not get the supplies he was demanding frantically day after day. Some crews struggled valiantly for most of the way, only to be forced to turn back when the target was practically within sight.

Here is the report of a Lancaster captain for the same night:

'Shortly after crossing the Channel we ran into thick cloud. The farther we went the worse it got. Then we struck an electrical storm. Vivid streaks of bluish light darted along the glass in front of my cabin and there were bright sparks between the barrels of the guns. At first we thought they were flashes of flak. The windows began to ice up and then we ran into driving snow. Very quickly the fronts of my windows and of the gun turrets were covered with ice and snow, which also interfered with the smooth running of my engines. We began to lose height. Three of my engines cut out for short periods and for about 10 seconds only one engine was working. The flight engineer got the engines running again, but I had to decide not to risk crossing the Alps. The weather was equally bad coming back.'

The year 1943 came and January passed with the struggle in North Africa working towards a climax. On 4 February Bomber Command returned in force to Turin, adding the port of Spezia to the night's agenda. The flak, the crews reported, was not up to the German standard. 'I saw one night fighter,' a Canadian pilot stated. 'He flew through the flak. I guess he knew Italian flak wouldn't hurt him.'

Ten days later it was Milan's turn and on this occasion 24 factories, three of them turning out war [supplies] on the number-one priority list, were pounded. On this February night [14/15th] a Lancaster's crew [in 101 Squadron] fought a memorable and gallant action. They had bombed and were on the home run, when a CR. 42 night fighter made a diving attack on them. The bomber caught fire amidships almost immediately, one engine stopped dead and two of the machine's petrol tanks were holed. The rear-gunner [Sergeant Leslie Airey] was wounded in the leg, but he sat at his gun button, waiting until the attacker was a bare 50 yards away, then he gave it a burst which set its engine on fire. The mid-upper gunner [Flight Sergeant George P. Dove DFM] likewise remaining at his guns, waited while the flames lapped his turret and, at the right moment, gave the fighter another burst, which sent it whirling down out of control, the flames from its engine spreading over fuselage and tail. Meanwhile the fire in the Lancaster was pronounced out of control and reluctantly the captain [Sergeant Ivan Henry Hazard] gave the order to prepare to abandon the aircraft.[10] However the intercom system had been wrecked and the rear-gunner with his injured leg could not make a parachute descent, so the captain decided to make a crash landing. But before he could find a spot to land the navigator [Sergeant William E. Williams] and the wireless operator [Pilot Officer Frederick W. Gates], working like men possessed, got the flames under control. The mid-upper gunner, though burned badly about the face himself, hauled the rear-gunner out of his turret. Again the captain revised his plan, determined to try to make his base on three engines. With a crew as stout-hearted as his, he could run any mortal risk and still expect to scrape through. He got up to 15,000 feet, staggered over the Alps and, with his tanks practically drained dry,[11] at length landed on an English flying-field [Tangmere].

The pilot of that plane was awarded the Conspicuous Gallantry Medal. The wireless operator, Pilot Officer Frederick W. Gates of Cheam in Surrey received the DSO. 'The pilot did a first-class job of work on that trip,' was Gates' warm tribute. 'He made three vital decisions in quick succession. After we were hit and set alight by the fighter the pilot put the aircraft into a spiral dive and pulled out about 800 feet from the ground. Bullets had hit incendiary bombs that were not released from our aircraft. We heard an explosion and, in 15 seconds, the fire was burning fiercely.'[12]

Flight Sergeant G. P. Dove DFM was also awarded the Conspicuous Gallantry Medal and he had this to add to the picture:

'My window was burned and ammunition began to explode. The smoke was so thick that I could scarcely see the fighter when I got him in my sights. Only one gun was working properly. I scrambled down and picked the rear-gunner out of his turret. But owing to the fire and a hole blown in the bottom of the aircraft by the explosion, I couldn't carry him forward to the bed and I had to prop him up near his turret.'

In April, Bomber Command was hammering again at the Italian armament centres. On the 13th, Lancasters flew 700 miles on an outward journey to Spezia, to strafe the San Vim arsenal, the shipyards and the submarine base. Flying Officer V. A. Wilson, the captain of the last Lancaster to leave the port, saw the dockyards burning furiously. 'I could see below me the interiors of the buildings looking quite black, but with the walls white-hot. And there were wide areas as red as the inside of a furnace.'

There was not much flak and the searchlights waved hopelessly, 'like grass in the wind'.

'In fact,' Wilson continued, 'the only dangerous moment we had was when we were over the Alps. I was looking at the white caps of the mountains and the dark valleys when suddenly everything seemed to blur. I looked at my instrument panel and I could see only a luminous haze. I realized that I was passing out and made a quick check of the oxygen supply. Somehow or other we had developed a bad leak and there was no oxygen left. Clouds then came between us and the ground. I asked the navigator if it was safe to lower. In a rather weak voice he said he didn't think it was. But by that time there was nothing else to do, as I knew I should become unconscious at any moment, so I put nose down and hoped for the best. We lost 5,000 feet and then found we were just clear of the mountains and over France. We began to feel less "muggy" and came home the rest of the way in good spirits.'

That, apparently, is the way Bomber Command comes through, by just sticking to the job and never letting up. It is the way the saga of the Trans-Alpine flights was written in the Command's log books. A member of any of the RAF four-engined bomber crews requires sound heart and clear brain. And possibly even more he requires that spiritual something so inadequately described as 'guts'.

The Lancasters were back over Spezia within a week, giving the port another gruelling workout. It was the same story. The defences were overwhelmed and the night fighters in the main were fight-shy. Perhaps the Italian defenders had lost heart, for the North African campaign was virtually over and the Italian Empire was a thing of the past. The great autumn to spring Trans-Alpine flights staged by Bomber Command had contributed in no small measure to the winding up of that empire. Henceforth the tactical pounding of the German-held Italian mainland could be safely left to their comrades in the RAF flying from newly won bases in North Africa.

Notes

1. Seventy-six aircraft – 56 Wellingtons, 13 Stirlings and seven Halifaxes - were dispatched. Four Wellingtons and a Halifax were lost. Smoke and haze affected bombing but good results were claimed in the centre of the city and on the Fiat steelworks.

2. One hundred and twelve Lancasters and the Pathfinders were sent to Italy to drop 180 tons of bombs on Genoa in a raid which was to coincide with the opening of the Eighth Army offensive at El Alamein.

3. One hundred and twenty-two aircraft – 53 Halifaxes, 51 Stirlings and 18 Wellingtons set out to bomb Genoa again but the target was almost completely cloud covered and it was later determined that Savona, 30 miles along the coast from Genoa, had been bombed. Two Halifaxes and a Stirling were lost.

4. Eighty-eight Lancasters were sent to attack Milan in daylight. This time a fighter escort of Spitfires accompanied the force across the Channel to the Normandy coast.

5. On the night of 6/7 November the Pathfinders lit up the port for the 72 Lancasters. Flak was heavier than before, especially from the dock area but the results obtained were described as 'very satisfactory'. Later it was found that most of the bombs had fallen in residential areas. Two of the Lancasters failed to return.

6. On the night of 7/8 November 175 aircraft – 85 Lancasters, 45 Halifaxes, 39 Stirlings and six Wellingtons took part. Four Halifaxes, one Lancaster and one Wellington were lost.

7. Group Captain Robinson DSO DFC* AFC was killed when his Halifax was shot down during the raid on Berlin on the night of 23/24 August 1943.

8. Squadron Leader George Holden DSO DFC* MiD, now commanding 617 Dam Busters Squadron was killed on the night of 15/16 September on the raid on the Dortmund-Ems Canal at Ladbergen.

9. Wing Commander Guy Gibson DFC* and Flight Lieutenant W. N. Whamond of 106 Squadron dropped the first 8,000lb bombs on Italy. Pilot Officer F. G. Healy had also set out carrying an 8,000lb bomb but as the Lancaster's undercarriage would not retract, its bomb had to be jettisoned into the sea. The award of the DSO was made to Gibson in November 1942 and a bar would follow in March 1943.

10. Pilot Officer Moffatt, the bomb-aimer, baled out.

11. After leaving his position to help with the fires, Sergeant James Fortune Bain, the engineer, returned to find the starboard tank holed and leaking. He turned on the balance cocks and manipulated the petrol system throughout the return flight with the greatest skill and on landing only 15 gallons of petrol were found still in the port inner tank. *In Action With the Enemy; The Holders of the Conspicuous Gallantry Medal (Flying)* by Alan W. Cooper, (William Kimber 1986).

12. Sergeants Bain, Airey and Williams were all recommended on 16 February for awards of the Conspicuous Gallantry Medal (CGM), Pilot Officer Gates the DSO, while Hazard and Dove were recommended for the Victoria Cross. These two latter recommendations went as far as the AOC of No. 1 Group, Bomber Command, who approved them but upon reaching the C.-in-C., were changed, on 11 March to immediate awards of the CGM. All five CGMs and the DSO to Gates were gazetted on 23 March. On returning after special leave Hazard was assigned a new Lancaster and on 20 March he took it up for an air test. He made a low pass over Hornsea beach but on pulling up at the end of his run, the tail wheel struck a concrete pill box on the beach. The impact caused the Lancaster to break up. All ten men including Hazard, Bain and Williams, were killed instantly. Cooper, op. cit. Pilot Officer Gates DSO died when the Lancaster in which he was flying, crashed when returning from Dortmund on 5 May 1943.

# Chapter 11

# Dam Buster – Dudley Heal

At the outbreak of the Second World War in 1939 I was an Assistant Preventive Officer in the (then) Waterguard branch of HM Customs and Excise, stationed in Southampton Docks. I had a close friend and colleague, Les Twentyman, who had joined the Service on the same day as me, 18 September 1936. As established civil servants we were exempt from call-up to the Armed Forces. Indeed, if we wanted to enlist we would have to obtain the permission of the Board of Customs before we could do so. Les and I frequently discussed this situation during the months of the 'phoney' war so that when the Board announced in March 1940, that after a certain date in May no Customs staff aged 23 or over would be allowed to join the Armed Forces it made our minds up for us. We were both 23! We forthwith applied for permission to enlist in the RAF. It was about this time that we got to know the Commanding Officer of No. 2 Embarkation Unit RAF, stationed in Southampton Docks. Squadron Leader Burt, like us, enjoyed a lunchtime glass of beer in the Canute, a pub just outside the dock gates. Learning of our intention to join the RAF as aircrew, he warned us that even if we were accepted it would be some time before we could expect to start flying training, thanks to the RAF having more would-be pilots than aircraft. 'You're both tall,' he said, 'I could use a couple of Service Policemen in my unit. Why not join the SPs while you're waiting for flying training?'

We both buried our faces in our glasses to hide the look of horror that had spread over them. Service policemen! A fate worse than death. 'What a good idea,' we cried, 'we'll bear it in mind.'

I learned one useful tip from the squadron leader, however – that the medical exam for aircrew included having to blow into a tube and hold a bulb of mercury at a certain point in the tube for a full minute. I should add here that as an asthmatic I had been apprehensive as to whether I would pass the medical exam for the Civil Service. In the event there had been no problems, but no blowing mercury up a tube either.

As soon as I was alone in my 'digs' that day I took my watch in my hand, inhaled deeply and held my breath. It ran out well short of a minute. From now on I practised this as often as I could.

In the meantime, Les and I had received permission from the Board to enlist, which we did forthwith and, in due course, were called to RAF Uxbridge for, among other procedures, a medical examination. Les had no trouble with it. For me the high point came when the Medical Officer handed me a tube and told me what to do as he stood there, watch in hand. Uttering a silent prayer and taking a very deep breath I blew the mercury up the tube to the required point and stood there watching it as the seconds ticked slowly by. Then I could hold it no longer and the bulb sank to the bottom of the tube. I looked at the MO. He looked at me for a moment and then indicated that I had passed. I believe it was touch-and-go. Thank you, Squadron Leader Burt for the warning. Everything else being satisfactory, we were told that we would be called up in due course and warned that we would probably have to wait for some time for aircrew training. During that waiting period we would have the choice of doing 'general duties' or of being – wait for it – Service policemen! Someone up there was having a good laugh at our expense. We had only the vaguest idea of what 'general duties' entailed but had enough imagination to guess some of the jobs under that heading so we chose 'Service police' and returned to Southampton to await our call-up.

This came eventually and, on 8 May 1940, we said goodbye to all our friends and colleagues and returned to Uxbridge. This was in effect the port of entry for all new recruits, in the south of England at any rate, to the Royal Air Force. Here one was given a service number and, of course, the lowest rank, that of Aircraftman, 2nd Class (AC2). Here one was documented, inoculated, measured for and fitted with uniform and generally indoctrinated into the basic rules of life in the Armed Forces. Also, by no means least important, one was introduced to the NAAFI, that supplier of all vital needs, such as a cup of tea.

The next few weeks confirmed Squadron Leader Burt's forecast of long delays before receiving aircrew training. One gets the impression that the RAF didn't quite know what to do with us at this time. We found ourselves at Hendon, for example, looking after the coke boiler in the airmen's quarters. I remember it particularly because of the Saturday afternoon when we were so unpopular because we'd let it go out and nobody could have a bath. Then there was Bridgnorth. Every effort was made to bring us and the rest of the course up to the required standard of physical fitness. We did 'square-bashing', arms drill and even bayonet drill, as there was the very real threat at this time of a German invasion; also cross-country runs as a change from exercise in the gymnasium.

From there we went to Wyton in Huntingdonshire where we seemed to spend most of time patrolling bomb dumps, usually at night. Quite by the way, I recall that during this period an adjutant at one of these stations did his best to persuade Les to give up the idea of aircrew and settle for being a Service policeman. I'm glad to say Les resisted this successfully – I must have been on leave at the time.

Our next move was to Southampton Docks. I don't know how it came about and can only think that Squadron Leader Burt had pulled a few strings. It was not unwelcome, however, as it meant that I could see my family frequently and we would be back amongst old friends again. Other memories of this period are of sitting in a train at Woolston Station while German bombers attacked the nearby Supermarine Spitfire factory – not a pleasant experience – and of one of the blitzes on Southampton. I remember Les and I leaving our billet in the docks, walking up through the town and, seeing a light on in an upper room of a house where the walls had been demolished during a raid, throwing stones at it to try and put it out.

The fact that fires were still burning all around seemed to have escaped our notice. We finally came to our senses and sat out the rest of the blitz in a shelter on Southampton Common.

Needless to say, our colleagues in the Waterguard were astonished to see us standing on the dock gates once again, this time in RAF uniform (with SP badges on our arms). We were to spend the winter of 1940/1 doing this, with a change of venue occasionally, but doing the same thing, at nearby RAF Calshot.

At long last we were posted to No. 8 Initial Training Wing, Newquay, Cornwall – the first real step towards pilot training. This was classroom stuff, really – trigonometry, mathematics, meteorology and so on, interspersed with a certain amount of physical exercise. As cadet pilots we now wore white flashes in our caps and had to be on our best behaviour at Newquay.

At the end of six weeks we took and passed the usual tests. I think we had hoped to stay together for a while but had certainly not dreamed of Les going to South Africa and myself to Canada! We made the best of it and said 'goodbye', not knowing when, or if, we should meet again. We went on leave and then parted from our families, for the time being at least. I headed for Liverpool where I and others from the RAF and Fleet Air Arm joined the merchantman *Northumberland* bound for Halifax, Nova Scotia.

We slept in the holds, in hammocks during the 10-day crossing, which passed uneventfully in convoy. From Halifax we were put on a train for Moncton, New Brunswick, RCAF, the centre for the receipt and disposal of all would-be aircrew. I remember it mainly for the enjoyable outings to Toronto, Montreal and Lake Ontario, thanks to the kindness of some of the Canadians at Moncton. Then the postings came through. For the group of which I was now a part it would not be Saskatchewan or Winnipeg but Pensacola, Florida, a holiday resort on the Gulf of Mexico. Some people are just lucky. It was a 36-hour train journey, not in uniform, since the States were not at war, but in grey flannel suits! Pensacola was the main Naval Air Base and comprised 30 landing grounds. It had a very high reputation for the quality of its pilot training so we were going to have to be pretty good. There was, of course, the usual classroom introduction but actual flying soon began on Stearman biplanes, similar to our Tiger Moths. My first flight took place on 8 September, my instructor being one Ensign Nelson. I have to admit that handling an aircraft did not come naturally to me but he was very patient and, in due course, I was put up for a test flight with another instructor. In my log book this is shown as 'NG'. Officially this meant 'failed' although as far as I was concerned it meant 'no good'. We persevered, however and on 7 October, after another test flight, the instructor stepped down from the aircraft and waved me off on my own. A proud moment indeed and I continued my training, flying more than 20 hours solo. It did not last, however and on 1 November I was up before a Board who decided that I would be better employed fulfilling some other function in the aircraft. As a matter of interest the item in the instructors' manual, which marked my downfall, says: 'Precision landings, 180 degrees, from 800 feet and its application in intermediate field approaches.' I have wondered whether that figured in the wartime RAF manual.

With other NG's I awaited my posting back to Moncton. I had made friends with American servicemen and civilians in the town so I had to say goodbye to them and thank them for their kindness and hospitality. So with other 'wash-outs' (the uncompromising term for those who had failed a course) I headed back to Canada, wondering what was in future for me now. At Moncton I was asked what other flying duty I would like to re-muster to and without hesitation, I replied 'navigator'. This was accepted and I waited again, this time in the depths of a Canadian winter, to hear about my next posting. It could be anywhere in that enormous continent, be it Canada or the USA.

On 15 January 1942 I boarded a train once more, this time with a number of would-be navigators, heading for the Gulf of Mexico and the spring-like weather of Pensacola, Florida. I renewed friendships there and got down to learning all those things which would enable me (hopefully) to answer a pilot's questions as to where we were and what course to steer to enable him to reach his destination. This was mainly classroom work at first, interrupted from time to time with sessions with a sextant, looking at the sun or stars. The climax of the course consisted of half a dozen flights, with several other would-be navigators in a Catalina, that marvellous flying boat, which could stay in the air for 24 hours, if necessary. Our trips took, on an average, about six hours nearly all over the Gulf of Mexico.

The course ended as usual with exams, in which I did fairly well and once more it was off to New Brunswick. Here we were told that the first six in the exams would fly home, the remainder going by sea. So I found myself heading for Dorval Airport, Montreal where I boarded a Lockheed Ventura which was being delivered to the Royal Air Force. I admired the American civil pilot who was undertaking this journey with a 'sprog' navigator and a 'sprog' wireless operator. He seemed fairly confident, I'm glad to say.

We took-off from Dorval and landed twice on the journey to refuel, first at Goose Bay, Labrador, next at Reykjavik, Iceland. Both these legs were uneventful and more or less according to plan. The third one from Iceland to Prestwick was not quite so smooth. We were well on our way when I left my seat and went back to the Elsan. Returning to my seat I tripped over something on the floor (it was the middle of the night and dark). I had, unfortunately, released the catch of the inflatable dinghy – which filled with air, more or less blocking the way to the Elsan should anybody else need to use it! I told the pilot what had happened. Neither he nor the wireless operator seemed particularly worried about it. When the time came for Scotland to hove in sight, according to my calculations, all we could see was the sea. The wireless operator began to look for the beam from Prestwick and eventually found it, necessitating a 90-degree turn to port and flying for quite a while until Scotland came into view.

It was now late May 1942 and I rejoined my family after an absence of nearly a year. After a joyous reunion and a spell of leave, I reported to No. 3 Advanced Flying Unit, Bobbington, Shropshire, where eventually I was reunited with the rest of my course from Pensacola, including friends I had made. Early in the course six of them were commissioned but not me. I was somewhat irked although it did not make any difference between my friends and me. I think however, that I worked even harder during the course and the end of term exams because of it. The result being that I came out top in the exams with 93 per cent. I mention this because it has a bearing on the rest of my time in the Service.

Our next move was to No. 19 Operational Training Unit, Kinloss. Here we crewed up with one or other of the pilots, bomb-aimers, wireless operators and gunners, all of whom were at the same stage in their training. I had no idea how this crewing-up was done but I soon found out. A day or two after my arrival I was walking through a hangar when three Canadians – pilot, a bomb-aimer and a gunner – stopped me. There was a never-ending influx of volunteers from all parts of the Empire, all anxious to take part in the struggle against Hitler. Although they kept their own uniforms or wore RAF uniforms with shoulder flashes such as 'RCAF' they accepted the routine and discipline of the RAF and were likewise accepted by us part and parcel of the overall struggle against Fascism.

'Your name Heal?' asked the pilot, a tall well-built chap. 'Yes' I said. 'Then you're going to be our navigator,' he said. I looked questioningly at him. 'Who says so?' I asked. 'I've just been to the Navigation Office' he said. 'You were top of your course at AFU so we want you to be our navigator.' I looked at the other two who were obviously in complete agreement with him. I liked the look of all of them and, if I considered it at all, my reaction would have been that here was someone who was interested in survival, which couldn't be bad. I agreed to join them without further ado. The pilot's name was Ken Brown. We shook hands; he introduced the bomb-aimer, Steve Oancia and the rear-gunner Grant McDonald and off we went to the NAAFI for a cup of tea. I can honestly say that I never regretted that decision. We then acquired a wireless operator, 'Hewie' Hewstone, and from that time on, our being together as a crew was everything.

Now we had to get used to each other, to a different aircraft, although Ken had already put in a fair amount of flying time with the Whitley, and to the fact that this was the last stage before real operations against the enemy. Most of our flying would be carried out at night and because much of it consisted of bombing practice we took it for granted that we were headed for Bomber Command. With one exception I enjoyed our time at Kinloss as we worked very well together as a crew. The exception was the sad loss of two Whitleys with their crews when they collided at night over the Moray Firth.

It came as something of a surprise when, having finished our course towards the end of October, we were posted to a Coastal Command base, St Eval, Cornwall. From here the crews carried out anti-submarine 'sweeps' in Whitleys. These could last anything up to 10 hours and ranged deep into the Bay of Biscay. To get one in daylight at this time of the year we had to be airborne by 0700 hours, which meant getting up at about 0430. From the time Bishop Rock disappeared from view behind us we would see nothing but the sea and the sky until, hopefully, Bishop Rock hove into view again. These flights were an excellent test for the navigator; also for the bomb-aimer in the nose of the aircraft who, from observation of the direction of the waves below with his drift sight, would keep the navigator informed as to wind direction, and for the pilot, on whose steadiness in maintaining the set course, would depend the accuracy of the track flown by the aircraft. This was in addition to his other responsibilities, as captain of the aircraft. Apart from this, all members of the crew would, as far as possible, keep their eyes open for submarines, aircraft and shipping. As we approached the Scilly Isles (hopefully) at the end of the 'sweep', all eyes would be alert for the first glimpse of land. Our crew made reasonable landfalls on all our 'sweeps' but I'm sorry to say that that was not always the case. One Whitley while we were at St Eval, made landfall on a Welsh mountain with the loss of all on board.

Our next move, early in 1943, was to Wigsley in Lincolnshire. Here we would convert, firstly to the twin-engined Manchester and then to its successor, the Lancaster. Here also we acquired two new crew members, Basil Feneron, flight engineer and Donald Buntain, mid-upper gunner. Now we learned to operate the Lancaster.

One memory of Wigsley is of arriving back from a cross-country flight to find the airfield swathed in fog. Rather than try and land somewhere else Ken had Steve drop navigation flares on a dummy run, after which we were able to land on the airfield. Ken had difficulty accepting mine and Basil's Christian names and ended by calling us 'D' and 'Buzz' respectively.

We were now posted to 44 Squadron, still in Lincolnshire. After the settling-in period Ken and I were detailed for our first operation over enemy territory, each with an experienced crew, I was bound for Wilhelmshaven in the capable hands of a certain Sergeant Forman. It was a clear, moonlit night and the navigation presented no problems. You could see the searchlights and 'flak' at the target long before you got within range. We bombed our target as accurately as we could and set course for Waddington. It was ironic that we should find the base swathed in fog and be diverted to Leeming in Yorkshire, returning to Waddington the next day.

Our first 'op' as a crew was to Munich. This was my first opportunity to use that marvellous navigational aid, *Gee*. We floated calmly down over southern England, the Channel and Northern France, checking our position at intervals with *Gee*. I worked out the change of course for Munich and shortly afterwards took another fix. To my horror we were well south of where we should be (if the fix was correct) and I told Ken so, working out a new course as I did so. This would be a long flight and we could not afford to waste petrol so I aimed directly for Munich. Eventually we began to see the same sort of picture ahead that I'd seen at Wilhelmshaven and I knew we were on the right track. We arrived over Munich 45 minutes after we should have done and had the 'flak' and searchlights all to ourselves. There did not appear to be any fighters about. (They were our main worry, of course, on a moonlit night.) I have always assumed that they had returned to base after the main force had turned for home and it was not considered worthwhile to get them airborne again for one bomber.

For the return journey I chose the shortest possible route and we landed back at Waddington long after everybody else, having been airborne for eight hours and fifteen minutes. The following morning the Navigation Leader sent for me. Eyeing my chart from the previous night he said, 'According to this you flew over every major city in the German Reich last night.' Restraining the temptation to say, 'Yes, that was how it felt to me,' I told him what had happened and we tried to find some explanation for it. I dismissed the thought that I had given Ken the new course to turn on over Northern France and for some reason he hadn't done so. It seemed just as unlikely to me that I had worked out the new course and had not passed it on to him. Anyway, the Nav Leader arranged to have the aircraft compasses swung, a process carried out on the ground whereby they could be checked for accuracy. No fault was found and the mystery remains to this day.

We flew to Essen, Duisburg and Berlin among other targets in that month of March and were then completely taken aback to be told, early in April, that we were being posted forthwith to Scampton, a few miles north of Lincoln and the base for 57 Squadron. We would be joining a new squadron that was being formed. We were not told why we had been chosen. We were on our way within 24 hours. At this time Ken was a flight sergeant and wore a crown over his three stripes while the rest of us were still sergeants. We found we were only one of some 20 crews, which would arrive within the next few days to join Squadron X. Then came the morning when we were all called to the briefing room where our new CO, Wing Commander Gibson, DSO* DFC* called us to order to tell us that the squadron had been formed to attack a particular target, the identity of which could not be revealed to anyone until briefing for the operation took place. Security would be at maximum and anyone caught talking about the squadron outside Scampton would be severely disciplined. We would be training for an unidentified period by night and at low level. With that we were dismissed.

During the next six weeks there were few days when we were not flying. At first it was just low level, say 200 feet above ground. As time wore on more and more flying was over water, the sea, rivers, or canals by day and then gradually by night. Tinted screens were affixed to the perspex around the cockpit in the daytime to simulate night flying. We practised flying over Derwent Water and attacking the dam with a newly designed bombsight that looked just like a dam, strangely enough. Of course, we all laughed at the idea that we might be going to attack a dam – we all knew that *Tirpitz* was the target. Spotlights were fitted to the underside of the aircraft, which converged to a point on the water when the aircraft was at the required height.

All this time 57 Squadron were steadily plugging over Germany at night and, no doubt, suffering the same percentage of casualties as the rest of Bomber Command. I don't think they thought much of 617 (as we now were).

While we were doing all this low-level flying, one incident comes to mind. We were flying along a canal and Steve called out, 'Bridge ahead'. Ken, of course, could see it and there was some discussion as to the size and height of it ending with Ken saying, 'Let's find out', whereupon he put the nose down and flew under it! I still remember those feelings as we were momentarily enclosed on four sides. I did not enter that in my log.

On 13 May the first of the bombs for our operation arrived. It looked like an outside garden roller and would be slung beneath the aircraft, the bomb doors having been removed and replaced by special fittings. Security at Scampton reached a high point over the next 48 hours. There was no chance of a trip into Lincoln.

In the early afternoon of 15 May the Tannoy came to life: 'All pilots, navigators and bomb-aimers of 617 Squadron report to the briefing-room immediately.' The great moment had arrived and we were to spend the next four or five hours learning all about the Ruhr dams, listening to Wing Commander Gibson and to Barnes Wallis, inventor of the bomb we would use. We studied models of the dams as well as the route we were to follow. Every known concentration of anti-aircraft fire would be noted as well as every possible landmark. No effort was spared to equip us for this op.[1]

We were dismissed, with the injunction that we were to tell nobody, not even our crew mates, what the targets were. Preparations continued on 16th and then all the aircrew were called for briefing. We learned that we would form part of the third, reserve wave to take-off, would set course for the Möhne dam but be ready to receive fresh orders en route. Soon after 2100 hours we watched the first wave of nine aircraft take-off in formations of three. This was most unusual for bombers. They lumbered over the grass (Scampton had no runways) with their bombs slung beneath the aircraft, and gathered speed slowly to clear the perimeter fence with little to spare. We silently wished them 'God-speed'. The second wave had taken-off a little earlier as they would follow a different route, rather longer, to distract the defences. We now had something like two hours to wait. I think most of us wrote a letter, just in case, collected our equipment and went down to dispersal to get organized in the aircraft and to chat to our ground crew who spent so many hours making sure that all was done that could be done to ensure that everything would work perfectly. We expressed our appreciation for their efforts.

It was 0020 when we, in our turn, lumbered across the airfield and climbed slowly into the air, as did the other members of the third wave. We set course according to the expected wind and headed for the coast. We would be in touch with base and had coded words with which to signal to base the result of any attack we made.

We flew as low as possible over the North Sea, 100 feet and less, to avoid attracting the attention of the enemy radar. At the Dutch coast we were a little off track so I made some adjustments. Steve kept me informed of any landmarks and I realized after a while that we had this tendency to drift off to starboard, so from then on I added or subtracted 5 degrees whenever the planned route called for a change of course. I was lucky that I had three pairs of eyes up front to report anything of interest to me – and other matters such as the loss of one Lancaster over Holland and another near the notorious Hamm marshalling yards. I was glad that we also had two pairs of eyes, which could see behind should fighters appear. Our mid-upper gunner, incidentally, was off sick and Dave Allatson from a reserve crew took his place. Both he and Grant, the rear-gunner, used their guns to good effect during this 'op'.

Some time before we were due to reach the Möhne dam, 'Hewie' reported that both it and the Eder had been breached and we were to aim for the Sorpe. We changed course, much encouraged by this news. Barnes Wallis' bomb was designed to be released by an aircraft heading over water towards a dam, the bomb then bouncing over water (like a pebble skimmed over the sea from the shore), hitting the dam and sinking to 20 feet, when it was set to explode. It had been realized quite late in the day that this was effective if the dam was built of concrete but no good for an earth dam, as the Sorpe was. Our instructions, therefore, were to fly over and along the line of the dam at 60 feet, releasing the bomb as near the centre of the dam as we could.

We found the Sorpe dam with no trouble and could see it quite clearly at the northern end of the Sorpe river. The ground rose steeply on each side, heavily wooded, with a church steeple on our line of approach, all, except the river and dam, swathed in mist. The only good point appeared to be that there were no defences. After two or three abortive runs, Ken decided to try the Wigsley 'gambit' of dropping flares along the approach route. We could see that the top of the dam was already damaged.[2] Eventually avoiding the steeple, dropping the bomb at 60 feet and pulling up sharply over the wooded hill we saw our bomb go off, causing an enormous water spout and an extension of the damage already done.[3] After a good look at it we set course for base, Hewie transmitting 'Goner', indicating that we had attacked but not breached the dam. Our homeward track took us near the Möhne dam and we stared in awe at the breach through which the Möhne river was rushing down the valley. After that the journey back was uneventful until we approached the Dutch coast and could see the sea ahead. Then, without warning, we were caught and held by searchlights and blasted by gunfire. Even in my curtained compartment I was blinded by those searchlights so how Ken and Basil coped I shall never know. Ken even put the nose down although we were already flying as low as seemed possible and we flew on. Then we were over the sea and I could see shells whizzing over our heads and hitting the water. The searchlights lost their effect and Ken handed over the controls to Basil, while he and I examined the holes in the fuselage. The starboard side of the aircraft at just above head height was riddled. I think there is little doubt that had we remained at the same height, or even attempted to climb, it would have been disastrous. (We learned later that Squadron Leader Young had gone down earlier at this same spot.)[4] Back at Scampton we were the last aircraft but one to touch down. Flight Sergeant Townsend landed about half-an-hour later, having attacked the Ennepe dam but, like us, failed to breach it.[5]

The importance with which the powers-that-be regarded this operation is demonstrated by the fact that Air Chief Marshal Harris, head of Bomber Command, attended the de-briefing of the returning crews, as did Barnes Wallis and the Station Commander, Group Captain Whitworth. I don't think any of us went to bed that night.

We were all given a week's leave now and it was during that week that IT happened. Halfway through the week I was sitting at the tea table with my parents and my brother, Les, (my other brother, Don, being at sea) when the doorbell rang. Being nearest, I got up and answered it. It was a telegram for me from Scampton. Back in the living room I held it up and said, 'I hope that isn't a recall from leave.' I opened it, everybody watching me apprehensively and read it aloud – it said, 'Heartiest congratulations on award of the Distinguished Flying Medal. Wingco.' We were all speechless. Then my father, who was secretary of the British Legion Club in Gosport, said, 'We're all going down to the Club tonight' – which we did.

Back at Scampton after the leave I found that Steve had also received the DFM while Ken had been awarded the CGM (Conspicuous Gallantry Medal). Basically, awards had been given to pilots, navigators and bomb-aimers who had reached and attacked their targets accurately, whether or not they had been breached. Where other members of the crews, gunners for example, had distinguished themselves in some way they could also have been decorated. The matter of rank was always a problem in this connection. Commissioned pilots had received the DSO, a most prestigious decoration, as Ken knew. Non-commissioned pilots received the CGM, which few people had heard of at that time – similarly, if I had been commissioned I would have received the DFC. I think Ken was, as a Canadian, miffed about this class distinction although he did realize that he had received one of the rarest 'gongs' of all. For my part I could not have been more thrilled if I had been awarded the Victoria Cross.

The raid received maximum publicity and does to this day thanks mainly to Barnes Wallis' 'Bouncing Bomb', but also to that excellent film, *The Dam Busters* with its marvellous music by Eric Coates. Scampton was honoured by a visit from Their Majesties the King and Queen and the decorations were presented by the Queen, (the King being in Africa), at a special investiture on 22 June 1943.

That over, 617 settled down to work again not, as most of us expected, to the hammering of German cities and industries but to specialized targets which needed accurate bombing by a small force. One such was the Antheor Viaduct in the south of France. This carried the railway between France and Italy and, as the Allies at this time were still fighting their way up through Italy, was being used to good effect by the enemy.

Because of the distance to Antheor it was arranged that after the attack the squadron would fly on to land at an airfield near Blida in Algeria. Here temporary accommodation was laid on and the aircraft would be refuelled. Here also, we found that we could fly home with a cargo of that commodity, at the time almost unobtainable in Britain – oranges. Three times we attacked this target, the third time in February 1944, a new arrangement was made. (I think Algeria had run out of oranges.) We flew first to Ford airfield in Sussex, topped up our fuel and then took-off for Antheor, returning to Ford after the op for refuelling, then back to base. This was when one of those incidents occurred for which no reason could be found. One of the flight commanders, taking-off from Ford to return home, in daylight, flew into high ground, just north of the airfield with the loss of all on board.

Also a casualty at Antheor was Squadron Leader Bob Hay, navigator to Mickey Martin, flight commander. Martin DSO* DFC* was one of the first choices for 617 when it was formed because of his known ability and predilection for low flying. On this occasion their aircraft was hit by a shell in the nose; Hay and Alan Whittaker, the flight engineer, were wounded and the Lancaster badly damaged. Martin managed to land in Sardinia, still with a bomb on board. Hay died from his wounds.

In August 617 moved to Coningsby nearby, where there were hard runways which Scampton lacked. Other long distance targets we attacked were power stations in northern Italy, on one occasion bombing Leghorn on the return trip. Factories such as the one at Limoges in France, Michelin, which were now producing material for the German war effort, were attacked with due care for the workers in them, the Lancasters flying over the factory two or three times, dropping flares at the same time and thereby giving the workers time to seek shelter.

Late in August it was noted that massive concrete structures were springing up in northern France. They were, of course, sites for the launching of V-1 and V-2 weapons, which would require accurate bombing with the biggest possible bombs. They would be 617 targets for the foreseeable future.

617, meanwhile, had moved again, this time to Woodhall Spa, near Coningsby, where we would be the only squadron. Accommodation was temporary at first and the nearby Petwood Hotel, taken over by the RAF, was our billet. In the hurly-burly of removal we found beds where we could and the first night I shared a room with members of another crew, the captain being Flight Lieutenant O'Shaughnessy. The next day they went off for some low level flying and bombing practice, ending up by flying into a rise in the ground off the beach. That night I shared a room with six empty beds.

It was in February 1944 that Ken began to have problems with his hearing and was occasionally unable to make out what was being said over the intercom. He reported to the MO, as a result of which our CO, now Wing Commander Leonard Cheshire, called us into his office to tell us that Ken would be grounded for the time being for medical reports. He went on to give us the choice of flying with another pilot or of being 'rested'. This was difficult, off the cuff. We had not yet completed the required 30 ops but we had been with 617 for nearly a year, not forgetting our time with 44 Squadron and with Coastal Command; altogether some 16 months under operational conditions. Added to this was the reluctance to change pilots – I said I would prefer to be 'rested'.

The other members of the crew felt as I did. Wing Commander Cheshire accepted our decision, shook hands with us and thanked us for our service. It was not long before our postings came through, mine being to Bruntingthorpe, near Rugby. I said 'Au Revoir' to the other members of the crew rather than 'goodbye'. The normal rest period was six months. It was now February 1944 and the war seemed likely to continue indefinitely.

At Bruntingthorpe I found that I would be teaching *Gee* to would-be navigators under classroom conditions. This left the evenings free, an unusual luxury, and after a while I began to spend some of those evenings with two or three fellow 'teachers', cycling to a village called, I swear, Willoughby Waterless, where we would play darts in the only pub, making friends with the locals. Occasionally we would cycle back to camp with a bag containing half a dozen eggs slung over the handlebars. These, with our names pencilled on them, were handed in to the Officers' Mess kitchen and eventually served up for our breakfast.

I should mention here that a new device was being used by Bomber Command in the year of the invasion. It was called 'Window'. It consisted of strips of metal, which were dropped from a bomber in large quantities and in some order over or near a target. This had the effect of disrupting the enemy radar and were put to good use by 617 on D-Day, 6 June 1944. By the most precise flying and dropping of 'Window' between Beachy Head and Calais the enemy were deceived into believing it was the invasion approaching.

I was now a Flying Officer, playing darts instead of helping the invasion. When I was approached by one of the pilots at Bruntingthorpe later in 1944 and asked if I would go back on 'ops' with him I did not hesitate for long. I had to smile when he said he would be joining a special squadron. When with 617 I had been a member of 5 Group, Bomber Command. The new Squadron was 214 in 100 Group (Radio Counter-Measures). They did not at this time carry bombs but carried three extra crew for operating the various sorts of radar equipment in the aircraft. This was all for disrupting the enemy defences. 'Window' was also used. I agreed to join Flight Lieutenant Johnny Wynne DFC and soon we had a complete crew of ten and joined 214 Squadron early in 1945.

We now changed to B-17s (Fortresses) and all had to make ourselves familiar with our new aircraft and freshen up our old skills. My new bomb-aimer colleague was one 'Tubby' Pow. For the next month we flew almost every day (or night) and, on 14th February, we did our first operation with 214. Since we weren't carrying bombs we didn't necessarily go to the main force target but could have quite a different programme. My log book, therefore, is no help in saying where we went.

It consists of entries like 'SD' (Special Duty), Ruhr ('Window') or Heilbron (*Jostle*) – *Jostle* was another form of jamming technique. In Fortresses we could fly higher than Lancasters or Halifaxes and were, in fact, required to do so, which is why these aircraft were used. We had, therefore, a good view of what was going on as we, Tubby and I, sat in the nose of the aircraft facing sideways. We had screens of course when we needed them.

On our 8th op we were required to drop down to 6,000 feet for the flight home; I don't know why. After more than an hour's flying in pitch darkness from the farthest point, we were suddenly caught by searchlights and hit by shellfire. The port inner engine began to burn. Johnny ordered the flight engineer to stop the engine, which he tried to do but without success. Johnny asked me where we were. I had seen nothing but darkness for over an hour but was fairly confident that we were something like 20 miles from the Rhine (the Franco-German border). We were losing height slowly and the damaged engine, apart from the fire, was causing considerable vibration. Any attempt to 'feather' the propeller didn't work. We were told to put on our parachutes. Johnny now gave the order to bale out.

I got up from my table, climbed the steps to the cockpit where Johnny and Dick, the flight engineer, were still fighting the fire in the engine without much success, gave them the 'thumbs-up' sign and went down again to help Tubby open the escape hatch in the nose. It appeared to be jammed but we got it open and I sat on the edge with my feet dangling in a black void, summoning the courage to jump. A blow in the middle of the back put an end to that and I was out. It was pitch black and absolutely silent. The contrast was unbelievable. I turned over and over and I stretched my arms and legs to see if I could stop spinning. Whilst doing this it suddenly occurred to me that I didn't really have time for that sort of thing. I pulled the ripcord and was brought up with the unexpected violent jerk and found myself swinging gently in the quiet and darkness. There was a faint white line in the distance, which I took to be the horizon but apart from that I could see nothing. Below, however, the area immediately beneath me seemed rather darker than the rest. 'My God,' I thought, 'it's a lake.' I was immediately proved wrong, however, because in the next second I landed – flat on my face on a hard surface. When I got my breath back I found that I was spread-eagled across the ridged roof of a large building with my parachute all around me. I carefully raised myself into a sitting position and collected the chute together before looking round to see where I was. I couldn't even see the ground; everything was so dark.

I thought I might have a cigarette and felt in my pocket for my lighter. Unfortunately it slipped from my fingers, rolled down the sloping roof and that was the last I heard of it. I had no idea how tall the building was or whether there were any other buildings around. I edged my way along the roof with my parachute and found that I was on a false roof with wooden panels, the main roof being two or three feet below me. I now heard the sound of a motor vehicle approaching and could see its dimmed headlights. It sounded very continental. It looked as if it was going to drive right past the building but it turned and came to a halt almost below where I sat. The night was so dark that I could not see it but I heard it stop and the engine was turned off. This was followed by the clatter of heavy boots and loud orders shouted in what, I'm sorry to say, was certainly German. I heard a door being forced open and then the boots again, this time inside the building, coming up the stairs and then right past where I huddled on the fake roof, my chute in my arms. I heard the boots clatter down again and out onto the truck. At that moment a torch shone on the roof as three shots were fired. I wasn't hit, I'm glad to say. Down from the truck, across the yard and into the building again, this time the boots stopped just where I was. The panel was broken open and arms reached out and pulled me inside – not roughly. I was taken down and put on the truck and I was the object of curious looks from members of the Wehrmacht. I spent the rest of that night, after the truck had unloaded us, walking in a convoy of soldiers and horse drawn vehicles to some unknown destination, clutching part of a loaf of bread a sergeant had given me (or was it a Feldwebel?).

The sequence of events during the next two or three days remain somewhat confused in my mind. They include sleeping one night in what was obviously an army barrack, or to be more specific, lying on the floor in the corner of a mess room where German soldiers sat at tables, eating and drinking. There was much coming and going and it was obvious that I aroused considerable interest as newcomers caught sight of me, tucked up in a blanket, and wanted to know who I was. I don't think I was very popular (after the recent heavy civilian casualties in Dresden, Cologne etc. from RAF bombing raids) and I was greatly relieved when I was taken away from there the following morning.

The next day I was put in an open truck once more, this time with civilians, apart from my guard. We drove through a town, which had suffered considerable bomb damage. It was Pforzheim. Seeing me looking at the buildings, a middle-aged man asked me, in English, how I felt about the damage. I said that I didn't like it but they had started it. We began to argue but my guard told him to shut up.

I was dropped at the local prison and on my way to a cell I caught sight of our wireless operator, Tommy Tate, in another cell. I didn't get a chance to speak to him at that time. While there I was taken outside and told to look after another RAF prisoner who had obviously been burned about the face and neck. He was heavily bandaged, particularly around the eyes and could not see. Since he could not tell if I was who I said I was, I refrained from asking any questions. I did what I could for him and eventually he was taken off to hospital. I should mention here that at some time during the night I found out that Tubby, our bomb-aimer, had landed in telegraph wires and broken a leg. He had, I was told, been taken to hospital. The next thing was that I was taken before a Luftwaffe officer for interrogation. He asked for identification and then asked what squadron I belonged to. I said I was only allowed to give him my name, rank and service number (which I had already done). I waited for him to ring for the Gestapo but he merely smiled and said he already knew I was one of the crew of a Lancaster from such-and-such a squadron, based at such and such an RAF station. I tried to look surprised and alarmed that he should know that but it didn't matter as he rang a bell and had me taken away. (I found out later that Tommy Tate had had exactly the same experience.)

Shortly after that I joined up with Tommy and Norman Bradley (another member of our crew) and we found ourselves in a sort of church hall with other RAF and British Army POWs. Life now took on some semblance of normality. Everybody spoke the same language and those who, like Tommy, Norman and myself, had been in a sort of solitary confinement couldn't stop talking.

Now I was able to learn what had happened to other members of our crew. Whereas Tubby and I had left the aircraft by the escape hatch in the nose, all of the others, with the possible exception of Johnny had left by the rear escape hatch. As there were seven of them it would have taken them longer to get organized and all out of the aircraft, so there would have been some distance between them and us when we were all captured. They had all been rounded up together and marched through the nearby town of Pforzheim, which had been heavily bombed before and the civilians had been very hostile. The prisoners, with their guards, were put into a cellar in the town overnight. During the night civilians, largely Hitler Youth, broke into the cellar, overpowered the guards and dragged the prisoners out into the street. There they were beaten up, then dragged off to a cemetery and were shot. Norman and Tommy managed to escape in the confusion. This was terrible news. It was not difficult to put oneself in the place of those unfortunate men and I could feel nothing but loathing for the so-called Hitler Youth. It personified all that was evil in fascism. I know now, I'm glad to say, that some of them were eventually brought to justice. [6]

This business also raised a number of questions in my mind. Was the information I had given Johnny as to our position accurate? Why did he order us to bale out so soon? And where was he now? Tommy, Norman and I discussed this endlessly without coming to any conclusions. Some light was shed on this much later.

Now we learned that we were going to start walking – away from the advancing Allies. There was some organization now in a larger group of prisoners. I acquired, among other things, a blanket and a diary, the latter being a gift from the 'European Student Relief Fund', based in Geneva. Both these items were most welcome, the diary in particular because it enables me now to read details and atmosphere I would have probably forgotten. Anything in inverted commas that follows is probably a quote from the diary, such as (first entry).

'Tuesday, 3rd April '45. Left Ludwigsburg at 10.30 last night. Walked fairly slowly until about 04.30 when we parked in a Stadium. Cold and damp. Set course again about noon. Walk very tiring. Arrived destination (WEIRLINGEN) about 6 pm.'

With variations this was to be the pattern for the next month or so. Friday, 6 April, was not a happy day: 'Bad night, rained half the time we were walking. Made 18 kms. Very cold and wet, No sleep. If I don't get pneumonia it'll be a miracle.' Things were to improve, however. We joined up with some 600 Indians who had been POWs since the war in the Western Desert and the Senior British Officer in charge of this growing band of POWs attached each of the RAF types to a company of these Indians. Mine were Gurkhas from northern India. They treated me like royalty. They received Red Cross parcels regularly and apart from the German soup ration I now had my first hot meal since being taken prisoner. It was midday. We were camped in a field and I sat in a circle with them, eating curry and rice from a large bowl with a spoon they had supplied. Life had definitely taken a turn for the better. We even had cups of tea. It is rather amusing that during this welcome period I carried a tin of spam, which someone had given me and I was unable to eat as it was offensive to my Indian friends.

For the next week or so we continued marching either by day or by night and sleeping in the open. If it was cold I shared blankets with Sergeant Kunwar Singh and Corporal Darwan Singh. They wore regular Army uniform and had been part of the Eighth Army. They did not necessarily come from the same region or even the same country. A group near to us were Gurkhas from Nepal and one of them gave me a haircut one day. I don't think he used his kukri.

My diary calls 14 April 'Black Saturday'. At an hour's notice that afternoon all Britishers had to march. 'Our leave-taking was quite touching. The Indians were too good, giving me tea, cocoa, milk.' I have never forgotten their kindness and companionship. We exchanged addresses of which more later. We now marched rapidly and crossed the Danube that day, sleeping comfortably in a hayloft at night. The following day we formed a group, Tommy, Norman, myself and Ted Pollock, an Army lieutenant. We were beginning to receive Red Cross parcels now and in a relaxed atmosphere due, I'm sure, to the nearness of the advancing Americans, were able to do a little bartering with the civilians, having luxuries like chocolate to offer; something most Germans had not tasted for many a day. My diary for Sunday, 15 April reads: 'We are staying the day here, so for supper we had dandelion roots, spuds, carrots, bread and toast. We did most of the cooking and it was very good.' We stayed in this village, sleeping in the hayloft for some days. It is quite obvious from my diary that food occupied much of my thinking, apart from the occasional entry such as: 'A night of feverish activity for the bed bugs' and 'I arranged with the old frau for a bath – and had a happy half-hour stewing in a tin bath – the first for over six weeks.'

We were beset with rumours at this time, the main one being that the Americans were close behind us. We continued walking again, staying overnight at the odd village. 26 April was a landmark. According to my diary, 'The Kriegsgefangenen' (the POWs) have just taken over the village and are strolling about at will, many of them being fed in the people's houses. The events of the following day confirmed that the guards had left. '4.20 pm. What a transformation! I haven't got used to it yet. In the square outside is a Sherman tank with a large white star on the side.' The American crew were friendly but very much on the lookout for unfriendly Germans.

We stayed in this village until 11 May. I had a hayloft to sleep in and I ate more pancakes than I'd eaten in the whole of my life before. My hostess was obviously able to get the necessary ingredients. I think we all got on well with the villagers. I found a piano in a former SS barracks and enjoyed myself, particularly with a book of sonatas. There was frustration, though, as we had no way of knowing whether the Allied Forces had any knowledge of our existence. We heard that a ceasefire had been signed on this day, so, somehow, Ted and I acquired a car, found out where the nearest airport was and drove there to badger the Allied presence about flying us home. As we had expected, Lancasters were already landing there and taking-off again, loaded with liberated POWs. I think we made ourselves unpopular but it worked. On that very day we got word that our little band would be collected and flown home as soon as possible. Sure enough, within the next day or two, a truck arrived from the airport and took us on board, a roll call having been taken to ensure that nobody was left behind.

In no time at all, it seemed, we arrived at the airport, were checked in and eventually put aboard a Lancaster. What a moment to listen to those Merlins starting up, to feel ourselves taxiing round the airport, lining up on the runway and then the roar of full power, the gradual increase of speed and then airborne. I don't think anybody spoke for a while. We just sat there on the floor of the aircraft trying to adjust to the knowledge that we would, in an hour or so, be landing in England.

We touched down at Dunsfold in Surrey where we were told that debriefing, medical examination and so on would take about 48 hours. Then we would be sent on two months' leave. I was surprised to be asked what RAF station I would like to be posted to when my leave ended. I had little time to consider this and said, 'No. 2 Embarkation Unit. Southampton Docks', my main ambition at that moment being to see something of my family again and perhaps, start living some sort of normal life again. My reply was accepted without question. I had been a prisoner for a mere two months. What must it have been like to have been captured at, say, Dunkirk?

I was able to send a telegram home and within 48 hours, opened the garden gate and was back with my family once more. It had been quite an experience for me, but must have been worse for them, wondering if I was still alive. The first intimation for them that I was, came with a telegram shortly after the war ended. It said, 'DUDLEY SAFE AND WELL GERMANY AWAITING TRANSPORT HOME. MAJOR GORDON.' He was a fellow prisoner who was one of the first to be flown home because he was ill. I had given him my address in the hope that he could let my parents know that I was alive. I am eternally grateful to him. I was relieved to find my mother and father in reasonably good health, as were my two brothers.

Now at last I learned what had happened to Johnny Wynne. I quote from a letter he wrote to my parents dated 24 March 1945. Having seen me give him that farewell wave before baling out, he says, 'When I attempted to leave the aircraft I became entangled in the oxygen leads and after much difficulty got free. Having relieved myself of the responsibility of the crew I felt it my duty to try at all costs to save my machine. I therefore decided to remain until the wing caught alight. So we flew on for half an hour and the flames subsided and eventually went out. Deciding to fly the aircraft home I went forward and got Dudley's maps and log and, in doing so, pulled my parachute, which had to be abandoned. A little later the engine caught fire again and this time without my chute I felt the end was inevitable. That the fire eventually burnt itself out and that with Dudley's chart and log we landed safely in Britain after 3 hours I can only attribute to Providence.'

Johnny landed at Bassingbourn in the Home Counties thanks to help he had from airfield beacons, searchlights and being able to fire off the colours of the day. He had been airborne 9 hours and 40 minutes.

The final bizarre touch to this operation came with a letter he wrote to me when he learned that I was back. He enclosed a photograph of the aircraft – it had a large hole in the nose, the damaged propeller having broken off on landing. Perhaps it was just as well Tubby and I were not sitting there at the time! I also wonder whether the aircraft would have struggled home as it did, with a full crew of 10 aboard.

Johnny and I kept up a correspondence for a while but it gradually faded as 'civvy' life, with all its demands, took over.

I also have two letters from my Indian friends, who I now learned were at a camp near Bury St Edmunds awaiting transport home. I replied to both letters and then received another (from Kunwar Singh) asking why I hadn't replied to his, I wrote again, sending it by registered post this time but it was returned to me from the camp, not having been delivered. I can only assume that my friends must have gone home.

During this leave the wheel turned full circle. Hearing footsteps coming up the garden path I looked out of the window – to see Les Twentyman. What a moment. We couldn't stop talking. He had passed the pilot's course and ended up flying Liberators over the Western Desert. He was still flying and would continue to do so until after VE-Day and demobilization. We came together again in the docks and had plenty of opportunities to talk over old times. Thanks to 617 Association, I still keep in touch with that crew and have seen Ken, Steve and Basil quite recently. We hope to meet again in May 1993, fifty years after the Dams Raid.

In due course I received orders to report to No. 2 Embarkation Unit again, not as a Service policeman, I hasten to add, but as an Embarkation Officer. I was a flight lieutenant by then.

In January 1946 I became a married man and the present took over from the previous six years. These had become an interlude, but something I would not have missed for all the tea in China.

Notes

1. Guy Gibson was sent to America on a publicity tour but he begged the Air Ministry to allow him to return to operations. On the night of 19/20 September 1944 he acted as controller for the raid on Rheydt. While returning over Walcheren both engines of Gibson's Mosquito cut and the aircraft crashed at Steenbergen, killing him and his navigator Squadron Leader J.B. Warwick DFC. Both men are buried in Steenbergen Roman Catholic Cemetery.

2. Brown made eight runs on the Sorpe but he was still not happy about dropping his mine. On the ninth he dropped incendiaries on the banks of the lake to try to identify the Sorpe dam through the swirling mist. On the eleventh run they saw the dam and Brown's mine was released. The mine exploded on impact, as it was dropped while flying across the dam and not dropped towards it as with the other dams. The explosion caused a crumbling of 300 feet the crest of the dam wall.

3. The Germans, unsure of the dam's integrity, were forced to drain off over 50 per cent of the reservoir's capacity until the structure could be inspected and repaired.

4. Young's Lancaster was hit by flak at Castricum-aan-Zee, Holland and crashed into the sea with the loss of all the crew.

5. Townsend was ordered to attack the Ennepe dam on the Schwelme River. He made three runs on the dam before his bomb-aimer, Sergeant Charles Franklin DFM, was satisfied. Their bomb was released, bounced once, and exploded 30 seconds after release. On leaving the target much opposition was encountered but by great determination on his part, plus the navigational skill of Pilot Officer Cecil Howard from Australia, they made it safely back, landing at 0615 hours. Most of the latter part of the homeward trip was flown in broad daylight.

6. 'Tubby' Pow, 2nd navigator, who had broken his ankle, was hospitalized. 1st navigator, F/O Dudley Heal DFM landed on the roof of a tall building in the centre of Buhl and became a POW. F/O Tom Tate, Special Operator, F/Sgt Norman J. Bradley DFM, one of the waist gunners, 40 year old F/O James W. Vinall DFM, co-pilot, twice Mentioned in Dispatches, F/O Harold Frost DFM, top turret gunner, F/O Gordon Hall, radio operator, F/L Sidney C. Matthews DFC, Gunnery Leader and F/Sgt Edward A Percival DFM, the other waist gunner

were rounded up. All were put in a school basement at Huchenfeld. Hans Christian Knab, the Nazi Kreisleiter (District Leader) of Pforzheim instructed the commander of the local Hitler Jugend, Sturmabteilung or SA and the Volkssturm to assemble with their men in civilian clothes and incite a crowd to murder the RAF airmen as a reprisal for the civilian losses in Pforzheim on 23/24 February. Wynne's crew were hauled into the street and were confronted by a lynch mob. Tate, in bare feet, managed to get away, was later apprehended by the Wehrmacht and taken into custody by two Luftwaffe soldiers who escorted him to POW camp in Ludwigsburg. Bradley and Vinall got away from their captors but Matthews, Frost, Percival and Hall were murdered in cold blood. Vinall was free for a day and then he gave himself up to Wehrmacht soldiers. He was handed over to the police at Dillstein, whose station was a few yards from a Hitler Youth barracks. Vinall was beaten up by a mob before being murdered by Gert Biedermann a 15 year old Hitler Youth, who shot him in the head. Biedermann, who had dug the bodies of his mother and five brothers and sisters from the rubble after the bombing of Pforzheim, was later tried, found guilty and sentenced to 15 years imprisonment. Bradley evaded re-capture and reached the village of Grunbach SW of Pforzheim. The five men of HB799 are buried in the Dürnbach RAF cemetery. In 1946 Knab was hanged following war crimes proceedings in Essen-Steele.

# Chapter 12

# The Malta Stories

The main island of Malta is only 95 square miles. It is just 17 miles long by 9 miles wide. The landscape of this rocky island is almost biblical with flat topped houses in honey-coloured limestone, set against stony hills. Contrasting with this is the brilliant blue sea and sky. Malta's strategic position in the middle of the Mediterranean, 60 miles south of Sicily, has made it attractive to all sorts of people – traders, colonizers and invaders – dating back to the Phoenicians. In 1530 Charles V of Spain granted the Knights of St John, ejected from Rhodes by the Turks, the islands as their new home. This move led ultimately to one of Christendom's greatest triumphs; the Great Siege of Malta in 1565 when the Knights and the Maltese withstood and eventually defeated the huge Turkish invasion fleet of Suleiman the Magnificent. More than two centuries of peace and prosperity followed under the rule of the Knights until the unwanted arrival of the revolutionary French Army. French rule lasted only two years. Blockaded by the Royal Navy, commanded by Admiral Lord Nelson and harried by the Maltese, the French occupying troops were forced to capitulate. Thus began the long association with Britain.

The Mediterranean island's most climactic episode was the second Great Siege of Malta during 1941–1942. Benito Mussolini, the Italian dictator, declared war against Britain and France on 10 June 1940 and the following morning, 10 Savoia-Marchetti SM79 tri-motor bombers attacked Valletta and surrounding districts. The first casualties were six Maltese gunners of the Royal Malta Artillery, killed outright by a high explosive bomb as they manned their guns at Valletta's Fort St Elmo at the entrance to Grand Harbour. Malta's only aerial defence at this time was a handful of Gloster Gladiator biplane fighters. Flying Officer Woods scored the first Gladiator victory when, south of Valletta at 1925 hours, he shot down a Fiat CR. 42 biplane fighter. The islanders now rallied to the Allied cause, promptly gathered their resources of fortitude and courage and immediately prepared themselves for a long and painful siege. Much would have to be done, since Malta was clearly defenceless at this stage. The immediate priority was to provide shelter for the civilian population. A gigantic programme to excavate underground shelters in all towns and villages, was quickly mounted. Old railway tunnels and historic catacombs were soon converted for this purpose. With the help of experienced miners from south Wales and Yorkshire, serving with the Royal Engineers in Malta, the authorities were successful in providing adequate protection for the population within a year. The early completion of this crash building programme greatly contributed to the relatively low figure of civilian casualties registered in Malta during the war. However, with some foresight, more lives would have been saved.

The *Regia Aeronautica* continued their bombing raids over Malta. Initially, only four Gloster Gladiators opposed the 200 plus aircraft. Legend has it that these were soon reduced to three and, nicknamed *Faith, Hope* and *Charity*, they battled alone, day and night for three weeks. Although probably apocryphal, the appendage is appropriate because they were fighting on an island on which St Paul was shipwrecked in AD59-60 and refer to his immortal words in his second letter to the Corinthians: 'Faith, Hope and Charity.' (I Corinthians 12:13).

On 28 June 1940 four Hurricanes en route to the Middle East were kept in Malta to help the stalwart defenders. On 13 July only one Gladiator and one Hurricane were serviceable but, by the end of the month, 12 more Hurricanes arrived. Against this stronger opposition, the Italian raids became noticeably less effective. Italy thus failed to subdue Malta in time. This would ultimately be most detrimental to the Axis effort in North Africa.

It was becoming increasingly clear that the Battle for Malta was also the battle for control over the 'waist' of the central Mediterranean. With the build-up of Axis forces in North Africa, their supply lines from Sicily were assuming more importance. The singular failure of the Italians to silence Malta and effectively blockade her supply lines, despite little or no opposition, proved to be of great concern to the German High Command. Clearly, Malta-based aircraft, shipping and submarines had to be prevented from ever taking to the offensive since the Axis lifeline from Sicily to North Africa would otherwise be jeopardized. For this reason, it was decided that the Luftwaffe should move in, take over from the Italians and finish the job in Malta once and for all.

With the Luftwaffe based on Sicilian airfields by December 1940 the siege of Malta commenced in earnest. During January 1941 the Luftwaffe made 57 raids on Malta but the Maltese anti-aircraft batteries were feared and respected defenders. They are perhaps epitomized by the spirit of men such as Lieutenant Micallef Trigona, a territorial officer of the 3rd Light Anti Aircraft Regiment, who commanded a Bofors gun position on the ravelin of Lower Barracca Gardens, which overlook Grand Harbour. He fired at the Stukas but as they pulled out of their dives they were flying out of Grand Harbour, past him but lower than his position. Trigona could not depress his gun barrel because of a depression rail designed to prevent him firing at the level of buildings. He could only look at the pilots grinning at him from their cockpit as they flew past. This was too much for Trigona. When the second formation appeared he ordered his men to remove the depression rail and depress the gun barrel. Maltese author Joseph Attard, in his book *The Battle of Malta*, says: '...The grin on the pilots' faces disappeared as they met the Bofors spitting fire at them and saw its commander standing on the ravelin crossing his right arm over his left transmitting the vulgar Maltese message which they understood. Shells which missed the planes hit the bastion of Fort St Angelo and one of the lighthouses on the breakwater of Grand Harbour, blowing half of it away, which is still missing today.'

With Rommel now preparing to redress Italian reverses in North Africa, German raids on Malta were intensified. This greatly assisted the Afrika Korps to win control of Cyrenaica, and Rommel was looking to invade Egypt. By spring 1941 Greece and Crete had also fallen. These gains now posed a serious threat to Malta's supply line from Alexandria. German strategy to strangle Malta into submission was clearly succeeding but in June 1941 Hitler attacked Russia and strikes on Malta from Sicily became fewer. Malta's strategic role in the battle for the control of supply lines in the Mediterranean now became vital. Rommel's victories in North Africa had been largely due to his relatively secure supply links with Italy and Sicily and these depended on the Luftwaffe's air superiority over Malta. Now for the first time the British in Malta went over to the offensive. Enemy shipping was attacked, Blenheims and Wellington bombers raided Naples and other Italian ports and Hurricanes and Beaufighters systematically attacked targets in Sicily and Sardinia, while Tripoli in Libya was raided repeatedly and the Axis powers in North Africa were blockaded and deprived of supplies. By the autumn of 1941 the Allies had made sweeping gains in North Africa.

Almost too late, the Germans realized that Malta was the chief obstacle to progress in North Africa and the airfields on the island fortress would have to be put out of action permanently. By December 1941 the Luftwaffe in Sicily was back to full strength and the bombing of Malta recommenced with a vengeance. Plans were also laid for a German invasion. That December the Luftwaffe made 169 air raids on Malta and, in early 1942, Malta was blitzed daily by the Luftwaffe. In January, the Luftwaffe made 263 raids on Malta and in February 1,000 tons of bombs were dropped. By April a peak of 283 bombing raids was reached and a total of 6,700 tons of bombs were dropped on the island. On 7 March 15 Spitfire Vbs were flown off the deck of the carrier *Eagle* and they landed at Ta'Qali. On 20 March 143 Ju 88s and Bf 109s made a massed attack on the islands and heavy raids continued for two more days before the Luftwaffe switched to bombing a convoy of merchant ships heading for Valletta. Airfields came under constant attack and soon the blockade of Malta began to have a telling effect on the island's reserves of stores, munitions and fuel. Food was in very short supply and 'Victory Kitchens' were introduced to feed the starving population. Sugar was unobtainable and even soap and matches had to be rationed.

Many towns and cities were reduced to rubble. In April 1942 alone, more than 11,000 buildings were destroyed or damaged. Because of their proximity to the Naval dockyards, the Three Cities were particularly badly hit. In Valletta too, many historic buildings were hit. The Royal Opera House, the Law Courts and some of the old auberges were totally destroyed. On 15 April the morale of the Maltese people received a welcome boost. The following message arrived from King George VI: 'To honour her brave people I award the George Cross to the Island Fortress of Malta to bear witness to a heroism and devotion that will long be famous in history.' That same month the American carrier USS *Wasp* sailed from the Clyde with 47 Spitfires aboard and, nearing the island, these were flown off to Malta. However, next morning only three Spitfires were serviceable at Luqa and by the evening only 17 of the original 47 were still in one piece following enemy air attacks.

Further reinforcement was provided on 20 April by the temporary transfer of eight Wellington bombers, 16 crews and a few ground crews from Egypt for raids from Malta on Axis bases in Italy. One of the Wellington aircrew who went was

Sergeant Wallace 'Wally' Gaul, rear-gunner in Sergeant Jim 'Cranky' Crank-Benson's crew. As a 19 year old working for Norwich Corporation 'Wally' had originally intended to volunteer for the Tank Corps but a raid by two Dorniers on Norwich during the afternoon of Tuesday, 9 July 1940, had altered the course of his destiny. Bombs dropped killed 27 people including several women workers leaving off at the famous Colmans Mustard Works. Wally was working on a road gang in Bracondale near Carrow Hill when a bomb crashed through trees and exploded at ground level as the women pushed their bicycles up the steep slope. He was so incensed that he volunteered for RAF aircrew. By April 1942 he had completed 31 ops in 148 Squadron flying from Kabrit, Egypt, but Gaul wondered how much longer his luck was going to hold out:

'On Monday, 20 April we took-off from Kabrit for ALG [Air landing Ground] 106. We flew in formation, as there had been an increase in enemy fighter activity in the area. A sandstorm was blowing at the ALG and made landing difficult. We stalled and hit the deck with one almighty crash. Although the aircraft was "bent up" a bit, there were no injuries. We took-off again at 2000 hours and after an uneventful flight, lasting 6 hours 20 minutes, we were on the circuit at Luqa. We were billeted at the Palace in Naxxar and told to stay out of sight when the raids were on. I woke up next morning to the sound of air-raid sirens. No one bothered to get up. Then we heard the guns opening up. Although the bombs were some distance away, the palace began to shake. There were slit trenches at the rear of the building so we made a dive for them. Naxxar is on high ground so we had a good view of the bombing.

'On 22 April ops were on. We were taken out to the aircraft to get ready for the "big one". At last we were going to get our revenge on Jerry. Our aircraft had survived the first raid of the day. I was busy in the turret when the yellow flare went up from Luqa. Soon the sirens were wailing and I could see the first wave heading for the island. Our kite was in a sandbagged enclosure. As I wondered whether to run for the slit trench, the first bombs were falling on the airfield at Ta'Qali five miles away. Hal Far airfield was only two miles away. A lorry arrived and I was whisked away to Luqa. We made a dash to the underground shelter. The next wave was bombing the airfield at Luqa and Safi Strip. On the way to the airfield another raid, on Luqa, had started. We had to scatter. Our kite was OK but the runway had to be repaired. We had lost quite a lot of kites in the bombing and the ferry crews bound for Egypt were diverted to Malta so that our squadron could take them on ops that night. (Most of the new kites were bombed the next day and the same thing would happen again.)

'A lorry took us out to our kite. A final check by the ground crew for any shrapnel damage. Everything seemed OK. The engines were started and we taxied along Safi Strip to wait for the green. Crank-Benson, who was flying on ops for the first time as captain, made a final check on the engines. We got the green and at last we were on our way. Sicily is only 60 miles from Malta and the target, the airfield at Comiso, was about the same distance inland. As we crossed the coast we were greeted with heavy flak. We were flying at 8,000 feet so most of the "stuff" was bursting above us. We ran into several of these heavy ack-ack sites on the way to the target and I could see other aircraft bombing airfields. Searchlights probed the sky. Flares drifted down to light up the target. Light flak spiralled up and bombs exploded on the airfield. The last of the aircraft in front of us had completed their bombing. Jim elected to go in over the mountains and make a low-level run over the target. The searchlights began to fade and the flak stopped. We had the target to ourselves. Jim said, "Going in now. Here we go." Over the mountain, a steep dive and we were running up to the airfield. Then the defences came to life again. Jeff Jefferies the navigator was having a hell of a job seeing the target. Then, "Hold it steady, Jim. I can see the target now. Steady…bombs gone!" Ack-Ack guns on the side of the mountain were having a go at us. I fired my guns in that direction but I knew it was useless. It took my mind off things down below.

'Our bombs were forty-pounders with a "mushroom" on the nose so that they scattered shrapnel across the airfield on impact. We left quite a few aircraft burning. I could still see the fires from several miles away. We ran into more flak but this was nothing compared with the target area. As we crossed the coast a hell of an explosion tossed the kite on its side. I told Jim there was a bloody great hole in the port side. Jim went back to take a look. He exclaimed, "Jesus Bloody Christ!" Was he praying? I don't think so. Soon the beacon at Malta was in sight. We landed and began the long taxi to the dispersal at Safi Strip. As usual I was the first to light up. Never had I enjoyed a fag so much before. A ground staff bod saw the damage and asked Jim, "How the hell did you get home?" "I didn't," said Jim. "The flak blew us back!" Our aircraft was U/S; two were shot down over the target; one was shot up and damaged. Total aircraft at daybreak…four!

'On 24 April Malta suffered a very heavy raid and our kite was hit. Two more kites were missing from the previous night's raid. The squadron was in a bad way. On 25 April we were told we were returning to Egypt. I was not sorry to hear this. I had completed 34 ops and the "old ring was beginning to twitter". At 1700 hours on Sunday 27 April, we left the Palace at Naxxar dressed in full flying kit to the cheers of the locals in the square. The *Maltese Times* gave us a big write-up about our bombing of enemy airfields in Sicily. This had raised morale no end. After briefing we had to wait for aircraft to arrive from Gibraltar. Soon, our kite arrived. It was refuelled and the gear stowed inside. The ferry crews, who would be shipped back to Blighty by sea later, were not pleased to lose their aircraft. We touched down at Kabrit at 0832 hours. As we left the aircraft we were greeted with, "Cor, you should have been here last night. We got raided by Jerry…one 'angar wos 'it." The Cockney driver prattled on and on.

"How many kites?" we asked.

"About 'arf a dozen He 111s" he said.

'We did not tell him that on the last raid on Malta 150 had taken part!'[1]

Flight Lieutenant Reg Thackeray was a pilot in 40 Squadron at Kabrit flying Wellington bombing raids when, in late November 1942, he and his crew were one of eleven Wimpy crews sent to Malta. He recalls:

'Eleven aircraft were briefed for the trip and 11 reached Luqa safely. We had *L for Leather*, a full crew, our kit, full tanks and an overload tank in the bomb bay, four mechanics with their kit and toolboxes. The run on take-off was very long and we flew west along the coast at 1,000 feet in rain. After passing Tobruk we made our final landfall at Ras el Tin and there started our run of over 500 miles to Malta. We climbed through 10/10ths cloud and came into the clear at 9,000 feet. Navigation was by D/F loop on the Malta radio beacon, supplemented by star sights using the bubble sextant and the astrograph, a sort of overhead projector in the navigator's compartment.

'ETA approached, we let down through the cloud and soon spotted the beacon at Luqa and the brilliant lights in the harbour at Valletta. Our approach to the runway was over the dockyards and we were glad to touch down at 0710 hours on Thursday 26 November, just as dawn was breaking. We landed with 400 gallons of fuel left – a useful addition to the island's reserves.

'About half the squadron aircraft and crews had flown to Luqa at the beginning of November. We were shocked at the thin, haggard appearance of our friends after only three weeks on the island. Although the blockade was virtually lifted by the arrival of the *Stonehenge* convoy from Alexandria, rationing was very strict and severe. On Friday morning we were on the detail for a double sortie to Bizerta in Tunisia. Take-off was set for 1930 hours. The straight line distance to the target was about 280 miles so we had a full load of 520 gallons and a bomb load of four 500lb and eight 250lb GP bombs, with dockside buildings the aiming point. The Met forecast was poor and the weather turned out to be very similar! The cloud base was around 1,000 feet when we went out to *L for Leather* and we were unable to start the engines owing to flat batteries on the starter trolley. It was 2100 hours before we were airborne and we were very much the last aircraft.

'We stayed below cloud at 800 feet and skirted the well-defended island of Pantelleria, heading for the coast south of Tunis. We were climbing on track and passed over Tunis at 10,000 feet. Bizerta was under a terrific bank of cloud and the heavy flak was spasmodic and inaccurate. Searchlights were ineffective in the cloud. Just before midnight there was a break in the cloud and Jeff Reddell, our New Zealand navigator, got a sight of the harbour. The break lasted long enough for him to bring me on to a straight and level heading at 10,000 feet and he set the *Mickey Mouse* for a single short stick.

'After "Bombs gone!" I closed the bomb doors and turned onto a reciprocal course. Almost immediately a large fire was seen and Wally Hammond, our English rear-gunner, reported a large explosion. The fire remained visible for 15 minutes as we lost height to "improve" the temperature. The oil in the constant speed units had frozen solid and it was quite some time before I was able to bring the revs under control. For long range economical cruising it was our habit to run the supercharged Pegasus XVIII engines on the highest available boost pressures but the lowest possible revolutions per minute. We were back over the Gozo radio beacon before 0200 hours but Malta was under cloud and Luqa took some finding. By the time we had landed, it was too late to bomb up and refuel for our second sortie so we turned in for interrogation.

'Our next sorties were to Sicily – two trips on the night of 30 November/1 December to Trapani aerodrome and two trips on the night of 3/4 December to the aerodromes at Catania and Comiso. We made two more trips on the night of 6/7 December to the docks at Bizerta and La Goulette; the deep sea port of Tunis. Then we had a fruitless trip to Tunis. There was 10/10ths cloud over the target. We had flown in cloud all the way and had had a wonderful display of St Elmo's fire on the way up to 10,000 feet where we came out into a clear starlit sky. Static electricity discharged itself round the propeller tips, between the machine guns in the turrets and on the windscreen as the raindrops hit the glass! There was no sign of the target on ETA so we turned back and made a very gentle landing with our full load of bombs!

'Next morning we were told that the main port engine bearing had failed so we had to say "goodbye" to *L for Leather* which had served us so well. She had taken me to Crete, brought me to Malta and we'd been out to Sicily and Tunis on eight occasions. Our next aircraft was DV566P. She took us to Palermo in Sicily early on the morning of 12 December following a report of bad weather over Tunis, which we had been due to visit the night before.

'We again took *P* to Tunis and La Goulette early on Sunday, 13 December. We were third off the runway at 1820 hours and set course as usual over the tiny island of Filfla off the south-west coast of Malta. There was little cloud and we pinpointed accurately on the coast south of Cap Bon. We could see flak bursting over Tunis and a good fire at La Goulette partly obscured by light cloud.

'There was no flak over the port so we stooged around and the cloud cleared by 2050 hours. There was a quarter moon giving good illumination of the target and we were able to go in to attack at 9,000 feet. We had four 500lb and seven 250lb GP bombs and decided on three sticks. Eric Laithwaite put the first stick near the electricity generating station, the second stick on the oil refinery and the third stick on two ships moored near the canal, just off the oil jetty. One ship was estimated at 8,000 tons and a fire was seen to start on this one. The fire, punctuated by explosions, was visible up to 40 miles away!

'We were safely back at Luqa for interrogation at 2255 hours. It was later confirmed that we had fired the ship and the report figured in the citation for my DFM – being a Pilot's Air Force, my navigator has always complained that he hit the ship but I got the gong!

'We were due for a return trip to La Goulette with take-off at 0030 hours on 14 December but we had to switch to DV647N as *P* had been grounded due to excessive oil consumption. All our Pegasus engines used a lot of oil – worn out by use and the sand in the atmosphere despite the Volkes air filters on the carburettor air intakes. Additional regular hours supplies had to be pumped by hand from a reserve tank carried in the fuselage. This was one of the second pilot's jobs and was jolly hard work at high altitude and low temperatures, which also caused high viscosity. As an example; in January 1943 HEII5N used two gallons of oil per hour, say 145 miles! Ten gallons of oil was hand pumped – 550 strokes on a "wobble pump" – on a sortie to Tripoli.

'On take-off at 0055 hours, the cockpit panel lighting failed and there was a terrific juddering on the control column. It was still possible to climb very gently. There was no improvement in the situation when the undercarriage and flaps had been cleared up, so I continued, straight ahead, up to 1,000 feet and made a wide circuit and long, powered approach, leaving the flaps up until the last minute. With 3,750lb of bombs and about the same weight of fuel I took great care to do a gentle "wheel" landing. Back at the dispersal it was found that the cooling gills on the starboard engine were jammed in the fully open (ground running) position and this had disturbed the airflow over the tailplane and elevator causing the "judder". I was only in the air 25 minutes! The problem was fixed quickly but the OC Night Flying cancelled our take-off since we should have returned to the island in daylight! (The *Times of Malta* reported this "Blitz on North African docks as the biggest bombing raid ever launched from Malta and the weight of bombs the heaviest ever to have been dropped in a single night by bombers operating from this island".)

'A double sortie to Tunis and La Goulette was made on the night of 15/16 December. Tunis was reached at 2045 hours and in the moonlight we found the flak very accurate as we did our first turn. We could see many shell bursts and we smelt the cordite smoke. Eric's first stick hit warehouses and his second fell across the railway marshalling yards. We were back at Luqa by 2300 hours and airborne again at 0050 hours, after sandwiches. The moon had set by the time we got back to La Goulette but there was a blazing ship in the canal entrance to light the target area. The first stick fell on the harbour works and the second stick caused an explosion in the generating station. We were "home" again at 0500 hours and found some flak damage to the starboard wing and flap.

'On Friday, 18 December, these double sorties came to an abrupt halt. We were briefed for Tunis and took-off at 1820 hours. But as we passed between the islands of Linosa and Lampedusa, Bert Ward, our Yorkshire wireless operator, reported that our engine-driven generator had failed and he couldn't promise that we would have sufficient voltage in the batteries to drop the bombs if we continued to Tunis. I turned back but it was evident that the voltage would "hold" for some time and the navigator gave me a course for Comiso in southern Sicily. We delivered our bomb load there before returning to Luqa and landing at 2100 hours. Between the double sorties, the aircraft were marshalled in a line alongside the runway for refuelling and bombing up, whilst all the crews took a breather and had a snack. Because of our generator failure in HX382/M, we had switched our kit, bombsight etc., to DV512/J and were preparing for take-off at 2330 hours. At 2300 the sirens sounded and shortly afterwards a concentrated dive bomber attack was made on Luqa. The squadron lost seven aircraft destroyed and three damaged. After this, every aircraft was put away in protected dispersals along the Safi Strip which ran across the island to Hal Far, the fighter aerodrome. The second pilot performed this arduous taxiing chore after the trip, whilst the captain, navigator, wireless operator and gunners proceeded to the Intelligence Section for interrogation. There were no casualties to air or ground crew during the raid. Most of us literally went to ground in slit trenches and shelters on the airfield. We were all very scared to be so directly on the receiving end and very lucky to survive.

'On 21 December five aircraft were available to operate against Tunis and ten aircraft took-off for Tunis (or Sousse as the alternative) at 1810 hours on 25 December. The weather forecast was dreadful – heavy cloud up to 12,000 feet. We had "N for Nuts" and didn't see anything on ETA at Sousse or Tunis so we brought our bombs back, as did most others. We felt relieved that we had not had to bomb on Christmas Day. (One crew ditched but were picked up by Malta ASR at dawn.) We had a tasty meal in the Officers' Mess on Luqa main camp before turning in at 0030 hours on Boxing Day.

'Attacks on Sousse, Sfax, Comiso, Palem and Tripoli followed during January and became almost routine. Some were more difficult than others. One night our bombs fell out, due to an electrical fault, when the bomb doors opened and undershot the target (Sfax harbour) and fell in the town. Another night we lost an engine over Tripoli but I managed to limp back to Malta (200 miles) losing oil from the "good" engine. Then on 22 January 1943 we flew back to Egypt for leave and did not return to Malta.'

In June 1943 King George VI visited Malta and he received a tumultuous welcome. In September the Italian Fleet assembled in Maltese harbours and Marshall Badoglio signed Italy's final surrender document in Malta. In November Winston Churchill visited Malta and saw for himself the devastation inflicted by the enemy. Three weeks later, Franklin D. Roosevelt arrived. The second siege of Malta, like the first, four centuries earlier, won the admiration of the world. Out of both sieges, Malta emerged in a state of utter devastation but totally unscathed in spirit and honour. From the last siege, Malta also emerged with the firm resolve to become at last the mistress of her own destiny.

Notes
1. On 6 May Wally Gaul flew his 35th trip, a single supply drop on Crete. On 8 May he flew his 36th with a bombing raid on enemy shipping in Benghazi harbour. They made it back on 10 May and he learned that it was his last trip. Next day, 11 May, was his birthday.

# Chapter 13

# It Just Couldn't Have Happened – Tom Wingham DFC

On the night of 29/30 March 1943, 329 aircraft of Bomber Command raided Berlin and 149 *Oboe*-guided Wellingtons bombed Bochum. Sergeant Tom Wingham, the bomb-aimer in Sergeant Dave Hewlett's Halifax II crew in 102 Squadron at Pocklington, Yorkshire was flying his 10th op (in *Q-Queenie* 'the oldest, clapped out Halifax on the squadron – quite notorious for its lack of climbing ability and poor ceiling').

'Like most crews who managed to survive, we were very close-knit, very rarely being off the station unless we were all together. Our pilot was Sergeant Dave Hewlett. Sergeant Harry Blackallar was navigator, Sergeant Eric "Joe" Holliday was engineer, wireless operator was Flight Sergeant Norman "Chiefie" Beale, who had previously done a first tour on Hampdens and Andy Reilly, rear-gunner and Sergeant Willie Hall, mid-upper gunner, completed the crew. We had our own crew song adapted from that well-known ditty "Sweet Violets", which had been sung to distraction in pub after pub since we had joined the Squadron at the beginning of the year. Having a rear-gunner from Dublin and a mid-upper from Belfast often led to interesting arguments on the Irish question when flying on the long grind to Holland or Denmark over the North Sea when life might have been quiet and otherwise dull.

'We had been to Berlin two nights before and Harris was determined to get in another raid on the Big City before the light evenings. The weather forecast at briefing was ghastly and our station Met officers unofficially predicted a certain "scrub". Came take-off time and the weather was on the deck with heavy rain from the occlusion running North to South over Yorkshire to Lincolnshire. Cloud as solid up to 15,000 feet with severe icing predicted. Take-off was put back and we knew there had to be a "scrub". The weather persisted and take-off was again put back. But Harris would not cancel and eventually we took-off. The occlusion tailed back over Yorkshire and almost as soon as we took-off we were in cloud as we set course over the North Sea. We flogged our way upwards through the occlusion and at 15,000 feet we were still in cloud and were unable to climb another foot. Our climb had been so slow we had taken the whole of the North Sea to reach this height. Now straight and level and still in cloud, we found ourselves with iced-up windscreen and turrets and a maximum IAS of 135 knots. At this point we must have been somewhere near Flensburg for we suddenly became the object of some heavy AA fire. Even the Germans didn't seem to believe an aircraft could be flying so slowly since most of the bursts seemed to be ahead of us. With everyone operating "blind" because of the icing, discretion now had to be the better part of valour. We dropped our bombs hoping against hope that they might give the German gunners earache but more in the hope of getting a bit more speed from the lightened aircraft.

'Thankfully, we turned for home and managed to re-cross the occlusion without incurring any further icing. As we reached the end of the runway we had to feather the starboard outer as the oil pressure dropped off the clock. Arriving at dispersal we got out and walked around the aircraft where one of the ground staff was getting rather excited. Both inner engines were shedding a steady flow of glycol. From one of the wing bomb bays two 4lb incendiaries were protruding with the other 88 lying loose in the bomb-bay doors. The IFF aerial had disappeared. Had we gone on to Berlin it seems certain that we would have either have run out of engines, had a wing on fire, or in the last resort, have been shot down by Fighter Command. Sometimes it was easier to fight the Germans.'[1]

Another long trip flown by Dave Hewlett's crew was to Pilsen's Skoda armaments factory on 16/17 April 1943 when 327 aircraft were dispatched. Eighteen Lancasters and 18 Halifaxes were lost but Hewlett's crew returned safely to Pocklington. Pilsen had been Tom Wingham's 15th op and it had been in a full moon. With the moon still full it was with some trepidation that he realized from the petrol and bomb loads that he was in for another long trip on 20/21 April. All told 339 aircraft (194 Lancasters, 134 Halifaxes and 11 Stirlings) were to visit Stettin, an 8½-hour round trip, while 85 Stirlings were dispatched to bomb the Heinkel factory near Rostock. Wingham recalled that: 'With briefing came enlightenment. Bomber Command had come up with a new plan to beat the German GCI – a low-level trip.'

Hewlett's Halifax climbed on take-off and crossed the North Sea at 10,000 feet, reaching the Danish coast near Esbjerg where they descended to 700 feet. Tom Wingham continues: 'Now began one of the most exhilarating trips I took part in as 350 heavy bombers streamed across Denmark between 400 and 700 feet. Lying in the nose map reading did feel a bit hairy as we were constantly being hit by the slipstream from other unseen aircraft. In the brilliant moonlight all the ground detail was clear and Danes came out of their houses flashing torches and waving. Occasionally, a little light flak came up to port or starboard as aircraft strayed off course or the sky was lit up as an aircraft hit the deck. We continued at low level across the Baltic doing a cruise among the islands until on our last leg with the north German coast on our starboard we climbed to a bombing height of 14,000 feet. As we approached the target, Stettin was well alight and, in the glare from the fires below and the brilliant moonlight, it was like carrying out an aircraft recognition test. It was the first time I had seen Fw 190s and Me 109s as well as 110s and Ju 88s, all clearly visible, flitting about among the silhouettes of Lancs and Halifaxes. Somehow we were not singled out for attention as we went in and bombed. Immediately after completing the bomb run we dived for the deck and went out the same way we had come. For such a long-range target, over 600 miles from England and well outside the range of *Oboe*, it was probably the most successful raid during the Battle of the Ruhr. There were a lot of very tired pilots when we got home. We still lost between 6–7 per cent[2], which was the going rate for the job, so presumably Harris felt there was nothing to be gained by repeating the exercise. As far as I know this was a one-off and the tactic was never used again on such a large scale.

'Dortmund on 23/24 May 1943 was our 20th operation as a Halifax II crew, although it was the first with us for Sergeant Jim Nightingale, who replaced "Chiefie" Beale. After our last operation he had been called to the adjutant's office and told that as he had completed 50 operations he was now "screened" and would not do any more ops. So we had had to find ourselves another wireless operator. Jim Nightingale was an experienced spare wireless operator on 102 Squadron, having lost his crew one night when he was unable to fly with them. So this was to be his first trip with his new, permanent crew. We took it rather hard that "Chiefie" had been taken away from us without a "by your leave". When we got to the briefing room and the target was revealed, there were the usual curses and trepidation at finding ourselves back on the "Happy Valley" run. But, as a crew, we couldn't complain since we had not operated since April. We had had, admittedly, a heavy month, visiting Essen both at the beginning and end of the month, with Kiel, Frankfurt, Stuttgart, Pilsen, Stettin and Duisburg sandwiched in between and a minelaying trip to the Kattegat thrown in for good measure. This was the March–July period that was later to be known as the Battle of the Ruhr.

'As the briefing commenced, we quickly found out that this was to be something different. It was to be the heaviest raid of the war. Up to this date, apart from the 1,000 bomber raids of 1942, which pressed everything into service that could take-off without necessarily being able to carry much of a bomb load, Bomber Command had only been sending between 300 and 580 aircraft on individual raids. Tonight, Dortmund was to suffer the mightiest blow that the Command could administer, with the use of 826 aircraft, the majority being "heavies" – Lancasters, Halifaxes and Stirlings – with 151 Wellingtons and 13 *Oboe*-marking Mosquitoes. This was presumably why Command had not operated for the previous nine days in order to get as many aircraft as possible serviceable.

'The weather forecast was good with no cloud cover over the target and at the duly appointed time we took-off and headed towards Holland. It was usual to expect fighters to begin to meet us 30 miles off the enemy coast and thereafter continue to make life difficult with the help of various flak and searchlight batteries dotted all over the place until we began to close in on the Ruhr. At that period all the German night fighters were operated in boxes and were directed against individual bombers. This was the reason for the bomber streaming – with so many aircraft flying through a box it was difficult for the ground control to pick out individual aircraft. Hence it was the stragglers and those outside the stream, port or starboard, higher or lower, which could be guaranteed to get most attention.

'As the bombers approached the Ruhr the game changed and masses of searchlights and guns took over. It was estimated at that time that several thousand AA guns protected the Ruhr and to meet them on your own was never a pleasant prospect. Again, as with fighters, if within the stream, it was difficult for the guns and searchlights to use radar to predict individual aircraft. So, once a raid got into its stride, the flak became more of a barrage, which had to be flown through, rather than fire directed at given aircraft.

'For Pathfinders and aircraft in the van of the attack, those early minutes of the raid were the most dangerous; the guns and searchlights had the opportunity to pick up individual bombers and send up very accurate predicted fire and always made the most of their chances. Anyone flying straight and level for more than a few seconds on their own could be certain of some near misses, if not direct hits. Because of their role in marking the target, PFF losses of heavies were very high at this stage since they had to follow in behind the *Oboe* Mosquitoes, which flew very much higher and put down continuous back-up markers on the Aiming Point. The control stations of *Oboe* could only operate one Mossie at a time, which meant a gap of 10 minutes between *Oboe* markers. By this time there had been another pair of stations installed, which meant that marking by *Oboe* could be carried out every five minutes, providing the equipment in the aircraft did not fail. Unfortunately, the equipment was rather temperamental and sometimes, when the first Mossie had failed to mark, there was a long wait for the PFF and Main Force until the next one came along.

'*Oboe* had proved to be the only reliable and extremely accurate marking system to overcome the notorious mist and smoke cover that had, for so long, prevented the Command from hitting the Ruhr. Therefore, since March it had been a cardinal rule that bombing on the Ruhr only commenced with the laying of an *Oboe* marker. It was then the job of the PFF back-up heavies to maintain continuity of the markers by aiming theirs, of a different colour, at the *Oboe* ones. This ensured that if there was a failure in an *Oboe* Mossie later in the attack, the aiming point would still be marked, although not quite so accurately.

'On this night, Halifaxes of 4 Group were leading the attack with 102 Squadron in the van. We had an uneventful trip at first, crossing the North Sea and Holland without any problems for ourselves, having as usual observed aircraft falling on either side of us. We continued across Germany before we turned on our final leg, which would bring us to Dortmund from the north. As we started to run down to the Ruhr the flak began to warm up and turned into the usual flashes and thumps so familiar to anyone who has experienced AA fire – quite frightening in its way. I checked the latest wind with Blackie and after switching on, fed this into the bombsight before checking that all the switches were on to ensure that the bombs were live and that the distributor would function. Taking the bomb tit release button in my hand, I settled down in the prone position over the bombsight ready to carry out my task.

'Everything was still dark, although it was a clear starry night with very good visibility. As we neared our target the flak intensified, although there were at this point no searchlights. Quite often the Germans would delay the use of these until the target had been marked in case, one presumes, the searchlights would give them away. Being in the forefront of the attack we kept on course to Dortmund. Even so, we were only a couple of minutes from our ETA and no markers were yet visible. Suddenly a vivid splash of colour appeared ahead and below us. Relief set in that this was the primary *Oboe* marker and we would not have to go round again.

'Now I took over and guided Dave through my bombsight. "Bomb doors open."

"Bomb doors open," repeated Dave.

"Left...left...steady...steady." I pressed the tit. "Bombs gone!"

'The aircraft jumped with the release of the two 1,000lb HEs. At the same time the photoflash left its chute at the rear of the aircraft and we now flew straight and level while I counted the 10 seconds. We carried a mixed load of HE and incendiary bombs which, unfortunately, had different terminal velocities. This meant that the HE bombs had a better forward travel than the smaller incendiaries, which would fall almost vertically. We still, therefore, had six small bomb containers of 30lb incendiaries and seven SBCs of 4lb to be dropped; these would be released in sequence so that the hundreds of incendiaries would cover an area over 100 yards long. The idea was that the HE should open up the buildings, then the incendiaries would follow to set fire to the exposed rubble. In order for this to happen there had to be a time lag between dropping the two types of bombs, hence the 10-second run. The bomb release had also set up the camera ready to record our position at the time of the impact of the bombs. Providing we maintained our run, which went on for a little longer after the release of the incendiaries, the centre of the photograph would indicate the impact point of our bomb load. It was not often that I had a virgin target to aim at with no other bombing except the *Oboe* marker. But of course this also meant that we were way out front, an ideal target for the gunners below and moreover, making life easy for them with the prolonged straight and level photo run. We had been getting a bumpy ride as the flak intensified almost to the point of realization of the old line shoot, "The flak was so heavy you could get out and walk on it."

'With the bomb doors closed we continued to cross the target going south and had just got our photo and were now free to jink about a bit to confuse the guns when there was an almighty bang. The aircraft almost shuddered to a stop and we seemed to be dropping out of the sky. There was confusion on the intercom, which had gone extremely fuzzy with the loss of the generator and for a brief moment there was a babble of voices as all the crew were enquiring what had happened. The rear-gunner's voice continued and Dave cut in to ask, "Who's that?"

"It's me, the rear-gunner. What's up Dave?"

The answer was very swift. "Prepare to bale out."

'With the loss of power the aircraft had swung to starboard and as we rapidly descended we were heading west along the Ruhr Valley with all the gunners turning their fire on us and searchlights seeking us out for the kill. Meanwhile, in the nose, Blackie and I clipped on our chutes and started to clear the navigator's chair away from the forward escape hatch. Ever since the first time I had seen the Ruhr being bombed I had made up my mind that I would never bale out over a German target on the assumption that the populace would be quite likely to tear aircrew to bits. This did happen in many instances, sometimes observed by their fellow crew-members. And here we were, falling out of the sky over the Ruhr of all places.

'To this day, I am not sure whether I would have jumped in those circumstances. All these thoughts were to be re-enacted a year later when I did have to jump but fortunately not in the target area. However, Dave was still wrestling with the controls and attempting to reduce our rate of descent. In the meantime, Joe had decided that maybe the petrol tanks had been holed and although he had, as normal, changed to full tanks before going in to the target, he hurriedly turned the cocks to switch to alternative tanks. By this time we were coned in the searchlights and were down to 7,000 feet with everything that was within reach beginning to bear on us. This now included light ack-ack with the frightening tracer, every one of which seemed to be heading towards the aircraft before it curled away.

'While all this was happening, I had looked back towards the cockpit and had been surprised to see a pair of white socked feet dancing by the side of the pilot. At the time I did not question what they were doing there and it was not until many years later when talking to Dave that I recalled the incident and asked for an explanation. Apparently, on the order "Prepare to bale out", Andy had shot out of his turret. His boots were ripped off as he scrambled out and had run up the fuselage to the cockpit, where he had shouted in Dave's ear words to the effect of, "Come on, Dave, this can't happen to us, you can't let it happen to us. Get it flying again. It can't happen to us." But then so many crews believed that it couldn't happen to them, only to other crews!

'At 7,000 feet the miracle occurred, as gradually the engines began to splutter again and Dave began to stabilize the aircraft. With power to our elbow, as it were, we now had a chance against the enemy, weaving to get out of the searchlights and above all, starting to climb to get some height again, having lost some 10,000 feet in our fall. As we were in the middle of the Ruhr we had no choice but to continue to fly westward through the best-defended area in Germany but we eventually made our way out and had an uneventful trip back to base.

'Arriving back at dispersal we now had the chance to examine the aircraft to see what had happened. We had apparently been hit by shrapnel from a rather near miss, as witnessed by some 20-plus holes in the aircraft, with one large piece slicing through the fire extinguisher buttons, setting them off in three engines and thus giving them foam rather than fuel to digest. Not taking kindly to this, they had given up. We lost 38 aircraft but it could easily have been 39. The same night and again just after dropping its bombs, a Wellington of 431 "Iroquois" Squadron was also hit. The pilot and rear-gunner baled out thinking that the tail had been lost, leaving a friend of mine, with whom I had trained in South Africa, trapped with the navigator and wireless operator in the nose. Sergeant Stu Sloan, an observer-cum-bomb-aimer like me, regained control of the aircraft with the help of the other two. In spite of two very rough engines, one of which had to be shut down, he not only managed to fly the Wellington back to this country but landed it for good measure. He was given an immediate award of the CGM, commissioned in the field and sent on a pilot's course. Without his efforts it could have been 40 lost that night.[3]

'The following morning it was arranged for us to meet up with an Engineering Officer for an inspection of our aircraft. When we got to dispersal we found him already wandering around, poking into holes at various places as engineers are wont to do. For a few minutes we all drifted around surveying the damage before we assembled in front of the Halifax with the Engineer facing us but keeping a few paces distance from us. Then began an encounter that will last in my memory until I die.

'The officer concerned had been a regular NCO in the inter-war years when all actions had to be governed by books of rules. He first addressed Dave by asking for an account of the events of the previous night. This Dave gave in full, answering questions as he went. There was a brief pause before the Engineering Officer asked Dave, "How far can a Halifax fly on one engine?"

Dave replied, "Not very far."

"Could you have flown back from the Ruhr on one?"

"That would be impossible."

"You would agree that three fire extinguishers have been operated?"

"Yes."

"What are the regulations about using an engine after the fire extinguisher has been used?"

"Normally, shut down the engine, feather the propeller and don't use it again – but this was different. The engines had not been on fire."

"The 'Book' says that an engine must not be used again after the fire extinguisher has been used. Three of your fire extinguishers have been used, therefore you could not have used those engines again. A Halifax could not have flown back from the Ruhr on one engine. It just couldn't have happened, otherwise you wouldn't be here."

'We stood there dumbfounded. Apparently, we were not where we thought we were. There was not the slightest sign of a smile on his face or humour in the situation as he turned away and arranged for our aircraft to have three engines changed and the holes to be patched up. At the tender age of twenty I had learned that, when using a Rule Book, always make sure that it is up to date and applied to the current situation when using it. When, later that morning, I visited the Photographic Section it was with great satisfaction that I found my developed photo showing a very clear picture of Dortmund with the Aiming Point right bang in the centre.'[4]

Notes

1. Twenty-one Berlin raiders and 12 Wellingtons of the Bochum force failed to return.

2. Twenty-one aircraft (13 Lancasters and 7 Halifaxes) FTR from Stettin and 8 Stirlings FTR from Rostock.

3. The rear-gunner had reported that he thought the aircraft was on fire. The pilot twice put the aircraft into a dive to evade the searchlights but was unable to do so. There was some confusion over whether an order to bale out was given by the pilot and the pilot actually did leave the aircraft. The bomb-aimer, Sergeant Stewart Nimmo Sloan, an Englishman, took the controls and eventually was able to shake off the searchlights. The navigator and wireless operator were still aboard and Sloan flew the aircraft back to England and made a perfect landing at Cranwell. He was immediately awarded the CGM, commissioned and posted to a pilot training course. The wireless operator, Flying Officer J.B.G. Bailey and the navigator, Sergeant G.C.W. Parslow, received immediate awards of the DFC and the DFM respectively. They later became part of the crew of Wing Commander J. Coverdale, the squadron commander, but were killed with Coverdale on the night of 21/22 June 1943 on the raid on Krefeld. Sergeant (later Flight Lieutenant) Sloan returned to Bomber Command as a Halifax pilot with 158 Squadron and flew on operations from January 1945 until the end of the war. In the post-war years he served with the King's Flight. *The Bomber Command War Diaries* by Martin Middlebrook and Chris Everitt, (Midland 1985).

4. Flying Officer S. T. 'Tom' Wingham completed his first tour in June 1943. On 28 March 1944 he and the Halifax III crew captained by Squadron Leader S. A. 'Stan' Somerscales DFC had arrived at RAF Holme-on-Spalding Moor to start their second tour with 76 Squadron. They made their 76 Squadron debut on 22/23 April when the target for 596 heavies was Düsseldorf. It was well known to Tom Wingham and all of the crew who had been there twice before during the Battle of the Ruhr April to July 1943. Somerscales' Halifax was one

of 37 RAF bombers shot down when the Halifax was hit by a Bf 110G-4 night fighter with *Schräge Musik* cannon, piloted by Oberfeldfebel Rudolf Frank of 3./NJG3 for his 43rd 'kill'. Somerscales and one of the crew were KIA. Three others survived and were POWs. Tom Wingham and another crewmember were able to evade capture and, after four and a half months, returned home to RAF service. On the night of 26/27 April, after having shot down two further RAF bombers, Frank also was shot down, near Eindhoven and killed with his crew. After two months' compulsory leave and being given an open invitation to decide his own posting, Wingham volunteered for Mosquitoes and after a navigation refresher course at an OTU ended up in 8 Group (PFF) on 105 (Oboe) Squadron at RAF Bourn at the end of March 1945, with whom he completed four ops before the war finished. In April 1946 on recommendation of AOC.-in-C. Bomber Command he was awarded the DFC, American, for his successful evasion, the list for British awards having been closed in June 1945.

# Chapter 14

# No Halt for the Lame – Bruce Sanders

Minnie the Moocher was her name. She was a Lancaster bomber [in 15 Squadron at Wickenby] which made the journey to Oberhausen on 14/15 June 1943 with a 4,000-pound 'cookie' tucked away in the bomb-bay.[1] Minnie's[2] pilot that night was Sergeant A. H. Moores of Bromley in Kent, an airman of uncommon determination and courage. He knew what the east-flying bombers could expect from the Ruhr defences in the days following the great attack on the Möhne dam. Happy Valley had not changed, except for the worse. But delivery of the giant 'cookies' was more urgent than ever. With the Italian islands surrendering one by one and the summer lull on the Russian front continuing, German industry had to be smitten; David smote the Philistine. It had to be put out of the fight. Well, Sergeant Moores was ready to do all he could personally to bring about that end. And what he could do personally proved to be plenty.

Thirty miles from the target – that is, about 10 minutes flying time – Minnie was accosted by three or four thugs in the guise of German night fighters. The gallant lady had quite a brush with these gentry before she shook them off. But the Germans had smashed the Lancaster's rear-turret and holed the fuselage badly and when they disappeared they left behind a disturbing reek of cordite, which gave Moores the impression that his aircraft was on fire somewhere in the region of the bomb-load. That was not a pleasant thought. But in the space of 10 minutes, if the great bomb did not explode before that time, he could drop the 4,000-pounder where it was scheduled to go. He decided to take a chance on lasting the vital 10 minutes. He could have jettisoned the big bomb there and then, or he could have ordered the crew to bale out. Minnie was lame. So far as he knew they were all in high peril. He would have been justified in any action he took to save his own life and the lives of his crew. But even as he pondered the questions and framed the alternatives, he saw the fires of burning Oberhausen ahead. That decided him. Minnie did not halt.

There is no halt for the RAF's lame. They go on till they drop and a surprising number come back to be made whole again. That night Minnie the Moocher got back to base. Moores told his story the following day. He said:

'My bomb-aimer, Sergeant J.D. Cushing, whose home is at Ealing, told me that there were two Junkers 88s below. The next thing I heard was the rear-gunner open up with a four-seconds burst. I think it was then that he was hit, because I heard nothing more and the intercom was cut off. The wireless operator, Sergeant Norcliffe, a Halifax man, thought that we were on fire and, in looking for the flames, knocked off his oxygen tube. He was so dazed that he said to me, "Are you the pilot of this aircraft?" We all believed that there must be a fire owing to the overpowering reek of cordite – actually it came from an enemy shell – and I was expecting our 4,000lb bomb to go off at any moment. But I was determined not to jettison the bomb after the distance we had flown. So we carried on to the target and when our full load had gone down I heaved a sigh of relief. I was amazed to find that the aircraft could still fly true and level. I turned for home. We hit the coast right where we wanted to. When our badly damaged Lancaster touched down at base we found that the rear-gunner had been killed by a cannon shell. It had smashed one side of the rear-turret. There were holes as big as coconuts in the fuselage and both starboard propellers had been hit. Luckily they had continued to function.'

Luckily indeed. But Minnie, apparently, had not been labelled 'moocher' lightly. She had mooched home not much more than 50 per cent operational. She had the one characteristic that all moochers have in common – she had arrived.

Pilot Officer Walter Scott Sherk of 35 Squadron won the bar to his DFC one night in April 1943 by getting his lame bomber back to base. He had three other Canadians with him; Flying Officer G.G. McGladrey, Flying Officer R.G. Morrison, both of whom were awarded the DFC, and Sergeant D.G. Bebensee, who got the DFM for his part in the operation. They were sent to attack Stettin and, when over the target area, were hit by falling incendiaries. One of these penetrated just behind the pilot's seat and jammed the rudder controls. In a matter of seconds there were flames and smoke in the cockpit and Sherk's clothing caught fire. The tail tipped up and the aircraft, already fairly low, began sliding down in an unpleasant dive, every instant becoming an easier target for the ack-ack gunners. At the control column Sherk tried desperately to regain control of the unmanageable machine, while behind McGladrey fought hard to beat out the crackling flames. Before the flames could be subdued much of the navigational equipment was ruined and rendered useless. The sergeant struggled to free the locked controls. The four men, in fact, were doing everything they could to prevent what seemed to be inevitable, a crash over Stettin. Their efforts were rewarded. The plane suddenly became manageable, to their great relief, and Sherk flattened out and circled round, preparing to head for home. McGladrey finished putting out the fire and then Morrison, who was navigator, tried his hand with what was left of his equipment. It took great deal of ingenuity to plot accurate courses in the circumstances but Morrison had all the ingenuity required. Bomber Command's navigators are usually well on top of their job. The four Canadians ran a gauntlet of danger all the way to the North Sea coast, for there was the possibility that the controls might jam again. It had taken Bebensee three-quarters of hour to fix them. A second jam might mean a different ending. However, before dawn the lame duck was home minus a few feathers, but otherwise undisturbed.

Squadron Leader Kenneth Holstead Burns, an American from Oregon, flew one of 97 Squadron's bombers to Dortmund, but lost the use of one engine on the outward flight. To continue offered the prospect of having to jink from night fighters and flak with a lagging aircraft that might at any moment become completely unmanageable. Burns continued, got to the target, pranged it and returned to base; that dead engine still giving no sign of life. A few nights afterwards he flew to attack a target in Czechoslovakia and, when all of 200 miles distant from his target, ran into a thick curtain of flak. His aircraft was hit and the air-speed indicator rendered unserviceable. Burns again went on, knowing he would have to come back over territory where gunners would be waiting for him and radio location minders ready to announce his coming. He again bombed his target vigorously – and got home.

He now wears the bar to his previously earned DFC.

Not all the lame ducks of the RAF get back from their long-range flights. The man who received the most laudatory official citation ever issued by the RAF was prevented from making base even when over the English coast. Flight Sergeant Middleton's 'devotion to duty', said the citation when the award of the VC was announced, 'in the face of overwhelming odds is unsurpassed in the annals of the Royal Air Force.' Middleton's famous flight was made to attack the Fiat works at Turin on the night of 28/29 November. He went down with his battered Stirling in the Channel, having brought his crew back to safety and when the great Channel storm in early February 1943 was at its height, the sea surrendered his body. It was washed up on the beach under Shakespeare's Cliff overlooking the most famous air battlefield of all time, the Straits of Dover.[3]

It is because men like Middleton die that others get back. They have an example to follow; a deed to emulate. Getting back to base after making an operational flight is part of the RAF's great living tradition. The captains and the crews of the bombers felt themselves honour bound to bring their aircraft back if the limits of human endurance allowed them. And it seemed, as the months went by and the scope of the RAF's all-embracing offensive widened to cover an entire continent, as though those limits were being stretched like an elastic band, stretched by the willpower of the men who flew.

Minelaying in enemy waters was a ticklish business. The Germans gave the minelayers of Bomber Command a really hot time while they were within range of coastal batteries. Night fighters too had special instructions to go in and engage minelayers, as a Lancaster minelaying off the Danish coast discovered. Actually the Lancaster was just leaving the Danish coast when the night fighter swept in to attack from astern. The German's fire was accurate and raked the bomber from nose to tail. The rear and mid-upper gunners were both wounded. Getting that shot-up plane back to Britain over 300 miles of open sea was no mean feat. Those of the crew who were able to work were struggling hard every minute of the way against the aircraft's tendency to slide down into the water.

'We heard the rear-gunner cry out,' the pilot related after landing 'and the wireless operator went to see what had happened. On the way he found that the mid-upper gunner had been wounded and was lying on the floor of the aircraft. His seat had been shot away from under him. When the wireless operator got to the rear-turret he found that doors were jammed and he had to break them down with an axe. Then with the help of the bomb-aimer he pulled the gunner out of the turret. They wrapped the two gunners in blankets and gave them orange juice and some morphia.' Then came the job of holding the damaged Lancaster on course. 'Meanwhile, I was trying to get the aircraft under control. When the fighter hit us the Lancaster went into a flat spin. The port aileron had been shot away and we dived down nearly 9,000 feet before I could get the Lancaster under control. The flight engineer then came to my help and by heaving on to the control column together we managed to right the aircraft. It was pretty exhausting work and we took it in turns to hang on to it. The flight engineer had to keep a check on the petrol-gauges, as two of the tanks had been holed and he was afraid that we might be running short of petrol. We found that we also had to keep the starboard rudder pushed hard forward. It was too much of a strain for me to hold it, so the bomb-aimer pushed it forward with a bar against a support and held it there.'

In short, controlling that Lancaster meant navvying thousands of feet above the North Sea at night in an aircraft with its radio aerial shot away, its tail-wheel punctured, both turrets riddled like sieves, two fuel-tanks holed, fuselage shot up and port aileron missing. It seemed a veritable miracle that the pilot should arrive home and make a perfect landing. We had the Air Ministry's word for it that he did.

Squadron Leader E. G. Gilmore had a tale to tell about his Halifax. He took it to Cologne on 2/3 February 1943, dropped his bomb load and then everything seemed to happen to it.

'We had just dropped our bombs on Cologne when one of the crew reported that fighters were following us. I swerved, but while we were still trying to get away we were caught in a cone of searchlights. Flak blew off the starboard inner propeller and the astrodome, punched holes in the fuselage, wings and aileron and threw the aircraft over on its back. All the engines stopped together and we whirled into a dive. The aircraft fell from 18,000 feet to 4,000 feet and I gave the order to bale out. The navigator almost got clear, but I called him back just in time. The rear-gunner told me over the intercom that he was hacking his way out of the jammed turret. In the twisting, turning, rolling dive a parachute broke loose and after smashing the master compass, got jammed between the control column and the instrument panel. Suddenly all the landing-lights went on. We were 4,000 feet above the target, lit up for the gunners to see us. Only two of my engines were working properly at this stage. Apparently they had started up during that headlong spiralling spin earthwards and we had lost so much height that it was no good trying to take evasive action. Besides, some of the bomb-doors were open and the Halifax was very difficult to manoeuvre. The only thing I could do was to fly straight and level. Somehow we got out of the searchlights without being badly hit again. The third engine had now picked up. We thought that our troubles were now over but when we got over the enemy coast we were caught by searchlights again. By good luck we escaped. Navigation was just about as difficult as it could be. We had lost the master compass and we had to find our way back to base on the bomb-aimer's compass. It was quite a trip.'

Very much it was quite a trip. The lame duck was all but plucked bare.

Shortly after this amazing example of a bomber crew sticking to the job and getting their aircraft home, another Halifax was badly mauled by a Ju 88 night fighter over Essen. The German fired everything he had at the British bomber, cannon and machine-gun fire and some of his cannon shells burst inside the fuselage, sending splinters in every direction. The rear-gunner continued replying until three of his four guns were knocked cold and he himself was wounded in the left leg. The flight engineer took a bullet through the chest, the navigator was hit by shell splinters in the back and one leg and the mid-upper gunner and the bomb-aimer were both wounded in the feet.

Five of the crew were casualties and the Halifax was badly holed. Their plight looked desperate indeed. The pilot, Flying Officer R. D. Johnstone of Glasgow, reported:

'I had no idea that the bomb-aimer had been wounded. He said nothing about it until we landed, but went about with the wireless operator giving first aid to the others. The wireless operator gave me great help. He told me how our fuel consumption was going and gave me the engine temperature – in fact, he took over the flight engineer's job. His wireless set was smashed and we were completely out of touch with home, so he went to and fro bandaging the wounded men and giving them coffee. In spite of his wounds, the navigator was able to give me an approximate course and we reached an aerodrome in the south of England. The wounded are getting on well and while the flight engineer may not be able to fly again, the rest of us hope to crew up once more. We were all trained together and have made twelve trips in company.'

Those men hoped to crew up again. They wanted to fly together. They were, in every sense, a real team. That is another fundamental reason why so many damaged RAF bombers got home when badly shot up. The crew were a team working in harmony. They flew as a team, they bombed as a team, they fought as a team and they carried on through adverse conditions as a team. Death alone could weaken their team spirit. The same simple truth applied to the Coastal Command crews who flew over the sea-lanes ploughed by the convoys. They went down in the drink only when it was no longer possible to remain flying.

On Sunday 30 May 1943 the story of the airborne lifeboat was released to the public.[4] The airborne lifeboat was a logical development of the service rendered for many months by ASR squadrons of Walrus and Lysander aircraft and by the RAF high-speed launches, which had had to carry on despite the murderous attentions of German fighter pilots. The new lifeboat was designed to help shipwrecked mariners and aircrews who had come down in the drink, to use one of their own graphic terms, too far from British shores and too near the enemy coastline to make rescue by Air-Sea Rescue launch or plane reasonably possible. With the stepped-up air offensive more bomber crews required aid when their shot-up aircraft had to be abandoned on the homeward flight. The airborne lifeboat was used operationally for the first time [on 4/5 May] when a Halifax [of 102 Squadron] captained by Flight Sergeant James Bowman of Durham had to be abandoned by its crew 50 miles out in the North Sea.[5] The Halifax had been on a heavy raid over Dortmund. Five members of the crew of seven were on their maiden operational bombing trip. Over Dortmund the Halifax had unloaded its bombs but had been badly shot up by the flak gunners. Three engines were put out of action and Bowman tried to get home on the one remaining but the aircraft had lost height and had gone on losing more. When out over the North Sea the order to ditch had to be given. The Halifax sank and the crew set to work firing the rockets stored in their dinghy.

Those rockets were spotted at six o'clock in the morning by the sharp eyes of Sergeant D. A. Workman, a Birmingham man, who was piloting a Hudson of Coastal Command which was out on patrol. The Hudson's navigator worked out the position of the marooned crew and radioed it back to base. The Hudson then began flying round and round the bobbing dinghy, watchful against the appearance of any German aircraft or E-boat. Workman was still watching over the Halifax men when another Hudson flew over. This aircraft had been dispatched by Air-Sea Rescue Headquarters and it carried one of the new parachute lifeboats. Flight Sergeant Hugh McGregor of Glasgow, the navigator of the Air-Sea Rescue Hudson, said:

'When we were briefed and told the dinghy was about 60 miles from the English coast and that we were to go out and drop the lifeboat, we were all excited. We flew over the dinghy and carefully estimated the strength and direction of the wind. Then we released the boat. I hardly dared breathe as it went down, for this was the first time it had been used except on trials. However, the parachute blossomed out beautifully and the boat settled in the water as neatly as could be. We all whooped with delight.' To this Workman, who watched McGregor's release of the lifeboat with anxious eyes, adds:

'I watched the launching of the lifeboat from the Hudson and it was an amazing job of work. The boat was dropped from about 1,000 feet and floated gently down, landing less than 20 yards from the dinghy.' Bowman, equally anxious, said afterwards:

'I've never been so frightened in my life as when this great boat came sailing down towards us from the air – we were sure it was going to hit us; it dropped so close. However, it landed all right and we soon scrambled in. I could hardly believe my eyes when I saw the engines. We got them going in a few minutes and they carried us forward for several hours at about six knots. The Hudson flashed us our course and we had got within about ten miles of England when were met by a naval vessel. We were given air protection nearly the whole way back.'

That strange meeting in the middle of the North Sea offered yet another demonstration of what a small world it had become. Sergeant Harold Mock, the Halifax's flight engineer, related afterwards how the crew of the Air-Sea Rescue Hudson came to see the men they had rescued next day in hospital, where they were recovering from their adventure.

'Imagine my surprise,' he said, 'to find that the pilot was a chap I knew well. He lived near me in Exmouth. That's what I call a pal.' Flight Sergeant A.H. Mogridge, the Air-Sea Rescue Hudson's pilot, shared that surprise. That smiling reunion in a hospital ward was a happy augury for the new service of aid and mercy for the east-flying bomber crews begun by the crews of the RAF's Air-Sea Rescue squadrons.

The lame ducks of Coastal Command were of the virile breed as were those of Bomber Command. Lame, they still fought, still got back to base. There was no halt for these ones. Some of them may have had as many as 1,000 miles to fly back. Distance and the long lapse of hours did not deter them.

Sergeant G.O. Ellergodt struck a bad patch when he was on his first operational flight as pilot of a Hampden torpedo-bomber. It was the depth of winter and he had to attack a German convoy sailing close in to the Dutch coast and under the coastal batteries. *F for Freddie* was his Hampden. He piloted it across the North Sea, found the convoy sneaking along in the darkness with no glimmer of light showing and went in low to drop his torpedo. He was met by a furious barrage. *F for Freddie* was hit again and again. Three shells burst inside the aircraft, one smashing all the flying instruments except the altimeter and the compass. The elevator trim was carried away into the winter night. *F for Freddie*'s tail went down and its nose elevated. The Hampden climbed steeply and would have gone on climbing had not Ellergodt, a brawny Canadian, thrown all his weight against the control column. Gradually the Hampden's nose came down again. But Ellergodt found that simply by using his hands he could not hope to keep the bucking machine on an even keel. He had to get more leverage. He obtained it by leaning far back in his pilot's seat, bracing one knee hard against the control column and raising his other leg and forcing his foot in the loop of the steering-wheel as though it were a stirrup. In this back-breaking position, by pushing as hard as he could with both foot and knee, he kept the Hampden steady. He remained in that position over a distance of nearly 300 miles while the battered torpedo-carrying aircraft flapped about on the route back to base. Ellergodt made his landing circuit over his base in just under three hours after taking up that position of strain.

And he put *F for Freddie* down safely.

There was a Hudson that got back to base three times after being badly shot up. Its favourite hunting-ground was along the enemy-held European coastline, where time and again it was sent on a 'strike'. The third time it came back damaged it had attacked a convoy and pranged an enemy vessel but had not got away before the flak gunners had blown a hole in the starboard wing big enough for three men to stand in.

'I was just congratulating myself' the pilot grinned afterwards, 'that we were clear of the flak when the kite seemed to jump about twenty yards in the air. We had been hit in the starboard wing near the trailing edge behind the engine.'

On the way home the Hudson behaved like a skittish colt, bucking and rearing suddenly, then sulkily lagging. It had to be coaxed along with a great deal of patience and a few fervid prayers that the wing would not buckle and break off. After landing safely, though somewhat faster than normally, the pilot said:

'We're getting quite used to it now. We don't worry any. We know that if the enemy leaves us one engine and pieces of wing and fuselage we can get the old kite home safe.'

That was no boast. It was the literal truth and the speaker spoke for all the lame duck airmen who touched down in safety after a rough passage back to base.

Notes
1. Oberhausen was cloud-covered but *Oboe* sky marking was accurate. Seventeen Lancasters from the 197 dispatched, failed to return.
2. A name derived from Cab Calloway's popular slow blues song, 'Minnie the Moocher'.
3. On the night of 28/29 November 1942, 228 aircraft including 117 Lancasters and 47 Stirlings, raided the Fiat Works at Turin. Flight Sergeant Rawdon Hume Middleton RAAF of 149 Squadron piloted one of the Stirlings (BF372). The aircraft met unexpectedly high headwinds over the Alps and had used so much fuel that many had to turn back. Middleton decided to press on and he went down to 2,000 feet in order to establish the exact position of the target. The Australian's Stirling was caught by anti-aircraft fire as he made his first approach but despite this he made two more runs over the city and, on the last, the Stirling was hit repeatedly. The windscreen was shattered and Middleton's right eye was completely destroyed. He was also badly wounded in the body but despite his fearsome wounds, he kept his aircraft on target until all the bombs had been dropped. Flight Sergeant Leslie Hyder the

second pilot, recovered consciousness from a head wound and struggled with Middleton to keep the crippled bomber airborne as they flew away from the immediate danger zone. When Middleton saw how badly Hyder was injured he ordered him to go back into the fuselage to receive first aid but, just as Hyder was doing this, Middleton suddenly lost consciousness and he slumped over the controls. Six thousand feet were lost and the Stirling was down to only 800 feet before the wounded Hyder could muster sufficient strength to check the descent and put the aircraft into a slow climb back on the homeward track. In the fuselage the wireless operator, Pilot Officer Norman Skinner and a wounded gunner, Sergeant Harold Gough received first aid from the uninjured crew members but both insisted on returning to their posts. The aircraft was badly damaged and fuel was short. Hyder assumed temporary command and ordered everything possible to be jettisoned. Even the guns were thrown out, leaving the Stirling completely defenceless. Middleton, conscious again but practically blind, called the crew around him to discuss the alternatives. They decided to stay with the aircraft and to try to make the English coast. For almost four hours Middleton kept the Stirling on track, taking evasive action as searchlights caught them over France. He must have suffered agony as the biting wind rushed through the shattered windscreen on to his hideously mutilated face. Fuel was running out as they were over the English Channel and Middleton gave the order to bale out. Sergeant John Mackie half carried the wounded Hyder to the escape hatch, placed the second pilot's hand on his parachute release and pushed him out. Gough, who was flying his 33rd operation, Flight Sergeant Douglas Cameron and Flying Officer George Royde jumped next, followed by the wounded Skinner. As they floated down they saw the Stirling turn back over the sea with Middleton, Jeffery and Mackie still on board. The bodies of Sergeant James Jeffery and Mackie, who was on his 31st operation having volunteered like Gough, to fly until his skipper had completed his tour, were washed ashore the next day. Middleton's body was not recovered for three months when he was washed ashore on Shakespeare Beach, Dover on 1 February. On 13 January 1943 Flight Sergeant Middleton was posthumously awarded the Victoria Cross, the highest award for gallantry. The official citation stated in part: 'His devotion to duty in the face of overwhelming odds is unsurpassed in the annals of the Royal Air Force.' On 5 February Middleton was buried with full military honours in the Military Cemetery in the churchyard of St John's Church in Beck Row. He was buried in the rank of Pilot Officer. News of his commission had not reached him before his death.

Flight Sergeant L. A. Hyder, Sergeant Cameron and Sergeant Gough were awarded the DFM. (Flying Officer Cameron later joined 635 Squadron and he was shot down on 4 August 1944 when he was flying with Acting Squadron Leader Ian Willoughby Bazalgette DFC RAFVR, who was awarded a posthumous VC. Cameron survived and evaded capture.) Middleton's medal is now on display in the Australian War memorial in Canberra. The RAF Mildenhall Officer's Club was renamed in his honour – Middleton Hall – in 2002. *RAF Mildenhall: Bombers, 'Blackbirds' & The 'Boom Years'* by Martin W. Bowman, (Tempus 2007).

4. The eventual production of the airborne lifeboat was largely due to the research and experimental work undertaken by Group Captain E. F. Waring DFC AFC the Deputy Director of Air-Sea Rescue. He realized that bomber crews must in the future be given the chance of getting themselves home if they could. Hitherto they had abandoned their aircraft and spent hours, sometimes days and weeks, in their rubber dinghies, often near to starvation, sometimes dying from exposure before the vigilance of searching Air-Sea Rescue craft was rewarded by sight of them in the vastness of the sea. The airborne lifeboat was a compact motor-boat, which could be carried under the fuselage of an ASR aircraft. It was dropped by parachute, which opened when the lifeboat was released and allowed the craft to drift downwind towards a bomber crew in their dinghy at the same rate of fall as an airman who had baled out. The lifeboat could be so accurately aimed by an experienced pilot that it struck the sea within a very few feet of a dinghy's occupants. Provision was made for rough

seas and freakish winds in that, no matter at what angle the boat hit the water, it automatically righted itself and floated right way up. It was fitted with special buoyancy tanks, which kept it afloat and uncapsizable in the roughest weather. In weather-protected compartments were two specially converted engines, with stores of clothes, medical equipment, food, and the various kinds of air-sea rescue signalling apparatus. Finally the fuel-tanks held enough petrol to enable the lifeboat to travel a considerable distance. For emergency use were a portable radio-transmitting set, sails and oars.

5. Seventy-five miles off Flamborough Head.

# Chapter 15

# The One who Didn't Get Away – Sergeant John Mattey

Flight Sergeant John C. Mattey and his crew were flying with 158 Squadron, 4 Group, stationed at Lissett, Yorkshire. On 8 October 1943 they took delivery of a new Halifax II, LW317 NP-P which they would fly that night to Hanover when just over 500 bombers took part. Their previous aircraft was shot up on their last operation, to Kassel on 3/4 October, where the rear-gunner shot down an attacking Ju 88. Take-off time on 8 October was 2030 hours. They were in the second wave, carrying incendiaries in the wings and HE in the bomb bay. Weather was broken cloud around 14,000 feet with clear skies above. The moon would not be up until after midnight and the flight out was uneventful until about 50 miles from the target. Parachute flares soon lighted up their route either side of their course. Soon 'Rebecca' was bleeping. They took evasive action and the bleeps faded. They could not see anything but they knew that they would have to run the gauntlet now until after the target. 'Rebecca' remained silent for some time but they gently weaved from time to time. Suddenly, the bleeps started again. They turned slightly to starboard and there was tracer coming from below and the port inner tank and engine were on fire. They were not equipped with self-sealing tanks or fire extinguishers, so the port inner started racing away. The propeller was immediately feathered and the bomb load jettisoned. Sergeant B.G. Anderson, the rear-gunner, reported that flames were licking round his turret. The fire from the burning petrol was like a giant Bunsen burner. Obviously it was not a healthy position to be in, so Mattey gave the order to abandon aircraft.

Having practised the drill many times, everyone was out in less than 30 seconds. However, the rear-gunner had not acknowledged, so Mattey did not know for sure that he had gone. With one engine out, it was not possible to trim for straight and level flight, particularly as the port inner drove the autopilot. Realizing that a power spiral would make it difficult to get out, he stalled the plane and it went into a stalled spin to port. He then was able to walk through the fuselage and check that the rear turret was empty. Finding that he was on his own, he returned to the cockpit and dropped through the escape hatch. The time was about 2330 hours and the height around 18,000 feet. Everything was suddenly quiet, then he felt a sudden jerk on his shoulders as the parachute opened and he was floating gently down, with the aircraft spinning in ever decreasing circles towards the ground. It hit and exploded when he was at about 10,000 feet. He actually felt the blast; then everything was quiet, except for the steady drone of the bomber stream heading for the target.

The sky was clear and the stars bright. Falling at about 1,000 feet per minute, he had time to re-orientate himself and he had no difficulty in deciding which way he would have to go. He landed in a meadow about a mile from the burning aircraft, which had fallen on some farm buildings.[1] This fortunately diverted any attention that might have been paid to a parachute descending. He did not stop to bury the parachute as instructed but made for a hedge some quarter of a mile away and in the opposite direction to the fire. Reaching the hedge he started walking westwards as quickly as possible. Suddenly there was a swishing sound from the other side of the hedge, as though people were walking through high grass. He stopped and dropped to the ground. The noise went on but did not seem to be coming closer. After what seemed an age, he crawled up to the hedge and peered through. What he saw were a number of cows moving slowly along, chewing the grass.

Recovering from the shock, he made for what appeared to be a small wooded area about a mile away and slightly to the left. He found that he had reached a fair sized copse with trees and brambles, so he pushed through about 50 yards and found a small clearing where he paused to take stock. Taking a razor blade from his pocket, he cut the tops of his leather flying boots, which were designed to become shoes. The whole crew had changed to this type of boot about a week previously. He then removed his brevet and stripes; for although his commission had come through, it had not been promulgated. He also removed his cap badge, opened the escape pack and had a look at the map, then decided that if he headed due west, with luck he should eventually reach Holland. The moon was now up and it was a clean, cold and frosty night, so he started his cross-country walk westwards, avoiding villages, roads and outlying farms as much as possible. He carried on this way until the sky began to lighten, then he found a suitable outlying copse to await dusk before continuing. He settled down and was soon fast asleep.

Waking about midday, he sorted through the emergency pack of Horlicks tablets, glucose sweets, chewing gum and bar of chocolate and decided on a couple of tablets, a sweet and a small amount of condensed milk which was in a tube. The bar of chocolate he put in his battle dress top pocket. Everything was quiet. Nothing stirred. The sky was cloudless, the sun warm; quite idyllic in fact. The whole area appeared to be for dairy farming which probably meant firm fields to cross. Dusk began to fall about 6 p.m. so it was time to get moving. Tucking his battle dress top under his arm, he set off. His sweater had been dyed navy blue some weeks ago, so he was not conspicuous. At about midnight he found himself on a farm track, going in the right direction so, as everything was quiet, he carried on. Walking was now a lot easier then, turning a slight bend, he saw a bench with four large milk churns on it. On examination they proved to be full, obviously awaiting collection. With great care he took off one of the lids, lifted the churn and poured about a quart of milk into the lid, then drank it down. Boy, did that feel good! Feeling much refreshed he set off with renewed vigour once again repeating the performance before dawn. Finding a suitable thicket, he holed up for the day.

Waking about midday again, he discovered that he was lying in full sun and with a cloudless sky. It was quite warm. He put his hand in the top pocket to get the bar of chocolate and found that it had melted in the heat. He salvaged what he could but most of it was wasted so it was back to the Horlicks tablets and sweets. Looking around, he saw that he was in an area of shrub land, no shelter or sign of habitation, so he waited until it was quite dark before continuing. After about a couple of hours the ground began to descend and a few sparse trees appeared, giving some shelter if it proved necessary. The ground levelled out and started to squelch and he realized he was in boggy land. He turned back quickly and followed the edge of the soft area, looking for a drier patch. It was quite slow going and eventually he found that he was on a riverbank. The river was about 40 feet wide. There was no way he could cross it, so he followed the bank as closely as possible.

The best part of an hour later, a bridge appeared in the darkness ahead, which meant a road of sorts and he would have to get on to that road. However, it was quite dark, the moon having not yet risen. Pushing through a hedge he paused for five minutes, making sure that the road was clear. He started walking over the bridge; all was quiet and he really had no option but to carry on. Luckily it was a typical country road and he walked on the verge as much as possible. Turning a bend, he was suddenly in a village. There was no turning back, so with a certain amount of trepidation, he pressed on. He heard voices and up ahead there was a knot of people chatting outside a garden gate. He quietly crossed the road so as to pass in the other side. As he came level with them, one of them turned and looked straight at him. Fortunately it was very dark and he was in dark clothes. 'Gute Nacht' he heard and with a heart beating nineteen to the dozen, he replied, 'Nacht' and waved an arm. The group continued chatting. Breathing a sigh of relief, he carried on until clear of the village. Then deciding that the road was going roughly, in the right direction, he would make up for lost time. He passed through another village, called out 'Gute nacht' to someone coming the other way. Coming to a railway crossing he had to wait for a goods train to pass. Crossing the railway, he kept on the road. Eventually he cut across country again; it was still a farming area but quite flat and more open, not nearly so much shelter. He was however, able to get a drink of milk but as time went on, the farms were given over to arable crops with very little cover. As it was now beginning to get light, he had to settle for a ditch at the side of a hedge and hidden by high grass and weeds. This proved to be quite safe and he slept soundly until about midday as usual.

On waking, he was surprised to hear voices. He stirred carefully but could see no one. He then realized that there were people the other side of the hedge, probably farm hands having a lunch break. Very soon they moved off and once again, all was quiet. He lay in the ditch until after dusk, not daring to move and suffering cramp now and again. Following a few stretching exercises, he set off once more across the fields, realizing that he would soon have to find out just where he was. Hitting a farm track, he followed it until he reached a road. Checking with the escape compass, he continued westwards, arriving at a small town. There were quite a few people about but in the blackout he was not noticed. He could hear a train in the station and people hurrying in that direction.

Finally, he came to a T-junction with a signpost. The town he had come through was Bentheim but best of all, the signpost pointed to Hengelo, which he knew was in Holland. The distance was 60 kilometres. He was well clear of the town by now. A deserted road and the occasional cottage or small house were the only signs of habitation. Glancing idly up the garden path of a cottage, he saw a bicycle propped up against a post. Quietly opening the gate, he crept up to the post. The bicycle was not chained up, so he lifted it up and carried it to the gate. The road was clear so he pedalled away as fast as he could, slowing down after about 20 minutes. He realized that he would have to cross the frontier in daylight, so he carried on for another couple of hours, then found a haystack to rest in and had a quick nap. Waking a little after dawn, he finished off the remaining sweets and tablets, burying the rubbish in the bottom of the haystack. Then he waited until there was a bit of traffic about.

He rode on until he came in sight of the border checkpoint; stopping a short distance away to watch the procedure. There were workers crossing both ways. Papers were checked, so crossing there was out. Realizing that he ought not to hang around there, he took a sight on some buildings that were obviously in Holland. He retraced his steps and then saw a track going off to the left which was negotiable with the bike. He went as far as he could until the track petered out. To the left was a thickly wooded area full of shrubs and brambles, almost impenetrable. However, he forced his way through a small gap, dragging the bike behind him. After about 100 yards he left the bike under a shrub well out of sight. Progress was now a bit easier although it was still a battle. After a good hour he broke through into a field. He stopped and looked around. Not very far away was a cluster of farmhouses and also a bit further on was the building that he had decided was in Holland. He had made it! He sat down and rested, deciding on the next step. Feeling refreshed after about half an hour, he made his way towards habitation. He decided that it would be best to find a place without any young children or a dog. The third house seemed to fill his requirements, so with a certain amount of trepidation, for this was make or break, he lifted the knocker and rapped twice. There was dead silence.

After what seemed an age, the door opened and an elderly woman appeared. He took his RAF wings out of his pocket and showed them to her, saying 'Englander' and, using sign language, tried to indicate that he was a flyer and had been shot down. She gave him a searching look and indicated that he should stay there, then promptly shut the door. Not knowing what she intended, he decided to wait. Then after about five minutes, the door opened again; this time by a man about 40, who, after a quick look around, invited him inside. He was shown into the living room where the family was gathered and he sat down with them. There was another man and woman, also the older woman who had opened the door. Communication was difficult but with mime and the wings and the cap badge, they realized who he was and with nods and smiles tried to make him feel at ease. He then had an inspiration. Taking out a packet of Players cigarettes he handed it round. This immediately broke the tension. By then he had established that they were indeed Dutch and would help him if they could. The first thing offered was a wash and shave, then a cup of tea and a couple of bacon sandwiches. After this, he was taken outside into a hay barn. There they hollowed out a space into which he climbed. Then he was shut in and they indicated that they would be back later. He fell asleep almost at once until roused in the evening.

It was dark when he went back into the house, where the evening meal was on the table. There was another man present, who was the village schoolmaster who could speak a little English but taught French at school. It proved a bit difficult at first, for although they both spoke French, the accents were quite different. However, writing down anything that the other did not understand solved the problem. The schoolmaster then interpreted into Dutch, so everyone understood what was going on. It was finally decided that he should stay at the farm while they contacted a friend of theirs in Arnhem who might be able to help.

In the meantime he spent his days in the haystack. They brought him food in the morning, and he came out of hiding after dark to join the family for the evening meal. On the third morning he was taken into the house for breakfast. A friend from Arnhem was there who spoke some English. He was given a civilian suit and an old navy raincoat. He had a bath and a shave and his uniform was parcelled up and they set off on bicycles to the nearest railway station, which was at Hengelo. He followed the guide about 10 yards behind. Arriving at the station, there was about an hour to wait, so they went into a cafe and had a cup of acorn coffee and, to while way the time, he pretended to read the morning paper. Just before the train came in, he was given a ticket to Arnhem and also a German propaganda magazine to read. This ensured that no self-respecting Dutchman would speak to him. They boarded the train and sat in the same third-class compartment but not together. He found himself isolated during the journey, as nobody would sit next to him. The journey was uneventful.

At the station there were two bicycles. His guide gave him a password and said that someone else who would use this word would pass them and he was to follow the new guide. Sure enough, after about a quarter of a mile a man who gave the password overtook him. He gave the reply and the new guide said, 'Follow me.' They arrived at a house in Amsterdamseweg, a three storey building. Leaving the bicycles inside the front door, they went up to the first floor. There he was shown into the living room; the only other person present was the wife of the guide. After a snack he was told that he would only be there one night and he would go into the country the next day. He was then given a questionnaire to fill in and then he was photographed for an identity card. The rest of the day he spent quietly. His hosts turned the radio on for the 9 o'clock news from the BBC, then a little later, to the overseas programme for any messages. Then the radio was hidden away. They all turned in at about 10:30 p.m. and he was able to sleep in a bed, which was the first time since setting out for Hanover.

After a good night's sleep, breakfast was very welcome. Then at about 9 a.m. he was relieved of the uniform parcel and he set off again on the inevitable bike ride and finally arrived at a remote farmhouse near Oosterbeck, where he was to spend two days. His host could not speak any English but they managed to play cards in the evenings. It was nice to be free to wander in the countryside. He then came back to Arnhem and spent one night at a different house. In the morning he was given an identity card and travel permits for a journey to Roermond. Once again it was on the train and on arrival the guide took him to a house. The street was Minderbroederssingel; quite a mouthful to remember! He was introduced to his new hosts who could speak good English and he was told that he would not be staying there but a few doors up the road. After dark he was taken to his new house, in the same block. They were all three-storey houses with attics.

His hosts were the Bremmers family and he was to be with them for four weeks. The household consisted of mother, father, grandfather, two sons, Jan and Willy, and daughter Lise. Father was an architect and the ground floor was his office and workroom. The others had various jobs and Willy was at the town hall and was able to get extra ration cards and any travel permits that might be wanted. He stayed indoors all day, mostly in his room in the attic and in the evening went for a walk round the streets for exercise, usually with Lise. During the day, he amused himself by trying to play the accordion that belonged to Willy and learning to type on an old machine from the office. Also, he had a few English books to read; even so he had difficulty in not getting bored.

At last the time came to move on. He was taken to Weert and over a cup of acorn coffee in a cafe, the guides changed over and he was taken to a gypsy caravan, prior to crossing into Belgium. The occupants were circus folk and also there was an American waist-gunner. They were to go over together. After dark there was a knocking on the door and two Dutch policemen came in. They obviously knew the gypsies and nodded to the two airmen. Being told that these were the two, the policemen then arrested them and they were told that they were to be returned to the Belgian customs authorities for smuggling. Then they were escorted to the frontier about three kilometres away and handed over with due ceremony and paperwork. The senior official shook hands with them and said, 'Welcome to Belgium gentlemen.' Then after the policemen had left, they were taken into the town to a big house and received by Mr and Mrs. Wijnen. The name of the town was Hamont. Their arrival called for a celebration, so a bottle of Bols was produced and duly dealt with in the accustomed manner. An hour later they had a meal and were then taken up to the top of the house, where an attic room was at their disposal. Next morning their host explained that he owned a factory that made straw rope and covers for wine bottles. He worked for the Germans and as it was not essential to the war effort, he felt it was justified; moreover he was able to support the resistance without coming under suspicion. He also entertained the German Kommandant from time to time and supplied him with gin from the black market, so consequently, quite a bit of local information came his way.

Later that morning, the resistance leader and two of his lieutenants called. Forms were filled in and a question paper was produced for them to fill in. Various other questions were asked, then they were photographed. They were told that if everything was satisfactory, they would be moved on in due course. Two weeks and many bottles of gin and cognac later, the resistance chief returned and said that they were to be moved in two days. Sure enough, two days later they were given identity cards and travel permits for Antwerp. Once there, they had an overnight stop, then next day they were collected separately and taken to Brussels. He did not see the American again.

Leaving the Brussels railway station with his guide, they walked to the Bourse, where he was handed over to Henri Maca whose English was quite good but once Henri found that he could speak French, then they got on well together. They boarded a tram and went out to Uccle, a suburb of Brussels. There he was taken to the home of M. and Mme Blanpain, where he stayed from 2 December until the second week in January. He was treated as part of the family and went shopping and occasionally was given a weekly ticket for the tram; so he got to know Brussels quite well. Christmas came and he was invited to a party on the other side of town; it was to be an all night affair. Curfew was lifted on Christmas Eve, so everyone went to midnight mass, then the party started. There were six other Allied airmen from different parts of the city and by 5.30 a.m. everyone just slept where they were. He was collected about 10:00 a.m. and arrived back at Uccle about midday.

The 8 January 1944 was to prove fatal. He left Brussels in the morning to move to Lille. The guide bought the tickets and another airman called Wells joined him. They travelled 2nd class, which he was not too happy about but concluded that the guide knew what he was doing. In the event, the guide proved to be careless and was being watched, for just after crossing into France, they were all arrested by the Abwehr. Mattey tried to bluff it out but as the policy was to arrest first and ask questions later, he admitted that he was a RAF pilot. Being dressed as a civilian, he was taken to the civil prison at Loos and put in a cell with five other French and Belgians waiting trial for various black-market and other crimes connected with the Resistance.

For the first week he was interrogated by the Gestapo, then on and off for the next two weeks. Finally, he was accepted as a military prisoner and transferred to the military jail, where he was kept in solitary overnight. The next morning he was taken to the railway station and with some 30 other assorted Allied airmen was bundled into a cattle truck, arriving at Dulag Luft interrogation centre, just outside Frankfurt-am-Main on 4 March. Here he was stripped of his civilian clothing and given prison clothes. Once more he was interrogated but as he had already been through the hands of the Gestapo, he was sent to the reception centre after only three days. Here he was given some RAF clothing and a Red Cross parcel. He was documented for the Red Cross and was able to write a postcard home.

There were 100 various airmen at the centre and two days later they were taken to the station, split up into groups and herded into cattle trucks for various destinations. Five days later his party arrived at Mulhlberg on the Elbe and were marched to Stalag IVB prisoner of war camp. Once there, they were documented, photographed and inoculated. Next they went to the showers where their clothing was taken away to be deloused; then finally after being read the camp rules, they were taken to the transit compound for allocation to the various huts. Once inside the hut they were visited by a number of other prisoners from the camp and he heard a shout of 'Skipper!' Turning round, there were Ron and Andy Anderson, his two gunners, as large as life. He was soon taken to their hut and met the rest of the crew, who had come through without a scratch. Mattey stayed there until 26 April 1945, when the Russians arrived. On 10 May they were all moved to Riga and handed over to the Americans on 23 May. They flew to Brussels and then to Dunsfold. While in Brussels he called on the Blanpains and found them safe and well. On 29 May he arrived at Cosford, was given a rail warrant and three week's leave.

Notes
1. At Wiedensahl, 16 km NE of Minden.

# Chapter 16

# Nearly a Nasty Accident (1) – Squadron Leader Bob Davies AFC

I joined the Territorial Army at the time of the Munich Crisis in 1938 (my mother was half-German). I enlisted in a searchlight unit that until 1942 was part of the British Army, the Royal Engineers. Believe it or not the anti-aircraft guns were also in the British Army but in the Royal Artillery. In retrospect it is so easy to argue that, like the Luftwaffe, all the UK air defences should have been an integral part of the RAF. Knowing the mentality of the Army top brass, they would have never surrendered any of their units to the RAF, the junior service. Nevertheless, there was no excuse for me and my fellow soldiers trying to find a German aircraft flying at 16,000 feet at night with a 1918 sound locator. Thank God all the radar early warning chains were manned and operated by RAF personnel!

In 1942 I transferred to the RAF and was sent to America to train as a pilot. I received my wings (Class 42H) in the USA, followed by one year's instructing the American cadets to fly the Vultee BT-13 Valiant 'Vibrator' for ten months at Shaw Field, South Carolina. My flight commander was a Captain Murray. When I said goodbye to him I thought the chances of our meeting again were remote to say the least. When I returned to the UK it was the usual sausage machine on Oxfords, Whitleys, Halifax IIs and then ops on Halifax IIIs with 578 Squadron at RAF Burn. It was the policy of Bomber Command to fly mainly at night. However at this period of the war the ever-cautious General Montgomery asked Bomber Command to abandon temporarily its night role and bomb tactical targets in daylight. This is how I came to be, on 3 September 1944, at 17,500 feet on the bombing run for Venlo airfield in Holland. The weather was good, there was light flak and so far as I could see, no fighter opposition.

At 1700 hours I remember my bomb-aimer, Sergeant P.E. Wells, saying 'Bombs Gone', when there was an almighty crash. My first thought was that we had taken a direct hit by flak, which was supported by the top gunner saying 'There's a fucking big hole in the top of the fuselage about 10 feet aft of my turret'. However, when the first moments of panic had died down a bit, I found that the aircraft was behaving normally. This, despite the news that there was an equally big hole in the floor of the fuselage and that the chemical closet and the flare chute had disappeared! A quick crew check revealed that the rear-gunner was beginning to suffer from lack of oxygen. I told him to leave his turret and plug into the emergency bottle. He declined my suggestion that he jump over the 'hole' and take up his crash position near the main spar. The nature of the damage to our aircraft dictated as to what we should do next – initiate an SOS and set course for Woodbridge (crash airfield on the coast) and slowly lose height to 10,000 feet. As we approached Woodbridge it was the decision of the whole crew (we were going on leave the next day) to cancel landing there and proceed to base (Selby, Yorkshire). However, deteriorating weather forced us to fly lower and lower and, at 800 feet in moderate turbulence 15 minutes from base, we were diverted to Old Buckenham, an American B-24 Liberator base in Norfolk. (Twelve of the original 18 aircraft that took-off landed away from base.) So back we went virtually on a reciprocal course. The circuit and landing were an anti-climax. Everything came down that should come down. We taxied to a halt and a very relieved crew went to debriefing and to their respective messes for a much-needed drink!

However, for me, fate still had two more cards to play. At the bar I was approached by a young officer who asked whether he could buy me a drink as he was the bomb-aimer of a diverted Lancaster who had watched one of his bombs go through my Halifax. (Why didn't the Lanc's bomb go off when it hit my aircraft? Was it a dud or is there another reason. I think I know the answer. RAF bombs had a wind driven propeller which spun off, then and only then was the bomb fully armed, i.e. the Lanc's bomb had not fallen far enough for it to be armed.) I accepted his drink and we shook hands. As I was finishing my drink I was tapped on the shoulder and a voice said, 'What are you doing here Bob?' It was my captain, now a major, from Shaw Field, South Carolina – now an operational pilot of a B-24 Liberator! It was and still is a small world.[1]

Notes
1. Bob Davies completed 16 ops on Halifaxes before being posted to North Creake in Norfolk where a new squadron, 171, was formed on 7 September 1944 for radio countermeasures duty in 100 Group (Special Duties) of RAF Bomber Command. He was promoted to squadron leader and became a flight commander in 214 Squadron on Fortresses. He did about 10 more ops before VE Day. *Confounding The Reich 100 (Bomber Support) Group RAF* by Martin W. Bowman and Tom Cushing, (Pen & Sword Books).

# Chapter 17

# The Great Escape – Pilot Officer Neville S. C. Donmall

My story begins just before Christmas in 1944. I was flying on ops as navigator with Flying officer G.S. Watson's crew of Halifax LK-X of 578 Squadron, 4 Group, based at Burn, near Selby in Yorkshire. Squadron briefing on 22 December was shortly after midday and we were informed that the target for that night was the Bingen marshalling yards, positioned on the Rhine 30 miles south-west of Frankfurt. One hundred and six aircraft were deployed on the raid: 90 Halifaxes, 14 Lancasters and two Mosquitoes. We learnt afterwards that two Halifaxes and one Lancaster had failed to return. Halifax LK-Y was airborne at 1611 hours, climbing to 18,000 feet on a cold sleeting December evening. We cleared cloud at 17,000 feet and set course for Southampton. Leaving our coast behind we were soon over eastern France where the cloud started to break. Fifty miles from the target there was only five-tenths cloud.

Our flight to Bingen was fairly uneventful, with moderate flak in places. There was also some flak over the target. All markers went down on time and the main force was assembled over the marshalling yards within seven minutes. On the run in we could see the Rhine and the target and our bombs went down directly on the aiming point. After bombing the target, we turned south for about 10 miles, then set course for home. Over Bad Kreuznach, after a few minutes on the new heading of 280 degrees, our gunners reported there was a Ju 88 on our tail. The enemy fighter-bomber and our rear and mid-upper turrets opened fire together. Both gunners reported hits on the Ju 88, which dived away beneath us. They also reported minor damage to our own tailplane and fuselage. About two minutes later the mid-under gunner called out that another Ju 88 was attacking from beneath us. Returning fire, our aircraft shuddered as more hits were registered on our starboard wing. Flames appeared near the petrol tank and our pilot ordered the crew to bale out. All crew positions acknowledged the call.[1]

Lifting my seat, I clipped on my parachute and released the emergency escape hatch beneath my feet. Positioning myself on the edge of the escape exit, I baled out at 17,000 feet. I recollect counting to three and pulling the ripcord but remembered nothing more until I found myself swinging beneath the parachute, with my jaw hurting and feeling a little sick. I must have been in the prone position when the chest-type chute deployed, for it had hit my chin and nearly knocked me out. I started to look for the ground but couldn't see it, due either to cloud or fog. The next second I clouted it with a hell of a wallop, once again hitting my chin, this time by my knee. Luckily I'd landed in a foot or so of snow, which somewhat reduced the full impact of my landing. Shaking my head and gathering up my chute, I got my compass out and set off at a run towards what I hoped was Luxembourg. I knew how imperative it was for me to clear the area before the Germans found me.

Discovering I'd landed in some hills, I kept running until I came to the shelter of a wood, then stopped for a rest. My tracks were showing but a light snowfall had started, obliterating my footprints. A few hundred yards inside the wood the snow was barely three inches deep and travelling was much easier. I turned south and walked about half a mile until I came out the other side of the wood. As I only had on my battledress and a roll-neck sweater I cut a few panels out of the chute to wrap around my body. Hiding the remains in a deep snowdrift, I retraced my tracks back into the wood. Checking my compass and turning west, I cleared the wood again, alternately running and walking in the snow for what seemed like an eternity. I appeared to be climbing higher in the hills and eventually came to a thicket of bushes with slit trenches to one side. Gathering a number of branches from the thicket, I laid them across the trench at one end, spread a panel of the chute from my body over them and added snow on top. Finding a suitable branch, I swept my footprints out from the area around the trench and got down inside. Pushing the snow from inside the shelter to the edge to form a wall to keep out the wind, I settled down to sleep. I was feeling really tired after my cross-country journey but I awoke after an hour or so feeling very cold. Dawn had broken and there had been another fall of snow.

Shortly afterwards I heard a horse and cart coming down the road. There were at least two people with the cart, for I could hear them talking to one another. Wide awake by then, I checked my RAF escape kit, which included Horlicks tablets, glucose sweets, water bag, tablets to purify water, a razor, soap, needle and cotton, waterproof matches and Benzedrine tablets, as well as German, Dutch and French currency.

Pulling my pullover sleeves down over my hand, I sewed between the fingers, so making myself a pair of mittens, which helped to keep my hands warm. I then put snow in my water bag and shoved it down inside my battledress to melt for drinking. I stayed in the trench all day, sleeping fitfully, being disturbed every so often by the sound of farm vehicles and people going down the road.

As soon as it was dark, I set out again; a couple of hours down the road I came across a village. I was about to walk through it when, by a building just a few yards away, someone lit up a cigarette. It gave me a bit of a shock and I vowed to keep clear of habitation as much as possible from then on.

After a further spell of walking, I came across a large wood on a ridge of high ground. On entering the wood, I found the going much easier, as the snow wasn't so deep. Keeping on a westerly heading by compass, I soon came out of the trees. After that the ground dropped away into a valley. Seeing the valley down below, I continued walking among the trees for a further two or three hours. Having travelled for so long and feeling warm out of the wind, I needed a rest. Sitting down with my back against a tree, I sucked some Horlicks tablets and had a drink of water. My water bag needed refilling and I packed it with snow and put it inside my battledress.

While resting, I kept on hearing what I thought was snow falling from the trees; I then noticed with some trepidation the ring of yellowish baleful eyes that surrounded me. Picking up a heavy branch near me, I charged at the animals, which scattered in all directions. They appeared to be stray dogs – probably turned out by their owners due to rationing of food in Germany. I didn't think it wise to stay in the area any longer, so I left the wood and went down into the valley. After a while I came across a railway line. Following the track, I looked for a place to hide, eventually coming to a large clump of bushes with a canopy of snow on top and sides acting as a windbreak. I crawled into the bushes and settled down to try and sleep. Waking with a start, I realized there was a man walking a push bike alongside the field and he was only a few yards away from my hiding place. It was light and a train came through on the railway line, otherwise I was undisturbed. Settling down to an exhausted sleep, I woke several times during the day due to the extreme cold. Time moved slowly – one hour seemed like three.

Dusk came at last and I decided it was time to continue my journey. After sucking two Horlicks tablets and a glucose sweet, I had a drink of water. With a compass setting of west, I made my way from the bushes on a heading of 270 degrees across the field. I needed more water and my luck was in, for I came across a small stream. Filling my water bag, I put in one purifying tablet. Though struggling through the snow was very tiring, I now felt much warmer.

Early the following morning, around dawn, I heard the crackling noise of a pulse jet roaring away behind me. From a small wood a V-1 was taking-off and it was flying directly towards me. I threw myself down and watched it as it rose about 300 feet, climbing above my head. As soon as it vanished I departed in a hurry from the area, as I knew there must be German troops close by.

It was getting towards daylight when, still travelling west, I came across a wood of fir trees. Checking it out carefully to make sure it wasn't occupied, I came across a number of thick cut-down fir branches propped against a tree in the shape of a tee-pee. Brushing out my footprints with a fallen branch, I pulled one log aside and slipped inside the shelter. As the light got brighter, I could see I was looking down on a largish town, with a river, a railway and marshalling yard. It must be Trier, I surmised, checking against my navigation and escape map. It looked as if it had been bombed recently, as there were fires and smoke all around, with what looked like bomb craters. (Later I found out that a bombing raid had taken place on the town of Trier during the night of 23 December 1944.)

During the morning, I heard voices – there climbing the hill below me were some soldiers and two young women. They were collecting branches of fir, also 'Window' (the metal strips dropped by our aircraft to jam enemy radar). The trees were covered with this foil – obviously they were collecting this for Christmas decorations. Luckily they didn't come too close to my hiding-place. I had little sleep that day – it was far too cold. I kept thinking about the Christmas dinner the Squadron was having in the mess, so I drank water and sucked Horlicks tablets and a glucose sweet for mine! At last it was dusk. I opened up my concealment and started to make my way down the hill. By my observations during the day I'd ascertained that there was only one bridge across the river, so I would have to reconnoitre the area to find out how easy it was to cross. Referring to my escape map I confirmed that it was the Moselle that lay in front of me.

On reaching the town, I found it reasonably easy to get near to the bridge. I could see military vehicles pulling other lorries along, so I gathered there was a shortage of fuel in Trier. Two tanks went by and I made a note of their military markings. There was a guard on my side of the bridge but a number of vehicles and people were crossing, both civilian and military. Making my way towards the guard, I could see he was watching me, so I deliberately went towards him. Taking a chance and speaking in a garbled version of the Spanish I'd learned at school, I asked the way. What I didn't know I made up in order to pretend fluency in the language and I was amazed when he gave up trying to understand me and just waved me across the bridge. The guard on the other side fortunately showed no interest in me whatsoever.

On going through the town I noticed far more bomb damage than I first thought when observing it from the far side of the river. Reaching the outskirts I came across a busy main road going north. Avoiding the road I continued in a westerly direction, eventually reaching a narrow country road that climbed up through some woods to the north-west. After walking along this road for some five or six hours, I came across a large farm. I was about to walk past when I heard the sound of someone moving about. There was a German guard in uniform standing there and I left the area in a hurry. After a further two to three hours' walk, still travelling west by compass, I stumbled across a large and deep trench that stretched to the left and right of me as far as I could see. Some 10 to 12 feet deep, I realized it was part of the 'Dragons' Teeth' anti-tank defence area that had been dug out by the Germans. I jumped down but getting out the other side was more difficult – I had to dig out hand- and footholds with my knife before this was accomplished. (I always carried a scout knife in my flying boot when going on an operation in case of emergencies.)

Successfully negotiating the steep side of the trench, I continued on past more slit trenches and coils of barbed wire. It was obviously a large defence area, so I proceeded with caution. After about half an hour I came across a steep valley with a river at the bottom. On my side, just below, was a vineyard but near the top were numerous pillboxes. Looking at my escape map, I realized I'd stumbled across the much-vaunted Siegfried Line, Germany's West Wall defence area with Luxembourg.

A little off the rim of the valley I discovered a small hut. Inside it I found farm tools, sacks and other agricultural implements. I decided to remain in the hut until the following morning in order to spy out the lay of the land. Pulling some of the sacks over me, for the first time since baling out, I slept reasonably well. Awakening with first light, I proceeded to study the layout of the valley. Down to my right was a small village at the water's edge, with a zigzag trench running down the valley side past more pillboxes and finishing near the village. About half a mile down on the other side was another small village. Along my side of the river was a 5 to 10 yard wide stretch of barbed wire. All I could do for the rest of that day was watch the movement of the German troops coming and going between pillboxes and the villages. As daylight faded the soldiers all went back to the pillboxes. It wasn't until then that I made up my mind to move. Negotiating the trenches and making my way down to the river in what daylight was left, I kept a sharp lookout for mines or tripwires. The trenches went along and through clusters of vines, which partly hid me from observation from the pillboxes above.

On arrival at the bottom of the valley, I could see a narrow road running alongside the river. Between the road and the river the barbed-wire defences had notices on them: 'Mines – Verboten!' Avoiding the mined area, I made my way along a trench until I came to the village. It was then getting dark. From my position I watched the village for signs of life, eventually making my way across the road, acutely aware that I was right below one of the pillboxes higher up on the valley side. Making sure I made as little sound as possible, I crossed into the village. Searching each building, I found the first few were empty. Growing in confidence I reached the end of the village, stopping about 10 to 15 yards away from the barbed wire. I could see the mines where they were just hidden under the mounds of snow. Finding two large gaps in the minefield I decided to make an attempt to cross the river at that point. Searching through a number of houses to find anything that would float, I found five planks of wood in one back yard, about eight feet long, six inches wide and two inches thick. I couldn't find any rope but in another house I discovered a ball of string and a sack filled with straw. In the same house I unearthed half a pot of jam, so I had something to eat for the first time since parachuting from the Halifax. Next, whispering a silent prayer that I wouldn't set a hidden mine off, I returned to the barbed wire, pushing and pulling the planks through to the other side before crawling through myself. At the river's edge ice had begun to form, even though the river was fast-flowing.

Starting to assemble my makeshift raft, I tied the planks together with the string I'd found and launched the planks as quietly as I could. Taking my flying boots off and clothing below the waist, I put the clothes in the straw-filled sack, tied the sack around my neck and boarded the raft. Sitting astride the planks, with great difficulty I started to paddle my way across the river. Since the planks were almost submerged, halfway across the raft started to break up – the string wasn't strong enough to hold the planks together. I was thrown in the water and forced to swim the rest of the way, the sack trailing behind me. The water was icy cold and I sighed with relief as I reached the opposite bank, thankful that the Almighty had seen fit to preserve me from a watery grave.

Shivering and gasping in my wet shirt and battledress top I emptied the sack, pulling on my trousers and socks, which luckily weren't too wet. My flying boots were full of water, so I walked in my socks to the village some 200 yards away. By the time I reached the village my battledress had started to freeze. Realizing it was imperative that I took my wet clothes off before succumbing to the intense cold, I broke into a house situated close to the river. It was empty but I found a duvet quilt on a bed. I stripped off and wrapped it around me, running round the room to get my circulation back. I couldn't feel anything in my fingers and toes and realized they were frostbitten. My manhood had temporarily disappeared after the enforced dip in the freezing water but after about an hour I felt better. I had had very little sleep during the past few days and I sank down exhausted on the bed. I must have slept for at least eight hours when I was woken by machine-gun fire. Dawn was breaking and I looked out of the window to see why the guns were being fired. It appeared they were being tested from the pillboxes.

In one of the rooms upstairs I found an old pair of boots. My flying boots were still soaking wet and as luck would have it, the replacement pair fitted. I also found a box of matches but couldn't find any food. In the kitchen there was a wood-burning stove, so I broke up some wooden furniture and with some paper lit a fire, hoping it wouldn't make too much smoke. Putting my wet clothes on the top of the stove to dry out, I heated some water and had a shave with the razor from my escape pack. After washing myself and having a drink of hot water, I felt ready to move.

By mid-morning, with my clothes dried out, I got dressed. Unfortunately my flying boots were still not wearable. Next I had to make a decision about travelling up the side of the valley. I could see the road that ran from the back of the village up and round the valley. Whether it would be safer to leave during daylight hours than at night, when the danger of hidden mines was a distinct hazard, gave me food for thought. I eventually decided to move by day, taking a chance that I wouldn't be seen from the pillboxes above. Slinging the sack over my shoulder, with my flying boots inside, I cautiously made my way from the far side of the house to the road. Then, with my fingers crossed, I continued walking. My luck held: no shouts, no machine-gun fire. Halfway up the side of the valley the road went round a bend, out of sight of the pillboxes. A little further on there were mines. The ground was so frozen; they were on the surface and only just covered by snow, their deadly presence shown by little mounds. Also across the road were stretched thin wires. These I would undoubtedly have walked into if I'd started out in the dark. Breaking into a cold sweat at the thought, I knew I'd made the right decision. Skirting the minefield, I left the road at the top of the valley and made my way across rolling terrain, entering a small wood of pine trees. It was mid-afternoon and the sun was shining when I left the wood. I could see a long convoy of troops and vehicles travelling along a road a few hundred yards away, so changed my direction to a north-westerly heading by compass in order to keep clear of the area. After going about a mile, I heard aircraft flying overhead, then the whistle of bombs coming down, so dropped flat on my face in the snow. There to the south of me all hell was let loose, with bomb-bursts and retaliatory fire from the convoy. One stick of bombs undershot and fell very close to me. Thinking I was a goner, I bounced up and down on the ground with bomb fragments screaming over my head. As soon as the bombing ceased, thanking my lucky stars that I was still alive, I went on my way at a run.

After a couple of miles, sweating at my exertions, I slowed to a walk. Another small wood was just ahead. Suddenly hearing low-flying aircraft behind me and the sound of machine-gun and cannon fire, I observed a P-38 Lightning being pursued by a Fw 190. As the planes approached I threw myself on the ground, with cannon shells and bullets flying all around me. As soon as the aircraft had passed over, I saw that the American plane was on fire – it crashed in the wood with a huge explosion.

I watched helplessly. There was no sign of a parachute and I knew I'd better get away quickly, for the place would soon be swarming with German soldiers. Veering south to get away from the wood, I later turned west again. It was almost dusk and I looked for a place to hide for the night. Just to the south of me was an area of shrubby farmland. Making my way towards the shrubs, I found a hollow in the ground, about 30 yards across, covered both sides with bushes. The ground level was about five feet below the surrounding area, so I was out of the wind and hidden from view in the hollow.

About two hours later, waking me from a fitful sleep, heavy guns opened up from a wood to the north of me – this went on for about five minutes, followed a few minutes later by return fire from the other side. Some of the shells fell very close to my hideout, shaking the ground, with shrapnel whizzing through the bushes above me. Eventually everything went quiet again, so I tried to get some sleep.

Next morning I moved off again. Dodging troops all that morning, I tried to keep out of sight as much as possible. After midday, I spotted more soldiers in the bushes and tried to get around them. This time I was out of luck. A shot went over my head and I was surrounded. There was no escape, for I was on open ground. After all my endeavours to reach friendly territory it looked as if my number was at last up. It wasn't until the troops got closer that I realized they were Americans! Breathing a huge sigh of relief, I shouted out that I was a RAF officer and had been shot down a few days previously.

Safe behind the American lines I was told they'd been watching me through binoculars for some time. They said they couldn't quite make out my uniform – it was almost the same colour as the Germans but a different design. When I told them I'd crossed a minefield safely, they said it was most likely because the heads had been frozen and my weight hadn't been enough to set off the mines. They were still suspicious and kept a gun trained on me until an officer came. He interrogated me thoroughly about my knowledge of London and shows that were on. As my home was a few miles south of the city and I'd been on leave there only four weeks earlier I was able to answer his questions satisfactorily. Convinced at last that I was a genuine RAF officer and I'd baled out of a stricken Halifax while flying as navigator on a raid on Bingen marshalling yards, I asked the American officer if they'd been shelling German positions the previous night. When he replied in the affirmative I told him they'd missed the German battery and gave them detailed directions of the enemy positions, my navigational training helping me to pinpoint the area. I was then taken to their main camp and given a wonderful meal – my first in many days. Luxembourg city was next for a bath and another good meal. I was fitted out with an American uniform with the bars of a captain and exchanged my flying boots with another American officer for a pair of his paratroop boots. I thought this was a good swap!

The following morning I was taken to a chateau nearby, which proved to be the headquarters of General Patton, to whom I was introduced and had lunch with. I was then interrogated by American intelligence officers about German troop movements before being sent off to Paris; en route to England by an Air Transport Auxiliary Anson. Even that flight wasn't without incident. I was sitting beside the civilian pilot and had to wind up the undercarriage. After leaving Paris we ran into heavy weather and got lost, so I asked him for his map. Noticing a break in the cloud to the south of us, we turned to fly over the area. I could see the French coastline below and identified our position. Informing the pilot where we were, I proceeded to map-read and navigate our way back to England. He couldn't understand why I could navigate, for I was still wearing the US captain's uniform without wing brevets and it was obvious I wasn't American. I told him I was a RAF officer and had been shot down on a raid over Germany, the uniform being supplied by the Americans when I reached their lines after escaping from Germany.

After the war I found out that the bombing of the Bingen marshalling yards our Squadron had attacked had been extremely accurate. All movements of supplies by rail through Bingen to the Ardennes battlefront had been dislocated. A few bombs fell into the Rhine and 150 houses suffered blast damage but not one civilian was killed or injured. The town wine store, however, received a direct hit!

Notes
1. NA501 of 578 Squadron in all probability fell victim to Oberleutnant Peter Spoden of 6./NJG6, for his 18th victory. Spoden claimed a Halifax shot down at 1859 hours and at a height of 4,000 metres in the Kylburg area. Watson and some of the crew were taken prisoner. The other four members of the crew were KIA. Hauptman Peter Spoden survived the war with 24 night and one day victories. He was awarded the *Deutsches Kreuz*.

# Chapter 18

# Harry's War – Harry Wheeler

I was fortunate to be one of a family of four brothers and two sisters and had the best one could wish for in my mother and father. I loved them all very dearly and hope that a percentage of all the nice aspects in them are somewhere in me. My story begins in 1940 when World War II was in its infancy. This was the stage in my life when I had to think as an adult, perhaps for the first time. I found difficulty in adjusting to the fact that I should join one of the armed forces and so take part in events, which would lead to a tragic loss of people from all walks of life. Everybody seemed to be keen to don a uniform and to get into the action to put matters in the world to right. I chose to join the RAF and confirmation that I had made the right choice was obvious when my elder brother Edwin (known always to me as Ted) resplendent in his uniform with brass buttons and badges came home on leave. I couldn't wait to follow his pattern and get myself kitted out. Ted had opted for a wireless operator/air gunner course and I felt that I was a long way behind him, so I joined the local ATC (Air Training Corps) at Alexandra Palace with a view to becoming a wireless operator. I was fascinated with Morse code and basic wireless and electrics and was soon able to receive and send Morse code at 12 words per minute which, I thought, would be beneficial when finally I entered the Service. Ted had passed his course and displayed his 'Sparks' badge and to me he could have been an Air Chief Marshal, such was his impression on me. The whole family was so proud of him.

I recall his leave because I thought I would capitalize on his expertise as a radio/electrics man, trained by the RAF to wire up an electric light in my bedroom. It would be no problem for AC2 Wheeler, E. RAF No. 647193 – or so I thought. In those days we had DC current as opposed to our present AC current. Ted professionally took a length of wire, stripped the ends and proceeded to divide the strands of wire into two, being the negative and positive connections to the fuse box in the basement and likewise a connection to the socket by my bed. When such an expert was in charge, who was I to suggest that negative and positive should be quite separate and not along the same wire? I was not going to make such a ridiculous suggestion! However, duly connected and quite rightly broken with an on/off switch, we were ready to bow to Ted's superior know-how. Somebody was needed to operate the switch and our lovely young sister, Doris, was duly delegated. I remembered that the air-raid sirens had earlier sounded the 'all clear' when the explosion took place and all the lights went out. Our immediate reaction was: 'That was close!' Smoke came up from the basement and on investigation, the fuse box was found swinging from its moorings. My faith in Ted's wiring was not as I had hoped. Ted made his excuses that he had urgently to return to his unit and left us all in darkness. The houses all down the street were also in darkness and this sparked off the investigation by the local Electricity Authority. After the fire subsided, the electrician said that: 'The wiring was rotten anyway,' and I accepted this to excuse Ted. Mother was informed that proceedings could be taken in view of the unlawful tampering with the Electricity Board's apparatus. Ted passed his Air Gunner's course and was promoted to sergeant, rapidly proceeding to an OTU (Operational Training Unit). He then went on to a distinguished wartime career that netted him a DFC and commission after two tours of operations in the European theatre of war.[1]

I was accepted into the RAF to train as a Wop/AG and my wireless training at Blackpool and Yatesbury was no problem; my experience with the ATC standing me in good stead. I qualified as a Wireless Operator and was proud to display my 'Sparks' badge. I was then posted to 116 Squadron at Hendon where I gained valuable experience on the key. I also had the opportunity to fly in Lysanders as W/Op, calibrating ack-ack and searchlights in the west country. Two months elapsed before my posting to Pembrey in Wales for my Air Gunners Course on Bristol Blenheims. This was my first experience of the cramped conditions in a bomber aircraft. How on earth would I even get into that gun turret and more pointedly, how on earth would I get out in an emergency? The stark reality of being a member of aircrew wasn't so appealing now. Finally, I passed the course and became a sergeant Wop/AG. My uniform took on a more glamorous appearance now but somehow it didn't seem the same as when Ted first appeared after being made up. I seemed to remember my brother being the only one of his kind. When I travelled by train or bus, it seemed that every other person was a Wop/AG, AC 'plonks' appeared few and far between.

My next port of call was 15 OTU at Harwell. I saw this as the 'Grand Hotel' where pilots, navigators, bomb-aimers, wireless operators and air gunners were thrown together for a 'getting to know you' programme. This was where crews were assembled, entirely from your own choosing and not influenced by the establishment. From my point of view, the priority was going to be the skipper (captain) and so I went looking for an Errol Flynn or James Stewart but on my first survey all I saw was a Danny La Rue or Franklin Pangbourne (comedy film star of the 40s). Because I was so anxious to be selective and discriminating, most crews had been made up and I was left with little choice. Of the two remaining pilots, one was a 'dead ringer' for Stan Laurel (of Laurel & Hardy fame) and the other a cut-down version of Clark Gable. I chose the latter who turned out to be a Sergeant W.A. Molyneux (Molly) and so I was fixed up and duly introduced to Dave Davison (navigator), Pilot Officer Joe Campbell (bomb-aimer) and Jimmy Velzian (rear-gunner). They seemed a great bunch of guys and turned out to be very good at their jobs.

After a week's ground training and classroom work, we started our cross-country flying exercises in daylight on Wellington ICs. We soon found out that the 'Wimpy' was a super aircraft for all crewmembers, certainly more comfortable than the Blenheim. There was so much more room to move about and with easy access to the 'Elsan', which subsequently became a very important piece of equipment as far as our navigator was concerned.

Our daytime exercises went off quite well with a few bumpy landings but on one occasion we did six 'overshoots' to land in very bad visibility. All and sundry watching down below were laying odds against us getting down at all. We were very glad to disappoint them, although when we finally touched down we were half way down the runway, failed to stop, went off the end of the runway and what was left of the grass beyond. We then ploughed through a barbed wire perimeter fence, across the main Didcot to Oxford road and straight into another Wellington, which also had overshot. Thankfully, we sustained no casualties but our confidence was shaken.

Night flying was next on the programme and this went quite well. We were adapting to each other's ability but one snag was that Dave, our navigator, was very often airsick and spent a lot of time sitting on the Elsan. Our only comfort was that we were assured of a warm seat! His sickness became a major problem as he became almost permanently attached to the 'loo', the bomb-aimer constantly having to take astro-shots to get positional fixes. Whilst this could be accommodated during training flights, what would happen when we were operational? We discussed the problem among ourselves and I personally thought we should make our predicament known to the Flight Commander. The remainder of the crew thought it would be disloyal to Dave and the consensus of opinion was to let the matter ride in the hope that the position would right itself.

Our last night exercise over, a celebration was the order of the day and the WAAFs in the Mess put on a farewell supper for us, consisting of eggs, bacon and fried bread, a rarity, but of course no booze. Twelve crews were passing out at OTU to join operational squadrons and one of these crews had a problem that came to light before a take-off. The rear-gunner of the crew, named 'Curly' (because he was as 'bald as a badger') was worried about his pilot, Sergeant Ayres (Lew) stating that he had been seen to be drinking double whiskies in the Sergeants' Mess earlier, after learning of his wife's association with another man. When we saw Lew we too were aware that he had been drinking excessively and the concern of his gunner was shared by us all. Nobody would confront him with the dangers that lay ahead and I failed to understand why it was not reported. Such was the misplaced loyalty of the day but it was considered disloyal to inform on another crewmember and to do so would mean being shunned by the others. We were ushered out to the lorries to take us to the aircraft on the dispersal areas and saw ironically that Sergeant Ayres was due to take-off first. I would gamble that 59 pairs of fingers were crossed as he lined up his aircraft on the runway.

The run up of the engines, the green light from control, the release of brakes, then the familiar sound of full power saw him move forward. The roar of the engines got fainter as he sped forward. The navigational lights were clearly visible for what seemed an eternity but slowly they lifted into the dark sky, banking as they went.

Fingers uncrossed, everybody was happy for Curly and at least his skipper had three hours or so to recover before facing a landing.

We ourselves had a straightforward exercise of three hours or so duration and on returning to base we were briefed to land on a satellite runway at Hampstead Norris. It was a clear night as we approached the circuit prior to landing. We were called by the control tower and advised not to land but to join the circuit at Harwell. This became obvious when we saw a Wellington burning fiercely yards short of the runway. No chance of there being survivors, we hadn't kept our fingers crossed long enough for Curly and other members of Sergeant Ayres' crew. I mention this incident as it has a bearing on another that happened much later.

Needless to say, an enquiry into the cause of the crash was opened. 'Why had the pilot been drinking and why on earth wasn't it reported?' The silent answer was loyalty.

At this moment in my life I was very fond of a young lady and was sure that she featured very strongly in whatever future I had. I was well aware that my chances of surviving a tour of operations were extremely low and I thought of the forfeit I would be paying in committing myself to the war effort. Nevertheless, my feelings, however strong, would have to be shelved for the duration of the war.

After leaving the OTU I was given seven days' leave but during this I was recalled to Harwell where we were to familiarize ourselves with a brand new Wellington being flown in from the Vickers factory – ferried by the tiniest female ferry pilot I had ever seen. Within an hour of its delivery, we were taking-off for a few circuits and bumps (landings) and we were delighted with the Mark III's performance.

Things were moving fast now and we were hauled into the Medical Inspection Room for injections, including one for yellow fever. This, we thought, was ominous and subsequently we were briefed to fly this aircraft to the Middle East area of operations within the next few days. With this impending overseas posting, I made a hurried phone call to my girlfriend Brenda in Palmers Green, which resulted in her arrival next day – chaperoned by her elder sister, Eileen. They were introduced to the crew and we had a farewell evening in the Crown Inn at Hampstead Norris. Our meeting had been so brief but we said our goodbyes in the right and proper manner.

The following day we flew to Portreath in Cornwall, stayed overnight and then were briefed to fly on to Gibraltar. We all knew what we were leaving behind in the UK but had not the slightest idea what was ahead of us. I recall listening to the BBC who were pumping out the *Warsaw Concerto*. It seemed to be more like being at the movies instead of going off to war. On the approach to the famous Rock of Gibraltar we were challenged by the aircraft carrier *Illustrious* by Aldis lamp calling for the appropriate letters of the day. As a member of a raw crew, I knew what the reply was to be but couldn't locate our Aldis lamp to make the response. Time was running short as we made our final approach to land; my first piece of action and I had blown it! So touchy were the Navy, there is no doubt that we would have been prevented from landing if we did not provide the response to their challenge. A quick thought and I loaded the colours of the day into the Very pistol and fired it off – praying all would be well. This obviously did the trick and with a sound of applause from all the lads, we were allowed to land. A few days on the Rock saw our aircraft fitted with extra fuel tanks to enable us to reach Fayid in Egypt. We had to take a dog-leg course over North Africa due to the fluid position of Montgomery's and Rommel's forces facing up to each other and we were in the air for 10 hours.

When we left England, we assumed that we were perhaps only ferrying aircraft to Fayid and would return to the UK to repeat the operation; after all we had not been issued with tropical kit. However, on delivering the plane, serial number HZ310, we were promptly advised that crews were a greater priority than aircraft, so what may have been a three-day trip turned out to be the beginning of a three-year term abroad. We kicked our heels in a transit camp at Heliopolis, Cairo, for a few weeks and so itched to be part of a squadron – which we made known to the powers that be. To keep us pacified, we were attached to 216 Group Ferry Command, flying old Wellingtons to Karachi in India, returning each time to Cairo by BOAC Sunderland flying boat. This was quite a pleasant experience until on one particular return trip the flying boat developed problems, making it necessary for us to land on the River Nile at Malakal, south of Khartoum in the Sudan. We were placed overnight in the BOAC hotel run by a Mr Sydney Baruch, a pleasant Romanian who made us so welcome and with whom I was to renew acquaintance in 1945.

Eventually, we were posted among 12 crews to 205 Group Bomber Command being divided between Nos. 70, 37 and 40 Squadrons and we were attached to the latter. We went by road from Cairo to an airfield at El Adem just south of Tobruk, where we joined our group. There was plenty of activity with daylight and night operations, quite awe inspiring, and we had our first glimpse of real bombs being trollied around. We were given a few days to settle in and didn't start flying as a crew, our skipper 'Molly' flying as co-pilot and navigator Dave as second navigator with a Canadian, Flying Officer Greenway. For familiarization, I joined them too as W/Op and Greenway's own W/Op stood down. Our regular gunners were also stood down.

I thought about my first operational flight and felt apprehensive about my ability to cope, thinking perhaps that I should have studied more thoroughly. My first operation was to be the docks in Piraeus in Greece and at briefing I paid particular attention to the location of the radio beacons that would be beneficial on the route. Principally, these were at Cairo West and Habbaniyah in Iraq. Whilst I had nagging doubts, I felt confident of being able to take bearings and a running fix, enabling a position plot to be made if the need arose. As it turned out, my main duties on this opening operation were to pour tea for the crew and to throw out an occasional flame float to enable the rear-gunner to take a 'wind drift' reading to assist the navigator. The only opposition came from a little light flak, not troublesome and I must say I was pleasantly disappointed. I thought it would be more traumatic.

The operation was repeated the following night with the same crew but our navigator Dave was due to play his first major role. He had been sick the previous night but the trip was quite straightforward across the Mediterranean. In spite of Dave spending most of his time on the Elsan, we didn't experience any real problems. I constantly took radio bearings in case they were needed urgently. I don't think the skipper even took a course to steer from Dave. Two trips had been achieved and there had been nothing frightening about them and we classed them as a doddle. Rommel and his Africa Korps were in hasty retreat to Tunis and so our group moved up to Benghazi.

Our next trip as a crew was to the docks at Taranto in Italy and it was our first taste of searchlight activity. This operation was more like what we had come to believe night bombing was all about. Our skipper was, I thought, somewhat ambitious when he decided to do a 'dummy run' over the target. The W/Op position in the Wimpy wasn't exactly the front row of the stalls, very little to see what goes on outside and one conjured up all sorts of alarming thoughts when evasive action was being employed and the cockpit brightly illuminated by probing searchlights. The stark white face of Dave climbing over the main spar heading towards the Elsan didn't help the situation. I thought, if only the captain would hum a little tune over the intercom to let us know he was happy and in control. We seemed to be over the target area for an eternity. Eventually, after a lifetime, those magic words of John Wayne's – 'Let's get out of here' – came over the intercom and, to our relief, we were heading back to base. By this time, a certain young man on the Elsan appeared to be throwing out at both ends, which made me feel somewhat insecure, myself. Then it happened. The captain requested a first course to steer on the three-legged track back to base but it was not forthcoming from the navigator, who had more important things on his mind. The skipper could only guess the first direction to steer – but for how long? Away from the target area, there seemed an awful lot of Italy to starboard.

I took radio bearings from Habbaniyah and Cairo but wasn't confident of plotting them myself, so with a map and torch I trundled them down to the unfortunate Dave in his newly appointed 'office' and somehow between us we managed to ascertain a course towards Benghazi. We finally reached the North African coast but didn't exactly know where. We could get no response to calls on our R/T (radio telephone) so I broke silence on W/T as it was an emergency, sent a signal to Benghazi and asked them to illuminate the Chance Light on the airfield so that we could pinpoint it. Within a short time, our rear-gunner spotted it and so we had a visual sighting for home. Safely down, it was inevitable at the debriefing that we should be asked: 'What went wrong?' We were so late on ETA that we were assumed lost. The skipper said that due to turbulence and violent evasive action, the navigator Dave had become unfit to navigate. When asked if this had happened before, he replied: 'No'. I wasn't very happy about this but found it too difficult to do anything about it in view of the rest of the crew's attitude. I thought of poor old 'Curly' at OTU. He had died because nobody would inform on his pilot: what a price to pay.

With the navigational problems we were experiencing, I realized the importance of my own job and so made a point of spending a lot of time in the ground signals cabin to digest more about my job than the normal training had given me. We had emergency transmitters installed in the aircraft that one could use if the need arose. Devices could be set up for the pilot to steer towards beacons with pin-point accuracy and a number of aids only sketchily touched upon at training school. After a few weeks elapsed, we were moved up behind the 8th Army at Tunis, being based at an airstrip named Kairoun. The 15th US Air Force shared the same strip – flying B-24 Liberators. They constantly practised low flying in the desert to get a coordination perfected in order to bomb the Ploesti oilfields in Romania. This they did eventually but with mixed success. During this period, I was absorbing as much technical data as I could on all the available radio aids.

The time arrived when Sicily was to be invaded by the Allies and as the Axis troops evacuated to the mainland via Messina, we started to bomb the Straits of

Messina bridgehead. All squadrons of 205 Group were called upon night after night and Sicily was plastered with bombs. We did three successive attacks on this one but the group's first serious losses had started. Night fighters shot down three of our original 12 crews from OTU. On one of the trips over the Messina beaches, I flew with Flying Officer Greenway, the Canadian skipper with whom I experienced my first operation, my own regular skipper being on stand-down. This trip was to be the most terrifying experience of my life so far. We had been losing aircraft on these sorties. The German and Italian searchlight defences made life so difficult. We were told by the skipper in advance that whenever we were 'coned' in searchlights, to grab a firm hold on the framework whilst he took violent evasive action – and of course to utter a prayer. The relatively short trip took us into the brightly illuminated target area with plenty of flak but this was indicative of the absence of night fighters. Photographs of the bridgehead were part of our duties, so accuracy was important and straight and level flying had to be carried out. The first run was relatively smooth but on the second run they picked us up and hammered us. Remembering the pilot's advice, I grabbed the geodetic frame firmly and prayed. Suddenly, it was as if we had hit a brick wall, there being a sickening shuddering effect and the nose went down sharply. We just dropped out of the sky it seemed, plunging into a blackness that was surely the end. Seconds later it was as if we had dropped into water, the impact was so violent. We had been flying at 12,000 feet so I knew that we couldn't have hit the sea so quickly. It transpired that when we were caught by the defences, the skipper selected full flaps, waited until the aircraft stalled, then pushed the nose down and whipped up the landing flaps which caused us to dive so sharply. How the wings stayed on, I shall never know. The pilot told us we were not to reveal his method of evasive action. I happen to know that the pilot, now retired Squadron Leader Greenway, is still alive in Canada. If he ever gets to read this, belatedly I say to him: 'You ought to have been bloody ashamed of yourself but at the same time accept my humble thanks for getting us out!' He might even recall how ill we all were and how he had to fly back on the beacon needles I set up for him on Blida and my handing him a map to choose his own course from Blida to Karouan.

Then a decision was made by group to send a number of Wellington crews on a conversion course to B-24 Liberators. Our posting was to Lydda in Palestine and after a very pleasant two weeks in a rest camp at Nathanya in Israel, we returned to Lydda airport. We were just four crews led by skippers Molyneux, Steele, Ells and Wright but there were only two aircraft available, *A for Apple* and *U for Uncle*. Our first experience of the Liberator was exciting. We clambered all over it. We found that you could get very intimate with it inasmuch as you had total access to the interior including the bomb bays and could be closely acquainted with the full payload, which was not possible in the Wellington. They appeared very cumbersome but the two extra powerful engines seemed to make up for its size. The gunners were far happier with their larger gun turrets, the navigator had more room and vision in the nose, pity there was no Elsan in that area. The most comfortable position was reserved for the wireless operator, on the flight deck immediately behind the cockpit, with plenty of space. From the radio compartment there was access to the bomb bays via a catwalk, which was no wider than 12 inches. The bomb doors rolled up the sides of the fuselage, revealing an enormous opening for the bombs' release. However, there was no way a crewmember could walk along the catwalk wearing a parachute, because the bomb rack carriers extended from the catwalk to the roof of the aircraft. The payload was invariably eight 1,000lb bombs or mines, dependent on the target. Four bombs were in the forward section and four in the rear, being released electrically by the navigator but manual releases were also available to be operated by – guess who? Yes, the wireless operator! If the electrics malfunctioned and bomb release was to be operated manually, most likely in darkness without a parachute, this became a daunting prospect for me. However, exit in an emergency was so much easier than it had been in the old Wimpy, so we were consoled.

The conversion course was mainly concerning the pilot, the equipment for the rest of us being identical to that we had previously experienced. The daily routine was to be 'circuits and bumps' with a 'screen' pilot additionally and two wireless operators for radio contact with the control tower. Four crews were undertaking this conversion course and we all knew each other well. One fellow, W/Op Sid Tucker and I were always playing cards as the opportunity arose and so we were never without a deck of cards and a cribbage board. Another good pal was a W/Op Sergeant John Hall, nicknamed 'Henry' after the BBC bandleader. Henry hailed from Wigan. A loveable character who was mad keen on rugby football. His habit was to stuff a towel into his flying helmet, call it the ball and taunt all and sundry, daring them to stop him from getting from one end of the hut to the other. Those of us who survived the war must still be carrying the bruises from those reckless days.

With the only two available aircraft, it was announced that I would be flying first with two pilots and another W/Op, Pilot Officer Rosmussen from New Zealand. The second aircraft was to carry two pilots and two wireless operators – including my pal, Sid Tucker. Awaiting the call when the aircraft would be pronounced 'Ready' we were playing cards and a reasonable kitty had been built up. The call came that A for Apple was ready. Henry Hall, who had been watching the game said, 'Carry on lads, I'll swap with Wheeler because I want to get away early and then I can visit my brother who is stationed nearby'. The 'swap' was mutually and thankfully agreed. Twenty minutes later, the second aircraft was ready so Sid Tucker and I left the game to do our stint, just routine circuits and landings. At the airstrip we watched as our friends in A for Apple made a perfect landing. We commented that the Liberator was so different from the Wimpy in that it made a long low approach and was dragged in on its 'fans' whereas the Wimpy made a much steeper descent.

We were alternating take-offs and landings with A-Apple. While in the circuit for a landing, the skipper asked me to call the control tower to report that a train on the railway line that ran at right angles to the runway had stopped and was making a lot of smoke, obscuring our visual approach. Sid took over the radio to pass on the message while I went aft to the beam gun position to get a closer look. I was horrified to see below me one of the unmistakable tail fins of the other Liberator sticking up out of the pall of smoke. It was immediately apparent that there could be no survivors. Further down the runway a smaller aircraft had crashed. It transpired that a Hurricane fighter plane was making an emergency landing and had collided with the Liberator. My own skipper, Molly, was not aware that I had changed places with Henry Hall and he was quite shocked when I stepped out of the belly of our aircraft. We saw the Hurricane pilot sitting on the side of the runway, smoking a cigarette and being attended by the medics. We thought he had only been badly shaken but it was revealed that he suffered internal injuries and he died later. In total shock we returned to the hut, saying very little. I spotted Henry's flying helmet that he had not used because it was only local flying. It was still bulging with the towel inside. I had a terrible feeling of guilt. But for Henry's offer to swap duties, he would have been alive and I would have met my Maker. I never really lost that feeling.

The next day saw us on the burial detail and the hearse was a truck with five coffins aboard, somewhat of a luxury really, seeing that most of our unfortunate colleagues were treated to a blanket stitched with bandages. Our crew were all pallbearers and it seemed ironic that I should take one corner of the coffin bearing my dear friend. They were buried in the cemetery at Lydda and I believe they remained there. I have always had the inclination to go back to Lydda and thank an old pal for giving me his life but I shall never ever forget him.

After a fortnight's training, we returned to our group at Kairoun and formed 178 Squadron, doing a sort of OTU in Tunisia while waiting to move to Italy which was being gobbled up by the 8th Army and the American 5th Army. During this period we were stood down to allow the UK based squadrons to operate their 'shuttle service' of bombing long range German targets and carrying on to North Africa, then doing a reciprocal bombing trip, landing back in the UK. The North African base for this was mainly at Blida, just north of us and sometimes at Maison Blanche. It seemed that Lancasters and Halifaxes were everywhere and unbeknown to me, my brother Ted had crashed at Blida after raiding Friedrichshafen, he being in one of the three PFF Lancasters on that operation. His crew suffered no serious casualties but he was at Blida for a whole week. If only I had known, I could so easily have made the trip to Blida to see him. We hadn't met for three years and the odds appeared that we would never meet again. Fortunately, this was not the case. We then moved into Italy, settling in at the very large base at Foggia, dominated by the presence of the US Air Force with seemingly hundreds of Flying Fortresses.

Of the original eight crews I was with at OTU at Harwell, only four now remained – which, I suppose, was a reasonable average. We were soon to lose yet another crew in our first week at Foggia. With only six Liberators, the squadron started operations to the north, mainly the marshalling yards at Vicensa. We carried only 6,000lb of bombs because the four Pratt & Whitney engines could not match the performance of the two Hercules Mk 3 engines of the Wellington. This being the case, my old card-playing partner Sid, had a first-class pilot named Flight Sergeant Ells and complained that his aircraft was underpowered and that he had doubts about there being sufficient runway to lift off with 6,000lb of bombs. The Commanding Officer, Wing Commander Dickie Smythe, was recognized as a hard taskmaster who rather belittled Flight Sergeant Ells by testing his aircraft with 4,000lb of bombs, lifting off just two-thirds of the way down the runway, assessing that the other third would adequately lift off the extra 2,000lb of bombs. So it was that Flight Sergeant Ells, Sid and crew started their run with 6,000lb of bombs. We all watched with fingers crossed. Every inch of the runway was used and at the perimeter, the pilot pulled her up but the rate of climb was painfully slow. We never saw that crew again; there was no Mayday distress call and no communication was forthcoming. We all developed a healthy hatred for old Dickie Smythe thereafter. At this stage, we said farewell to Dave, our navigator, who was posted back to 40 Squadron and quite frankly I had a sense of relief. A Canadian, Flying Officer Woods, replaced him.

With just four operational aircraft we took on a different role. Nuisance bombing became the name of the game and we worked in conjunction with the Yanks. Marshalling yards to the north and dock areas were our targets. We operated in pairs, one aircraft running in to the target area would drop the bombs singly whilst the other would orbit and drop bundles of 'Window' – tin-foil strips that would play havoc with the radar below, thus confusing searchlight and flak units. This would go on throughout the night hours, very boring for us but we had little opposition to worry about. The Yanks would take over throughout the hours of daylight with their pattern bombing. The idea was to prevent or disrupt the unloading of supplies from trains or ships. This procedure became a regular chore, just like a bus route.

On one occasion, Genoa was the focus of our attention for 'nuisance' bombing. Six runs over the target were timed to perfection. To offset our boredom, at around 2130 hours I picked up a BBC broadcast on my Marconi receiver and we had a sing-along with Anne Shelton. All seemed to be going smoothly but complacency made me miss the half-hourly broadcast from base – this being an immediate recall of all aircraft to base. We all had the feeling that light flak at 11,000 feet was nothing to worry about. Don't believe it! A direct hit amidships shook us rigid. An almighty bang, with showers of sparks etc. through the bomb bays, promptly put paid to our sing-along.

The skipper brought us out over the Mediterranean with no apparent malfunction of the plane and I went aft to assess the damage. On either side of the top main spar was a gaping great hole. Apparently the AA shell found the oxygen bottles which duly exploded and took out quite a lump of fuselage. Our gyrocompass was also affected. I went to the flight deck to report the damage and all seemed to be well, except that our compasses gave different readings. No coastline was visible. Not knowing the possible consequence of events, we decided to transmit an emergency signal on our IFF transmitter. This was a transmitter to provide identification between friend or foe but it also had an automatic SOS signal built-in.

We still had four 1,000lb bombs on board so the navigator made them 'safe' and jettisoned all four together. While I was trying to aid the pilot by setting up a homing procedure on a radio beacon at Ban in southern Italy, we were joined by a Bristol Beaufighter off our starboard wing tip. To see this aircraft suddenly loom up initially frightened the life out of us but he took immediate evasive action. Then we realized that possibly this was our ticket home. Unable to establish R/T contact with the Beaufighter who, no doubt, could see our damage, we followed him but with great difficulty. We slowly descended until eventually we sighted the volcanic islands of Stromboli ahead and with a calculated turn to starboard, it was not long before we sighted Foggia, which had been specially illuminated for us by the Chance Lights. We landed safely to be greeted by 10 anxious people.

Some three or four months elapsed before we were given leave and this took us to Rome and the Vatican. At St Peter's Church an Irish priest met us and before

long we had an audience with Pope Pious. The priest volunteered to show us
around the Vatican and, in the course of conversation, our skipper said how
wonderful it was that both opposing sides in the conflict had agreed to spare Rome
from bombardment and make it an open city. The priest concurred but said 'In fact,
bombs did fall into the Vatican City but failed to explode.' His belief was that this
was done purposely by one side to discredit the other, creating the impression that
the agreement to spare Rome had been broken. Later on we were struck by the
thought. 'Could these bombs to which the priest had referred have been the ones
which we jettisoned "safe" in the emergency?'

On our next trip to the Vatican, we could not locate our Irish priest but
approached another one, with a view to making discreet inquiries of the said
bombs. He volunteered the information that two unexploded bombs had been
found in the Vatican but would not divulge their size, make, or even when they
were dropped. Studying the map of Italy, Genoa, Rome and Stromboli are virtually
in line and the time of jettisoning could be assessed as it would take a Liberator
about one hour to fly from Genoa to Rome. Our minds boggled at the thought that
we could be responsible for this incident but if only two bombs were found, were
there still two others waiting to be found?

It was now spring of 1944, the Allies were driving ahead well north of Rome and
our operations were becoming spasmodic. The US Air Force was still doing its daily
chores but there seemed little for our three remaining Libs to do. That is, until some
bright spark thought we could be usefully employed laying mines in the River
Danube. Prior to starting on this new venture, we fitted in a few trips over
Yugoslavia, not with our usual hardware but with Navy and Army personnel
complete with radio equipment. Strange to see these poor guys going out of the
bomb bays instead of our usual bangers. We thought, 'This is a doddle, just suit us
till the end of hostilities', until returning to base after one of these sorties, we found
that we had lost yet another crew. Subsequently, we were told that the crew had all
baled out but their skipper, Captain Blake, a South African, had been shot by his
captors – purportedly trying an heroic escape. The theme of *Ten Little Nigger Boys*
kept going through our minds.

However, two more clapped-out Liberators joined us to bring our strength up to
four and then we started our trips to various stretches of the Danube. We carried
four 1,000lb mines, fitted with parachutes to slow their entry into the water. They
were magnetic in operation to detonate when shipping came into the near vicinity.
It seemed that the surrounding terrain to the Danube was somewhat hilly and as
we were directed to drop the mines from only 1,000 feet this was decidedly dodgy
unless we had the benefit of moonlight. One consolation was that there was no
ground activity or interference from any source. Nevertheless, in view of our
previous experiences, we were all decidedly on edge. Even the skipper, a dedicated
man to his job, would sweat profusely prior to take-off. I had always been
concerned for the welfare of the other crewmembers and made a point of studying
their duties and attitudes. For example, the mid-upper gunner was located in his
turret immediately above the wireless operator's position and he was completely
mobile including his oxygen supply. I made it my duty to keep his oxygen supply
topped up from the main source. I was aware when he was running low on oxygen
because the regular rotation of his turret would cease and he would drift into a

pleasant sleep. OK for him but this would constitute a danger to the rest of us as a fighter attack could be over within seconds. Our gunners, other than when they were testing their guns, hardly ever fired a round of ammunition. So, this task became boring and tiresome, making them too relaxed and lethargic, unlike the experience of the gunners in the European theatre of operations who were faced with the prospect of constant attacks by night fighters.

To get over the problem of sleeping or dozy gunners, I enlisted the help of the ground crew and persuaded them to drill a hole in the perspex, the purpose being to allow the inlet of a draught of air. This did the trick for a while until the resourceful Jimmy Velzian, hailing from the Orkneys, used a well-chewed piece of gum to plug the hole in the perspex, so we were back to square one.

My crew position was immediately behind the cockpit, no bulkhead door separating us. Prior to take-off I would mentally go through the cockpit drill with the pilot, a routine that was of paramount importance to safety. On our first minelaying operation, we wondered how this could possibly help the campaign but then reckoned that the mines were surplus to requirements and this was the best way to dispose of them. The skipper went through his cockpit drill and I watched closely. He made his selections of mixture, flaps etc. and through to 'cowgills closed'. This procedure referred to the segments at the back of the engines and these would normally be opened while on the ground or taxiing etc. to prevent the engines overheating. However, on take-off it was essential for the cowgills to be closed as otherwise they would act as a brake and seriously affect the take-off. Cockpit drill completed, we started our run down the runway and I sat down and braced myself. Suddenly I realized that I hadn't seen the pilot operate the closing of the cowgills although he had voiced it as part of his cockpit drill. I quickly jumped up to a small window on the flight deck, overlooking the main plane and to my horror saw that the gills were all fully open. Rushing back to the cockpit, having no time to switch on my intercom, I lifted the pilot's earpiece and shouted 'Cowgills'. We were a quarter of the way down the runway so had ample time to abort the take-off. The pilot informed control that he was concerned about an engine noise, no reference to the cowgills of course. Molly, the pilot, gave me a full dressing-down for interfering and this I failed to understand. What might have happened if we had carried on? My mind boggled as we made our grand second run which was satisfactory. On arrival at the dropping zone, we found it virtually impossible to get to the directed height of 1,000 feet on a stretch of water that snaked through high ground surrounding it. Two attempts were made before deciding to abort. How many times have aircrews said, 'Sod it, let's drop them anyway and get out of here?' Molly wouldn't do that and decided to look for another suitable stretch. This kept us over the target area twice as long as was allowed for. The remainder of the crew were unanimous that we should get out but the skipper insisted on trying again and again. Finally, we did drop the mines but none fell into water; a wasted effort.

I decided it was a bit late in the war to become an Errol Flynn and was increasingly agitated with all that seemed to be happening. I was convinced that the odds were shortening against us. We lost yet another aircraft during these operations and this lessened confidence even further. I felt already that I had been living on borrowed time since the accident in Lydda and what was happening now seemed to be so futile. The Wellington squadrons in the group were also minelaying now. Nobody was 'hogging' trips now. 'Hogging' meant that any crew member, other than the pilot, could volunteer to take the place of members in another crew, in order to complete the requisite 40 operations to finish a tour and thus enjoy a well-earned rest from flying.

The war in Europe was going very well for the Allies now and it was just a matter of time but the end of hostilities was in sight. We had a quiet period for a while as we went from 1944 to 1945. The weather improved and we were back into minelaying again. At that time, if we had flown the previous night, it was highly unlikely that we would be called again to fly the following night. Sergeant Birkbeck, a friend who was not attached to any particular crew, in fact a spare bod in the pool of aircrew, managed to get two tickets for a show the Yanks were putting on in Foggia. It was suggested that we get into Foggia early, have a meal and go to the American bathhouse to freshen up and then on to the show. But firstly, it was necessary to go to SHQ to establish who, if anybody, was on flying detail that night. These flying orders were put into a clipboard and displayed on the Crew Notice Board. A quick glance told us that we were not among the crews selected which seemed in order as we had flown the night before. We duly signed out at the guardhouse and grabbed a lift into Foggia. A good evening was enjoyed, after which we returned to base. On signing in we were immediately placed under open arrest for apparently being absent without leave (AWOL). We thought this was crazy. We were informed that we had both been detailed to fly that night but there had been a delay in take-off times. The fact that we were not at briefing would have provided plenty of time to obtain replacements from the aircrew pool of spare bods.

The recurring problem of 'keeping mum' about crewmembers came up again. My skipper had said nothing but hoped I would get back in time to fly. His so-called 'loyalty' did me no favours; the problem would never have arisen had he declared that I was not available and in such circumstances another standby wireless operator could have been allocated. As it was, at the last minute the CO's bosom pal, Squadron Leader Wells, the Navigational Officer stepped into the breach as my replacement and of course this led to a Court of Enquiry. Subsequently, I was to appear before the CO to answer the charges of AWOL. Prior to going in to the CO's office, I was briefed by Warrant Officer Paddy Kelly, who was a fatherly figure, well respected by all aircrew members. Taking me to one side, he said that I would be formally charged and that I would be given the option of accepting the CO's punishment or alternatively going before a Court of Enquiry. It was generally the practice to accept the CO's punishment but Warrant Officer Kelly expressed the view that I should opt for the Court of Enquiry which would take some considerable time to come about – during which time I would be grounded. I was given 30 minutes to make my decision. My skipper, Molly, was at hand and I asked for his advice. He replied that the decision had to be mine but added, 'If I were in your position, I know what choice would be obvious to me!' Flying had become so hazardous, his comment convinced me to opt for the Court of Enquiry, so I had made my decision. I was grounded pending the outcome of the enquiry which, I was informed, was to be held in Naples on a date to be advised. My defence would be that I could see no listing of our crew for flying detail on the night in question. Rumour had it that someone unknown had removed the said notice to the Mess to study it but this was not substantiated.

Early the following morning, I was awakened by a pilot, Flight Sergeant Les Steele, with the news that Molly and my old crew had failed to return from a raid on Bucharest. I was stunned but frankly not surprised. I had the same awful feeling I had when Henry Hall had taken my place in Lydda and was killed. Who said that fate plays a hand in who should live or die? Les Steele was the sole surviving skipper from the eight who had left Harwell OTU together. I was duly posted to Naples where, in a transit camp, I had time to reflect on all that happened over those months in North Africa and Italy. The only consolation I had was that a certain young lady was waiting for me back home and until now I didn't think I would ever see her again. But now I had something to hold on to and look forward to. I was placed in a Services canteen for a while, to supervise its operations; just for something to occupy my time and to alleviate the boredom. Eventually I was summoned to SHQ to be informed that I had been tried at the Court of Enquiry and found guilty. I was not even allowed to attend the court to present my defence. The outcome was that I was stripped of my stripes, downgraded to LAC (Leading Aircraftman) and posted to Africa, a staging post 200 miles south of Khartoum in the Sudan. I had no rights of appeal against the Court's decision. I weighed up all the pros and cons and came to the conclusion that being alive compensated for all the bad things that had happened. Constant memories of Molly, Jimmy, Ken, Harry and Henry Hall, are and always will be, etched on my mind to the end of my days. I think also of Warrant Officer Paddy Kelly who counselled me at a time when I was prepared to walk the other way, so, 'Thank you, Paddy!'

No. 28 Staging Post was a lonely airstrip called Malakal on the River Nile. This was where I was to spend my last five months in the RAF. I was put into the Transmitter & Receiver Radio Station to maintain contact with the Dakota aircraft ferrying from Italy to South Africa, mainly taking South African service personnel home. The war was now over in Europe and I had survived where so many others had perished. I heard that my brother Ted had made it against overwhelming odds and I was so delighted that the Wheelers had come through. My delight was blunted when I received the 'My Dear Harry' letter from Palmers Green telling me that what I had been looking forward to for so long was not to be. Three and a half years were, I suppose, a very long time for anybody to wait but I slowly began to understand what the war had done to us. I was getting older now, in fact I was 23 but felt I had lived a lifetime in a comparative short number of years.

Malakal was perhaps the best place to recuperate. Our duties were minimal, discipline was not tight and we had plenty of time to appreciate the wonderful wildlife in the area. However, 'ere long, I was caught up by a bloody mosquito that knocked me out with two types of malaria. I was convinced that I was going to die and that this was some sort of retribution for what had gone before. It was very nearly the end until a South African doctor was flown in from Khartoum to give me a lumbar puncture, which, eventually, broke the fever and I slowly recovered. The lads in our group were a super bunch and they laid on a party to celebrate my recovery. They booked into the local BOAC hotel to which crews from Sunderland flying boats would go after landing on the River Nile. Earlier, I mentioned that when we were attached to 216 Ferry Command, ferrying Wellington ICs to Karachi in India, we used to come back by BOAC flying boats and land near Malakal. It was there that I met the manager of the hotel, a Romanian named Sidney Baruch, totally pro-British and who loved the RAF. It was my pleasure to meet him again at this party and he did us really proud. He supplied all our food and service at his own expense, while we paid for the booze. During the meal, we heard that a Sunderland had made an unscheduled stop and a few passengers had disembarked to stay at the hotel. Of these, one turned out to be the Aga Khan together with his wife, the Begum. Apparently, he had felt uncomfortable and decided to break his journey at Malakal and stay overnight. He joined us at our table and when he learned of the purpose of our celebration, he settled our bills for us. It was a very pleasant experience. He returned shortly after and we remained in the lounge with Sidney Baruch, who insisted that we all keep singing *Land of Hope and Glory*, which we did until the tears ran down his cheeks.

1946 came; time for me to be demobilized but until this day I feel that the whole mantle of my life was spent in the war years. My best friends and family are very dear to me and will always be so. I particularly remember the very young men I was privileged to be associated with and feel sadness that the circumstances that befell me never came their way. I believe many of them would have welcomed such opportunities – especially when I recall my old skipper Molly saying, 'Harry the choice is yours but I wish I was in your situation to make such a choice!'

I say now to all surviving members of aircrew, your experiences must all have been similar to mine and those memories will be engraved on your minds for the rest of your days. Rightly so, because you and the families of lost ones will only remember those lads as they really were super guys who are as real today as they were then. I truly hope that they did not give their lives in vain. We will remember them!

Notes
1. *Flying Into The Flames Of Hell* by Martin W. Bowman, (Pen & Sword Books, 2006).

# Chapter 19

# Nearly a Nasty Accident (2) – Flight Sergeant Ken Westrope

I didn't hear it. I felt it, an almighty thump and our Liberator just fell out of the sky. We were on the bombing run. We had just dropped our bombs and got the photo. The intercom and hydraulics had all gone. The only thing to do was to get out of the turret, unplug the intercom and oxygen, open the doors, get out and put your parachute on. It was 16 March 1945 and our target was the Monfalcone shipyards in northern Italy. Our bomb load was six 1,000lb and six 500lb, fairly general for all aircraft on these raids. I was 25 years old and the rear-gunner on *V-Victor* in 37 Squadron, 205 Group, the only RAF heavy bomber group in the Middle East, based at Tortorella airfield near Foggia. This was my 20th or 21st operation. We flew 'Wells' up to Christmas 1944 in 37 Squadron and changed over to 'Libs' in January 1945.

Our Liberator had plunged 5-6,000 feet. It just dropped down and I thought 'This is it'. I just didn't know what had happened. We had experienced nothing like this. We had had one or two things happen because of duff engines. During a training flight on Wellingtons we had been forced to land at Beirut airport on a single engine but we didn't suffer any damage from enemy action. Flak had been the main threat, more than fighters. We had done all sorts of trips, including supply dropping to Tito's troops and dropping mines outside the northern Italian ports.

I hadn't given such dangers as bombs hitting us a thought. There had been the odd problem on supply drops when parachutes came down through when some aircraft were flying higher but you were able to see and avoid them. It wasn't in our minds. We didn't realize or think it could have happened. As far as I could gather, I had been watching this aircraft, *R-Roger*, a 70 Squadron Liberator, flying more or less parallel and coming up on our port side. I got in touch with our mid-upper gunner and told him to watch it.

'OK', he said, then I lost sight of him.

Then he came alongside and suddenly must have turned left and come straight over the top of us. When bombs drop, they do not just drop straight down. They go forward.

By the time I could get out of the turret, unplug and open the doors, Squadron Leader Lionel Saxby, the skipper, had *V-Victor* under control. Then eventually we got on a level course again. I went forward and I saw this big hole in the aircraft. It was a bit shaky. The hole was about 6 feet by 4 feet. The bomb, or maybe there were two bombs, had fallen on the mid-upper turret. Wally Lewis was jammed in his seat. I don't know if he was unconscious; he was a bit bruised but miraculously not badly hurt. Cliff Hurst, the wireless operator, got the worst of it. He was sitting on the starboard side with his back to the hole. Oil and steam were pouring out of the port inner but there was no fire in the engine. However, the prop was completely knocked off.

Pieces of the engine had entered the wireless operator's back. He was a tent-mate of mine. At first we laid him on the flight deck. He was unconscious for some time and then he came to. I suppose he must have felt the pain but there was no question of being able to do anything about it. You could not give him morphia. That would have knocked him out and he never asked for it. His set, everything, was out of order and even though he was wounded, he managed to repair the wireless and get a message through to base to tell them what had happened. I held his parachute harness away from his back so it did not chafe on him.

It was a bit of a struggle on the flight back and obviously we slowed down. Lionel Saxby was a very experienced skipper. We just sat hunched up on the flight deck so that if anything happened we could all get out together, or attempt to get out, as there was no intercom to warn us when to go. You could not hear anything. It had to be by signs.

We all got into ditching positions for the landing. They cleared all the runway and were waiting for us. We did not know if the wheels were locked. We had to be prepared for anything. As it was, we left bits and pieces of wreckage strewn on the runway. Cliff Hurst made a full recovery and was awarded the DFM. The pilot was not decorated. He got a green endorsement in his logbook, which represented a 'good show'. We did not think about decorations. We just did what had to be done.

# Chapter 20

# Operation Plunder – Squadron Leader Malcolm Scott DFC

For more than a week during March 1945 the Mitchells and Bostons of 2 Group had been pounding targets in the Rhineland in close support of the 21st Army Group fighting its way to the great river barrier; 22,000 British, Canadian and American casualties had been suffered in clearing the area between the Maas and the Rhine. Xanten, one of 2 Group's earlier targets and more recently the recipient of a devastating night raid by Bomber Command, was now occupied by British and Canadian troops. The last strong bastion of the German troops on the west side had fallen and within a few days the rest of the territory was cleared and the Allied armies stood on the west bank looking at the remains of the Wesel bridge blown up by the retreating Germans.

For the six squadrons of 137 and 139 Wings in 2 Group (I was a Mitchell navigator in 180 Squadron) the targets now shifted to the east side of the Rhine. At least two, occasionally three, raids were made each day on marshalling yards, communication centres and bridges, oil dumps, billeting areas and barracks, artillery emplacements and troop concentrations. Some penetrations were deeper to important rail centres but mostly attacks were concentrated in the Weser-Emmerich-Munster area where *Plunder*, the code name for the overall operation covering the Rhine crossing, was to take place. Maximum effort had been ordered and quite often up to 15 aircraft per squadron took part instead of the usual dozen aircraft in two boxes of six.

Montgomery's preparations for the Rhine crossing were, as always, massive and painstaking; troops being ferried to the rear echelons to practise 'boat drill' and the handling of small craft up and down the muddy banks of the River Maas at night in preparation for the real thing. There could be no misleading or attempted feints this time. Within a mile or two, the Germans could estimate where the Allied crossing would be made. As Kesselring wrote: 'The enemy's operations in a clearly limited area, bombing raids on headquarters and the smoke-screening and assembly of bridging materials, indicated their intention to attack between Emmerich and Dinslaken with the point of the main effort on either side of Rees.'

The only questions facing the enemy were when and how. Always before, the Allies had launched a parachute and glider attack as a prelude to the full force of the main assault. Kesselring could but wait to see where the paras dropped, or so he thought.

In the meantime, RAF medium bombers and Typhoons and the 9th USAAF Marauders and Thunderbolts carried on with their now familiar role of softening up the area around the chosen points of the great river and the hinterland of the proposed bridgeheads on the east bank. One important road and rail junction town and troop-billeting area was Bocholt, which became the object of almost daily attacks and quickly gained a reputation for providing a very warm reception. On 18 March it was bombed and again two days later. We all got back but with our aircraft and a few aircrew heavily peppered by shrapnel.

The next morning, 21 March, Bocholt was again listed as the target. On the bombing run No. 1 in the box was badly damaged and an air gunner's leg was almost shot away but the pilot retained control and made an emergency landing at Eindhoven. No. 2 in the box received a direct hit as the bombs fell away and virtually disintegrated, taking down No. 3, an all-Australian crew, from which one parachute was seen to emerge. This belonged to an air gunner who, although captured on landing, was freed eight days later by advancing British troops. The pilot of No. 4 was severely injured, shrapnel smashing through his right thigh bone but he managed to retain consciousness long enough to get his aircraft back over friendly territory after bombing, before passing out. The mid-upper gunner then took over the controls and managed, under the pilot's guidance, to crash-land at the first airfield en route without further casualties. The leading aircraft of the second box was seriously damaged by flak, wounding an air gunner but the pilot pressed on, bombed and led his formation back over the Rhine before breaking away to force-land at Eindhoven. Bocholt deserved its thick red ring on the map as a place to be avoided if possible. Of the twelve 180 Squadron Mitchells that had left Melsbroek earlier, only seven returned to base, all with varying degrees of flak damage and some with wounded aboard. (Only six aircraft took part in the afternoon show but the other two squadrons operated 24. The next day they were joined by 11 aircraft from 180 Squadron, attacking an enemy strongpoint near Dingden in the morning and Isselburg in the afternoon.) Notification was received of an immediate award of the DSO to the wounded pilot, Pilot Officer Dick Perkins, a CGM to his air-gunner, Flight Sergeant J. Hall, who carried out the emergency landing and a DFC to the leading pilot of the second box, Flight Lieutenant G. Howard-Jones.[1]

On 23 March the Mitchells and Bostons bombed strong-points near Wesel in the morning. On return from a second visit to Isselburg in the late afternoon, we were told at debriefing that this was 'R-Day' and that British, Canadian and American troops would be crossing the Rhine that evening at various points on either side of Wesel and Rees. An early night was suggested and while we slept Bomber Command put in a heavy attack on Wesel.

Long before dawn on the 24th, 'R-Day + 1', we were called to attend briefing at 0530. The target was set in the forest of Diersfordterwald, north-west of Hamminkein, where we would be making the final bombing raid before *Operation Varsity*, the airborne assault, came in. Our bomb load was six clusters of 20lb APs. The bombing height was to be between 11,000 and 12,000 feet and the approximate heading on the bombing run 075, turning right off target after bombing.

By 0735 we were checking over our individual equipment in the aircraft and half an hour later we took-off leading 'Grey' Box, while 'Brown' Box tucked in behind as we set course. We picked up our Spitfire escort as we set course for Xanten, where we contacted 'Cosycoat', the MRCP controller. Within minutes we crossed the Rhine but the flak was minimal and not particularly accurate. Bomb doors were opened as the pilots followed the instructions given by 'Cosycoat' on the run-in to the target and the six clusters dropped clumsily away from each bomber. Flak was now more accurate but judged by earlier standards, only moderate. 'Cosycoat' signed us off and took control of another box running in. It all seemed very impersonal as the bombing details were entered in the log and the pilot was given the new course and it was not until we'd made our right turn off the target that I became aware of all the activity taking place below. Even during the Ardennes breakthrough in the snow of the previous December and January I saw nothing to match the scene below us.

On either side of the river we could see the ripple of flashes from gun batteries and tanks and the occasional puff of dust and smoke as a flurry of shells landed. The little boats (from our height) handled by the Navy were ploughing back and forth across the river and we could see the spans of the demolished bridges lying in the water. Already pontoon bridges were being thrown across the great waterway looking like threads of cotton. We knew, although we couldn't see them, that the Army and Marine Commandos alongside various infantry units were fighting around Rees and Wesel and our tanks were already in action on the east bank, having 'swum' across during the night and early morning. Smoke was still drifting about and we could see Tempests, Typhoons, Mustangs and Thunderbolts diving in to attack enemy positions. We learned afterwards that Churchill was there on a high vantage point with Alanbrooke, Eisenhower and Tedder but I don't think they got the marvellous view we did.

As we left the Rhine behind us we could see, coming in from the west, several thousand feet below, the vanguard of the Airborne divisions. Dakotas, C-46 Commandos and C-47s loaded with paratroopers and their equipment occupied the first waves of the assault, heading three great columns stretching back as far as the eye could see. Following the paratroops came the gliders towed by Halifax, Stirling and Albermarle tugs and, of course, the ubiquitous Dakotas. Our south-westerly course was gradually taking us away from this awe-inspiring sight. We hoped our bombing had been of support and had reduced in some measure the opposition that the Airborne were bound to encounter.

Our fighter escort left us over Goch and we were all back at base by 1010. There was the inevitable 'turn round' call; the bomb trolleys were waiting to fill the empty bellies of our aircraft as we taxied in. Another briefing was on at 1045 and the Squadron was airborne again by 1250, attacking another strong-point near Brunen. The great colonnade had gone. All that remained of it were masses of 'broken' gliders and splashes of discarded parachutes. Smoke and gunfire were still in evidence but it was not the same. The morning of 'R-Day + 1' was the only time that I really appreciated to the full our true role in tactical air support.

Notes
1. Flight Sergeant James Mansfield Hall came from Jamaica where his father was the Assistant Director of Medical Services. He had completed 72 operations with 180 Squadron.

# Chapter 21

# The Skylark and the Psychology of War – Dennis J. Gill

*To know war is to know there is still madness in the world.*
President Lyndon Johnson

I now ask myself why, at the age of 18, in 1942 I volunteered to enlist in the RAF as a bomber aircrew air gunner?

Teenagers have always been gullible material for wartime recruitment propaganda, especially in relation to the RAF and the false glamour it depicted, of brave young men going to war, killing the enemy and returning as heroes.

I quickly discovered there was no glamour about being committed to carry out 30 bombing operations over enemy territory and that the chances of not surviving the war, or of being seriously injured, were much more likely than returning as a hero.

Like all teenagers, other volunteers and myself believed ourselves to be immortal. We all subconsciously believed that others would be killed or injured, but not ourselves.

It was not long before this outlook would change. One soon realized, after watching other aircraft being shot down, that the doomed aircrews in those aircraft also believed that they were immortal. With the true reality of war and the realization that one is not special or immortal, fear begins to permeate one's mind and is then with you on every operation over enemy soil.

The psychological effect of war upon bomber aircrews is still a taboo subject, since the heroism myth of men at war must be maintained. Films about war thrive upon this largely false concept. The aircrews that I knew did not equate with these celluloid heroes; they were ordinary human beings whose sole interest was to survive and not to be seen as either brave or heroic.

When our bomber aircraft touched down after our 30th operation it was, to us, like being reborn. We could shed our fear and had our lives ahead of us.

In our seven months' of operational flying we had metamorphosed from innocent teenagers to serious adulthood. We had witnessed the dark side of human nature – but also learnt the lesson everyone must know, which is that war, in all its forms, can only be seen as the ultimate form of madness.

Creating an aircrew in the RAF was a very informal procedure. A number of pilots gathered together with a number of other bomber aircrew members in a large room with tea and cakes available. The pilots sized up the aircrew available and then enquired to various individuals if they would become a member of the aircrew they were each trying to create. A pilot officer pilot tapped me on the shoulder and asked if I would be an air-gunner in his aircrew. He was older than the other pilots were. He was of slim build, about five feet seven inches in height and quietly spoken. I said, 'Yes' and later realized that this was a big mistake on my part. When our pilot began his conversion at our OTU (Operational Training Unit) to fly Wellington bombers prior to going onto the bigger Stirling four-engine bomber, he turned out to be quite unsuitable to fly Wellington aircraft. After numerous hair-raising landings accompanied by some equally hair-raising language from his instructor – 'Are you trying to fucking well kill us all?' – he was withdrawn from our aircrew. He was replaced by a tall, fair haired 20 year old of an entirely different character – Pilot Officer Wood – with whom we eventually began our tour of operations with 199 Squadron based at North Creake in Norfolk.

An amusing incident happened while flying on Wellingtons with our first pilot. Our crew was instructed to fly in daylight from our OTU airfield in the Midlands on a dog-leg training flight to Scotland and back. The navigator obviously had to inform our pilot when to change direction on this dog-leg course. Towards the end of the outgoing course the instructor called up the navigator and suggested that it must be time that we were changing course. No answer from the navigator. The instructor repeated his question – still no answer. He then instructed the engineer to find out why the navigator was not replying on the intercom. The engineer then called back on the intercom that the navigator was sound asleep. He was awakened and it was later revealed that the previous night, until the early hours of that morning, when we had an early take-off he had been out drinking and with a consequent lack of sleep had fallen asleep in our aircraft.

The instructor, an officer, was livid and with numerous expletives informed our navigator that on our return he would be arrested on a charge of dereliction of duty.

We then realized that we were lost. We were over thick cloud and the instructor told the air-gunners to look out for breaks in the cloud cover to identity where we were over the sea whilst our dog-leg routes were entirely over land areas. This brought forth further bad language from the instructor against our navigator but eventually our W/Op was able to fix our position via local radar stations and our navigator got us back to base.

Here he was taken into custody by the station police and later court-martialled and sentenced to a period in a RAF 'glasshouse'. I often wondered what happened to him. I presume that he was later put back on operational flying. Perhaps he became a casualty of war. His night out drinking might have cost him his life – whereas if he had stayed in our aircrew he would have survived the war.

The sky was an inverted blue bowl over the flat greenness of the marshland. As I walked the bridle path in the spring sunshine, the song of a skylark drifted down from above. I looked up and found it, high up on fluttering wings and my mind went back to a wartime Norfolk airfield on a summer evening in 1944.

I was 20 then and with six other members of our aircrew we were sprawled out on the grass beside our aircraft as the sun neared the distant horizon, waiting to begin another operational flight over German soil. I remember a skylark hovering above us in the sky, pouring out its song, as if saying to anyone who wanted to listen – 'Isn't it good to be alive?' To us below it was a wasted message. Would we survive this, our seventeenth, operation? With 13 more to go, we knew by the law of averages our luck was fast running out.

Our aircraft, a Stirling bomber, stood beside us like a huge black praying mantis. A war machine, without a conscience, it waited there, Dracula like, to embrace the coming darkness and bring destruction to whatever lay in its path.

A green Very light arced up over the airfield – our signal to prepare to take-off. We climbed aboard our aircraft. Inside, stark and metallic, it reeked of high-octane petrol. The door closed and secured, we were encapsulated within the bowels of our war machine. The explosive roar of starting aircraft engines shattered the peace and quiet of the airfield. The skylark dropped to earth to shelter fearfully in the long grass.

Our turn arrived to take-off. The airfield dropped away and soon we were swallowed up in the darkness of the night and set course for our other world of death and destruction.

Below us at the target area, the velvet black darkness was broken by the continuous flashes of exploding bombs. Soon a red sore developed in the darkness below. As the city burned the sore spread and seemed to pulsate with a macabre intensity – in the flames below, schools, hospitals, homes and families, were being destroyed. This area of carnage was but one definition of the madness called war.

Above the target area, a vast demented, murderously intent barrage of anti-aircraft fire began to trawl our aircraft from the sky. They fell like autumn leaves into the inferno below. Some exploded in the air; others fell in flames, as numerous searchlights swept the menacing darkness.

These individual lances of white light captured their victims for the master searchlights – batteries of searchlights from which there was no escape. The captured aircraft, like silver moths, were soon plucked from the sky by the accurate radar controlled anti-aircraft guns. Two aircraft collided as they left the target. The flaming wreckage gyrated slowly earthwards. A searchlight almost caught us, its nearness lit up the interior of our aircraft as it swept past.

Then the madness stopped. The last bombs had fallen. The sky was free of gunfire. The searchlights became still sentinels of light, marking the site of yet another act of man's inhumanity to man.

'Isn't it peaceful here?' It was a woman's voice. Peaceful here?

My mind clawed its way back to reality. 'Yes' I answered, as she walked past, 'It is peaceful here.'.

I closed my eyes, soaking up the peacefulness of this other world. I felt solitary and alone – almost ashamed of being a survivor.

I looked up to find the skylark but the skylark had gone.

Throughout the ages, man has been engaged in warfare. Permeated with violent genes created over thousands of years, since man evolved from his ape like origins, he has existed in an environment governed by nature's law of survival of the fittest and 'kill or be killed'.

The harsh conditions in which he existed over thousands of years, without warmth or shelter from freezing cold, or medical treatment for bodily pain and suffering, created a human animal that was brutalized and without conscience or compassion, and on the same level as the animals he hunted and slaughtered.

But like all animals he enjoyed an aspect of life that was totally natural and accepted as such – he was free. Time had no significance to him, neither was he burdened with any responsibilities.

All this however was to change.

Man's inherent intelligence led him to exploit animal husbandry and agriculture for food, housing and fire for shelter and warmth and the smelting of bronze and iron to fashion tools. Specialist tradesmen emerged, bartering as a means of exchange evolved to coinage and paper money and society changed from serfdom to that of employer and employee. Virtually overnight a capitalist society came into being and for a capitalist society a new type of man was required, a subservient employee class, devoid of his primeval freedom and subjected to long working hours. This new man must also be responsible and law-abiding to serve his employers to their satisfaction.

Religion was used as the basis of the new industrialized society. The primeval nature of man to kill must now be moulded by the Ten Commandments and in particular, compliance to the rule 'Thou shalt not kill'.

But with one exception. And this will be if the state and its lawmakers, for reasons of greed power or politics decide to go to war. But when this happens the lawmakers have a problem. They need cannon fodder and they need it fast. And the lawmakers are clever, they know that this imposed way of life we call civilization can be easily peeled away. The lawmakers who also control the media now create the required propaganda for war and the populace awake to discover that they suddenly have an 'enemy'. However, rest assured, God is on our side. Conscription is enforced, but volunteers are also needed and encouraged to prove to their womenfolk what brave fellows they are and shame their male contemporaries to also prove their courage and patriotism.

The lawmakers have a public school understanding of human nature. They know that patriotism is the Achilles heel of every human being and appealing to this side of human nature sidetracks logical thinking and reaps rewards in cannon fodder. Furthermore they also know that the masses are poorly educated, respectful of their superiors and trust the lawmakers to know what is best for them – hence, if we are told we have an enemy and there is a call to arms, to arms we must go.

They also know that there is no cannon fodder like young cannon fodder. The young cannon fodder believe themselves to be immortal. God, after all, knows they are special individuals. They will go off to war, kill the country's enemies and return heroes. When they are called to arms the state supplies them with a smart uniform specifically designed to appeal to the opposite sex and adorn it with coloured ribbons, if earned, to depict how brave they have been in killing the lawmakers' enemies. They are clothed, fed, given shelter and told to forget their civilized responsibilities.

Now the process of unveiling recruits' primeval instincts must begin; they must be liberated from the restraints of civilized behaviour and law and order. Religious teaching: 'Thou shalt not kill' is now buried.

Next the military procedure of teaching recruits their primeval freedom to kill and maim their enemy begins. Initially the reborn primeval man is given a rifle and bayonet and ordered to attack a straw effigy of a human being and told to emit a primeval scream as he thrusts the weapon into the stomach area and twist it for good measure.

After that, the lawmakers' patriot is introduced to the machine gun and hand grenade and told to imagine the carnage these new toys can wreak upon his new enemy. Then, if the recruit is made of the right stuff, better killing machines, such as tanks and aircraft, are available for better killing results. Finally, if you are seen to have a psychopathic mind, one can be put in command of an atomic missile, programmed to fall upon civilian cities to wipe out thousands of human beings regardless of age or sex.

Now man's primeval instincts are released.

Unrestricted by civilized laws he has regained his primeval freedom. He drinks to dull his mind – sings bawdy songs to stop himself thinking – and then there is the sex. This is the one thing upon which the military man can concentrate his mind. In the pursuit of whoring he scores points in the eyes of his comrades. It elevates his standing with them and there is the added bonus of describing in detail how your conquests have been made – but then, when you are not killing and maiming your fellow human beings, what else is there to do?

But eventually all good things come to an end.

Whichever side wins, the politicians of both sides get together and wine and dine each other. The dead are buried, the maimed are patched up. The cannon fodder has done its job. Now, after peering into hell, they have served their purpose.

You are told to take off your uniform, hand in your weapons, kiss your tank or aircraft goodbye and are then taken to a large area where you can choose from rows of clothing to wear on your return to civilization. There is a door marked 'Exit' and without the preparation you were given to learn to kill, you are pushed through it, having served the purpose of the lawmakers and are expected to overnight become a caring law abiding citizen again.

But then, as time passes, reality kicks in.

As you get older and wiser you start to question things: was the war you fought a just war? Were you really defending your country so far from its shores? Or were you and your comrades victims of misguided patriotism and the pawns of clever politicians and international vested interests?

When you retire at night, cloaked in darkness, thoughts fend off sleep. What you have done and seen, your less fortunate comrades, the scenes of destruction, your victims, the dead and the dying, return to haunt you and, plagued by your conscience, you find there is no escape from the madness of war.

# Index